Fusebox:
Developing
ColdFusion®
Applications

Contents At a Glance

Fusebox:
Developing ColdFusion® Applications

Jeff Peters
Nat Papovich

New Riders

www.newriders.com

201 West 103rd Street, Indianapolis, Indiana 46290
An Imprint of Pearson Education
Boston • Indianapolis • London • Munich • New York • San Francisco

Fusebox: Developing ColdFusion Applications

Copyright © 2003 by New Riders Publishing

FIRST EDITION: June, 2002

International Standard Book Number: 0-73571-269-7

Library of Congress Catalog Card Number: *2002100323*

06 05 04 03 02   7 6 5 4 3 2 1

Interpretation of the printing code: The rightmost double-digit number is the year of the book's printing; the rightmost single-digit number is the number of the book's printing. For example, the printing code 02-1 shows that the first printing of the book occurred in 2002.

Printed in the United States of America

Trademarks

Warning and Disclaimer

Publisher
David Dwyer

Associate Publisher
Stephanie Wall

Production Manager
Gina Kanouse

Managing Editor
Kristy Knoop

Acquisitions Editor
Elise Walter

Development Editor
Frederick Speers

Product Marketing Manager
Kathy Malmloff

Publicity Manager
Susan Nixon

Project Editor
Stacia Mellinger

Copy Editor
Karen Gill

Indexer
Ginny Bess

Manufacturing Coordinator
Jim Conway

Book Designer
Louisa Klucznik

Cover Designer
Brainstorm Design, Inc.

Cover Production
Aren Howell

Proofreader
Debbie Williams

Composition
Amy Parker

Table of Contents

About the Authors

Jeff Peters has been messing around with computers since "terminal" meant a teletype. He is currently a program manager with Operational Technologies Services in Vienna, Virginia, a member of the Fusebox Council, and an occasional seminar speaker and instructor. When Jeff's not pushing bits around, he can often be found remodeling rooms with his wife and daughter, or noodling around on bass and guitar. Jeff maintains a Fusebox-related web site at www.grokfusebox.com.

Nat Papovich, as a member of the Fusebox Council that oversees the development of the standard, has contributed to the formalization of many popular Fusebox concepts and was instrumental in the release of version 3.0. Nat is a Senior Partner and Lead Architect at fusium, offering application development and project consulting, Fusebox training and mentoring, along with tools and products for developers. In addition to being a frequent speaker at ColdFusion events and conferences nationwide, he has written and contributed to many other Fusebox publications. Currently residing in Portland, Oregon, Nat enjoys climbing, biking, and astronomy. He can be reached at nat@fusium.com.

About the Technical Reviewers

These reviewers contributed their considerable hands-on expertise to the entire development process for *Fusebox: Developing ColdFusion Applications*. As the book was being written, these dedicated professionals reviewed all the material for technical content, organization, and flow. Their feedback was critical to ensuring that *Fusebox: Developing ColdFusion Applications* fits our reader's need for the highest-quality technical information.

Michael Smith is president and founder of TeraTech Inc., a Rockville, Maryland-based ColdFusion, Database, and Visual Basic consulting company. Michael has written articles on ColdFusion programming for *CFDJ* magazine, Macromedia Developer Center, CF Advisor, Fusion Authority, and CPCUG monitor. He has spoken at many ColdFusion conferences, including CFUN-2K, CFNORTH, CFSOUTH, and Sys-Con's ColdFusion Edge. Michael runs the Maryland ColdFusion User Group (MDCFUG) at `http://www.cfug-md.org/` and has taught programming and methodologies at USDA, VOA, AOC, and FDA.

He wrote his first program in 1976 on a mini-computer in BASIC. Of that he says, "I had to handwrite the program—in very neat block caps—for data entry by the punch card folks. The results came back on line printer paper the next week. Boy, did it make me careful not to make typos in my code or have bugs in my program! We used to bench run the programs out loud before submitting to be sure they worked before the computer got hold of them..." Fortunately, programming languages have improved greatly in the past twenty-five years!

Michael has been programming for more than 20 years and has been coding in ColdFusion since version 1.5 in 1997. He has coded in more languages than he sometimes wants to remember, including BASIC, Clipper, FoxPro, Visual Basic, C, Fortran, ASM, Oracle, and SQL.

Michael is on the board of ByteBack (`http://www.byteback.org/`), a non-profit organization that provides computer training for unemployed and under-employed inner-city residents.

You can reach Michael at `michael@teratech.com` or 301-881-1440.

Steve Nelson is one of the original creators of Fusebox. He has been the chairman of the Fusebox organization for the last 4 years and was also a member of Team Allaire for 3 years. Currently he is a consultant for SecretAgents.com and assists companies with building projects using the Fusebox Lifecyle Process. Steve built SecretAgents.com to connect programmers and companies, allowing companies to instantly obtain an army of programmers to complete their software within 24 hours.

Acknowledgments

From Jeff Peters

I usually read acknowledgments in the books I buy, and many of them seem to be quite similar, thanking all kinds of folks who helped get the book together. Having finished this, my first book, I understand why that is the case. This book would not be in your hands without the great work of a whole bunch of people. I'd like to thank Nat for his ability to hang with me and see this project through; Michael Smith at TeraTech, for believing it would happen; Steve Nelson, for being the biggest Fusebox cheerleader in the world; Elise Walter and Fred Speers at New Riders, for having the vision to drive us into producing a much better book (without making us crazy!); Hal Helms, for daring me to start writing about Fusebox—I may never forgive you; the members of the Fusebox community, whose ideas challenge the status quo every day; and my wife Kathryn, for the forbearance to learn what it means to be married to someone who not only gets lost in computers, but then spends *more* time to write about them. Finally, I would be remiss in not thanking Jesus Christ, whose example of an orderly universe is the inspiration for much of how I see orderly systems like Fusebox. Thank you all for being part of the adventure!

From Nat Papovich

One of the more pleasurable tasks of being an author is to thank the people who contributed to the success of the book. My greatest thanks goes to Jeff for his amazing productivity. I would like to thank my family and friends, particularly Hood Frazier, for really believing in me; Corey Snow, for giving me a chance; my partner Erik Voldengen, for inciting a much-needed change; and my parents, for leading by example.

Many Fuseboxers had a hand in this book, especially Michael Smith for directing us toward New Riders; Hal Helms & Paul Mone, for the laughs; Steve Nelson and Gabe Roffman, for sharing their creation; and Craig Girard, for the original, much-needed effort.

Most of all, my love, appreciation, and thanks to my wife and editor, Sarah. No words can describe my gratitude in having her beside me.

Tell Us What You Think

As the reader of this book, you are the most important critic and commentator. We value your opinion and want to know what we're doing right, what we could do better, what areas you'd like to see us publish in, and any other words of wisdom you're willing to pass our way.

As the Associate Publisher for New Riders Publishing, I welcome your comments. You can fax, email, or write me directly to let me know what you did or didn't like about this book—as well as what we can do to make our books stronger.

Please note that I cannot help you with technical problems related to the topic of this book, and that due to the high volume of mail I receive, I might not be able to reply to every message.

When you write, please be sure to include this book's title and author as well as your name and phone or fax number. I will carefully review your comments and share them with the author and editors who worked on the book.

Fax:	317-581-4663
Email:	stephanie.wall@newriders.com
Mail:	Stephanie Wall
	Associate Publisher
	New Riders Publishing
	201 West 103rd Street
	Indianapolis, IN 46290 USA

Foreword

It's customary for authors to gratefully acknowledge the labors of the many people whose work goes into putting a book together. It's all true: In addition to the hundreds of hours Jeff and Nat have devoted to this book, editors have poured over the text for any slips in grammar or spelling, technical reviewers have examined every bit of code looking for possible bugs, graphic artists have labored to make concepts visually clear, and the publisher has gone to great efforts to ensure that *this* book got into *your* hands.

All of which means nothing to us readers. Our time is scarce and the demands on it are great. This book asks us to devote a little of our money and a good deal more of our time to learn about Fusebox 3's framework and methodology. Should we? It seems to me that there are three questions we want answered first.

What's so great about the Fusebox framework? As a web developer, I want a framework that gives me something I couldn't have easily done myself. Why learn something new if new isn't better? If you talk to some of the thousands of active Fusebox developers, you'll hear them speak passionately about how Fusebox makes it easier to develop complex web applications. These Fuseboxers talk about the framework that promotes reuse, making applications easier to maintain and better able to scale. Unlike the glowing reports we hear from many frameworks vying for adoption, these aren't coming from the pens of highly paid PR professionals. These are letters from the front, so to speak.

What's so great about the Fusebox methodology? Talk to these same Fuseboxers and they'll tell you this: The Fusebox Lifecycle Process (FLiP) is a methodology that is proven to work in the diverse environments that Fuseboxers work in. In fact, the methodology grew from the frustrations with project failures, and it represents the best practices that produced successful deployments. Fuseboxers find that FLiP provides a space in which developers of differing skills and levels can work productively together. Ask Fuseboxers what the community of Fusebox developers is like, and they'll tell you how warmly the community welcomes newcomers and how quickly requests for help receive answers.

What's so great about *this* book? It's rare when the authors of a technical book are not only guides, but also guiding lights in the technology about which they write. Stated simply, Fusebox 3 would not be what it is without the contributions Jeff and Nat have made to it. Their unique perspective on the goals and philosophies behind Fusebox 3, as well as the details that make it work, will help you understand not only *how* to do things, but *why*.

Because Nat and Jeff are both full-time developers, they can offer you help using Fusebox amidst the stresses of pressing deadlines and pointy-haired bosses with no understanding of the technology they manage. This grounding in reality means you won't waste time learning something that you'll never use.

Anyone who has tried to write clearly knows how devilishly hard this is to achieve. So many technical books suffer from the same problem: The people who know can't write, and the people who can write don't know. When done well, though, writing becomes transparent, leaving the reader the space to learn. Luckily for us, their readers, Nat and Jeff have crafted their words with the same care with which they write their code. The happy results are this book, which you now hold in your hands. Nat and Jeff have admirably done their job of writing. Now, it's up to us. Let's get reading!

—Hal Helms

Introduction

"Brody, cut off the techno tunes and answer the phone! If it's Janice, I'm not here."

"Hello, SB Consulting. No, Stan's not here. Can I take a message? Oh hi, Janice." Brody spins around to face Stan and flashes an evil grin. Leaning on the doorframe, soda can dangling limply in his hand, Stan looks pale and sickly. "Yes, I'll tell him you called—the admin module, right." Brody hangs up the phone.

"I was up all night fixing bugs in the admin. Every dang time I fixed one, two more popped up. Betcha Janice wanted somethin' else added to it," Stan slurred every other word between slurps of Mountain Dew.

"Yep. She said something about processing prepaid checks. She wanted to know how much time it would take."

"I swear, Brody, our next job isn't gonna be like this one. Janice is cool and all, but I'm sick of all the changes."

Happy that he is not in Stan's shoes, Brody swings back around to his desk and slaps his headphones back over his ears, his stylish sideburns sticking out beneath. Stan closes his eyes, exhales, and slowly turns around, trying to remember the last time he ate.

Sound familiar? Many developers struggle to launch projects on time and under budget without staying up all night to do it. Those of us who are successful often wonder how we can improve our success rates. We need advice about communicating with our clients. We need a standard process to make the project manageable. We need a framework to serve as a base for our applications so we stop reinventing the wheel every time. We need a system that simplifies maintenance and requests for change during development.

We need Fusebox.

This book is about making ColdFusion applications reliably successful by following a standardized system. At the heart of the system is simplicity: a framework consisting of a set of helper files and organizational principles, and a methodology consisting of a set of best practices for managing web projects. Used by application designers, developers, and architects, the system addresses development problems such as unmanageable complexity, wasteful redundancy of effort, time-consuming code maintenance, and slow development speed. Fusebox is not a new creation. In answer to the problems plaguing software development over the past few decades, the framework and methodology described here have been used by thousands of developers to build tens of thousands of applications. This book documents the practices of a large and growing community of users who have not been able to refer to a definitive guide—until now.

One aspect of Fusebox is an application framework. This framework includes guidelines to follow regarding file naming, directory use, and file content. More important, it has a set of core files—files that implement the Fusebox specification, a set of requirements, and an application program interface (API). These core files create the Fusebox framework, which contains powerful features such as variable inheritance and nested layout control.

Fusebox is also a development methodology—a step-by-step process consisting of a set of guidelines and best practices for the entire application development lifecycle. Some of the phases are framework independent; they are especially useful for Fusebox applications, but they are relevant and helpful no matter what application framework is used.

What Is this Book About?

Because Fusebox is a grass-roots effort that is not owned or sold by any commercial group, until now developers have not had a single point of reference. Information has been spread out, hard to find, and occasionally contradictory. We have collected and sifted the information to create this book as a new definitive reference. As a master guide, this book will cover the following topics:

- **Understanding the benefits that Fusebox provides for application development**—Because Fusebox is a community-driven, free, and formalized framework and methodology, some managers might need convincing.

- **Using the Fusebox core files as a framework for writing Fusebox applications**—The core files are an implementation of the Fusebox specification. They provide a framework that cultivates modularity, maximizes cohesion, and promotes reusability.

- **Preventing re-invention of the wheel when it comes to design, architecture, and methodology for ColdFusion**—Using an established framework and process for creating ColdFusion applications decreases your development time because you are able to focus on the business problem and requirements rather than how you are going to implement your solutions.

- **Using the Fusebox Lifecycle Process (FLiP) to increase the chance of a successful project**—Born from the successes of projects using Fusebox, this process greatly increases the chance of completing web projects successfully. Although it has specific implications and advantages when used in concert with the Fusebox framework, the lessons learned from it are beneficial no matter what web application language or architecture is used.

These topics are addressed in three sections that make the fundamentals of Fusebox easy to understand and implement in your own work. In this book, you'll find explanations of the specific benefits of Fusebox, a technical Fusebox reference, and a step-by-step Fusebox application so that you can see the process in action.

What Is this Book Not About?

Because Fusebox is a web application framework, it does not address mastery of a web application language. As such, this book is not about the following:

- **How to program in ColdFusion**—This book assumes that you understand basic ColdFusion constructs and principles. If you are not familiar with such tags as `<cfinclude>`, `<cfoutput>`, and `<cfswitch>`, we recommend you check out one of the excellent books available that are specifically devoted to ColdFusion programming. We recommend any book on ColdFusion published by New Riders; check out www.newriders.com for more information.

- **How to create web pages using client-side technologies such as Flash, HTML, or JavaScript**—Although Fusebox eases some of the development pains of dealing with highly dynamic applications and presentation issues, Fusebox is not a methodology designed to aid in structuring presentation-tier technologies. Thus, we will not cover these topics.

- **How to implement best-practices based "back-end" technologies**—Fusebox is a software framework, not a technology. As a result, we will not cover topics such as databases, web server security, or network configuration.

Now that we have a basic understanding of what Fusebox is and what this book will cover, who should be reading this book? Before we answer that question, it is important to briefly discuss the larger history of web applications so that we can see how Fusebox came to be.

Web Development Issues

You might be familiar with large, dynamic web sites containing content that changes depending on user interaction. Many e-commerce sites up- and cross-sell products based on which products you have already shown interest in. Portions of those e-commerce sites are available only after you have logged in and, depending on who you are, you see personalized information such as your previous orders.

Dynamic, personalized sites are not limited to e-commerce. Corporate intranets and business-to-business (B2B) applications are rapidly gaining popularity as more companies realize the savings that are involved in hosting applications online. Such sites are often highly customized to individual employees by displaying reports and providing access to tools via complex security systems.

Hard-coding such dynamic sites in HTML would be ridiculously expensive. Maintenance of such systems would require an army of HTML coders, and anything above the simplest sites would be nearly impossible to create. To overcome this, we write web-based applications that mimic some of the features and powers of traditional desktop applications. Web applications are the answer to most problems that are introduced by attempting to create complex systems from pure HTML. As a web application programming language, ColdFusion allows us to solve many business problems, such as interacting with external systems like databases (via `<cfquery>`), other web sites (via `<cfhttp>`), email systems (via `<cfpop>` and `<cfmail>`), and file systems (via `<cffile>` and `<cfdirectory>`).

However, when ColdFusion applications become complex, the costs begin to increase out of proportion to the benefits. Maintenance becomes nightmarish due to the lack of an application framework. Individual pages are haphazardly linked to one another, and changes to one page produce unexpected changes in others. Eventually, we as developers are scared to make changes to the application because we do not know what effects these changes will have on the application as a whole. The answer to our problems lies in adopting a standardized web application framework—Fusebox. By adopting Fusebox, we can freely modify and add to our application because we know how the system will respond.

A Brief History of Frameworks

Modern-day standardized frameworks began as design patterns that were applied to traditional software engineering. A design pattern is a technique that is applied to similar software problems. The discussion of design patterns was popularized by the *Gang of Four:* Erich Gamma, Richard Helm, Ralph Johnson, and John Vlissades in their 1994 work, *Design Patterns: Elements of Reusable Object-Oriented Software.* The Gang of Four's work made developers realize that mastery of a computer language did not guarantee the success of their projects. Programmers had to learn to apply the reusable elements of one application to another application.

The Gang of Four were the first to document commonly used software patterns, but their work was focused on object-oriented (OO) software design, which ColdFusion cannot efficiently duplicate. The web is a different environment from the software that the Gang of Four was addressing.

In fact, some of the strength of ColdFusion comes from the fact that it is not object oriented. Line for line, OO programming is more time consuming to write than non-OO programming, which makes for slower development times. Also, a large proportion of ColdFusion developers do not come from traditional programming backgrounds, which makes OO programming foreign to them. The main benefits of ColdFusion over other languages have been speed of development and ease of use. However, along with those benefits come problems. It can be difficult to find a design pattern that works with ColdFusion.

The Problems

ColdFusion programmers have had no models to follow, no patterns or frameworks identified and documented on which to base their work. And because ColdFusion has traditionally been the easiest web scripting language to employ successfully, many developers have never placed a premium on architectures, which has led to problems of complexity, redundancy, maintenance, and slow development time.

Complexity

Creating ColdFusion applications beyond a few pages can be difficult. Without using a structure, pages are pieced together haphazardly, global variables are difficult to control and create, and it is difficult to get components to communicate with each other. Layouts and user presentation become cumbersome to manage as the site grows. Requirements often change during development, which can cause major setbacks to the delivery timeframe because the application was not created to allow for additional modules. If the system is highly dynamic, managing the different layouts and options can be a major difficulty.

Adopting Fusebox in ColdFusion applications allows the system to increase in complexity without the code increasing in complexity. Controlling layouts and constants is organized with Fusebox, and there are specific ways of dealing with both. Slipstreaming changes in the application during development is simplified by breaking down the application's functionality into modules. Controlling complex layout states becomes manageable because of the specific and powerful separation of logic from display.

Redundancy

Often, ColdFusion developers find themselves repeating code in multiple places. The same query might be written three times in a single application, each time embedded on a different page. (Imagine a product detail lookup used on the catalog page, the administrative page, and the best sellers page.) If one element of the query needs to change, it must be duplicated wherever it is used. A single display might be used multiple times in an application to accomplish the same task with a few modifications for each one, such as the form action. (Think of a user-entry form used to create a user, edit a user, and allow an administrator to create and edit a user.) If one form field needs to be added or removed, it must be done four times.

Fusebox cultivates code reuse by separating display from logic and by encouraging code to be broken into the smallest possible unit needed to accomplish a discrete task (called a fuse). This allows code to be referenced and reused throughout the application. Fusebox's powerful nested layouts functionality allows header files that display a universal navigation element to be created and instantiated once, and the entire application becomes embedded in the page layout.

ColdFusion programmers often take advantage of the built-in functionality of `application.cfm` to create global-style constants and application-wide settings. However, most `application.cfm` files for decent-sized applications are unnecessarily complex and are limited in power because of the way ColdFusion implements `application.cfm` functionality. Fusebox allows much finer control of global elements for true inheritance among application sections (called circuits).

Maintenance

Imagine that you are maintaining an application, trying to resolve a few bugs. You fix a bug in the most likely location only to discover that it has produced a bug in another seemingly unrelated part of the application.

Alternatively, imagine you have been maintaining a system that was created by a group who is no longer employed by your company. Every day is a struggle. A "small" change request comes in and you spend all week trying to update one page.

Traditional ColdFusion applications can be difficult to maintain because there can be little structure and compliance of communication between sections. Developers have no common ground on which to base their applications. Maintainers have to understand what the application does as well as how it does it.

We always find that the launch of a new web site is just the beginning. The maintenance spending on a web application can quickly outgrow the initial development costs. That means that any application architecture or framework that ignores maintenance ignores what most ColdFusion programmers do all day long. Few developers regularly start new applications from scratch. Therefore, many developers' greatest concern is ease of maintenance.

Fusebox has three important aspects that directly contribute to ease of maintenance. First, we use Fusedocs, a powerful documentation system. Second, there are Exit Fuseactions, which eliminate dependence between application modules. Finally, a central controller file, the Fusebox, serves as a starting point for all debugging as well as application modification. Using Fusebox is sure to reduce the amount of time and money spent on maintaining applications.

Slow Development Time

During the dot-com blitz of the late 1990s, the winner in a market was usually the first one to make a showing. If you got into a market a month too late, chances were that you did not make it. Even today, many developers spend too long figuring out how to create a framework and not enough time implementing specific business solutions. Also development teams often have difficulties with integrating individually built components into a cohesive application. Often one person holds an inordinate amount of knowledge and is the only person who feels comfortable making changes to the application.

By adopting Fusebox, developers can more easily focus on the requirements of the system; they know they have a framework that can be used to solve any set of business requirements. Developers have used this framework in the past, so each new application is just another recurrence of the same system, with different requirements attached. Team members can work in synchronicity, each one performing his strongest task the fastest, confident that after the created components are wired together, they will function flawlessly because they are all created with a common architecture.

By using web applications created in ColdFusion, we can create highly dynamic sites that overcome the limits of static HTML pages. Also, by adopting Fusebox as a ColdFusion framework, we can allow those web applications to increase in complexity without becoming too complex to control. Our applications contain more recycled and reused code and are easily maintainable. All this translates into decreased development times. Your project is completed faster, cheaper, and more easily. We have found our framework—Fusebox.

Who Should Read this Book?

This book is designed to teach you Fusebox, even if you have no Fusebox experience and only know as much as you have gleaned from flipping through this book and reading this far.

If you are an HTML developer and want to create your first dynamic application using ColdFusion, then this book is for you. Pick up a companion ColdFusion syntax book and learn Fusebox alongside ColdFusion. You will be starting the right way by learning how to create robust web applications as well as how to accomplish basic ColdFusion tasks.

If you are an intermediate-level ColdFusion developer who has created a few applications but are planning ahead for the next big, scary project, then this book is for you. You might have a firm grip on ColdFusion Markup Language (CFML), but you are wondering how to put it all together into a major application. Fusebox is the answer, in the form of this book.

If you are an experienced ColdFusion developer who has completed several successful projects and you are wondering what the Fusebox buzz is all about, then this book is for you. You will be adding feathers to your cap with more ease and speed than ever. If you have been using your own homegrown architecture, you might find many similarities to it and Fusebox.

Finally, if you are a team leader, senior programmer, or project manager looking for a way to increase the productivity and effectiveness of your developers, especially when it comes to enterprise-level corporate systems, then this book is for you. The discussion of FLiP in Part 3, "Fusebox Lifecycle Process (FLiP)," will be of particular value to you.

Our Cast of Characters

Because this book is based on implementing Fusebox in ColdFusion applications, we use a few characters to help relate our discussions to the real world. You will see more of these characters in Part 3 when we create a Fusebox application from start to finish. You might even be able to relate with one or more of these characters:

- **Janice the Client**—Janice is in her mid-forties and owns a bicycle shop called Third Wheel. She has been doing brisk retail business in her shop but wants to expand to become an e-retailer. Janice has a successful business plan and real-world system, so she just needs assistance in transforming her model to the web. She is almost an ideal client except that, like most clients, she knows little about the web. The good news is that Janice totally trusts that we will do a good job.

- **Brody the Designer**—Brody graduated from Columbia University a couple of years ago with a major in fine arts and a focus in new media design. We have completed a few projects with Brody already, so we can vouch for his talents. Although he is not at all familiar with ColdFusion ("cold fusion will never happen," he usually jokes), he is great with user interfaces and always makes our applications look as good as they really are. Brody is proactive, easy to get along with, and is already hard at work creating design proofs for the Third Wheel web site.

- **Stan the Developer**—A native of Arizona, Stan dropped out of college in his third year to open a web development business. He started off creating simple HTML web sites but has recently completed his third Fusebox application. He is a regular whiz when it comes to SQL and databases and is a great Fusebox architect. Stan will be working with us as our lead developer in creating the Third Wheel web site.

Hopefully, you will not miss our characters until we see them again in Part 3.

Parts and Chapters

This book is divided into three parts. Part 1, "Fusebox Basics," covers the basics and benefits of Fusebox. Upon completing this part, you will understand what Fusebox is all about and why you should use it. Part 2, "Fusebox Coding," covers technical Fusebox in detail. It serves as a reference for Fusebox, covering the seven major points. Part 3 covers the Fusebox Lifecycle Process (FLiP) and our team's work on Third Wheel Bikes in that context. After you have completed Part 3, you will understand the FLiP process from beginning to end.

Part 1, "Fusebox Basics," begins with Chapter 1, "The Arrival of Fusebox," which sets the stage for a technical discussion of Fusebox by working through some of the most basic concepts of code and application organization.

Chapter 2, "Is Fusebox Right for You?," explains all the benefits of Fusebox and why you should use it.

Part 2, "Fusebox Coding," begins with Chapter 3, "The Fusebox Framework," which covers the five main Fusebox framework files: `application.cfm`, `index.cfm`, `fbx_fusebox30_CFxx.cfm`, `fbx_circuits.cfm`, and `fbx_savecontent.cfm`.

Chapter 4, "Handling a Fuseaction," covers the process and files that are used to control the flow of a Fusebox application, including `fbx_settings.cfm`, `fbx_switch.cfm`, `fbx_layouts.cfm`, the layout file, and `fbx_errorCatch.cfm`.

Chapter 5, "The Fuses," explains what fuses are, what rules cover fuses, and what they're used for.

Chapter 6, "Exit Fuseactions," explains what exit fuseactions are and how they can benefit you.

Chapter 7, "Fusedocs," explains the documentation system used in Fusebox to increase cohesion among files.

Chapter 8, "Nesting Circuits," discusses the power and functionality of the nested circuit model in detail, including inheritance of circuit settings.

Chapter 9, "Nested Layouts," covers the power of Fusebox's layout features, which allow detailed control of page layout and the complete separation of logic from display.

Chapter 10, "Nested Coding Concepts," covers the specifics of where to place code to interact with the different levels of a Fusebox application.

Part 3, "Fusebox Lifecycle Process (FLiP)," begins with Chapter 11, "Introduction to Development Methodologies and FLiP," which serves as both a plea for the need for development methodologies as well as an introduction to FLiP.

Chapter 12, "Wireframing," explains the first step of the FLiP: the phase of formalized requirements gathering.

Chapter 13, "Prototyping and DevNotes," explains the second step of the FLiP, where a full-scale representation of the completed application is created.

Chapter 14, "Construction and Coding," explains the architectural decisions that are involved in making a schematic of a Fusebox application, as well as consideration in documentation and fuse interaction.

Chapter 15, "Unit Testing," explains the power and benefits of unit testing fuses before integrating them into the final application.

Chapter 16, "Application Integration and Deployment," discusses considerations to ensure that deploying completed Fusebox applications is uneventful.

Chapter 17, "Best Practices," covers some of the techniques that have developed out of the use of Fusebox.

Chapter 18, "Fusebox Exotica," covers some of the fringes of the Fusebox world, such as Fusebox in languages other than ColdFusion.

Chapter 19, "The Adventure Continues," finalizes our discussion of Fusebox and takes a glimpse into where Fusebox is headed along with how to get involved.

Part 4, "Appendixes," begins with Appendix A, "Fusebox 3.0 Specification Reference," a no-nonsense reference for the Fusebox 3.0 specification designed for quick review.

Appendix B, "Fusebox Glossary," is a glossary of terms that are used throughout the book. Use this appendix while reading the rest of the book to refresh your knowledge or learn unfamiliar terms.

Appendix C, "Fusedoc Data Type Definition," is a reference of the data type definition (DTD) for the XML-based Fusedocs.

Appendix D, "Fusebox Version 2 to Version 3 Comparison," is a comparison of the previous version of Fusebox (2.0) with the current release (3.1). It is helpful for Fusebox developers who are experienced with version 2.0.

Appendix E, "Fusebox Resources," is a listing of places to go for Fusebox information and tools.

Conventions

This book follows a few typographical conventions:

- A new term is set in *italics* the first time it is introduced.
- Program text, tags, statements, variables, and other "computer language" are set in a fixed-pitch font—for example, `www.thirdwheelbikes.com`.
- When a line of code wraps to a new line, a code continuation character (➡) is used to indicate.

The Book's Companion Web Site

If you check out `www.newriders.com`, you will find this book's companion web site. It serves as a resource warehouse for use while reading this book as well as a jumping-off point for all things Fusebox. It is crucial to consider the content of the web site and the content of the book as two pieces of a whole. The web site includes the following:

- Databases, files, and code from this book
- Current enhancements and revisions to the material in this book
- Links to other Fusebox resources
- The latest updates to the core of Fusebox, for whatever version we might be up to

In addition, you'll find our sample site application at `www.thirdwheelbikes.com`. We refer to this application throughout the book.

The Journey Begins

If you have made it this far, you have decided to join us on the trip. You have your roadmap in hand, and you have a good idea of what to expect ahead. You are in great shape so far. Often, the hardest step is the first—allowing change and admitting the possibility of success. This book will be your companion guide to solving many problems that have plagued your development efforts. Congratulations for starting. We'll see you on the other side.

1

Fusebox Basics

"...doctrine is not the point of arrival but is, on the contrary, the point of departure..."

—Joseph Brodsky

1

The Arrival of Fusebox

Lᴏɴɢ ʜɪᴅᴅᴇɴ ɪɴ ᴛʜᴇ ᴡᴏʀʟᴅ ᴏꜰ ᴀᴄᴀᴅᴇᴍɪᴀ, the World Wide Web began to attract the attention of businesses in the early 1990s. Initially unsure of how to best utilize the power of "infinite communication," companies were finally realizing the potential of the web. At the same time, emerging technologies were making it possible to create increasingly capable sites.

However, along with new desires and tools came new problems, and many well-intentioned development efforts were mired in problems inherent to working on the web. Programmers who were familiar with traditional desktop or client-server environments encountered a host of difficulties while trying to solve business problems in this new, stateless, request-and-receive environment. Chief among these problems was the lack of a computer language designed specifically to operate in a web environment.

> **Note**
>
> I used to work in a software development shop that did both desktop applications and web applications. The desktop team always had a good laugh at us on the web team because we could not "maintain state." I never quite figured out what was so funny about it, but I think those people are not laughing now, considering the growing popularity of the Internet.

Allaire's ColdFusion was the answer. ColdFusion was easy to use, and developers could quickly create web applications with it. A group of ColdFusion developers including (among others) Gabe Roffman, Joshua Cyr, Michael Dinowitz, Robi Sen, and Steve Nelson started discussing common solutions to the problem of reinventing the wheel with each new site development. The "House of Fusion CF-Talk" mailing list became home to the discussion. Threads on a better way to organize applications progressed, and ideas began to form within the group. Example frameworks were discussed, but a catalyst was needed to finalize the system.

That catalyst arrived when Steve and Gabe (both independent consultants at the time) started sharing an office in Charlottesville, Virginia in the spring of 1998. They began to swap notes and ideas about their own development practices and how they related to some of the CF-Talk ideas. Discussions of the state problem and design patterns led to ideas about organizing applications, controlling system actions, and separating functionality of pages.

Before long, Steve finalized his idea for a centralized controller page within each directory of a site. Gabe noticed the resemblance of this model to the breaker panel of a house. This "fuse box" ColdFusion application system was documented in a white paper as the first specification for Fusebox version 1.0. Joshua Cyr wrote an example calendar application based on that specification.

Impressed with the system, Robi Sen hired Gabe and Steve to create the first full-scale Fusebox implementation at `eBags.com`. This e-commerce site was a magnificent success and is still going strong today as the largest online retailer of bags. And the rest, as the saying goes, is history.

Since its inception, Fusebox has been based around an open exchange of ideas—a community. This community has been pivotal to Fusebox's success and growth. Make no mistake, we have come a long way since that first basic concept, but the fundamental ideas of Fusebox remain intact. These ideas are what make Fusebox the best web application framework for ColdFusion.

What Is Fusebox?

To explain what Fusebox is, let's look first at what it is not. Fusebox is not a software package—there is nothing to buy. Fusebox is also not a development environment, a compiler, or a code library, although there is some standard code involved with it.

However, Fusebox *is* a web development specification. People who use Fusebox (*Fuseboxers*) use a standardized development methodology and framework to help their projects succeed. Fusebox has the strongest and most dynamic community of ColdFusion developers on the Net today.

What is Fusebox all about in practice? There are two major aspects of Fusebox:

- Basic concepts of the purpose of Fusebox
- Fundamental Fusebox principles in practice

Each of these aspects is made up of other pieces, so let's take them one at a time.

Basic Fusebox Concepts

Fusebox borrows many of its essential concepts from other systems. First, Fusebox is a way to organize program code. Second, Fusebox is a way to manage growing applications by organizing the application directories in a hierarchy. Third, and perhaps most fundamentally, Fusebox is a way to think about applications and the art of building them. Comparisons have been drawn between the Fusebox controller file and computer networks. Now let's discuss each of these essential concepts in more detail.

A Way to Arrange Code

A great deal of thought has gone into the idea of organizing applications into some kind of logical framework. Code organization schemes are as old as computers. Back when computers used punch cards, programmers kept routines in tidy order. If you got a card out of sequence, your program did not function properly. And heaven forbid you drop a box of cards on the way to the computer! More discussions of code organization choices appear in Chapter 14, "Construction and Coding," such as the popular Model-View-Controller (MVC) framework.

The easiest concept to observe about Fusebox is the impact it has on your application's code—where you store files and how you arrange your directories. The Fusebox specification defines how to arrange your program's code into easy-to-manage chunks. What is the big deal with organized code?

Although many people quickly recognize the value of using a standard approach to arrange code, some of the benefits are often overlooked.

ColdFusion has been an incredibly successful language primarily due to its low entry threshold. That is, ColdFusion does not require a great deal of study and knowledge of programming to get started.

Because so many people who have had no formal background in programming or application development get involved in developing ColdFusion applications, a great deal of ColdFusion code is disorganized or poorly written.

Sure, it does the job, but unfortunately, ColdFusion's reputation has unfairly suffered as a result. Instead of recognizing that ColdFusion accommodated an amazingly wide spectrum of experience from complete novice to application guru, rumormongers proclaimed that ColdFusion could not scale well.

Scaling means that a completed application will be able to successfully handle workloads larger than those for which it was originally designed. In the case of web applications, it usually translates to a large increase in the number of page requests or simultaneous users that the system handles.

Database issues aside, when an application is poorly designed and constructed, it is generally not able to scale very well. Program logic that works well for one or two users might overstress the server when several hundred users all try to use it at once. Many ColdFusion applications are poorly designed and constructed, simply because their creators never considered the issues involved in effective application design.

However, ColdFusion's reputation as a small-scale application server is not deserved, and indeed has been greatly reduced in recent years. Projects such as RoomsToGo.com (the largest retailer of furniture online) and Autobytel.com (one of the largest car sales sites) have proven that ColdFusion can scale effectively when the application is properly conceived and executed. Both of these high-volume sites are not only ColdFusion efforts, but they also both use Fusebox as their architecture.

> **Note**
> Still quite Fusebox, you may notice that AutoByTel.com uses ?action= rather than the familiar ?fuseaction= in the URL.

A Way to Manage Growing Applications

The responsibilities of a manager can be defined by a constant struggle to determine when a project will be completed and how much it will cost. If, as a manager, you do not have a good idea of how the application's code is organized, then the uncertainty factor rises rapidly. Fusebox project managers can use this framework again and again, regardless of the size of the project, which aids in code reuse. For example, you might have written a report for accounting last week. This week, you can literally copy and paste it into the whole intranet without changing a thing.

Using Fusebox is good for project managers, but Fusebox also mimics the way managers work. If you have ever managed a project, you know that most of your time is spent coordinating the efforts of others. Managers do not tend to produce much, but they encourage and allow those underneath them to produce more, better, faster. They are skilled at assigning tasks, which helps manage a project's size. A comparison of Fusebox and corporate managers reveals that they share some of the same methods for getting work done. Fusebox encourages code to be highly specialized and focused. The structure helps to control all the smaller pieces. The controller files excel at delegating tasks.

If you are a reader of the *Dilbert* comic strip, you are quite familiar with the Pointy-Haired Boss (PHB), the epitome of a manager without a clue. *Dilbert* is funny because we can relate to the title character; most of us have worked for a PHB at one time or another. Consequently, it might be hard to imagine corporate managers as a model for solving a problem, but there is a reason that management hierarchy rules the structure of companies today.

People can only process so much information in any given day. Using a flat organization (where managers are nonexistent and everyone is an equal), every member of the group must communicate his ideas and information to every other member of the group on a regular basis. Obviously, this is inefficient and can easily grow to the point where everyone spends all his time involved in communication, with no time left to actually get work done.

ColdFusion applications that lack a real structure act similarly. Every page can link to every other page. In fact, every page must link to every other page to get something done. If you add a page, all the other pages must be updated. Every page must be aware of every other page in the system.

This is where the manager comes in. Sacrifice one person's ability to directly produce but give that person the role of facilitating communication, and everyone else gets more done. By filtering out all the other stuff that goes around other parts of the organization, team members can focus on the skills for which they were hired in the first place.

The manager can see the "big picture" of the organization—what projects are currently underway, what areas of uncertainty lie ahead, and what teams need resources to complete their job. A good manager is a master delegator. If a manager goes "into the trenches" to produce and directly contribute, communication suffers and projects slow down.

PHBs notwithstanding, by organizing and regulating the flow of information between teams, managers streamline business. Fusebox's controller file duplicates the purpose of a manager by passing requests off to focused portions of the application. It an employee needs to arrange a meeting with another department to complete a project, the manager knows whom to contact and facilitates the communication. Similarly, if a web site user wants to see a list of all products on sale, the Fusebox controller knows which files accomplish that task.

A Way to Think About Applications

When you sit down to work with an application, do you have a mental concept of it in your head? What does it look like in your mind's eye? Can you fit it all into your head at once? Do you think of the application's code as being organized in a particular way, or does it all just sort of run together in a big jumble?

Part of the problem of working with unorganized code is just trying to envision the application. Without a defined model, the picture that forms tends to be abstract. It is hard to imagine what happens when a particular template runs, how information is passed from one template to another, and what a change in one template does to another template. You might tend to think in terms of web servers and page requests or maybe streams of ones and zeros flying around if you understand that kind of thing. Although there is nothing wrong with this view, there is nothing tangible about it either. You cannot visualize the application. Or, as Beethoven said:

> "[The work] rises, it grows, I hear and see the image in front of me from every angle... and only the labor of writing it down remains..."

Beethoven was a musical genius who was fully capable of composing a complete symphony in his head. Most folks are not as good at programming as Beethoven was at composing; we need a structure to our applications. Thankfully, we use things every day that can give us some valuable models for our applications. One example that closely resembles Fusebox is a computer network router.

Fusebox Mimics Networks

Over time, routers have helped organize network traffic immensely. Two of the most successful early network topologies were ring and bus architectures, shown in Figure 1.1.

These two architectures had one thing in common: They were based, as are all networks, on the idea of broadcasting packets of data from one machine to another.

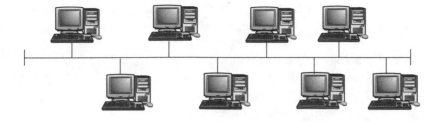

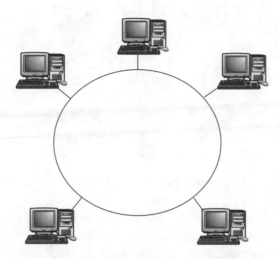

Figure 1.1   Ring and bus networks.

As you can see in Figure 1.1, the bus architecture (at top) worked by machines sending packets addressed to other machines onto the bus, the central line in the figure. Each machine would check the address on every packet that went by. If the packet belonged to the machine, it would make a copy of the packet and read it. Otherwise, the packet would be ignored.

Acting somewhat like a bus network in a loop, IBM's Token Ring worked by each packet attaching a token that carried the address of the recipient. When the token passed the recipient machine, the machine stripped off the packet. If the token passed a non-recipient machine, nothing happened and it continued around the ring.

As you can imagine, both of these approaches meant that a lot of packets were flying around on the wires. Then came a new topology, and the problem got worse.

The newer topology, called a star, used a central hub to send packets from one machine to another. A hub was a simple concept; it took whatever came in one port and sent copies of it out on all the other ports. This made great sense when you had a single hub at the center of several computers. Shown in Figure 1.2 is the classic star network.

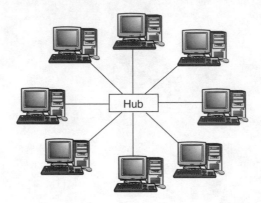

Figure 1.2   Star network.

Networks based on hubs eventually reached a practical limit on the number of ports, so network engineers expanded the capacity of the hub by linking hubs together. However, that technique was not scalable. If you linked too many hubs, the multiplied traffic would cause collision problems, with traffic moving slowly.

The answer to this problem was the router. A router is the hub's smarter cousin. Whereas a hub simply copies what is received in one port to all the other ports, a router sends a packet only to the destination. Using strategically placed routers, network planners were able to create huge networks. In fact, the Internet is a series of interconnected routers.

By organizing and regulating the flow of traffic between workgroups, network routers streamlined the networking industry. Routers act as a big switch. If one computer wants to talk to another computer, the router essentially connects those two machines to each other. Similarly, Fusebox uses a master controller file to directly pipe a page request to the correct set of files. The controller file handles every action that the system can perform.

Traditional ColdFusion applications have no hub. Page requests are all point-to-point. As the system grows in size, developers can't remember which pages link where. It becomes extremely difficult to keep a clear picture of the application in your head. Imagine trying to memorize exactly what a pile of spaghetti looks like and where each noodle winds. Tough, huh? Now imagine a map of the interstate freeway system. That is a lot simpler, isn't it? It is pretty simple to find your way from Atlanta, Georgia to Atlanta, Idaho even if you have never been to either of those places. Freeways have structure, like Fusebox. Spaghetti has no structure, like traditional ColdFusion applications.

Back to Thinking About Applications

We started this discussion with the idea that applications are difficult to think about in tangible terms, and that Fusebox provides an easier concept to grasp. Each of the real-world examples (network routers and managers) is tangible if you are familiar with it. When someone mentions one of these examples, you instantly have an idea of what it is about and how it works.

Fusebox does something similar with applications. As you gain experience with Fusebox, you will become more comfortable with the associated terminology, and your applications will be easier to visualize. Now we just have to tell you what Fusebox really is.

Technical Fusebox Principles

If you are like us, you are probably thinking, "Okay, enough with the metaphors. Just what makes a Fusebox application in the real world?" Well, Fusebox has many technical aspects. Some people use all the ideas that have ever been labeled "Fusebox," whereas others only use some core components. For an application to be considered "Fusebox," it needs to exhibit all of the following characteristics:

- Use the Fusebox method of file and directory organization.
- Use the Fusebox core files.
- Switch on a "fuseaction" to control the flow of the application.
- Employ exit fuseactions (XFAs).
- Have all fuses contain Fusedocs.

What happens if an application only uses some of the five characteristics? Usually we call it "my own version of Fusebox." It might work perfectly well for you, in your own development environment, for your own application, but what would happen if everyone wrote applications differently? You could not proclaim that you "knew Fusebox" because you write it differently from others. Shared applications could not be said to be "written in Fusebox." The power of a widely used framework and methodology is lost. Most industries standardize on a certain set of specifications. When that happens, the industry booms.

In Part 2, "Fusebox Coding," we will discuss these concepts in greater detail. Throughout the book, we will look at other ideas and practices that (although not all Fusebox developers use them) are considered Fusebox "best-practices." For the following sections, we will give you some background so that you understand how the whole picture fits together. Welcome to technical Fusebox. Put on your thinking caps!

File and Directory Organization

Any time you have more than a few files, it makes sense to reorganize them into a set of folders. Imagine you start a new school semester with a new laptop computer and you stick all your schoolwork in My Documents. After the first week, you have 10 files in there—a few Word documents, maybe an Excel spreadsheet of your class schedule, a Mind Map you created in Biology class (more on Mind Mapping in Chapter 14, "Construction and Coding"), and a handful of text files of notes. By next week, the number of files has doubled to 20. Sensing impending disaster by file overload, you wisely create folders for each of your classes and segregate your files. This works wonderfully through the end of the school year, but the next fall rolls around and you have all those folders from old classes—too many of them to quickly access folders for your current classes. You create a new folder called Freshman Year and move all your class folders from last year into that new folder. "Hey, I'm getting organized," you think. And you are right. Using folders to logically and physically separate files and subfolders is mandatory after you get a good number of them together.

What do we mean by "logically and physically"? Determining that you had too many files and putting them into separate folders is the physical separation. However, you didn't just create folders called folder1, folder2, and folder3 and randomly stick files in each one until they were equally full. You carefully named your folders Biology 101, Intro to Java, and Women's Studies and placed the files that you created for each of those classes into the corresponding folder. That is what is meant by "logically." Maybe your Intro to Java folder has twice as many files as Biology 101, but it makes sense to organize them according to class, not according to count.

The way we organize files and folders in Fusebox is nothing radical; it is just an extension of logical organization. Take, for instance, this site map of a couple HTML pages pictured in Figure 1.3.

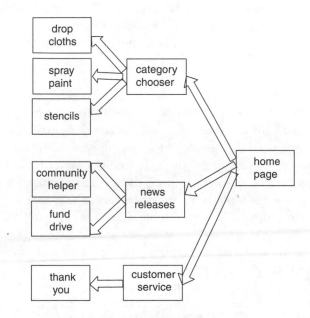

Figure 1.3   Simple HTML site map.

The site map in Figure 1.3 is an example of the directory structure shown in Figure 1.4.

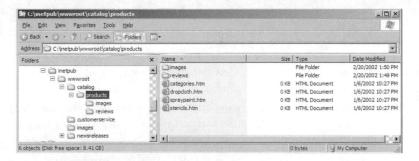

Figure 1.4   Simple HTML site directory structure.

If the web site shown in Figure 1.4 were a Fusebox application, then the sub-folders `customerservice`, `newsreleases`, and `catalog` would be called *circuits*. On the most basic level, a Fusebox circuit is just a directory. In Windows terminology, there are folders and subfolders, but in Fusebox, there is only one name for any directory, regardless of how deeply nested it is. Frequently, Fusebox developers refer to a circuit as being a *child* circuit of another circuit. That just means that a circuit is nested inside another circuit.

Circuit Inheritance

Circuits are more than just a collection of files. When you (using your imagination) organized your freshman year class folders into one folder, what benefit did it bring? It reduced the number of folders in one location, but it also allowed you to apply security (if you had some important files in those folders) to one folder and have subfolders inherit the security settings from their parent folder. If you were to mark the folder Freshman Year as read-only, you would not be able to modify files in subfolders of Freshman Year. Imagine if this feature were not built into Windows; you would have to go through each file and modify its properties by hand, which would be quite time-consuming.

Fusebox has the same system of inheritance. In fact, it is even more powerful than Windows's version. Inside each circuit is a file called `fbx_settings.cfm`. Variables set in `fbx_settings.cfm` are available to the rest of the circuit, including any nested circuits. This means that you can apply security to check whether a user is logged into one circuit's `fbx_settings.cfm` file; then every file in that circuit can forego its own security validation. Because the files in the circuit that contain the secured `fbx_settings.cfm` inherit its settings, they cannot be accessed unless the user is logged in. We will further discuss the security of circuits and the `fbx_settings.cfm` file in later chapters.

> **Note**
>
> *Inheritance* is a term used in object-oriented programming, but in Fusebox, it basically means what it sounds like it means—a child circuit can use the variables from its parent circuit.

One good way to decide how to partition your application into circuits is to determine what parts of your application might be considered miniature applications. If we were building an e-commerce site (which we will do throughout Part 3, "Fusebox Lifecycle Process (FLiP)"), we would make the catalog/product viewer a circuit, as well as product reviews, checkout, customer service, search, and user management. Let's not forget about the home circuit, too. Every application needs a home circuit, which is used to tie all the circuits together into one application. Just as we applied a setting to `fbx_settings.cfm` and had all files in that circuit inherit those settings, we can apply settings to the home application, and every circuit in the entire application will inherit those settings.

File Organization

To review the terminology acquired thus far, a folder or directory in Fusebox is called a *circuit*. Any subfolders or subdirectories are said to be *child circuits* of the main circuit, which might be called the *parent circuit*. We would be remiss if we did not correct ourselves by replacing the term *file* with *fuse*. Often, ColdFusion files are called *templates*. Although the terms *template*, *file*, *page*, and *fuse* are relatively interchangeable, a file that is used in a Fusebox application carries two unique distinctions that any old ColdFusion template or file does not necessarily have: structured naming conventions and rules of use.

Fuses Versus Plain Templates

The first distinction is that Fusebox fuses follow a carefully defined yet extensible file-naming system. The content that can and should be contained in a fuse depends on its file prefix.

Table 1.1   **File Prefixes for Fuses**

Fuse Prefix	Fuse Type	Description
`dsp_`	Display	Only fuse type that can contain display, be it HTML, WML, or SOAP packets.
`qry_`	Query	Only fuse type that can perform database interactions, whether it be via `<cfquery>` or `<cfstoredproc>`. Always returns a recordset.
`act_`	Action	Any ColdFusion that does not fall into the previous two fuse types. Used primarily for data manipulation, form validation, and external systems interaction such as `<cfmail>`, `<cfpop>`, and so on.
`lay_`	Layout	These files assemble the page request for presentation to the user by handling headers, footers, and embedded fuseactions.
`fbx_`	Fusebox framework reserved fuse	The seven reserved Fusebox fuses use the `fbx_` prefix. No user-defined files should use this prefix.

For the majority of files in your Fusebox application, exactly what code should get which of the preceding four fuse prefixes is a no-brainer. A fuse that runs a

`<cfquery>` tag to get a recordset of all products in a database with prices over $30 would use the `qry_` prefix (that is, `qry_GetProducts.cfm`). A fuse that loops over the recordset created by a `qry_` fuse and displays each row formatted into a `<table>` would use the `dsp_` prefix (that is, `dsp_showProducts.cfm`). A fuse that performs some complex validation based on the results of a user-submitted form would use the `act_` fuse prefix (that is, `act_validateProduct.cfm`).

The `fbx_` prefix is used for the reserved Fusebox framework files—those files that get the Fusebox job done by creating the inheritance structure, creating the central controller file, handling the layout and nesting of displays, and other tasks. For now, you should understand that nearly every fuse with an `fbx_` prefix is not a file you create, although you do edit the contents of some of those files. We will talk more about `fbx_` fuses starting in Chapter 3, "The Fusebox Framework."

The second distinction between a plain ColdFusion template and a Fusebox fuse is that each fuse should perform a discrete task. If a user is placing an order at the end of a checkout process, an example system has a number of tasks to perform, including checking the inventory, verifying and processing the credit card, updating the inventory, inserting the order into the database, sending an email to the shipping and accounting departments, sending an email to the customer, and finally displaying a "thank you" page to the customer. Each one of these steps would be a fuse. A good Fusebox developer would not combine these steps into one fuse, as tempting as it might be. A good rule of thumb is that most query and action fuses should fit on one screen in ColdFusion Studio.

Fuse Rules

A complete discussion of fuses and fuse content comes in Chapter 5, "The Fuses," but in the meantime, some hard and fast rules are available to keep in mind about what kind of code can and cannot be in certain fuse types.

For action fuses that use the `act_` prefix, there can be no display. Whether the requesting client is a browser, a WAP phone, a web service, or a `<cfmodule>` tag, `act_` fuses can only contain CFML logic and service calls. Use of `<cfoutput>` should be strictly limited to looping over query resultsets to perform manipulations of the data. In rare instances, an action fuse can perform database queries if, for example, you are trying to emulate the functionality of a stored procedure by running a query, looping through it, and performing subsequent queries based on the results of the first query. However, it would be wisest to `<cfinclude>` that nested query as a `qry_` fuse. Here is an example of an action fuse that creates a name list:

```
<!--- act_nameBuild.cfm --->
<cfset nameList="">
<cfloop collection="#attributes.stName#" item="aName">
  <cfset nameList=ListAppend(nameList,aName,)>
</cfloop>
```

This code takes a structure of names (`attributes.stName`) and creates a list of the key values (`nameList`).

Like action fuses, query fuses that use the `qry_` prefix cannot present display to the client. Query fuses should be as modular as possible to allow maximum reuse of the query. This means that the only code that should be contained in a `qry_` fuse is the `<cfquery>` (or `<cfstoredproc>`) tag, a few `<cfparam>` tags to create defaults for the query, and *maybe*, just maybe, some looping afterward to rearrange the data output if it could not be accomplished in the query. Query fuses must always generate a recordset. It is also a good idea to name the recordset (via the `name` attribute in the `<cfquery>` tag) the same name as the fuse, minus the file extension and fuse prefix. For example, the fuse `qry_customerDetails.cfm` has a recordset called `customerDetails`:

```
<!--- qry_customerDetails.cfm --->
<cfparam name="attributes.customerID" default="0">
<cfquery name="customerDetails" datasource="#request.dsn#">
  SELECT * FROM customers
  WHERE customerID=#attributes.customerID#
</cfquery>
```

Unlike the previous two fuses, display fuses are the only type that can present output to the client. As a consequence, display fuses should contain a minimal amount of ColdFusion logic. Common ColdFusion tags that are used in display fuses include `<cfoutput>`, `<cfloop>`, `<cfset>`, `<cfparam>`, and `<cfif>`. Of course, you are free to use whatever tags are necessary to get the job done for a fuse, but if you find yourself writing blocks of ColdFusion code, it should probably be moved into an action fuse. Here is an example of a display fuse:

```
<!--- dsp_customerDetails.cfm --->
<table border="1">
<tr>
  <td>Name</td><td>Managers</td>
</tr>
<cfoutput>
<tr>
  <td>#customerDetails.name#</td><td>#nameList#</td>
</tr>
</cfoutput>
</table>
```

Because Fusebox encourages different kind of code to be created in different fuse types, the result is a complete separation of display from logic. Due to this separation, debugging is easier, development is faster, and the entire application has increased cohesion, bringing many benefits, discussed further in Chapter 2, "Is Fusebox Right for You?"

> **Note**
> *Cohesion* relates to how well a fuse, fuseaction, or circuit performs exactly one function or achieves a single goal.

The Fusebox Core Files

Applications that were developed in early versions of Fusebox consisted of a "federation" of circuits; in a metaphysical sense, each circuit lived in its own world, only vaguely aware of ties to other circuits. Circuits did not share the benefits of inheritance. To simulate inheritance, it was commonplace to tie circuits together, which reduced modularity. Extended Fusebox (XFB), created by Hal Helms, was developed to solve these problems. XFB gave circuits complete independence from each other but also created a true structure among the circuits, uniting them into one "wrapper" application. In the latest release (version 3), Fusebox builds on XFB by using a formalized set of core files that sets up a structure for the circuits, creates the system of inheritance and settings, provides for the switch-case that controls the application flow, and controls layouts and nested displays. Each core file uses the `fbx_` prefix.

Table 1.2   **The Core Files**

Processing Order	Filename	Description
1	fbx_fusebox30_CFxx.cfm	Commonly referred to as "the core file," this file sets up the entire Fusebox framework that calls the other core files and fuses. The `xx` denotes ColdFusion version-specific files.
2	fbx_circuits.cfm	Establishes the relationship of circuits to each other by "registering" circuits with the application.
3	fbx_settings.cfm	One per circuit, this file allows circuit-wide (and child circuit) settings and inheritance.

Processing Order	Filename	Description
4	fbx_switch.cfm	Little more than a `<cfswitch>`/`<cfcase>` statement, this file controls the application flow, based on the fuseaction.
5	fbx_layouts.cfm	One per circuit, this file controls which layout file to use for the request.
N/A	fbx_savecontent.cfm	Fusebox relies on `<cfsaveco-tent>`, introduced in CF5. This file emulates the native tag's functionality for people using versions of ColdFusion earlier than version 5.

All these files might sound confusing at this point, but fear not; they will be discussed fully in Part 2.

Controlling the Flow

Unfortunately, we both find ourselves flying more than we would like. Last year, we flew cross-country at least a half-dozen times and over the course of one two-month period, we flew nine times combined. But out of all those frequent-flyer miles accumulated, few were on delayed flights. We never got "bumped," and for the most part, the tickets were inexpensive and we were able to get on the flights we wanted, even on short notice.

But if this were 1950, it's unlikely we would have had such success. Back then, airlines were frequently late, ticket prices were higher, and direct flights were the only way you could fly. If you wanted to go from Los Angeles to New Orleans, you had to wait for a long time for a direct flight, or take any number of flights, each one quite expensive, and there was little guarantee that you would not miss a connecting flight. Airlines were operating on a point-to-point system but recognized that something needed to change to allow an increase in cities served, passenger volume, and profits realized. In the early 1960s, United Airlines created the world's first hub-and-spoke system of airports, linking western U.S. routes with eastern U.S. routes via major connecting hubs. At the time, the other major airlines nay-sayed this model, claiming it would destroy the industry. However, after a few short years, all the airlines had their own hub-and-spoke systems.

The system used by the airline industry these days is similar to the system used by Fusebox. In addition, the system used by the airline industry up until the early 1960s is similar to most non-Fusebox ColdFusion applications. Non-Fusebox ColdFusion applications tend to rely on page-to-page links. A form that is collecting information submits to a form-processing page. The form-processing page has a "thank you" section at the bottom. In Fusebox applications, every page links and submits to one controller file, which then processes the user's request. If you are on a page with a form, it submits to the Fusebox, which then passes control to the form-processing page. Because all links, form actions, JavaScript redirects, `<cfmodule>`, and `<cflocation>` tags go through the Fusebox, the hub-and-spoke system is duplicated in web applications.

Figure 1.5 shows a comparison of point-to-point versus hub-and-spoke systems in airlines and web applications. Point-to-point models can work well in small sizes, but they must be upgraded to hub-and-spoke systems to handle increases in traffic and complexity. This hub-and-spoke is most obvious in the "controller file," called `fbx_switch.cfm`.

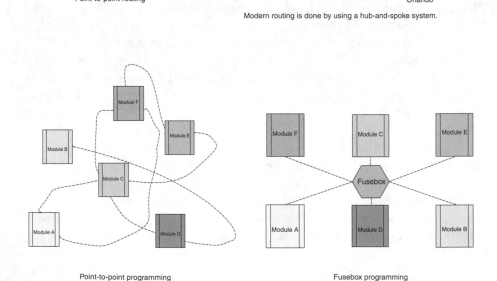

Figure 1.5 Point-to-point versus hub-and-spoke.

A Look at *fbx_switch.cfm*

So what makes a Fusebox application actually run? In ColdFusion, you point a browser to a .cfm template, and the web server picks up the request and passes it off to ColdFusion Server. From there, ColdFusion processes the Application.cfm file—including any files referenced—and then processes the page, again including any files needed. When ColdFusion is done, the page goes back to the web server and you get your page. But in Fusebox, instead of pointing to individual fuses, you always point to one file: the default web document, which is usually index.cfm.

This index.cfm file includes the core file (fbx_fusebox30_CFxx.cfm), which runs code to set up the Fusebox framework, including <cfinclude>ing the fbx_settings.cfm fuses from the circuits. Next, it includes the fbx_switch.cfm for the target circuit, and then finishes off by handling any layouts to be used. But again, where do you stick your code—the stuff that actually does something?

All the fuses—your code—gets <cfinclude>d from the fbx_switch.cfm file. Here is an example fbx_switch.cfm file:

```
<cfswitch expression = "#fusebox.fuseaction#">
  <cfcase value="main">
    <cfinclude template="act_ReadFiles.cfm">
    <cfinclude template="act_MakeFileIntoStruct.cfm">
    <cfinclude template="dsp_map.cfm">
  </cfcase>
  <cfcase value="admin">
    <cfinclude template="act_getAllDirs.cfm">
    <cfinclude template="dsp_admin.cfm">
  </cfcase>
  <!-- ... other <cfcase> tags here... -->
</cfswitch>
```

That is all there is to an fbx_switch.cfm file. We will do a little more explaining later, but for now, just think of the Fusebox as a big switchboard, running different code depending on a user-supplied variable.

Fuseactions Control Flow

If the user wants your application to run the "main" fuseaction, the request that follows will do it. The <cfswitch> statement switches on fusebox.fuseaction, which is passed on the URL string like this:

```
<a href="index.cfm?fuseaction=home.main">
```

or in a hidden form field like this:

```
<input type="Hidden" name="fuseaction" value="home.main">
```

or in a `<cflocation>` tag like this:

```
<cflocation url="index.cfm?fuseaction=home.main">
```

Being an astute reader, you are probably wondering where `fusebox.fuseaction` comes from if we are only passing around `url.fuseaction` and `form.fuseaction`. Remember how we mentioned that the core file sets up the Fusebox framework? One job that the core file has is to take any incoming Fuseaction variable, no matter what the scope is, and copy the second part of it (after the dot) into a variable called `fusebox.fuseaction`. Referencing `fusebox.fuseaction` is similar to referencing `ListLast(url.fuseaction, ".")`. Instead of needing two `<cfswitch>` blocks, one switching on `url.fuseaction` and the other switching on `form.fuseaction`, we can have one that does the job no matter what scope it is. It even works if you pass in the variable `fuseaction` in a `<cfmodule>` tag:

```
<cfmodule template="index.cfm" fuseaction="home.main">
```

Now we have four different ways to call a fuseaction, and only one set of code to handle all those requests.

Every time `index.cfm` (or whatever your default web document is) is run, it expects the variable `fuseaction` to be passed in. However, sometimes that variable is not passed in. This case occurs when a user types in something like this:

```
http://www.thirdwheelbikes.com/
```

There is no `?fuseaction=main.welcome` in that URL, so Fusebox needs a default fuseaction. Default fuseactions are key to understanding how a Fusebox application responds. You set a default fuseaction in the root `fbx_settings.cfm` file for your application like this:

```
<cfparam name="attributes.fuseaction" default="main.welcome">
```

Now for every request of the Fusebox application, we can be assured that the variable `attributes.fuseaction` is available. Now the system can respond appropriately. Now that a fuseaction is known, how does the framework know which circuit to go to?

Which Circuit Runs?

The fuseaction variable always contains two values in what we refer to as a *compound fuseaction*. We know that the second part of the fuseaction is the actual fuseaction; it determines which set of fuses is run for a given user request. Imagine that a user requests the `order.basket` fuseaction like this:

```
<form action="index.cfm?fuseaction=order.basket" method="post">
```

We know that the basket fuseaction will be run, but we also know that the `fbx_switch.cfm` file in the order circuit should handle the request for that fuseaction. Using this compound fuseaction, we can specify any fuseaction in any circuit to be run. The first part is the circuit, and the second part is the fuseaction.

Imagine that a customer is buying a product on your e-commerce site. Halfway through the checkout process, she decides to review your company's privacy policy. All of the fuses in the checkout process are in a circuit called `checkout`, which is off the root of the site. The page that she wants to see, `dsp_privacy.cfm`, is in the `policy` circuit, also off the root. How would you write the link from the checkout page to the privacy policy fuseaction? How about this:

```
<a href="index.cfm?fuseaction=policy.privacy">
```

The first file that runs is `index.cfm`, which is the file that the link requested. The Fusebox framework file (`fbx_fusebox30_CFxx.cfm`) is included from the `index.cfm` page. The core file establishes the framework and calls the `fbx_switch.cfm` file from the policy circuit, which looks like this:

```
<cfswitch expression = "#fusebox.fuseaction#">
  <cfcase value="privacy">
    <cfinclude template="dsp_privacy.cfm">
  </cfcase>
  <cfcase value="security">
    <cfinclude template="dsp_security.cfm">
  </cfcase>
</cfswitch>
```

The `dsp_privacy.cfm` file is processed because the second part of the fuse-action (the part after the dot) matches the `<cfcase value="privacy">` tag. After the Fusebox core file finishes processing, your display file is presented to the customer, who is satisfied with the privacy of your site and happily completes her purchase.

Exit Fuseactions

By now you might be imagining the `fbx_switch.cfm` as something of a roadmap for a circuit. In one easy-to-read page, it shows every possible action that can occur, every possible page that can be displayed, along with each fuse used to accomplish the job. Each fuse is specialized and knows its job well ("I insert a new customer into the database." "I display the privacy policy," and so on). But because each fuse contains links, form actions, and <cflocation>s, each fuse must know where those links go—what the circuits are called and what fuseactions are in which circuits. That is a tall task for a measly little fuse. Fuses should be designed so that they contain as few dependencies on the rest of the application as possible. It is with this in mind that we use XFAs rather than hard-coded fuseactions. Here is a sample XFA:

```
<form action="index.cfm?fuseaction=#xfa.submit#" method="post">
```

It's not too complicated, huh? XFAs are nothing more than fuseaction values as variables. They are set in the fbx_switch.cfm just before <cfinclude>ing the fuse:

```
<cfcase value="privacy">
<cfset xfa.continue="policy.payments">
<cfset xfa.back="policy.security">
<cfinclude template="dsp_privacy.cfm">
</cfcase>
```

This allows the fbx_switch.cfm file to control where each fuse it calls is allowed to go next. In the preceding case, the file dsp_privacy.cfm has two links: most likely a forward and backward button to guide an inquisitive customer through the array of site policies. Because each fuse should not be required to be aware of its surroundings, its own exit locations must be dynamic. This becomes especially important if a fuse links to another circuit. If the target circuit is moved or no longer exists, the fuse does not need to be updated—only the fbx_switch.cfm file does. XFAs also promote reusability of code. By using XFAs, we can write the fuse once but use it in different locations, and the links can go to different places. XFAs are completely discussed in Chapter 6, "Exit Fuseactions."

Fusedocs

Because an individual fuse is supposed to be designed and coded as if it were unaware of the larger application using it, a formalized method needs to exist to describe everything that the fuse can assume and everything that it cannot. By carefully documenting every variable that a fuse is allowed to reference (#variable#) and every variable that a fuse is supposed to create (<cfset foo="bar">), we can be assured minimum coupling by our most discrete units.

A Fusedoc appears at the top of every fuse. Using XML, a Fusedoc describes all the variables that the fuse needs to get its job done as well as all the variables that it needs to create. It identifies the scope, structure, mask, and potential values of those variables. Following is an example Fusedoc. It is for an action fuse that deletes a task. Do not worry if all the code is foreign to you. A full explanation follows the listing.

```
<!---
<?xml version="1.0" encoding="UTF-8"?>
<!DOCTYPE fusedoc SYSTEM "http://fusebox.org/fd4.dtd">
<fusedoc fuse="act_deleteTask.cfm" language="ColdFusion"
➥specification="2.0">
  <responsibilities>I delete a task and any user_tasks associated with
  ➥that task.</responsibilities>
  <properties>
    <history author="Nat Papovich" date="08/10/2001" email="nat@fusium.com"
    ➥role="Architect" type="Create"/>
  </properties>
  <io>
    <in>
      <list name="taskID" scope="attributes" optional="False"/>
    </in>
    <out>
      <boolean name="success" scope="variables"/>
    </out>
  </io>
</fusedoc>
--->
```

If you have not picked up XML yet, do not fear. Fusebox.org has tag chooser and tag insight files available to plug into ColdFusion Studio, which greatly simplifies creating Fusedocs:

```
<fusedoc fuse="act_deleteTask.cfm" language="ColdFusion"
➥specification="2.0">
```

Starting at the top (below the mumbo about XML versions and doctypes), the tag <fusedoc> wraps the whole Fusedoc. Anything that falls within the opening and closing <fusedoc> tag is considered part of the Fusedoc. The <fusedoc> tag contains a number of attributes, including the name of the fuse:

```
<responsibilities>I delete a task and any user_tasks associated with
➥that task.</responsibilities>
```

Next, the <responsibilities> tag describes what this fuse accomplishes, in plain English:

```
<history author="Nat Papovich" date="08/10/2001"
➥email="nat@fuseboxtraining.com" role="Architect" type="Create"/>
```

The <history> tag is like a stamp of who did what when to this fuse. This example shows the creator of the fuse:

```
<io>
  <in>
```

```
      <list name="taskID" scope="attributes" optional="False"/>
   </in>
   <out>
      <boolean name="success" scope="variables"/>
   </out>
</io>
```

The final section describes the input and output (<io>) of the fuse: what variables are coming in and what variables need to go out. This example shows that a variable called taskID in the attributes scope is available and that a variable called success in the local variables scope should be created.

We now have an understanding of the benefits that Fusedocs offer to our applications. If you are uncertain about the XML format in which to write Fusedocs, don't worry; www.fusebox.org has a free Fusedoc toolkit that plugs into ColdFusion Studio and makes writing Fusedocs a snap.

That about covers the basics of Fusebox except for one thing—a common scope for variables that users can modify.

A Common Scope

One final characteristic that is fundamental to Fusebox is a shared scope for incoming variables. We have already mentioned how the Fusebox core file copies the second part of the incoming form, URL, or attributes-scoped variable fuseaction into a variable called fusebox.fuseaction. That is how the fbx_switch.cfm knows which <cfcase> tag to run for the request. However, the core file also copies all URL and form-scoped variables to the attributes scope. This feature is commonly referred to as "form URL to attributes" because it was originally accomplished using a custom tag created by Steve Nelson called formurl2attributes.cfm.

Having a single scope to refer to user-defined variables means that portions of Fusebox applications suddenly become incredibly reusable. Imagine you have a <cfquery> tag like this:

```
<cfquery name="customerDetail" datasource="#request.DSN#">
   SELECT * FROM CUSTOMERS
   WHERE customerID=#form.customerID#
</cfquery>
```

This bit of code is saved into a file called qry_customerDetail.cfm, but it can only be used if the previous page contains a form with a field named customerID. If you also want to be able to pass the customerID variable on a URL string, you would have to rewrite that query file to be something like this:

```
<cfquery name="customerDetail" datasource="#request.DSN#">
   SELECT * FROM CUSTOMERS
```

```
    <cfif IsDefined("form.customerID")>
    WHERE customerID=#form.customerID#
    <cfelseif IsDefined("url.customerID")>
    WHERE customerID=#url.customerID#
    </cfif>
  </cfquery>
```

The code is generally the same as the earlier code, but it now takes into consideration `customerID` coming from two different scopes. This is a kludge. What happens now if you want to be able to use this query file from `<cfmodule>`? You would have to add yet another `<cfelseif>` to the growing code to accommodate. In addition, you would have to add this chain of `<cfif>`s to every query you wanted to reuse.

Because URL, form, and attributes scope are all available for users to write to, Fusebox uses the attributes scope as a catch-all for those scopes. Early in the processing of the Fusebox core file, all variables in the form and URL scopes are copied to the attributes scope. Now you can write the same query like this:

```
  <cfquery name="customerDetail" datasource="#request.DSN#">
    SELECT * FROM CUSTOMERS
    WHERE customerID=#attributes.customerID#
  </cfquery>
```

By using one scope to reference all incoming variables, our applications gain a huge boost in reusability. We are no longer concerned with exactly how a request is being made. We do not need to differentiate between a `<cfmodule>` request and a form post. Reusability rules.

That Was Fusebox

A long time ago, a really smart Neanderthal knocked the hard edges off a big stone and made a wheel. That kind soul shared the invention with others, which enabled us to evolve into a highly intelligent bunch of people. Although no Fuseboxer claims to be as smart as that one Neanderthal tens of thousands of years ago, we do take pride in creating a solution once and sharing the results. When a developer shares a technique that is particularly helpful, it can eventually be combined into Fusebox. Developers also make and share tools to speed up coding time. We can benefit by sharing our common knowledge. That is how Fusebox started—a couple guys found something great and shared it with the world.

Fusebox solves many problems, both by encouraging a way of thinking about applications and by providing cold, hard, technical solutions. The

Fusebox framework files have been created for you, and you can focus on making applications quickly. The system of file and directory naming and organization helps you manage growing applications. In Fusebox, ColdFusion developers have found a methodology and framework that enables their applications to scale easily while they get to work less.

Should a solution be used just because it works? If you are in the middle of making a cake and realize you need some more butter, should you use the grocery store's online shopping and have it delivered to your door for an extra ten bucks? What about your cake? It will be waiting for the delivery to arrive. Maybe driving a couple of blocks to the store is a better idea. The latest technology should not be used blindly just because it is cool.

Expounding on technical specifications might convince some of you to use Fusebox, but for most of you, you are probably wondering what good Fusebox is. How will it save you time, money, and stress? Transitioning from a traditional point-to-point model of building ColdFusion applications to the more rigid Fusebox framework might seem like too much work. Just wait for us to cover the benefits of using Fusebox in the next chapter.

2

Is Fusebox Right for You?

WHEN STAN'S CLIENT JANICE WAS INTRODUCED to Fusebox, her first reaction was a glazed look in her eyes. (For a formal introduction to Stan and Janice, see this book's Introduction.) She had a sense of good things ahead, but Stan was having a hard time trying to express the benefits of using Fusebox. After scratching his head a bit and thinking about exactly *why* he wanted to use Fusebox, Stan was able to give Janice some good answers to her questions about Fusebox in relation to her projects. This chapter will explain those answers so that we can successfully talk to Janice at your next team meeting.

We'll start this chapter by looking at Fusebox as a development methodology and looking at why methodologies are used in general. Then we'll explore some of the benefits of Fusebox, including speed of development, simplicity, maintainability, and extensibility. Finally, we'll look at what kinds of applications can be built with Fusebox.

Fusebox and Other Methodologies

What makes a well-designed application? This is a complex question, but the answer can be boiled down to a simple concept: organization. In general, applications that are well organized tend to be better applications in terms of meeting design goals, user needs, and maintenance requirements. A good methodology provides organization throughout an application's development cycle, including everything from the development team's organization to the way code is organized within a program. As we saw in Chapter 1, "The Arrival of Fusebox," a variety of methodologies are available for web developers. Many companies even create their own proprietary methodologies and implement them religiously. Methodologies are generally recognized as good. But why are they good?

When it comes to Fusebox, we can talk about a number of benefits. Clients in the web development world seem to be interested in two factors: cost and time to deployment. Sites are wanted faster and cheaper than ever before. The marketplace is putting increasing pressure on developers to build high-quality, robust applications with increasingly fewer resources. This creates a precarious balancing act in which the developer must choose which factors are most important: time, cost, or quality.

The use of a methodology like Fusebox is an opportunity to optimize those three factors. We can build high-quality systems on reasonable schedules at lower cost. To do this, care must be taken at every step of the development lifecycle. Fusebox helps us exercise that care.

Fusebox's separation of processes throughout the lifecycle offers time advantages by allowing focus on one aspect of the development at a time. If you're a one-person code factory, this can be a critical advantage simply because you don't have to constantly change your focus from one type of task to another as you move through the development. You also have a clearly defined set of steps that must be performed, so it's easy to see where in the process you are and estimate how much longer it will take you to get through the remaining steps.

If you're fortunate enough to be working in a team development environment, this same modularity of process allows the team to focus the talents of its members well. We'll get to more specific material on teamwork later; for now, it's enough to understand that Fusebox, perhaps more than any other web methodology, can leverage team environments to a high degree.

In the following sections, we'll discuss the benefits to development in terms of speed and cost, benefits to maintainability of the system, benefits to scalability, and some less quantifiable benefits, such as the Fusebox community and Fusebox's extensibility. We'll also discuss team development issues and porting existing applications to a Fusebox framework.

Speed of Development

Where the Internet and e-commerce is concerned, few things are stressed as heavily as the "need for speed" in terms of application development. As time passes, a growing plethora of tools is developed to help generate HTML more quickly. This has engendered a certain expectation on the part of clients about how quickly applications can be developed and presents a real risk for application developers. Is it possible to produce quality products at a fast rate?

We'll take a look at that question and how Fusebox helps increase the speed of application development while encouraging practices that contribute to higher quality. This balancing act is followed by a look at how Fusebox can provide time savings to both teams and individual development efforts.

Speed and Quality

Although it's competitively advantageous to be fast in your development, it's never good to be fast at the cost of quality. As the old saw goes, "You can have it fast, good, or cheap: Pick two." Fusebox is decidedly a way to gain a speed advantage in your development efforts without sacrificing quality.

That last word is critically important. In a recent discussion with a colleague (who shall remain nameless to protect his otherwise excellent reputation), we compared notes about how long it took to develop an application with Fusebox. Our colleague's reaction was that he could have generated the same application much more quickly using his favorite set of coding tools. Although skeptical of his claim, we started to compare development techniques and realized that we weren't talking about the same application. Our colleague's approach, although fast, overlooked some aspects of the project that were a natural result of using Fusebox. For example, he did not have a method to ensure that all his templates were well documented.

The fact of the matter is that using the methods of the Fusebox Lifecycle Process, which we'll talk about in Part 3, "Fusebox Lifecycle Process (FLiP)," a team is able to perform a solid, quality application development lifecycle in a fraction of the time it would take without such a well-defined process. After the application is thoroughly defined, the coding in a Fusebox application becomes a trivial exercise instead of a time-consuming major effort. Instead of spending a great deal of time worrying about a world of issues while writing code, the programmer is narrowly focused on the immediate task of writing great code.

This is the part our colleague didn't understand. When discussing time to market, he was considering only the time estimated to write the code for the system. He hadn't thought about everything that happens *before* we start writing code. He also overlooked the maintenance profile of the finished application. His approach, although rapid in terms of creating an initial application, would have built a system that would be difficult to maintain, particularly if it were left alone for a period of months and then taken up again for upgrade purposes. The longer we talked about these ideas, the more he began to see how Fusebox's high degree of organization does save time while building a better product.

In fact, practically everything about the Fusebox process is designed to leverage speed without sacrificing quality. The process of defining a new application is so well defined that you can clearly communicate the process to a new client in just a few minutes. This means you can actually get to work gathering requirements soon after your initial meeting.

Speed and quality give us a competitive advantage, but they're nearly impossible to achieve without a plan that works for the team. Another of Fusebox's great strengths is its adaptability to both team-development environments and one-person code shops.

Teams and Loners

We've mentioned before that Fusebox is well suited to use in a team-development environment. In fact, much of the thought that has gone into the development of Fusebox and the Fusebox Lifecycle Process has been aimed directly at development teams.

What makes Fusebox so great for teams? In a word, it's focus. Fusebox allows you to focus the talents of the members of your team on the areas they know best. This happens because the code of the application is divided into fuses that are identified by their category of responsibility. Display code is separated from database code, which is in turn separated from other business process code. Under this scenario, it's clear that you can assign your database guru to write query files, your HTML/JavaScript guru to write display files, and your CFML/CFScript/backend guru to write business processes.

You might be thinking that this is only a marginal advantage, in that each of these people will still need to talk with the others to get the flow of information correct throughout the application. All this interaction will cause friction when one person has to wait for another, so the gain will be nominal at best.

If that thought occurred to you, you're going to love Fusedocs. The original intent of Fusedoc was to provide the application architect with a way to describe the purpose of a fuse in sufficient detail that a coder could pick up the Fusedoc and any related HTML (together called a "fuse stub") and complete the coding of that fuse.

This means that after the architect writes the Fusedocs for an application, the coders can proceed, each at their own optimal pace, to create the required code.

It also means that the team's manager has built-in structure to help monitor the progress of the coding. In fact, the entire Fusebox Lifecycle Process is well defined and consequently, quite easy to manage. With built-in checkpoints in the process, the manager has cues about when might be a good time to communicate with the client about specific aspects of the project. We'll get into this in much greater detail in Part 3.

Fusebox's highly organized nature also lends well to the use of standardized custom tools for managing and participating in team projects. For example, with the information in the project's Fusedocs and a local procedure for annotating a file's coding progress, you can create a tool to monitor the coding status of every fuse in your project. You can also make use of some interesting third-party tools to aid in the design process.

Even if you aren't working in a team environment, Fusebox's well-organized nature makes it much easier for you to "switch hats" and focus on the various aspects of your development project in an efficient and organized way. To shorten the story, using a framework like Fusebox opens the door to a world of tools and methods that can improve your development practices.

Fusebox is a general-purpose methodology, unlike some of the canned solutions that have been introduced in the ColdFusion world. Fusebox is not a content-management system, an e-commerce framework, or a portal site system. However, you can certainly build content-management, e-commerce, or portal sites using the Fusebox techniques.

Because you can apply Fusebox to such a wide variety of sites, you don't have to learn (or relearn) a set of custom tags or objects when you move from one type of project to another. Of course, if your line of business would benefit from the creation of a customized environment for its particular type of pages, you can always create it using Fusebox. The more you get into using Fusebox, the easier it becomes to see new projects as not only possible, but quite straightforward. That benefit alone serves to make Fusebox one of the best development accelerators around; new tasks don't carry the weight of the unknown nearly as much as they do when you don't use a standard methodology.

Fusebox can go a long way toward improving your ability to quickly develop quality applications, thereby helping to lower development costs. Fusebox is also one of the simplest development frameworks available.

Simplicity

If you've been involved in web development for any length of time, you've probably been introduced to some other methodologies and products that are designed to help your development efforts. For example, you might have seen Allaire's Spectra product or Ralph Fiol's CFObjects. These products are designed to allow the development of complex applications while simplifying the amount of work the developer must do. It's worth taking a look at these two to see how Fusebox compares with them.

Fusebox Isn't Spectra

Spectra is a framework that is aimed at creating content-management systems—that is, web sites where the content changes on a regular basis, such as news or portals. To that end, Allaire created a large library of custom ColdFusion tags to help manage the creation of such sites. This library was sold as Spectra. Spectra was quite good at its intended goal, but it was also a complex system. Using it required the developer to spend a long time learning the library of tags. In fact, learning Spectra has been compared to learning an entirely new scripting language. This is not a bad comparison, in that there are far more tags in Spectra than in ColdFusion. Learning Spectra takes more time than learning ColdFusion in the first place.

Fusebox, in contrast, minimizes its use of custom tags. In fact, as of version 3.0, all the custom tags that had been used in previous versions have been rolled into the single core file, so the developer doesn't need to learn them at all.

Fusebox has a definite "Eureka moment." When someone first encounters the Fusebox concept from a programming perspective, the gestalt is rarely understood early on. However, after some exposure to what Fusebox is all about (such as with the contents of this book), the person says, in effect, "Eureka! It makes perfect sense! What a great way to do things!" at a specific point in time. You might be laughing at our hyperbole, but you'd be surprised at how many people have described having this experience with Fusebox in similar terms.

Go back to the idea of simplicity. Whereas Spectra has a large library of tags to learn, Fusebox has none. Linguistically, a good ColdFusion programmer doesn't need to learn anything to use Fusebox. It's all in the technique.

Fusebox has different design objectives from Spectra. In somewhat similar fashion, Fusebox can be compared to CFObjects, a product that is designed to bring object orientation to the ColdFusion world.

Fusebox Isn't CFObjects

According to Ralph Fiol (http://www.cfobjects.com), "CFObjects is a simple, elegant, and efficient framework for implementing inheritance, polymorphism, and encapsulation with CFML." If you haven't been exposed to the terminology of object-oriented programming, that statement probably didn't say much to you.

As its name implies, CFObjects is aimed at bringing the ideas and concepts of object-oriented programming to ColdFusion. It has succeeded admirably. It's fascinating to look at Fiol's work and see how he has enabled ColdFusion coders to create and manipulate objects in code. The CFObjects site even has a one-hour (estimated) tutorial on how to get started.

If you haven't had exposure to object-oriented programming, you'll need to get some foundation there before (or along with) learning CFObjects. After all, what do inheritance, polymorphism, and encapsulation mean?

Now, don't get the wrong idea—CFObjects is a cool and powerful concept. As you get involved in the Fusebox conmmunity, you'll find that many of our ideas have grown out of object-oriented programming disciplines. In particular, Hal Helms' background is in Smalltalk, one of the first truly object-oriented languages. We're not trying to disparage CFObjects or object orientation—far from it.

No, the point here is that Fusebox is just ColdFusion organized in a particular manner. Fusebox doesn't offer an abundance of new concepts—just ones you've seen before (such as organization, or documentation of code) arranged in a particular fashion. Although many people come to Fusebox thinking of it in mystical terms, it's not. The learning curve with Fusebox is quite gentle.

In fact, we like to think that a new ColdFusion developer who learns Fusebox from the start of the ColdFusion experience will be much better equipped than the average developer.

By helping the developer with some defined techniques for breaking applications into meaningful pieces, Fusebox simplifies the application design and construction process. Another natural outgrowth of Fusebox's organization is the maintainability of Fusebox applications.

Maintainability

Another benefit of using Fusebox is the impact it has on the concept of maintainability. *Maintainability* refers to the level of effort that is required to make modifications to an application after it has been deployed. This is a factor that is often lost in the fervor for rapid initial development.

The vast majority of any application's lifespan is spent in maintenance. We define maintenance as that period of time that follows the initial release of the system. If you think about any program you have developed, you can easily see that the time spent with it after it was originally written was probably much longer than the time it took to get that first working version up and running.

Maintenance Perspectives

Maintainability can be looked at from two different points of view: future maintenance by the original author and future maintenance by unknown parties.

In the former case, you might have had the uncomfortable (although usually amusing in some respects) experience of picking up a program you wrote some number of months in the past, only to spend a great deal of time figuring out what you were trying to do with some section of code. This is a common experience among programmers.

In the latter case, you might have also had the even more uncomfortable experience of being given someone else's program to enhance and maintain. Unless the program in question was thoroughly documented, the question, "What was he thinking?!" probably crossed your mind.

The tried-and-true solution to these maintenance issues is good documentation. Good documentation when it comes to program code can be summed up in a single word: comments.

From the beginning of software development history, programmers in every language that had the ability to embed comments have been told to comment their code. In most cases, though, developers haven't been told *how* to effectively use comments. Have you ever picked up a program with a comment that looks like this one?

```
<!--- Delete this line before beta test --->
```

Your first question is, naturally, "Which line is 'this'—the one before the comment or the one after it?" On the other hand, you might have been fortunate enough to learn from someone who had developed an effective means of documenting his code.

Fusedoc and Maintenance

When you use Fusebox, you get the expertise of just such a person in the deal. The Fusebox standard includes the use of Fusedoc, a documentation concept that Helms originated and Javadoc inspired.

Fusedoc instructs the system architect to start each fuse with a piece of standard documentation called a Fusedoc. This chunk of information is intended to give a programmer all the information needed to write the code for that fuse.

As we'll talk about in Chapter 7, "Fusedocs," after you are familiar with the Fusedoc format (which takes little time), you'll find this little gem at the top of each fuse to be an invaluable reference work as you're programming. This is particularly true in the case of that old program you pick up a few months later. A quick perusal of the Fusedoc will bring you right back to the purpose of the fuse in short order.

Fusedoc was designed to be a means for an application architect to communicate the technical details of a fuse to a coder. It makes sense, then, that Fusedoc also provides a wonderful built-in mechanism for the communication of these same details to maintenance coders who might inherit the application in the future.

Fusedoc isn't the only feature of Fusebox that increases the inherent maintainability of Fusebox applications, though. One of Fusebox's greatest strengths is the independence of its components, which we call *circuits*.

Component Independence

When you think of circuits in Fusebox, think of the circuit breakers in your house's breaker panel. If your house is old enough or located in the proper part of the world, you might even have a genuine fuse box. Either way, the idea is the same. When a circuit breaker or fuse blows in a panel, the capabilities of that circuit are not available to the house. The other circuits, though, are unaffected. Like separate circuits in a panel, Fusebox circuits are intended to be collections of functionality. As such, they are independent and can be reused in other applications, or they can be removed from an application altogether for modification.

This is sometimes a difficult concept to imagine, so let's look at a couple of examples. In the case of reusability, imagine a circuit that contains all the code you need to let a user log in to your site to maintain his account information. You might call this circuit "Users."

Then you get a request to develop a new application for a different client. The new site requires the same user functionality that you already built in the Users circuit. Instead of rebuilding the same functionality for the new application, you simply take a copy of the Users circuit from the first application and drop it into the second application.

If you need to modify a site, it's easy to disable individual circuits without disrupting the rest of the site. Let's imagine that your site processes customer orders with credit cards. One night you get hacked, and the next day all the news wires are reporting that your site allowed credit card information to get out. What do you do? The drastic approach (and one I've seen taken) would be to place a "site down for maintenance" notice on your home page, and then proceed to make the fixes as quickly as possible.

This really isn't much of a solution, though. It would be much more effective if you could allow users to do everything they normally do at your site except check out. Then you could fix the credit-processing features and turn the Check Out feature back on. Meanwhile, the disruption to regular visitors is minimized. If your site is a well-designed Fusebox site, this approach is actually trivial. You could control access to your credit-processing circuit while you make changes, and then reopen access after you're done. That sounds like a much lower-stress plan than the first. The independence of Fusebox circuits makes it all possible.

Application Flow

The final point we'll discuss, relative to maintenance, is application flow. How do you know what an application is supposed to do? Where in the application will the user go next if he clicks the Submit button?

The answers to these questions might require a great deal of research on most web applications. To get all the answers to the "Where next?" questions, you'll have to cruise through the templates in the site, checking each one's form actions, links, and redirects to see where they might lead.

In Fusebox, though, the entire application flow for a circuit is represented in one file. You just open the switch file (fbx_switch.cfm) to see all the actions that circuit can handle, and where the user will be sent if a given action is performed.

Fusebox Is Proven

Many concepts come and go, but the best ones stick around and get better. Fusebox continues to be a dynamic, growing framework with a terrifically active community. In fact, a Google search of the Internet in January 2002 showed about 1,050,000 URLs that exhibited characteristics of Fusebox. According to Google's metrics, that's about 1/20th of 1% of the entire web! Fusebox also represents about 7% of all sites that were developed with ColdFusion. Add to these figures the knowledge that many sites use Fusebox without being quite so obvious about it, and it's quite clear that Fusebox is indeed a popular methodology.

Some of the more high-profile sites that use Fusebox include these:

- Rooms to Go (`http://www.roomstogo.com`), America's largest furniture e-tailer
- The Boeing Store (`http://www.boeingstore.com`)
- eBags, the first e-tailer to use Fusebox (`http://www.ebags.com`)

The Scalability Issue

ColdFusion has long suffered from the reputation that it "doesn't scale well." Many folks throughout the ColdFusion community, right up to Ben Forta, have committed a great deal of time and explanation to the debunking of this popular myth.

ColdFusion's bad reputation on this issue grew out of the simple fact that it provided a great way for non-programmers to get into dynamic web site development. With its shallow learning curve, ColdFusion has always been attractive to a broad spectrum of site developers, from the complete neophyte to the seasoned veteran. Because of the ease of the language, many sites were constructed without some basic understanding of program design and performance issues. When sites like this became popular, they often suffered great performance hits as their user load increased. When the site broke down under increased load, the finger was often pointed at ColdFusion instead of at the poor design of the application.

Users of Fusebox understand quite well that ColdFusion can scale up nicely to handle heavy loads if the application is well designed. That's where Fusebox drops into the mix. Fusebox gives a developer the structure needed to plan great sites. With its highly modular design characteristics, Fusebox allows performance gains to be realized by clarifying the entire design of the system. This allows developers to focus on those areas of the system that will benefit from performance tweaking, while leaving the other parts of the system undisturbed. In similar fashion, the DBA can focus on performance tuning the database-related aspects of the application without impacting the developers. Fusebox is also specifically designed to be well behaved in a clustered server environment, allowing it to scale from a single-server implementation to a high-traffic environment.

Much can be said about the scalability issue and ColdFusion, but that's not really the focus of our book. If you're interested in more information on this subject, visit the ColdFusion Developers Journal site (`http://www.sys-con.com/coldfusion`) and look for Ben Forta's two articles on scaling. Doug Nottage, Director of Advanced Technology for AutoByTel, has also spoken frequently on scaling ColdFusion. He has some great information on his site at `http://doug.nottage.com`.

The "Performance Problem"

Somewhat like ColdFusion and the scalability rumor, Fusebox has been subject to a variety of rumors regarding performance of sites that were constructed using its methods.

Numerous questions have been posed about Fusebox's performance because the basis of Fusebox is a collection of `<CFINCLUDE>` statements. The concern is that the performance hit caused by using numerous includes will cause a site's response time to degrade to an unacceptable level.

Our first reaction to this concern is to state that Fusebox certainly doesn't seem to hobble the large e-commerce sites that use it. This, however, is as anecdotal a response as the original concern. Wherever possible, we prefer to address concerns, anecdotal or otherwise, with factual responses.

To that end, we took a Fusebox application and timed the load of a particular page over five trials with caching disabled. We then created a ColdFusion page that was the result of processing all the `<CFINCLUDE>` tags required to create the Fusebox page in the first test. The results shown in Table 2.1 might surprise you.

Table 2.1   **Testing Fusebox Page Load Times**

	With Fusebox	Plain CFML Without Includes
Initial Page Load	250ms	350ms
Avg. Page Load (5 Trials of Immediate Refresh)	200ms	173ms

With a Fusebox application, every page request is tantamount to an initial page load because of the dynamic nature of the Fusebox file. Even though each request is for the same page (normally index.cfm), that page changes its "shape" with every call, according to the request string. Rarely does a Fusebox application call the same URL twice in succession.

Fusebox wins the race unless you "cook the books" by immediately refreshing the page several times, taking advantage of ColdFusion's caching of the static page to overcome Fusebox's intial page load advantage.

In the typical application scenario in which you proceed from one distinct page call to another, the caching doesn't get a chance to affect the race, and the Fusebox version wins by 40%. How can this be?

As it turns out, Fusebox inherently takes advantage of ColdFusion's caching with every page call. Because every page call goes through a single file (typically index.cfm), the ColdFusion server gets to use its cached version of that file, as well as cached versions of the Fusebox core file and some of the other files that are included along the way. The end result is that, instead of hauling all the code out of P-code to run it, ColdFusion can use a large percentage of the code from its cache. Although this has never been a design objective of Fusebox, we think it has turned out to be a rather nice benefit.

We should mention that although we enjoy this little performance benefit, Fusebox has never been an exercise in performance tuning. We firmly believe that performance is an issue that should be addressed within the context of whatever framework you use, as opposed to designing a framework specifically for performance. This seems imminently logical, in that the best-performing solution would be written tightly in well-crafted machine language, consequently being indescribably difficult to create and maintain. We strongly encourage every development shop to make a strong investment in a good SQL head. Tuning the performance of your application's individual queries will get you much more in the way of performance gains than just about any other performance-related pursuit.

The Community

No discussion of the benefits of Fusebox would be complete without some mention of the Fusebox community. An amazing collection of people are using Fusebox worldwide, and a large number of them actively participate in the community at large.

The predominant means of participating in the Fusebox community is through the use of email lists. The main Fusebox list is at `fusebox@topica.com`. This list is home to some of the most knowledgeable folks you'd ever hope to meet. The discussion on this list covers whatever aspects of Fusebox you're curious about, as well as announcements about conferences, courses, updates, and so on.

The Fusebox.org web site is the official repository of Fusebox information. This is the place to visit for copies of white papers, the latest version of the Fusebox files, and contact information for Fusebox training. The site is run by the Fusebox Council, which as of this writing consists of six members:

Hal Helms (`hal@teamallaire.com`)

Steve Nelson (`m@secretagents.com`)

Nat Papovich (nat@fusium.com)

Jeff Peters (jeff@grokfusebox.com)

John Quarto-von Tivadar (jcq@mindspring.com)

Erik Voldengen (erik@fusium.com)

In addition to the Fusebox Council, a Standards Committee is responsible for maintaining the Fusebox standard and voting on changes to it, and an Advisory Committee makes suggestions to the Standards Committee regarding the specification. More information on these aspects of Fusebox organization can be found on the Fusebox.org site.

The community is perhaps one of Fusebox's strongest features, even though it's not really a feature of Fusebox. Fuseboxers are working worldwide, so it's likely that if you post something to one of the lists, you'll get a response fairly quickly, no matter where you live.

According to a straw poll taken at the 2001 Fusebox Conference, Fusebox is in use on every continent with the exception of Antarctica. Who knows—maybe one of the researchers down there is running a site that uses it!

Extensibility

Another of Fusebox's strengths is its ability to "work and play well with others." This is sometimes referred to as *extensibility*. Simply put, using Fusebox does not force you to use a restrictive set of tools or libraries.

You're free to draw from the extensive collection of custom tags that is freely available on the Net, as well as to augment your style with any code inventions you might have devised.

Most development shops find that, instead of restricting the way they work, Fusebox actually allows them more time to create innovative methods instead of plowing through the drudgery of building poorly organized applications.

What Kinds of Applications Can I Build?

Occasionally we're asked this question by someone who thinks he might be interested in using Fusebox. An underlying assumption seems to be that Fusebox is designed to help build specific types of applications.

Usually this question arises from the questioner's previous experience with products that are designed for specific types of site development, such as content mangement or e-commerce. However, Fusebox isn't geared toward any specific type of site. Its benefits are availabe regardless of what type of site you want to build, be it e-commerce, an intranet application, or a web service. The next sections take a look at each of these application types and how Fusebox can help. Of course, these are only three of an infinite variety of application types. We offer them because they are common web-development tasks.

Fusebox and E-Commerce

E-commerce is one of the leading reasons for building a web site. After all, the lure of being able to market something on a worldwide basis for the cost of building a web site is appealing.

Fusebox has been used for a wide variety of e-commerce sites. One of the primary reasons for this is the ability to reuse Fusebox circuits after they've been built.

E-commerce is particularly well suited to reuse of circuits because every e-commerce site has some things in common with every other e-commerce site. For example, your visitors need a way to view your products, specify what they want to buy, and give you their payment and shipping information. The system needs to validate the payment information and process the order. Many of these processes can be reused from one site to the next simply by adding the circuit in question to the new application. Fusebox can also make moving into and out of secured (SSL) pages a simple matter.

Fusebox and Intranets

Intranets are an often overlooked opportunity for web developers. The possibilities are endless for internal applications using Fusebox. Sales information, corporate contacts, task management, and a wide variety of other areas can be streamlined using custom applications.

Typically, intranets grow from small initial application ideas into larger corporate portal sites. This progression of growth is perfectly suited to Fusebox, which allows you to build a new circuit and plug it into the existing application. This goes a long way toward lowering the overall stress involved with adding features to a site. In fact, it's possible to have different teams working on different additions to the site, entirely independently of one another.

Fusebox and Web Services

The past year or so has been filled with buzz about web services—those chunks of applications that are exposed to outside use through a web interface. Web services promise to allow you to build applications that leverage a collection of unrelated servers anywhere in the world to build a comprehensive application.

One of the concerns in building web services is the ability to create datasets for retrieval by client systems. Fusebox 3.0 has been tuned to streamline this sort of activity. For example, if you create a fuseaction to build an XML output dataset, Fusebox ensures that you don't have leading whitespace in the returned dataset, which can be a problem for SOAP and other web service implementations.

"Porting" Existing Applications to Fusebox

When evaluating Fusebox, a company might be thinking in terms of updating its existing applications to use the new methodology.

Examining whether to rewrite an application must happen on a case-by-case basis, and we can't simply say, "Of course, you should rewrite everything in Fusebox." Depending on the size of the application, the rewrite might be far from a trivial matter.

However, Fusebox rewrites can provide benefits in many cases. Original applications are often difficult to maintain, particularly if they were developed without the benefit of a controlling methodology. If the application in question has a long life ahead of it, it might be useful to consider a Fusebox redux.

The primary question for rewriting has to be, "Does it do what it's supposed to do?" If the answer is "yes," then the payoff for rewriting it probably isn't great. If the answer is, "yes, but…," then it's a good idea to start considering the problems that exist from the perspective of making the answer a simple "yes."

How to Decide if Fusebox Is Right for You

In trying to decide whether Fusebox is right for you, you must consider several factors. Do you already use a methodology? Does that methodology work well, or does it have problems that you want to fix? Are you working alone or on a team?

This chapter addressed some of the areas where Fusebox provides benefits for web applications, including rapid development, simplicity, maintainability, and extensibility. This combination of features makes Fusebox a compelling methodology, and worth a look.

Unlike purpose-specific methodologies and products, Fusebox isn't designed to assist in the development of particular types of sites or web applications. Rather, its general approach to organization and consistency is applicable to any development project.

The selection of a methodology is an important decision that deserves deliberate consideration. After looking at Fusebox, you might decide that something else would provide a better solution for your team's needs. We don't try to pretend that Fusebox is a panacea for every shop's development problems. We have, however, found that Fusebox stacks up well in the vast majority of situations we've examined.

Hopefully, this chapter has given you plenty of food for thought, as well as a good impression of how Fusebox might improve your development processes. The rest of the book will make sure you're steeped in enough Fusebox information not only to make reasonable decisions about using it, but also to build terrific web sites and web applications with Fusebox.

Let's get started with that information. The next chapter jumps into the nuts and bolts of what makes Fusebox work—the Fusebox framework files.

2

Fusebox Coding

3

"*And since geometry is the right foundation of all painting, I have decided to teach its rudiments and principles to all youngsters eager for art...*"

—Albrecht Dürer

The Fusebox Framework

As we begin Part 2, "Fusebox Coding," you might be wondering how all the parts combine to create a Fusebox application. There are fuses of different types, there are controller and core files, and there are places to put circuit-wide code. Applications are called with an accompanying fuseaction, which always goes through the default document—usually `index.cfm`. What is inside the "core file"? How does it work? What is the rest of the Fusebox framework, and how do all the pieces fit together? How can plain old ColdFusion be used to build a complete application framework?

Starting with this chapter, Part 2 answers all those questions and more, in addition to serving as a reference guide to technical Fusebox. In this chapter, we explain how a request is processed by a Fusebox application—all the steps that ColdFusion goes through to execute your page. By the end of this chapter, we will be halfway through an analysis of the core file. Chapter 4, "Handling a Fuseaction," finishes up the request, but here we will cover all the pre-processing, such as `Application.cfm` and `index.cfm`. We will also cover the first six sections of the core file. Before we start, though, there are a few things to cover.

Notes About the Framework Files

Throughout this book, we refer to the "core file" (or occasionally the "core"). The *core file* is the file available from fusebox.org that contains the code that sets up the Fusebox framework with each page request. Some people think of it as "the Fusebox," but a more apt phrase might be: "the engine that drives Fusebox."

The filename of this engine varies depending on the version of Fusebox, the version of ColdFusion, and which operating system is running. Versions are optimized for different ColdFusion versions from 4.0 through 5 in both Windows and UNIX-based operating systems. There are currently no core files for any ColdFusion versions prior to 4.0. At the time of this printing, Fusebox is in version 3.0 and the core files are as follows:

Table 3.1 **Core Files**

Filename	Description
fbx_fusebox30_CF40.cfm	ColdFusion version 4.0, 4.5, 4.5.1, 4.5.2, and Windows OS
fbx_fusebox30_CF45.cfm	ColdFusion version 4.5.2 SP2 and Windows OS
fbx_fusebox30_CF45_nix.cfm	ColdFusion version 4.5.2 SP2 and UNIX-based OS, including Solaris and Linux
fbx_fusebox30_CF50.cfm	ColdFusion version 5 and Windows OS
fbx_fusebox30_CF50_nix.cfm	ColdFusion version 5 and UNIX-based OS, including Solaris and Linux

Although many members of the Fusebox community contributed to the theory involved in the 3.0 core implementation, John Quarto-Von Tivadar and Nat Papovich built the majority of the code in the core files as a collaborative effort based on a loose specification. We will dive into fbx_fusebox30_CF50.cfm shortly, after we make a few comments about it.

The goal of many members of the Fusebox community is to evolve Fusebox into a specification that is complete enough for any party to create a core file from it, instead of just having one copy that everyone uses.

The existing core files were created based on the feedback and wishes of the Fusebox community along with current common practices that were not officially part of Fusebox. The core file was not created from a true specification. If a certain feature sounded like a good idea, it was added to the core. If something needed tweaking, it was done. Only after the Fusebox 3.0 core was released in November 2001 did the creators realize that the core was in fact an implementation of a specification. The specification did not yet exist, but it could be created off of the existing core file.

The Fusebox specification that the community hopes for has not yet emerged, but we suspect that it will soon. When developers use a Fusebox specification rather than a product, we are not locked into using the core file as available from `fusebox.org`. This way, we achieve vendor independence. Similar in practice to the J2EE specification, individuals or organizations can develop their own compatible core files, each following the same set of rules and creating the same API, but each might be optimized for a certain environment or also include extended features. An API (application program interface) is the method prescribed by a program by which a programmer writing an application can make requests of the program. In other words, it is the interface between the application and the program. This way, any applications built using a core file that follows this specification will be compatible with any other application using a different, but also compatible core file.

However, at the time of this writing, there exists only one set of core files; those files are available from fusebox.org, and this book deals with Fusebox as implemented in those core files.

Starting the Request

In Chapter 1, "The Arrival of Fusebox," we discussed the basics of Fusebox and how all page requests go through the `index.cfm`. All `<href>` links, form actions, JavaScript redirects, `<cflocation>` tags, and `<cfmodule>` tags should point to `index.cfm`. But how do we guarantee that? Aren't there problems if a user requests `qry_DeleteUser.cfm` directly from a browser? At best, the misguided user sees an error message. At worst, the user is able to delete users in the system. How do we fix this problem?

Application.cfm Always Runs First

There is a template that ColdFusion processes with each page request: `Application.cfm` (the capital "A" is for UNIX case sensitivity). In fact, ColdFusion processes `Application.cfm` before processing any other template. You request `http://www.thirdwheelbikes.com/index.cfm`, and ColdFusion processes the `Application.cfm` file in the same folder as `index.cfm` first. If ColdFusion cannot find a file named `Application.cfm`, then the processor looks in the next highest folder. In our case, if `http://www.thirdwheelbikes.com/index.cfm` were in `c:\inetpub\wwwroot\`, ColdFusion would first look in the web root—`c:\inetpub\wwwroot\`. If there was none to be found there, ColdFusion would then look in `c:\inetpub\`. If no `Application.cfm` was found there either, ColdFusion would look in `c:\`.

If any `Application.cfm` file was found in any of those folders, ColdFusion would stop looking up the tree.

There is no known way to get around this feature, which is a good thing. Many applications rely heavily on `Application.cfm` to run for each request. Some developers place security code in `Application.cfm`. Fusebox relies on the `Application.cfm` file for security too, but in a different way. Check out this code snippet commonly placed in the `Application.cfm` for Fusebox applications:

```
<cfif listLast(cgi.script_name,'/') neq "index.cfm">
  <cflocation url="index.cfm">
</cfif>
```

In essence, this code *forces* all requests made in this web root to go through `index.cfm`. Let's think carefully about this. We know that ColdFusion does not process requests without first processing the `Application.cfm`. Our Fusebox applications have one `Application.cfm` file—in the web root. This `Application.cfm` contains code that forces page requests made for anything other than `index.cfm` to the root `index.cfm` file. Now we can be assured that no one is bypassing the `index.cfm`. These two important steps ensure that all requests made of a Fusebox application go through our default document. All `<href>`, form action, and `<cflocation>` code that we write points to `index.cfm`. Any request that slips through or is created by an errant user also is pointed to `index.cfm`.

index.cfm Is Requested

Because `index.cfm` is the only file that is directly called, it is here that we call the Fusebox core file. The `index.cfm` that comes with the core files downloaded from `fusebox.org` looks like this:

```
<cflock type="READONLY" name="#server.coldfusion.productVersion#"
➥timeout="10">
  <cfset variables.fuseboxVersion=Replace(Replace(ListDeleteAt
  ➥(server.coldfusion.productVersion,4),",","","all")," ","","all")>
  <cfset variables.fuseboxOSName=server.os.name>
</cflock>
<cfif variables.fuseboxVersion lte 450>
  <cfinclude template="fbx_fusebox30_CF40.cfm">
<cfelseif variables.fuseboxVersion lt 500>
  <cfif variables.fuseboxOSName contains "Windows">
    <cfinclude template="fbx_fusebox30_CF45.cfm">
  <cfelse>
    <cfinclude template="fbx_fusebox30_CF45_nix.cfm">
  </cfif>
<cfelseif variables.fuseboxVersion lt 600>
```

```
<cfif variables.fuseboxOSName contains "Windows">
  <cfinclude template="fbx_fusebox30_CF50.cfm">
<cfelse>
  <cfinclude template="fbx_fusebox30_CF50_nix.cfm">
</cfif>
</cfif>
```

Let's look at this code from the top. `server.coldfusion.productVersion` is a ColdFusion built-in variable. The server scope is readable and writeable, but most developers wisely avoid using it. You must exercise great caution when writing to the server scope because variables there are persistent (they are stored across page requests) and they are available to all users in all applications. The application scope is available to all users in a specific application, but if multiple sites are running on one server (as is the case in shared hosting environments), all applications share the server scope. Thankfully, reading the server scope is not as dangerous. For now, let's get back to the variable `server.coldfusion.productVersion`.

`server.coldfusion.productVersion` contains the value of the ColdFusion server version. If you are running ColdFusion version 4.0.1, this variable contains the value `4,0,1,0`. If you are running version 5, the value is `5,0,0,0`. We mentioned previously that different versions of the core file are available for different ColdFusion versions. Well, this is the code that decides which one to use. This code also uses the variable `server.os.name` to determine which operating system is running. Regardless of the final choice, the `index.cfm` `<cfinclude>`s the appropriate core file. Refer to Table 3.1 to find out which core file is used for which operating system and ColdFusion version.

Portability Is the Key

You might think it makes more sense to remove all the logic and make a single `<cfinclude>` to the appropriate core file. After all, you are running on one operating system and one ColdFusion version, right? And how often does that sort of thing change? It might change more often that you think. If you can imagine coming into your office one day and hearing your boss say that the entire company is moving to Linux—servers and all—then maybe this logic is a good idea.

Also, if your environment consists of a development server and a production server, then the possibility exists for different ColdFusion versions to be running on those different machines. Maybe the production server is a Solaris box and you prefer to develop on a Windows server. Or maybe you host applications on a shared server, where you cannot be in control of when the servers are upgraded. This logic in the `index.cfm` will allow you to run the same application on different servers without changing a thing, provided that the application code you write is cross-platform and written for the earliest ColdFusion version.

However, if you are a one-man, one-computer shop or you run the same platforms and versions on all your servers, then you can crop out all the logic in `index.cfm` and leave just the `<cfinclude>` for the core file. You might shave off a few nanoseconds of page execution time.

Now that we have worked through the `index.cfm`, you might be wondering what the point is of calling the `index.cfm` if all it is going to do is call the core file. It is certainly not doing anything right now. However, because it only calls the core file, you can include it from outside your web root, increasing application security.

A Web Site Outside the Web Root

Although `index.cfm` includes only the core file, it can do a whole lot more. We have already discussed how the code in `Application.cfm` ensures that all requests go through `index.cfm`. In 1999, a vulnerability was found in Microsoft IIS 4.0 and 5.0 that allowed a malicious user to view the source of any file in the web root without preprocessing. By adding a couple characters to a common URL string, users could see the ColdFusion source code without ColdFusion getting a chance to process it. Because ColdFusion was not able to process the `.cfm` page before IIS passed it on to the user, it also was not able to process the `Application.cfm` file. This meant that users could see any file in the application. Whether it was `index.cfm` did not matter.

Microsoft created a patch very quickly, but this opened up the eyes of many developers. If one hole was found to make our source code readable by hackers, then others might exist. How could we avoid this in the future?

One excellent answer lies in the `index.cfm`. Because this file `<cfinclude>`s the Fusebox core file, and the Fusebox core file `<cfinclude>`s the rest of the application, we can place the entire application directory outside of the web root and essentially cut it off from the web. Figure 3.1 shows an example of how a directory structure might be set up.

As you can see in the figure, the directory that contains our application `thirdwheelbikes` is placed outside of the web root. Now the `index.cfm` needs to be modified to accommodate the application being in a different location:

```
<cfinclude template="../../thirdwheelbikes/fbx_fusebox30_CF50.cfm">
```

By setting up our application this way to take advantage of some of the power of `index.cfm`, we have removed all but two pages from the web root. Now, users can only request `index.cfm`, and no other fuses or templates can be accessed directly.

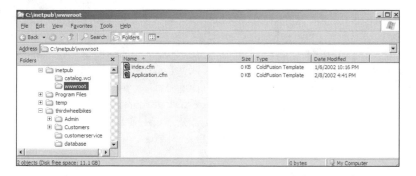

Figure 3.1   Secure directory structure.

Closing Notes on *Index.cfm*

Throughout this chapter, we have used the filename `index.cfm` to be our default web server document. But this might not always be the case. What happens if your default document is `default.cfm` or `home.cfm`? In those cases, Fusebox has you covered. So far, the only hard-coded reference to `index.cfm` is in `Application.cfm`, where you declare which file can be accessed. If you use `default.cfm` instead of `index.cfm`, your `Application.cfm` would look like this:

```
<cfif listLast(cgi.script_name,'/') neq "default.cfm">
  <cflocation url="default.cfm">
</cfif>
```

Now you know that whenever we refer to "index.cfm," we are really referring to whatever the default document is, which is most likely `index.cfm`.

Now that we have covered all the preprocessing, we are ready to take a look at the core. This is where the Fusebox-specific code runs, and where the Fusebox framework files are processed.

Notes on the Core File

In this section, we will discuss some general background about the core and its purpose before we jump into the code inside the core. Throughout this section—and in fact, throughout the course of this book—our examples and discussions use the core file for ColdFusion 5 on the Windows platform: `fbx_fusebox30_CF50.cfm`. At times, we will make a reference to how other core files accomplish tasks, but this is the exception rather than the rule.

It is important to note that we are documenting the current state of the Fusebox core files. We are not trying to guess where Fusebox officially will be in six months or a year. Despite this caveat, the current status of Fusebox is stable, and the basic principles documented here are unlikely to change.

It is also important to remember that this book is about developing solutions—it is Fusebox in practice. This chapter and the next are technical documentation of the current core files, as are available from www.thirdwheelbikes.com. If you are interested in learning how the latest version of Fusebox differs from the version presented here, you should visit fusebox.org. This book is relevant regardless of the current version.

Frozen ColdFusion Core

The core file should be a frozen file. That means that any modifications to it are done at your own risk and are not advised. Modifications occur to fix bugs, increase functionality, or reduce execution times. By using the core file as it is released, we can be assured that upgrading to a new core will be as simple as copy and paste. If we decide to extend the functionality of the core file ourselves, we risk being cut off from the community's progress.

One major concern with new releases is backward compatibility. The API (more on the API later in this chapter) might gain some power, or new functionality might appear, but applications built using previous versions will always work with new versions.

Just because the core is frozen in code does not mean that it is frozen in time. Changes that community members propose are frequently adopted into the code. Therefore, if you think a particular addition to the core would benefit all developers, please do not hold it to yourself. Sign up at fusebox.org and share. That is how Fusebox evolves!

No Custom Tags in the Core

In an effort to improve scalability and simplicity, the core uses no custom tags during processing. If you are familiar with previous versions of Fusebox, you might remember `<cf_formurl2attributes>`, `<cf_bodycontent>` and `<cf_nesting>`. Although those tags were quite clever, Fusebox relied on them for every page request. In the case of `<cf_nesting>`, the same custom tag was called multiple times for each request. Fuseboxers realized that this model was not sustainable because ColdFusion processes custom tags in a separate memory space from the currently running request. That meant that for every Fusebox request, multiple threads were being consumed by ColdFusion to handle all the extra custom tags being used. It just did not make much sense.

In Fusebox 3, the core subsumed the custom tag functionality of `<cf_formurl2attributes>`. The power of the nested circuits model provided in part by `<cf_nesting>` was duplicated by some code wizardry in the core, also. Macromedia finished off the job for us by creating a native tag, `<cfsavecontent>`, which exactly mirrors the functionality of `<cf_bodycontent>`. (We consider Steve Nelson's `<cf_bodycontent>` the finest five lines of Cold Fusion code ever written. It is no wonder that Macromedia "borrowed" it.)

If you are still using a ColdFusion version prior to 5, you do not have `<cfsavecontent>`, so the core files for those versions continue to use the custom tag version of that tag, renamed to `<cf_savecontent>`. Now you have one more reason to upgrade—no Fusebox custom tags.

Fusebox in JSP and PHP

Mostly due to the similarities in the languages, a core file has been developed for JSP (by Ben Edwards and Stacy Young) and PHP (by David Huyck). These core files closely duplicate the functionality found in the ColdFusion version and are available from `fusebox.org`. The community of developers who are using them is not as numerous or as vocal as those who are using ColdFusion, but we expect the numbers to grow.

Don't worry about having to learn a new framework if your boss comes into your office one day and says that all new development is to be done in JSP. You can just use it as an opportunity for some excitement!

CFScripted for Speed

CFScript, a server-side scripting language, was introduced in ColdFusion 4.0. It provided some CFML functionality in JavaScript-like syntax, without tags. It also gave developers a way to speed up some kinds of ColdFusion code. Unfortunately, translations aren't available for all ColdFusion tags in CFScript, so the core uses a combination of CFScript and tag-based CFML to increase performance. During early core file tuning, a nearly 40% reduction in execution time was achieved in part by using CFScript.

If you are unfamiliar with CFScript, you might want to take a moment to review the syntax in the ColdFusion documentation. It is not hard to learn, but it is used heavily in the core walkthrough, which comes next.

Now that we have enough background covered, let's start our investigation of the core. For the rest of this chapter, we will cover sections 1–6 of the core file. Each section will appear in the text, followed by an explanation of what it accomplishes and how it fits into the rest of the core and the framework. We also recommend that you open a copy of the core file in your favorite code editor so that you can easily see the whole file, including color-coding, which makes for easier reading. The sections are labeled in the file so that you can easily find your way around.

During our examples, we will discuss how the framework handles a variety of requests, whether they come via a URL, a form post, or a `<cfmodule>`. However, the one request we will completely track through the core is this:

```
<a href="index.cfm?fuseaction=reviews.read&productID=1392">
```

Upon requesting this URL, the application displays the page in Figure 3.2.

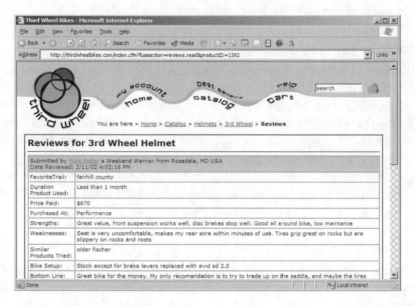

Figure 3.2   Product review page.

This figure shows a page containing all the reviews for a product called 3rd Wheel Helmet.

The Very Top of the Core

Following is the code that appears before Section 1 begins. We can call this Section 0:

```
1 <cfsetting enablecfoutputonly="yes"><cfprocessingdirective
  ➥suppresswhitespace="Yes">
2 <cftry>
```

Wait a minute! What happened to all the comments?

During our discussions of the core files (and in fact, throughout the entire book), we have removed comments from code regularly included inline with the text. We have done this mostly for compactness. Explaining the comments here would be redundant because we wrote most of the comments in the actual core. The inline comments will probably prove to be helpful when we begin dedicated development, but learning Fusebox from them would not be very easy.

The amount of comments in this section is indicative of the rest of the core; it is approximately 20% comments. Do not worry about ColdFusion having to parse unnecessarily through dozens of lines of comments. It is incredibly fast at the job, and the couple of fractions of nanoseconds' penalty is well worth it. The core would be a pretty difficult maze if there were no comments!

Line 1 contains the only code in this section. It opens two tags designed to control whitespace generated by ColdFusion. Those tags are closed at the end of the core file.

The rest of the code in this section is comments, describing what each section of the core file does. Because we are going to cover all of that in this chapter and the next, there is no need to explain it here. But it does provide a useful reference if you find yourself working inside the core without this guide. We are all done with Section 0, so let's move on.

Section 1: The Fusedoc

Here is the code that appears in Section 1. It is a Fusedoc. Do not worry if you cannot read Fusedocs yet; that will be discussed in Chapter 7, "Fusedocs."

```
1  <!-- ... -->
2  <fusedoc fuse="fbx_fusebox31_CF50.cfm" specification="2.0">
3    <responsibilities>
4    I am the code behind Fusebox 3.0 that handles nesting, layouts--oh,
     a bunch of stuff, really. PLEASE BE VERY CAREFUL ABOUT MAKING ANY
     CHANGES TO THIS FILE, AS IT WILL RENDER IT NON-COMPLIANT WITH THE
     STANDARD NOTED ABOVE. There is no need to modify this file for any
     settings. All settings can occur in fbx_settings.cfm. Because
     this file requires a tag introduced in CF5 (cfsavecontent), it can
     only be run on CF5+.
5    </responsibilities>
6    <properties>
7      <property name="version" value="3.1" />
8      <property name="build" value="1b" />
9      <history author="John Quarto-vonTivadar" date="27 Sep 2001"
        email="jcq@mindspring.com"></history>
10     <history author="Nat Papovich" date="Oct 2001"
        email="mcnattyp@yahoo.com" type="Update">Converted to cfscripting,
        bug fixes for final release.</history>
```

```
11      <history author="Nat Papovich" date="Nov 2001"
        ➥email="mcnattyp@yahoo.com" type="Update" />
12      <history author="Nat Papovich" date="Jan-Feb 2002"
        ➥email="mcnattyp@yahoo.com" type="Update">Added integrated error
        ➥handling.</history>
13  <note>Portions of code contributed by Hal Helms, Patrick McElhaney,
    ➥Steve Nelson, Nat Papovich, Jeff Peters, John Quarto-vonTivadar,
    ➥Gabe Roffman, Fred Sanders, Bill Wheatley, John Beynon, Bert
    ➥Dawson and Stan Cox.</note>
14    </properties>
15    <io>
16      <out>
17        <structure name="fusebox" scope="variables" comments="this is
          ➥the public API of variables that should be treated as
          ➥read-only">
18          <boolean name="isCustomTag" default="FALSE" />
19          <boolean name="isHomeCircuit" default="FALSE" />
20          <boolean name="isTargetCircuit" default="FALSE" />
21          <string name="fuseaction" />
22          <string name="circuit" />
23          <string name="homeCircuit" />
24          <string name="targetCircuit" />
25          <string name="thisCircuit" />
26          <string name="thisLayoutPath" />
27          <boolean name="suppressErrors" default="FALSE" />
28          <boolean name="useErrorCatch" default="FALSE" />
29          <boolean name="rethrowError" default="TRUE" />
30        <structure name="circuits" />
31          <string name="currentPath" />
32          <string name="rootPath" />
33        <structure name="cfcatch" />
34          <string name="defaultFuseactionString" />
35        </structure>
36        <structure name="FB_" comments="Internal use only. Please
          ➥treat the FB_ as a reserved structure, not to be touched." />
37      </out>
38    </io>
39  </fusedoc>
40  --->
41  <cfscript>
```

This Fusedoc documents all the variables in the Fusebox API. These variables
are available throughout the processing of the core file and all the subsequently
included files. Each of these variables will be discussed further, throughout the
course of this chapter and the next. The next section starts the real code of the
core file.

Section 2: The API

Just after the Fusedoc documenting the API, all the variables are declared in this section.

```
fusebox = structNew();
if (findNoCase("cf_", "," & getBaseTagList()))
  fusebox.isCustomTag=TRUE;
else fusebox.isCustomTag=FALSE;
fusebox.isHomeCircuit=FALSE;
fusebox.isTargetCircuit=FALSE;
fusebox.fuseaction="";
fusebox.circuit="";
fusebox.homeCircuit="";
fusebox.targetCircuit="";
fusebox.thisCircuit="";
fusebox.thislayoutpath="";
fusebox.suppressErrors=FALSE;
fusebox.circuits=structNew();
fusebox.currentPath="";
fusebox.rootPath="";
```

Although it is not necessary to declare variables before using them in ColdFusion (unlike other programming languages), the core file does so here for clarity. Most of these variables are simply being created with empty values in preparation for being supplied real values later in processing.

fusebox.isCustomTag

The first variable, `fusebox.isCustomTag`, is set now. This variable is a boolean variable. (You can confirm this via the Fusedoc in the previous section.) `fusebox.isCustomTag` does just what is sounds like it does; it says whether the current request is being processed as part of a custom tag call. The way it determines this is by using the `getBaseTagList()` function to retrieve a list of tags that have been opened, but not yet closed, prior to this section of code. By "opened," we mean ancestor tags, such as `<cfoutput>`, `<cftry>`, and `<cfif>`. Those tags are open and close tags. You must close each tag. Tags such as `<cfset>` and `<cfparam>` as well as any open and close tags that have been closed, such as a `<cfif><cfelse></cfif>` block, would not appear in this list if they had been run before this code.

When the getBaseTagList() function is run, it returns a string that looks like this:

```
CFTRY,CFPROCESSINGDIRECTIVE
```

The result reveals that those two tags (`cftry` and `cfprocessingdirective`) were opened but have yet to be closed. (They are closed at the end of the core file.)

With this list in hand, the core file checks to see whether the string "cf_" is included in any of the tags in the list. Based on the output of the preceding function, no match should exist. But here is where ColdFusion tricks us somewhat.

<cfmodule> Is a Custom Tag

Files can be `<cfmodule>`d in two different ways. We can use the `<cfmodule>` syntax like this:

```
<cfmodule template="myfile.cfm" variable="one">
```

We can also use the custom tag syntax if the target template is in the custom tags directory, or in the same directory as the currently executing template:

```
<cf_myfile variable="one">
```

If, in myfile.cfm, we output `#getBaseTagList()#`, we see that `CF_MYFILE` is included in the list no matter which syntax we use to execute the template. Somewhere behind the scenes, ColdFusion converts all `<cfmodule>` tags to their custom tag counterparts. Although it does not make much sense, Fusebox uses this feature to its advantage.

Because the core file is checking for the existence of "cf_", it is found whether the core file is being called via `<cfmodule>` or as a custom tag. Therefore, if you `<cfmodule>` a Fusebox application like this:

```
<cfmodule template="index.cfm" fuseaction="home.main">
```

the value of `fusebox.isCustomTag` will be `TRUE`. Therefore, in reality, the core does not determine if the current request is only called as a custom tag. It will be `TRUE` whether called as a custom tag or `<cfmodule>`.

You can use this variable to control layouts, display output, or manage application initialization throughout your application. We will come across a few references to this variable as we follow the application.

You need to be careful while using this variable. You should not `<cfinclude>` a Fusebox application from within another request because (among other problems), `fusebox.isCustomTag` might be incorrectly set to `TRUE`. If, for example, you are running ColdFusion 4.5 and you set a new fuseaction, then `<cfinclude>` a Fusebox application like this:

```
<cfset attributes.fuseaction="help.feedbackForm">
<cfinclude template="index.cfm">
```

You would expect `fusebox.isCustomTag` to be `FALSE`. After all, you are not calling the application via `<cfmodule>` or as a custom tag. But because Fusebox for ColdFusion 4.5 uses the custom tag `<cf_savecontent>`, the core file would find that tag in the list of `getBaseTagList()` and set `fusebox.isCustomTag` to `TRUE`. Although it is correct, it might be confusing.

The lesson, therefore, is never to `<cfinclude>` a Fusebox application; always use `<cfmodule>` or call it as a real custom tag.

Section 3: The *FB_* Structure

This is the code that appears in section 3 of the core:

```
FB_=structNew();
```

This section certainly is short. Is it even worthy of an entire section to itself? Yes, it probably is because of the importance of this one line of code.

The `FB_` structure created here is for use by the core file only—it is considered a "private" structure. The core file creates variables while it processes all the rest of the included files, and this structure is where all those variables are grouped together.

It is important that you never try to use this structure in your own code without a complete understanding of it. Also, do not try to create your own structure with the same name. The `FB_` structure should be considered a reserved word in Fusebox. You don't need to be aware of keys in this structure; you don't need to reference keys to use Fusebox. Occasionally, some keys are duplicated into the Fusebox API (discussed previously) if they need to be accessible to developers.

Section 4: formURL2attributes

We call section 4 of the core the "formURL2attributes" section. Earlier in the chapter, we mentioned that Fusebox 3 doesn't have custom tags unless you are running earlier versions of ColdFusion. Section 4 is one of the former tags that is now built into the core.

```
if (NOT fusebox.isCustomTag) {
   if (NOT isDefined("attributes")) {
       attributes=structNew();
   }
   structAppend(attributes, url, "no");
   structAppend(attributes, form, "no");
}
</cfscript>
```

The Fusebox framework encourages the use of the attributes scope as the one user-input scope. This is the code that copies all form and URL variables to the attributes scope. By using one scope, you can call a Fusebox application in three different ways:

- `<a href="index.cfm?fuseaction=basket.show">`
- `<form action="index.cfm" method="post">`

  `<input type="hidden" name="fuseaction" value="basket.show">`
- `<cfmodule template="index.cfm" fuseaction="basket.show">`

The variable `fuseaction` can be referenced as `attributes.fuseaction`, regardless of whether it was originally in the form, URL, or attributes scope. Talk about reusability!

Section 4 is the first section that has dramatic differences between the different core file versions. The ColdFusion function `structAppend()` was introduced in ColdFusion 4.5.2 SP 2, so versions of the core other than `fbx_fusebox30_CF50.cfm` use different code to get the same job done.

Section 5: *fbx_circuits.cfm*

Sections 5 and 6 of the core file handle the `circuits` structure. We like to think of the `circuits` structure as the family tree for the application.

The `circuits` structure looks something like this:

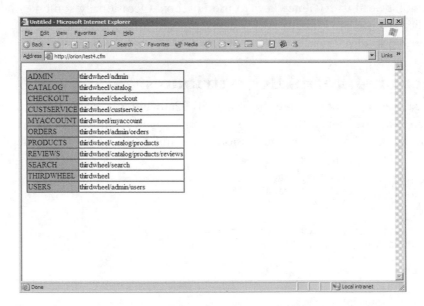

Figure 3.3   `<cfdump>` of the `circuits` structure.

As you can see in Figure 3.3, the left side of the output is the circuit name. Each circuit is a folder in the application, and each circuit gets one key in the `circuits` structure. The right side of the output is the location to the circuit, starting from the root. The root of the application is arbitrarily given a name that does not necessarily have to be the name of the web root. In our case, the `thirdwheelbikes.com` application is running in the web root, but we gave it the name `thirdweel`.

The `circuits` structure provides a map to each circuit's actual location from the root. This allows any circuit to be aware only of where it is in relation to the root, but not to any other circuit. If each circuit were responsible for knowing the location of other circuits, it would be difficult to maintain control of the entire application.

Control with Circuit Mappings

Fusebox 2 didn't have a `circuits` structure. If a circuit wanted to link to another circuit, it did so like this:

```
<a href="../../catalog/products/index.cfm?fuseaction=detail&ID=1021">
```

This is not a good way to link circuits to each other because if the location of the products circuit changes, this link breaks. In Fusebox 3, the link looks like this:

```
<a href="index.cfm?fuseaction=products.detail&ID=1021">
```

The core file uses the `circuits` structure to look up the location of the `products` circuit to complete the request. We will have a closer look at exactly how the core file does this lookup and processing in the next chapter, but for now, remember that the `circuits` structure contains the locations of all the circuits.

Including the Circuits Map

Following is the code that appears in section 5. It mainly `<cfinclude>`s `fbx_circuits.cfm`, but it has some error handling built in.

```
<cftry>
  <cfinclude template="fbx_Circuits.cfm">
  <cfcatch>
    <cif fusebox.suppressErrors>
      <cfoutput>The Fusebox framework could not find the file
      ➥fbx_Circuits.cfm. If you think this error is incorrect, turn off
      ➥the Fusebox suppress error messages flag by setting
      ➥fusebox.SuppressErrors to FALSE, and you will receive ColdFusion's
      ➥"normal" error output.</cfoutput><cfabort>
    <cfelse><cfrethrow></cif>
  </cfcatch>
<cftry>
```

Stripped of all the error handling, this code contains one `<cfinclude>` tag:

```
<cfinclude template="fbx_circuits.cfm">
```

A Fusebox application has only one `fbx_circuits.cfm` file, which must be in the root, alongside this core file. After it's included, the `circuits` structure is available to the core.

Here is the `fbx_circuits.cfm` file for our example site, Third Wheel Bikes:

```
<cfscript>
fusebox.circuits.thirdwheel="thirdwheel";
fusebox.circuits.catalog="thirdwheel/catalog";
fusebox.circuits.products="thirdwheel/catalog/products";
fusebox.circuits.reviews="thirdwheel/catalog/products/reviews";
fusebox.circuits.myaccount="thirdwheel/myaccount";
fusebox.circuits.search="thirdwheel/search";
fusebox.circuits.checkout="thirdwheel/checkout";
fusebox.circuits.custservice="thirdwheel/custservice";
fusebox.circuits.admin="thirdwheel/admin";
fusebox.circuits.users="thirdwheel/admin/users";
fusebox.circuits.orders="thirdwheel/admin/orders";
</cfscript>
```

This file's only job is to populate the `fusebox.circuits` structure with one key per circuit to be used in the application. The left side is the name of the circuit to be used in the compound fuseaction passed like this:

```
<a href="index.cfm?fuseaction=reviews.read&productID=1392">
```

The right side tells the core file that the `reviews` circuit is nested under the `product` circuit. The `product` circuit is nested under the `catalog` circuit, which is under the root circuit, `thirdwheel`.

In the previous example `fbx_circuits.cfm`, we used CFScript to populate the `circuits` structure for our application. However, we could have used straight CFML like this:

```
<cfset fusebox.circuits.reviews="thirdwheel/catalog/products/reviews">
```

Remember that the `fbx_circuits.cfm` file needs only to populate the `circuits` structure. Exactly how you go about writing the `fbx_circuits.cfm` file is up to you.

Dynamic Circuit Mappings

When architecting large projects, particularly intranets, the situation arises in which the application has to be flexible enough to handle dynamic circuits. Bear with us for a minute, while we set up a realistic but fictional situation.

Stan has just started a new project: a global intranet for a big Fortune 500 company. (For a formal introduction to Stan and his friends, see this book's Introduction.) It seems daunting, but he has already begun some initial tinkering around with architecture. It will mostly consist of a content management system with some extended file sharing and collaboration tools. The bulk of the benefit to the company will come in the consolidation of dozens of other mini-applications into the new intranet.

For the past few years, a parade of consultants and junior programmers has been creating everything from one-page report generators to applications with a few dozen pages. Human resources has tools that allow them to quickly create new employee records and generate all the right emails to other departments. Marketing has a few single-page reports that allow them to monitor the activity on the public site. Accounting has a report in which they can quickly get headcounts of all employees grouped by department as well as by manager so they can get their budgeting straight.

For a while, these solutions worked well. But for the past few months, things were starting to boil over. Everyone wanted more features added to existing tools and more tools created to make their jobs easier. Things were starting to get out of control with dozens of applications spread all over the network. At last count, close to 30 Microsoft Access databases were serving data to more than 50 different mini-applications. Something had to be done, and this new intranet was the answer.

Stan realizes that it would be folly to attempt to assemble all those applications into one master architecture. There are just too many of them! How can he create a system that is flexible enough to combine dozens of mini-applications, some of which he knows nothing about?

And what happens after the intranet is completed when the operations and facilities department wants an application built that allows them to track room reservations online? Stan's system will have to accommodate their request, so how can he plan for such future additions to the `circuits` structure?

The answer is to store circuit names and mappings in a database. Stan can create a simple form to add, edit, and delete circuits (accessible only to himself and the IT manager). Each mini-application that is already developed (and new ones that come along later) can be created separately, and when it comes time to include it into the master architecture, a row can be added to the `circuits` table.

Now, Stan's `fbx_circuits.cfm` file looks like this:

```
<cfquery name="circuits" datasource="#request.DSN#"
⇥cachedwithin="#CreateTimeSpan(d,h,m,s)#">
  SELECT circuitName,mapping FROM circuits
```

```
</cfquery>
<cfloop query="circuits">
  <cfset structInsert(fusebox.circuits,circuits.circuitName,
  ↪circuits.mapping)>
</cfloop>
```

If you want to use this system, you need to replace
`cachedwithin="#CreateTimeSpan(d,h,m,s)#"` with values appropriate for the
length of time you want to cache the query. The `cachedwithin` attribute of the
`<cfquery>` tag tells the ColdFusion server to cache the result of the query in
memory, and for subsequent requests, to use the cached copy of the data,
bypassing the database altogether. Although this will speed up an application
significantly, it can be problematic. If the data changes in the database, it will
not be used until the cache expires, which means the application could be
using incorrect data. For more information, consult the ColdFusion
documentation.

Although we have not yet used the `circuits` structure, we can see its value.
It serves as a map to the application, containing the names and mappings to
each circuit. In the next section and in the next chapter, we will use the
`circuits` structure to handle much of the processing of the Fusebox framework.

Error Handling and *fusebox.suppressErrors*

So far, we have only discussed what the `fbx_circuits.cfm` file does and what
the importance of the `circuits` structure is. A lot more code is in section 5.
What does the rest of it do?

The entire section is wrapped in a `<cftry>` block to catch any errors that
might occur. If an error occurs, a message is displayed to the browser right
away:

```
<cfif fusebox.suppressErrrors>
  <cfoutput>The Fusebox framework could not find the file
  ↪fbx_Circuits.cfm. If you think this error is incorrect, turn off
  ↪the Fusebox suppress error messages flag by setting
  ↪fusebox.suppressErrors to FALSE, and you will receive ColdFusion's
  ↪"normal" error output.</cfoutput><cfabort>
<cfelse><cfrethrow></cfif>
```

This code references an API variable, `fusebox.suppressErrors`. This is a
boolean variable that the developer can set in section 2 of the core. It decides
whether or not to suppress ColdFusion's native error.

If there is an error attempting to `<cfinclude>` `fbx_circuits.cfm`, the output
looks like Figure 3.4.

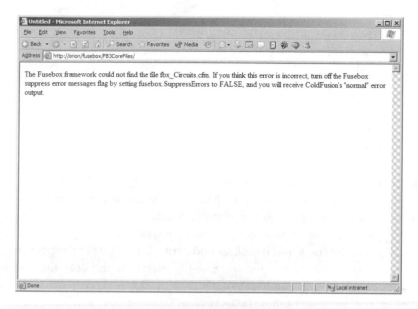

Figure 3.4   Core error message.

Notice the core's short error message at the top of the page in Figure 3.4.

In the error throwing and messages code, we replaced long sections of text with ellipses. Those sections of text are pleasant and helpful error messages that describe the error encountered as well as some guidelines to fix the error. They were removed for compactness because they were quite extensive.

Now we are all done with section 5. The `circuits` structure is created. The core file can now continue processing the request.

Section 6: Reverse Circuit Structure

Section 6 creates a mirror image of the `fusebox.circuits` structure. Instead of the keys in the `circuits` structure being the circuit names and their values being the directory mappings, this structure's keys are the directory mappings and the values of those mappings are the circuit names. The reverse circuit structure is used throughout the rest of the core to look up the circuit name of whichever circuit is being accessed at that moment. Here is the code:

```
<cftry>
  <cfscript>
  FB_.ReverseCircuitPath=StructNew();
  for (aCircuitName in fusebox.Circuits){
    FB_.ReverseCircuitPath[fusebox.Circuits[aCircuitName]]=
    ↪aCircuitName;
```

```
    if (ListLen(fusebox.Circuits[aCircuitName], "/") EQ 1){
      fusebox.HomeCircuit=aCircuitName;
      fusebox.IsHomeCircuit=TRUE;}}
  </cfscript>
  <cfcatch>
    <cfif fusebox.suppressErrors>
      <cfoutput>The circuits structure does not
      ➥exist...</cfoutput><cfabort>
    <cfelse><cfrethrow></cfif>
  </cfcatch>
</cftry>
```

At the top of section 6, we notice an opening `<cftry>` tag. As we progress
through the core file, you will notice that many sections are wrapped in
`<cftry></cftry>`. You will also notice that many of them handle errors the
same way, especially in regards to `fusebox.suppressErrors`.

Putting aside all the error-handling code (the last half of the section from
the first `<cfcatch>` to the ending `</cftry>`), notice how the core file does not
store the reverse copy in the `fusebox` structure. It is not an API variable, unlike
`fusebox.circuits` and `fusebox.isCustomTag`. Because only the core file uses
this reverse structure, it is stored in the `FB_` private structure.

Nestled in the code to produce the reverse structure, we can see references
to two more API variables: `fusebox.homeCircuit` and `fusebox.isHomeCircuit`.
As the reverse structure is being built, it captures the root circuit by looking
for only one directory as a value, rather than multiple directories, as is the case
for all the other circuits. Remember that our root circuit's mapping looks like
this:

```
fusebox.circuits.thirdwheel="thirdwheel";
```

And the other circuits look like this:

```
fusebox.circuits.reviews="thirdwheel/catalog/products/reviews";
```

Notice the preponderance of forward slashes in the mapping to the `reviews`
circuit over the root circuit, `thirdwheel`. Because the root circuit contains no
slashes, the API marks it as the home circuit, and the circuit name is stored in
the variable `fusebox.homeCircuit`.

The second API variable referenced in this section is
`fusebox.isHomeCircuit`. Unlike `fusebox.homeCircuit`, which stores the value of
the home or root circuit name as a string, this variable is a boolean (all the
boolean API variables are easily differentiated from the string counterparts by
the word "is" in the variable name) whose value is `TRUE` if the currently executing circuit is the home circuit. So far, the core file has only processed files
in the root circuit—`fbx_circuits.cfm`—and itself, `fbx_fusebox30_CF50.cfm`.

Because those two core files are always in the root, they do not need the variable `fusebox.isHomeCircuit`. However, in later processing, when the core is including different files, this variable is set and reset depending on the currently executing circuit.

In our case, we are requesting the `reviews` circuit. So when we get there, this variable will be `FALSE`. However, the next file the core processes is the root `fbx_settings.cfm` file (section 7 of the core file, covered in Chapter 4), so this variable is set to `TRUE` in anticipation of that event.

Halfway Through the Core

By this point, the core file has finished all the "pre-processing." It has created the API and populated some of the values for further use. It has run the formURL2attributes code to create a single user-input scope. It has processed the `fbx_circuits.cfm` file, which creates the `circuits` structure, and it has done a lot of heavy lifting to get everything ready to go to execute the fuseaction and the code written in the fuses.

This chapter covered steps that the core file takes regardless of the circuit or fuseaction. Chapter 4 discusses the remaining framework files. The next sections of the core file include the `fbx_settings.cfm` files as well as the target `fbx_switch.cfm`, where our fuses get executed.

*"But since why is difficult to handle,
one must take refuge in how."*

—Toni Morrison

4

Handling a Fuseaction

IN CHAPTER 3, "THE FUSEBOX FRAMEWORK," we got all the way to section 6 of the core file by discussing how it processes a request and how the Fusebox framework is created. We are tracking the URL request:

```
http://thirdwheelbikes.com/index.cfm?fuseaction=
➥reviews.read&productID=1392
```

We walked through ColdFusion's processing of `Application.cfm`, the default page (`index.cfm` in our case), `fbx_fusebox30_CF50.cfm`, and `fbx_circuits.cfm`. We also covered some of the "overhead" that the Fusebox framework sets up, including the `circuits` structure and the `formURL2attributes` section.

This chapter continues the discussion from sections 7–11. We recommend that you open up a copy of the core file and follow along with us. Remember that an understanding of how the core files work is not necessary to effectively use Fusebox, but it can allow you to make use of many of the features built into the core file.

Most of the elements of Fusebox that were covered in the previous chapter are not things that you need to visit frequently. In fact, of the four files discussed, two should be considered read-only (`fbx_fusebox30_CF50.cfm` and `index.cfm`), and the other two (`Application.cfm` and `fbx_circuits.cfm`) are usually built once and only infrequently reviewed. You modify `fbx_circuits.cfm` when adding, removing, or relocating circuits in the application, and you modify `Application.cfm` even more infrequently when you're creating code to be run for the entire application.

Now we are five files into the Fusebox framework. ColdFusion is working its way down the core file, processing logic and including files. Where does the actual work get done? Where do we write code?

In this chapter, we will discuss the four framework files that Fusebox developers spend most of their time working with. These framework files are the place to write inheritable code, manage circuits, identify the steps to be taken for a fuseaction, encapsulate fuses, and control the layouts used. These four files are spelled out in Table 4.1.

Table 4.1 **The Final Four Framework Files**

File	Description
`fbx_settings.cfm`	Required in the root circuit, this file is optional in children circuits. Write circuit-wide settings here, including security and inheritance.
`fbx_switch.cfm`	Required in all circuits, this file is the hub of the circuit, running code for each fuseaction. It consists of a `<cfswitch>` and one `<cfcase>` for each fuseaction.
`fbx_layouts.cfm`	Optional in all circuits, this file provides the nested layouts functionality by allowing a layout file to be chosen, thus facilitating reusability of fuseactions.
Layout fuses	Optional in all circuits, this file contains the "wrapper" layout—including headers and footers—and serves as the assembly file for layout.

Let's discuss each of these files in the order that the Fusebox framework processes them. One thing to keep in mind is that `fbx_settings.cfm`, `fbx_layouts.cfm`, and the layout fuse each get called once in each circuit. If a fuseaction is being run in a child circuit, then those three files will be run from the child circuit and from the parent circuit.

If some of that sounds confusing, don't worry; the explanation in this chapter will clear any confusion.

Section 7: Root *fbx_settings.cfm*

We left the processing of our page request between sections 6 and 7 of the core file `fbx_fusebox30_CF50.cfm`. Section 7 is where we will start. It looks like this:

```
<cftry>
  <cfinclude template="fbx_Settings.cfm">
  <cfcatch>
    <cfif fusebox.suppressErrors>
      <cfoutput>The Fusebox framework could not find the file
      ➥fbx_Settings.cfm...</cfoutput><cfabort>
    <cfelse><cfrethrow></cfif>
  </cfcatch>
</cftry>
```

We already discussed the error handling in the core file in the previous chapter, so forget about everything from the first `<cfcatch>` to the last `</cftry>`. That leaves a remarkably slim section:

```
<cfinclude template="fbx_settings.cfm">
```

This does just what it looks like: It includes the root `fbx_settings.cfm` file. By "root," we mean the folder from which the core file is being run. For example, if you are running the core file from your web root (`c:\inetpub\wwwroot`), then it will look for the `fbx_settings.cfm` file alongside it, in `c:\inetpub\wwwroot`.

Now the core has included two files: `fbx_circuits.cfm` (first) and `fbx_settings.cfm` (second).

Exactly what should go into the root `fbx_settings.cfm` file? Remember that this file is the first user-created file that has been processed, after `fbx_circuits.cfm`. Not only is `fbx_settings.cfm` the *first* file to be processed, but it is also the file that is processed with every page request, regardless of the fuseaction or circuit that is requested. The core file has not done anything specific to a fuseaction so far. That means that anything you want to be run with every page request should go in this file.

This sounds like ColdFusion's `Application.cfm` file, doesn't it? Remember though that `Application.cfm` has already been processed and that Fusebox discourages using it for anything other than file redirection. (Check out Chapter 14, "Construction and Coding," to see why using `Application.cfm` is not a good idea). This means that the root `fbx_settings.cfm` file can assume some of the responsibilities that `Application.cfm` has in traditional ColdFusion applications.

Here is the root `fbx_settings.cfm` file for our example site, `thirdwheelbikes.com`:

```
<cfparam name="attributes.fuseaction" default="home.main">
<cfset xfa=structNew()>
<cfset request.dsn="thirdwheelbikes">
<cfif fusebox.IsHomeCircuit>
  <cfapplication name="thirdwheelbikes" clientmanagement="Yes"
  ⇒sessionmanagement="No" setclientcookies="No"
  ⇒clientstorage="#request.dsn#">
  <cfif not IsDefined("cookie.cfid")>
    <cfcookie name="CFID" value="#client.cfid#">
    <cfcookie name="cftoken" value="#client.cftoken#">
  </cfif>
</cfif>
```

Exactly what you put in the root `fbx_settings.cfm` file for your application is up to you. For the most part, this file can serve as a replacement for `Application.cfm`. However, because each circuit gets its own `fbx_settings.cfm` file, the code in the root `fbx_settings.cfm` should only be code that must be run for every fuseaction, regardless of the circuit.

Only one line is required in the root `fbx_settings.cfm` file:

```
<cfparam name="attributes.fuseaction" default="[circuit.fuseaction]">
```

This line creates a default fuseaction for the entire web site. The value `circuit.fuseaction` should be replaced with the actual circuit and fuseaction to be defaulted. As of this point in the processing of the core file (section 7), the variable `fuseaction` that was passed in on the URL string (`&fuseaction=reviews.read`) has been copied to the attributes scope. Therefore, the variable `attributes.fuseaction` has been created, and this line of code will not overwrite the fuseaction. This `<cfparam>` is needed if no fuseaction is passed.

Doesn't the variable `fuseaction` have to be passed on each request? Yes it does, but look what happens if the user types in a URL like this:

```
http://www.thirdwheelbikes.com/
```

No fuseaction is passed. The application responds with the default fuseaction, which is set in the root `fbx_settings.cfm`.

Now that the root `fbx_settings.cfm` file has been included, we can be assured that the variable `attributes.fuseaction` has been declared. The next section takes over here.

Section 8: Preparing the Fuseaction

Section 8 of the core file prepares the compound fuseaction to be handled
separately as a circuit and a fuseaction. We have stripped the error-handling
code from this section for compactness in this text. We will go back and cover
it fully later. Here is section 8 from the core file:

```
<cfscript>
FB_.rawFA = attributes.fuseaction;
if (ListLen(FB_.rawFA, '.') is 1 and Right(FB_.rawFA,1) is '.')
  fusebox.fuseaction = "fusebox.defaultfuseaction";
else
  fusebox.fuseaction = ListGetAt( FB_.rawFA, 2, '.' );
fusebox.circuit = ListGetAt( FB_.rawFA, 1, '.');
fusebox.TargetCircuit=fusebox.circuit;
</cfscript>
```

This is the first section of the core that is mostly CFScript. Why isn't more of
the core in CFScript?

More of the code is not in CFScript because script equivalents aren't
available for many important CFML tags, including `<cfinclude>` and
`<cftry>/<cfcatch>`. When it is feasible, the core uses CFScript.

This section's primary purpose is to set three keys in the `fusebox` structure
based on `attributes.fuseaction` and to utilize one more previously set API
variable. The first variable it creates is `fusebox.fuseaction`, done so by the first
`if/else` block. (The variable `FB_.rawFA` is in the private structure `FB_`. The first
line in section 8 sets `FB_.rawFB` to the value of `attributes.fuseaction`, essentially copying it.)

This variable is created in one of two ways. It is either copied from
the second part of the fuseaction, or it is created as the string
`fusebox.defaultFuseaction` if the second part of the passed-in fuseaction is
empty.

The string `"fusebox.defaultFuseaction"` was arbitrarily chosen to be the
default fuseaction name. It can then be used in your `fbx_switch.cfm` like this:

```
<cfcase value="main,fusebox.defaultFuseaction">
```

When creating page links, you can take advantage of this default fuseaction
functionality:

```
<a href="index.cfm?fuseaction=home.">
```

Notice how the fuseaction is a circuit name followed by a period, and how
nothing follows it. Usually, the fuseaction appears after the period, but by
leaving it off, we are asking the core to change the `fusebox.fuseaction` to
`fusebox.defaultFuseaction`.

Therefore, `fusebox.fuseaction` gets set to the second part of the fuseaction or, if blank, gets set to `fusebox.defaultFuseaction`. What are `fusebox.circuit` and `fusebox.targetCircuit`?

Section 8 creates the second variable with this line:

```
fusebox.circuit=listGetAt(FB_.rawFA,1,'.');
```

This line is simple. It copies the first part of the fuseaction into the API variable `fusebox.circuit`. This variable is referenced further during the processing of the core. It is also helpful during coding to perform certain actions depending on the current circuit. We will discuss this API more during the discussion of layouts and during the application tutorial in Part 3 of this book, "Fusebox Lifecycle Process (FLiP).

The last API variable set in this section is `fusebox.targetCircuit`. The difference between this variable and `fusebox.circuit` is that this variable is the circuit alias that was found in the `circuits` structure as opposed to the circuit that was requested. In all non-error situations, `fusebox.targetCircuit` and `fusebox.circuit` will be the same. The distinction will become clearer as we discuss how the core file uses each one differently.

Section 9: Children *fbx_settings.cfm*

So far, the core file has included `fbx_circuits.cfm` and the root `fbx_settings.cfm`. It has also converted `attributes.fuseaction` into its API counterparts: `fusebox.circuit` and `fusebox.fuseaction`. In addition, the core file has set up the path to the target circuit based on its mapping in the `circuits` structure. The next step is to include the `fbx_settings.cfm` files, in top-to-bottom order, down to the target circuit, by following the `circuits` structure mapping. Stripped of all the error handling, section 9 of the core file looks like this:

```
<cfscript>
FB_.fullPath=ListRest(fusebox.Circuits[fusebox.TargetCircuit], "/");
FB_.Corepath="";
fusebox.thisCircuit=fusebox.HomeCircuit;
</cfscript>
<cfloop list="#FB_.fullpath#" index="aPath" delimiters="/">
  <cfscript>
  FB_.Corepath=ListAppend(FB_.Corepath, aPath, "/");
  fusebox.IsHomeCircuit=FALSE;
  fusebox.currentPath=FB_.Corepath & "/";
  fusebox.rootPath=repeatString("../", ListLen(fusebox.currentPath,
  ➥'/'));
  </cfscript>
<cftry>
```

```
      <cfif StructKeyExists(FB_.ReverseCircuitPath,
    ⤷fusebox.Circuits[fusebox.HomeCircuit] & "/" & FB_.CorePath)>
        <cfset fusebox.thisCircuit=FB_.ReverseCircuitPath
        ⤷[fusebox.Circuits[fusebox.HomeCircuit] & "/" & FB_.CorePath] >
        <cfif fusebox.thisCircuit EQ fusebox.TargetCircuit>
          <cfset fusebox.IsTargetCircuit=TRUE>
        <cfelse>
          <cfset fusebox.IsTargetCircuit=FALSE>
        </cfif>
        <cfinclude template="#fusebox.currentPath#fbx_Settings.cfm">
      </cfif>
      <cfcatch>...</cfcatch>
    </cftry>
  </cfloop>
```

This section does two things: It sets up each circuit's API variables, and it calls the `fbx_settings.cfm` file per child circuit. Let's take these one at a time.

Prepare the API

The first part of section 9 creates two keys in the private `FB_` structure. `FB_.fullPath` holds the value of the target circuit's mapping, minus the first directory. This variable is first used in the next section of the core. The fuseaction from our URL (`&fuseaction=reviews.read`) requests the `reviews` circuit whose mapping looks like this (from `fbx_circuits.cfm`):

```
fusebox.circuits.reviews="thirdwheel/catalog/products/reviews";
```

That means that `FB_.fullPath` will contain this value:

```
catalog/products/reviews
```

The next key created is `FB_.corePath`. This variable is used during the looping in the next section to hold the value of the directory path that is currently being accessed. Right now, it's blank; it is set and reset soon.

The next thing that this section does is set another API variable, `fusebox.thisCircuit`, to the value of `fusebox.homeCircuit`. It's set to the home circuit because the home circuit is currently being accessed. In the next core section, other circuits are accessed. As they are, this variable is set and reset.

Following the closing `</cfscript>` tag, this section begins a loop. The loop is based on the list of `FB_.fullpath`. The core file just finished setting `FB_.fullpath` based on the mapping of the target circuit, like this:

```
catalog/products/reviews
```

The `<cfloop>` tag uses the delimiter of / (forward slash), which means that this section will be looped three times—once for each element in the list. Each time, through, the index `aPath` will contain the value of the current circuit: first `catalog`, then `products`, and finally `reviews`.

The rest of this section sets some variables in a CFScript block. The first one is `FB_.corePath`, which was set to blank in the previous section. In this code, the current circuit stored in `aPath` is added as a list element to `FB_.corePath` using / (forward slash) as a delimiter. This builds the directory path down to the target circuit, starting at the top directory. We'll see more of `FB_.corePath` in just a second.

fusebox.isHomeCircuit

The next three lines set three API variables. We have already seen `fusebox.isHomeCircuit` in section 6. This code sets it to `FALSE` because the core file is no longer processing the home circuit. Why should it be set to `FALSE` every time through this list? Why not set it once because it will always be `FALSE`?

`fusebox.isHomeCircuit` is repeatedly reset because it is a writeable variable. Although it is not recommended to do so, a developer might set it to `TRUE` in her code. Because it would be incorrect if this happened, the core file takes the extra step to make sure it is `FALSE`.

fusebox.currentPath and fusebox.rootPath

The next API variable that is set is a new one—`fusebox.currentPath`. This variable contains the path from the root circuit to the path that is currently processing the circuit, in directory notation, with a trailing slash. This variable is used just a few lines later to do the actual `<cfinclude>` of `fbx_settings.cfm` files, but it is also available to the developer in his own code.

When used in a fuse, `fusebox.currentPath` is extremely helpful to resolve the path to the current directory. Because of the way that the Fusebox framework operates, every fuse gets `<cfinlude>`d into the root of the application—wherever the `fbx_fusebox31_CF50.cfm` is running. This could cause problems if you have a directory structure like the one shown in Figure 4.1.

If you have a fuse in the "products" directory and want to show images from the "images" directory nested below it, the HTML would look like this:

```
<img src="images/glove1.jpg" width="250" height="250" alt="glove">
```

This would work fine in normal HTML, but in Fusebox, all requests go through the `index.cfm` in the web root. By the time your fuse with the `<img>` tag is finished processing, the browser thinks it is being run from the root. The Fusebox framework `<cfinclude>`d the `fbx_switch.cfm` file in the target circuit, which `<cfinclude>`d your fuse. The browser cannot find `glove1.jpg` in the Images directory below the root. The tag would have to be changed to read

```
<img src="catalog/products/images/glove1.jpg" width="250"
➥height="250" alt="glove">
```

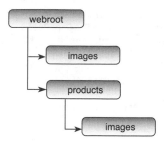

Figure 4.1   A common directory structure for images.

All solved, right? Unfortunately, no. Remember that one of the major aims of Fusebox is to create completely removable, independent components. If a fuse hard codes the value of its location relative to the root of the application, some of that severability is lost. If the location of the products circuit changes, all the image tags in all the fuses have to be modified. What a pain!

The answer is to use the variable `fusebox.currentPath` to refer to the location of the current template to the root:

```
<img src="#fusebox.currentPath#images/glove1.jpg" width="250"
⮡height="250" alt="glove">
```

The next variable set is a reverse of `fusebox.currentPath`. `fusebox.rootPath` creates a string of `../` (dot dot slash) up to the root of the application from the current template. It looks like this:

```
../../../
```

This variable allows any circuit, regardless of where it is in the directory tree, to access files in the root circuit. It can reuse fuses, such as `fbx_savecontent.cfm`, which are in the core directory, or it can allow you to reuse certain directories, such as a global images directory as opposed to an images directory for each circuit.

Each of these variables is set each time the loop repeats, and it contains the value of the current loop's circuit mapping.

Call the Right File

After the API is created for the current circuit in the loop, the `fbx_settings.cfm` is almost ready to be included. Just to review, we are looking at the second part of section 9:

```
<cftry>
  <cfif StructKeyExists(FB_.ReverseCircuitPath,
  ⮡fusebox.Circuits[fusebox.HomeCircuit] & "/" & FB_.CorePath)>
```

continues

```
      <cfset fusebox.thisCircuit=FB_.ReverseCircuitPath[fusebox.Circuits
      ⮡[fusebox.HomeCircuit] & "/" & FB_.CorePath] >
      <cfif fusebox.thisCircuit EQ fusebox.TargetCircuit>
        <cfset fusebox.IsTargetCircuit=TRUE>
      <cfelse>
        <cfset fusebox.IsTargetCircuit=FALSE>
      </cfif>
      <cfinclude template="#fusebox.currentPath#fbx_Settings.cfm">
    </cfif>
    <cfcatch>
      <cfif fusebox.suppressErrors>
      <cfelse><cfrethrow></cfif>
    </cfcatch>
  </cftry>
```

At the top of this code section, the core file runs a `<cfif>` to determine if this code block should be processed. The core looks up the currently executing circuit in the `circuits` structure to see whether it is defined. If it is defined, processing continues; otherwise, the rest of this section is skipped. (If you look carefully, you might notice that the lookup does not occur in the `circuits` structure. It happens in the `FB_.reverseCircuitPath` structure based on the current mapping. Looking up the circuit mapping in the reverse structure is functionally equivalent to looking up the circuit name in the `circuits` structure.)

This is our first time through the loop, so the `<cfif>` returns TRUE because the circuit `catalog` exists. (Remember that `catalog` is the first circuit in the path down to `reviews` from the root.) Now, the variable `fusebox.thisCircuit` is set to the name of the current circuit ("catalog").

The next code is a `<cfif>` block; its purpose is pretty obvious. If the target circuit is the current circuit, the variable `fusebox.isTargetCircuit` is set to TRUE. Otherwise, the variable is set to FALSE. Now, in each `fbx_settings.cfm`, you can check the value of `fusebox.isTargetCircuit` to allow specific code to be run based on whether the `fbx_settings.cfm` is the target circuit. We will see more of this when we get into Part 3 of this book.

After all those API variables are set, the `fbx_settings.cfm` file for this circuit is `<cfinclude>`d. At this point, the Fusebox API looks like the one in Table 4.2.

Table 4.2   **API Variable Values at Section 9**

API Variable	Value
fusebox.isHomeCircuit	FALSE
fusebox.isTargetCircuit	FALSE
fusebox.homeCircuit	thirdwheel

API Variable	Value
fusebox.fuseaction	read
fusebox.circuit	reviews
fusebox.targetCircuit	reviews
fusebox.thisCircuit	catalog
fusebox.currentPath	catalog/
fusebox.rootPath	../

So far, the Fusebox framework processed everything except your code—the stuff that does the work when a user requests a page. We have covered Fusebox framework through section 9 of the core file, including setting up the framework and all the request-specific processing of the settings files—in essence, setting up the application for the current request. Now, we will complete our investigation of the core file by running the fuseaction that is defined for the request in the correct circuit and applying the layout templates to the generated content. We like to think of the last part of the core file as "fuses and layouts."

Section 10: Target *fbx_switch.cfm*

This section includes the target circuit's fbx_switch.cfm file. The fbx_switch.cfm file decides which fuses to run based on the value of fusebox.fuseaction. Here is the fbx_switch.cfm file from the reviews circuit:

```
<cfswitch expression = "#fusebox.fuseaction#">
  <cfcase value="read">
    <cfset xfa.addReview="#fusebox.thisCircuit#.reviewForm">
    <cfinclude template="qry_reviewByProduct.cfm">
    <cfinclude template="dsp_reviews.cfm">
  </cfcase>
  <cfcase value="reviewForm">
    <cfset xfa.submit="#fusebox.thisCircuit#.addReview">
    <cfinclude template="dsp_reviewForm.cfm">
  </cfcase>
  <cfcase value="addReview">
    <cfset xfa.continue="#fusebox.thisCircuit#.read">
    <cfinclude template="qry_addReview.cfm">
  </cfcase>
</cfswitch>
```

No more code was left out. The fbx_switch.cfm consists only of a switch/case statement, switching on fusebox.fuseaction, which was set previously in the core file, based on the second half of the compound fuseaction.

Our request looks like this:

```
<a href="index.cfm?fuseaction=reviews.read&productID=1392">
```

The value of `fusebox.fuseaction` is "read," which means that the first `<cfcase>` block will be run, setting an exit fuseaction. (You will learn more about exit fuseactions in Chapter 6, "Exit Fuseactions.")

Section 10 Code

After those files are included and processed, this section is done. Here is the code for section 10:

```
<cfscript>
fusebox.thisCircuit=fusebox.TargetCircuit;
fusebox.IsTargetCircuit= TRUE;
FB_.fuseboxpath=FB_.fullpath;
if (Len(FB_.fuseboxpath)){
  FB_.fuseboxpath=FB_.fuseboxpath & "/";
  fusebox.IsHomeCircuit = FALSE;}
else
  fusebox.IsHomeCircuit = TRUE;
fusebox.currentPath=fb_.fuseboxpath;
fusebox.rootPath=repeatString("../", ListLen(fb_.fuseboxpath, '/'));
</cfscript>
<cftry>
  <cfsavecontent variable="fusebox.layout">
    <cfoutput><cfinclude
    ↪template="#FB_.fuseboxpath#fbx_Switch.cfm"></cfoutput>
  </cfsavecontent>
  <cfcatch>
    <cfif fusebox.suppressErrors>
      <cfoutput>I could not find #FB_.
      ↪fuseboxpath#fbx_Switch.cfm...</cfoutput><cfabort>
    <cfelse><cfrethrow></cfif>
  </cfcatch>
</cftry>
```

The top CFScript portion of this section sets Fusebox API variables that are already familiar. Because the target circuit is the only circuit in which the `fbx_switch.cfm` is run, `fusebox.thisCircuit` is set to `fusebox.targetCircuit`. The core determines if this is the home circuit and sets `fusebox.isHomeCircuit` appropriately. Finally, `fusebox.currentPath` and `fusebox.rootPath` are updated so that they can be used in fuses for this fuseaction.

The next lines include the target `fbx_switch.cfm`, which processes all the fuses for the fuseaction. Just like that, all your code is processed for this fuseaction. What about that `<cfsavecontent>` tag?

<cfsavecontent>

<cfsavecontent> traps all output that occurs between its opening and closing tags in the variable specified in the name attribute. Here is a short example of its use:

```
<cfsavecontent name="foo">
  Help! I'm trapped!
</cfsavecontent>
This is the content:<br>
<cfoutput>#foo#</cfoutput>
```

Even though the text Help! I'm trapped! appears before the rest of the output on the page, it is not displayed until the variable foo is referenced. When run, this page looks like this:

```
This is the content:
Help! I'm trapped!
```

This tag is new to ColdFusion 5, but earlier versions of ColdFusion can gain the same functionality via the custom tag <cf_savecontent>, which is what the core file for those versions uses.

Because the fbx_switch.cfm is included inside <cfsavecontent>, any output that the fuseaction generates will not be displayed. Instead, it will be trapped in the variable fusebox.layout. This means that although the combination of the fuses qry_reviewByProduct.cfm and dsp_reviews.cfm will produce a well-formatted page showing all the reviews of a particular product, nothing will show up on the page yet.

We are going to maintain the secret of where the output is actually presented for a little longer. Just remember that the output of the fuseaction is stored in fusebox.layout; we'll come back to it soon.

Section 11: *fbx_layouts.cfm* and Layout Files

Fusebox has a place for everything. Application-wide settings such as variable constants and DSN names go in the root fbx_settings.cfm. Circuit-wide settings such as security logic go in each circuit's fbx_settings.cfm. The fbx_switch.cfm serves as a roadmap to a circuit by showing the fuses that make up each fuseaction. The individual fuses do the work of the application and run the code needed to satisfy each request. What about layouts: headers, footers, and nested tables?

Two pieces make up Fusebox's layout structure: circuit-level fbx_layouts.cfm files and layout files. In short, the fbx_layouts.cfm file tells the framework which layout file to use for this request, and the layout file contains the page elements and the results of the fuseaction execution. Let's cover them one at a time.

fbx_layouts.cfm

The first part of section 11 looks like this:

```
1  <cfset FB_.circuitalias = fusebox.Circuits[fusebox.TargetCircuit] >
2  <cfset FB_.layoutpath = fusebox.Circuits[fusebox.TargetCircuit] >
3  <cfloop condition="Len(FB_.layoutpath) GT 0">
4    <cfif StructKeyExists(FB_.ReverseCircuitPath, FB_.circuitalias)>
5      <cftry>
6        <cfset fusebox.thisCircuit =
         ⮡FB_.ReverseCircuitPath[FB_.circuitalias] >
7        <cfcatch>
8          <cfset fusebox.thisCircuit = "">
9        </cfcatch>
10     </cftry>
11     <cfscript>
12     if (fusebox.thisCircuit EQ fusebox.Targetcircuit)
       ⮡fusebox.IsTargetCircuit=TRUE;
13       else fusebox.IsTargetCircuit=FALSE;
14     if (fusebox.thisCircuit EQ fusebox.HomeCircuit)
       ⮡fusebox.IsHomeCircuit=TRUE;
15       else fusebox.IsHomeCircuit=FALSE;
16     fusebox.ThisLayoutPath=ListRest(FB_.layoutpath,"/");
17     if (Len(fusebox.thislayoutpath))
       ⮡fusebox.thislayoutpath=fusebox.thislayoutpath & "/";
18     fusebox.currentPath=fusebox.thislayoutpath;
19     fusebox.rootPath=repeatString("../",
       ⮡ListLen(fusebox.thislayoutpath, '/'));
20     </cfscript>
21     <cftry>
22       <cfinclude template="#fusebox.thislayoutpath#fbx_Layouts.cfm">
23       <cfcatch>
24         <cfset fusebox.layoutfile = ""><cfset fusebox.layoutdir =
         ⮡"">
25       </cfcatch>
26     </cftry>
```

Lines 1 and 2 create two FB_ structure variables to hold the currently executing circuit. Line 3 begins the looping of nested layouts. Starting at the target
circuit, the entire rest of the code in this section will loop once per circuit.
Each time through the loop, lines 6 and 8 set the value of
fusebox.thisCircuit to the currently executing circuit. Lines 13–15 continue
to create variables that are available for use in the fbx_layouts.cfm and layout
files. These same API variables were set in section 9, discussed earlier.

The real action of this code occurs in lines 16–22. fusebox.thisLayoutPath
contains the path to the current circuit. The first time through the loop, this
path is the same as the path to the target circuit. Each time through the loop,
however, the core file resets this variable to the appropriate path to reach the
fbx_layouts.cfm file for the current circuit. You might notice that

fusebox.thisLayoutPath contains the same value as fusebox.currentPath. We recommend not using fusebox.thisLayoutPath in favor of using fusebox.currentPath. fusebox.thisLayoutPath is superfluous and might become deprecated in a future release.

Now that fbx_layouts.cfm is included, what does it do? What is its purpose?

Here is an example fbx_layouts.cfm:

```
<cfif dateCompare(now(),createDate(year(now()),"12","26"),"d") LTE 0>
  <cfset fusebox.layoutFile="#fusebox.rootPath#layouts/
  ➥lay_christmas.cfm">
<cfelse>
  <cfset fusebox.layoutFile="#fusebox.rootPath#layouts/
  ➥lay_default.cfm">
</cfif>
```

Similar in brevity to fbx_switch.cfm, fbx_layouts.cfm sets only one variable: fusebox.layoutFile. That API variable tells the core file where to find the layout file relative to the circuit. This fbx_layouts.cfm example seems simple; you will find that in real applications, fbx_layouts.cfm files often are simple. Most applications use one layout file per circuit. The entire site is usually wrapped in one "global" style wrapper containing the top-level navigation links. Some circuits might also add their own navigation links. For the most part, however, the fbx_layouts.cfm's job is a simple one.

That does not mean that fbx_layouts.cfm's job *has* to be simple. fbx_layouts.cfm can contain any code you want. Here is a slightly more powerful example:

```
<cfparam name="client.layoutScheme" default="white">
<cfset fusebox.layoutFile="#fusebox.rootPath#
➥layouts/lay_#client.layoutScheme#.cfm">
```

Using this example, the application can present an individualized layout for each user, depending on chosen preferences. If John Barker likes the "peasoup" layout scheme, his layout file would be lay_peasoup.cfm.

This might seem like an unnecessarily complex system just to manipulate the colors of the web site. After all, that sort of functionality is commonly referred to as "candy." It usually does not satisfy system requirements, but it can be fun.

If all you did with different layout files was create new color schemes, then you would not be taking full advantage of the power of nested layouts. Although we will cover them in detail in Chapter 9, "Nested Layouts," let's discuss briefly how they relate to the Fusebox framework that is processing a request.

Layout Files

After the core file includes the `fbx_layouts.cfm` file, the resulting API variable—`fusebox.layoutFile`—is set. This is the second half of the code in section 11:

```
1    <cftry>
2      <cfif Len(fusebox.layoutfile)>
3        <cfsavecontent variable="fusebox.layout">
4          <cfoutput><cfinclude template="
           ➥#fusebox.thislayoutpath##fusebox.layoutdir##
           ➥fusebox.layoutfile#"></cfoutput>
5        </cfsavecontent>
6      </cfif>
7      <cfcatch>
8        <cfif fusebox.suppressErrors>
9          <cfoutput>I could not find the
           ➥layoutfile...</cfoutput><cfabort>
10       <cfelse><cfrethrow></cfif>
11     </cfcatch>
12   </cftry>
13 </cfif>
14 <cfset FB_.layoutpath = ListDeleteAt(FB_.layoutpath,
     ➥ListLen(FB_.layoutpath, "/"), "/")>
15 <cfset FB_.circuitalias = ListDeleteAt(FB_.circuitalias,
     ➥ListLen(FB_.circuitalias, "/"), "/")>
16 </cfloop>
```

Based on the value of `fusebox.layoutFile`, this section of code `<cfinclude>`s the layout file to be used for this request. Line 2 decides whether to run this code section. If the `fusebox.layoutFile` is set to `""` (blank), then no layout file is to be used, and this section is skipped.

Line 3 opens a `<cfsavecontent>` tag. The results of `<cfinclude>`ing the layout file will be stored in the variable `fusebox.layout`, as specified in the `variable` attribute of the tag. Doesn't that overwrite the existing value? The core file already has content saved from the processing of `fbx_switch.cfm` and all the fuses.

That brings up an interesting feature of `<cfsavecontent>`. Here is an example of it:

```
<cfoutput>
<cfsavecontent variable="layout">
I am the fuseaction
</cfsavecontent>
<cfsavecontent variable="layout">
  TOP<br>#layout#<br>BOTTOM
</cfsavecontent>
#layout#
</cfoutput>
```

In this example, the variable `layout` is not overwritten. As we want it to, the output appears like this:

```
TOP
I am the fuseaction
BOTTOM
```

To output the initial results of the `<cfsavecontent>` tag, we had to output `#layout#`. That occurs between lines 4–14. The layout file is `<cfinclude>`d, and the layout file is what outputs the value of `fusebox.layout`. Here is an example layout file:

```
<!DOCTYPE HTML PUBLIC "-//W3C//DTD HTML 4.0 Transitional//EN">
<html>
<head>
  <title><cfoutput>#app.page.title#</cfoutput></title>
</head>
<body>
<table cellspacing="2" cellpadding="2" border="0">
<tr>
  <td colspan="2"><cfinclude template="dsp_navigation.cfm"></td>
</tr>
<tr>
  <td rowspan="2" valign="top"><cfoutput>#fusebox.layout#
  ➥</cfoutput></td>
  <td valign="top"><cfmodule template="#request.self#"
  ➥fuseaction="news.topStories"></td>
</tr>
<tr>
    <td><cfmodule template="#request.self#"
    ➥fuseaction="horoscopes.readToday" DOB="#client.DOB#"></td>
</tr>
</table>
<div align="center">Copyright &copy;Third Wheel Bikes,
➥thirdwheelbikes.com</div>
</body>
</html>
```

This layout file contains the HTML formatting to correctly display the page to a browser. It contains some navigational controls in the top row of a table. The rest of the table contains three elements: the output of the fuseaction, which is stored in `fusebox.layout`; the output of another fuseaction, which by the name of the fuseaction, tells us that it outputs the top news stories for the day; and the output of another fuseaction, which displays the horoscope that is customized for the user's date of birth. Finally, the layout file displays copyright information to appear on every page and closes the HTML formatting.

What if the application gives the user preferences as to which portal elements to display? If the user does not want to see horoscopes, then some CFML logic can surround the `<cfmodule>` tag in that table cell. By arranging page elements together into one display page, the layout file serves as a master layout control. A web designer mocks up complex pages with multiple elements on each display. Then, you extract the sections into fuseactions and reassemble them into the total page layout.

A complete discussion of nested layouts occurs in Chapter 9 "Nested Layouts," so hold your questions until then. For now, the core file is only concerned with outputting the value of fusebox.layout.

Let's finish the code in section 11. Lines 7–11 handle missing layout files. If the fbx_layouts.cfm file specifies a non-existent layout file, then the error is caught here. Lines 14 and 15 finish off section 11 by removing one level of the circuit mapping in preparation for the next circuit to be handled. Remember that section 11 is run inside a <cfloop>, which loops from circuit to circuit, up the circuit chain to the root circuit.

Nested Layouts

The <cfinclude> of fbx_layouts.cfm and the layout file that is defined there occur once per circuit, starting at the target circuit, and proceeding up to the root circuit. The effect that this nesting has on layouts is more dramatic than the error handling. Because the circuits are nested one inside the other, the effect is that of a Russian doll; the parent wraps each circuit up to the root. Of course fbx_layouts.cfm is completely optional, so you can leave out a circuit with no ill effect. Doing so just removes that layer's wrapping. In most cases, each circuit does not apply its own layout. Occasionally, some circuits have their own wrapper, and the root almost always contains the global wrapper.

That is it for nested layouts for the time being. Although more could be covered, we cannot do it all here. You are probably wondering how much more of the core there is to cover! We have saved a complete explanation of the benefits and practical uses of nested layouts for Chapter 9.

Finishing the Processing

We're finished! The entire request is nearly done processing; the result of the entire fuseaction, including all the nested layouts, is stored in the API variable fusebox.layout. All that is left is to output the variable:

```
1 <cfoutput>#trim(fusebox.layout)#</cfoutput>
2 </cfprocessingdirective><cfsetting enablecfoutputonly="no">
```

Line 1 is the magic line of the core file; it outputs the complete value of the entire contents of the request. Any output in a file that the core file has called is stored in fusebox.layout. The trim() function crops whitespace from the final output, which allows Fusebox to be used to generate SOAP-based web service requests as well as requests from Flash.

It's All Under the Hood

Although understanding all the nuances of the core file is not necessary to become an excellent Fusebox developer, it is compelling to do so. We are programmers, and programmers like looking under the hood.

It is okay if you did not understand everything in these chapters. You can review the chapters at your leisure when you really want to explore all the API variables. Alternatively, you might want to "optimize" the core. These chapters should serve as a useful guide to the existing core. The rest of Part 2, "Fusebox Coding," is much more important—a complete discussion of all the rest of the technical points of Fusebox.

"The chess pieces are the block alphabet which shapes thoughts..."

—Marcel Duchamp

5

The Fuses

EVEN THOUGH WE HAVE COMPLETED THE DISCUSSION of the Fusebox core file and the supporting framework files, such as `fbx_circuits.cfm` and `fbx_settings.cfm`, we have yet to talk about where to write the application code. Where do the queries go? Where do you write the forms and other files?

We have discussed how the `fbx_switch.cfm` in the target circuit `<cfinclude>`s files to accomplish each fuseaction. What are those files? They are the fuses of the application, and we are going to discuss them in this chapter. We will cover the 10 "fuse rules" that guide the creation and use of fuses. We will also provide plenty of example fuses of all the different types so that you can see how the rules are applied in practice.

ColdFusion files go by different names: Some people call them *files* and some people call them *pages*. The ColdFusion documentation calls them *templates*. Regardless of the name, they all contain the same stuff: ColdFusion code. In Fusebox, those files are called *fuses*.

Fuses are small files that do all the request-specific work. Because `fbx_switch.cfm` is the manager, delegating application responsibility to individual fuses, it should be the best manager it can be by delegating only small tasks.

With that in mind, here is an interchange that you are not likely to hear:

"Jim, can you tackle the entire company rebranding yourself? I don't think you'll need any help."

"Umm sure, boss. I'll get started right away."

The relationship between managers and employees is not like that because different employees are best suited to accomplish different small jobs, leaving managers to tie it all together.

The 10 Fuse Rules

Now that we have some background covered, let's cover the 10 rules of fuses. Why exactly 10? Well, it takes 10 points to cover using fuses in every scenario we could think of. No doubt, odd situations might require extrapolation of the purposes of some of these rules, but these 10 should cover most development.

Rule 1: A Fuse Is Length Challenged

Fuses do not like to be long. They can become hard to control and take on lives of their own. The last thing you want is a fuse that starts giving you back-talk in the form of unsquashable bugs. All fuses should be as short as possible. If many of the fuses you write are longer than one screen in ColdFusion Studio, you are probably writing longer fuses than you should be. Let's take a look at a typical fuse:

```
<!--- qry_validateUser.cfm --->
<cfquery name="validateUser" datasource="#request.DSN#">
  select * from users
where email='#attributes.email#' and password='#attributes.password#'
</cfquery>
<cfif selectUser.recordcount is 1>
  <cfset success=TRUE>
<cfelse>
  <cfset success=FALSE>
</cfif>
```

This fuse does a simple, discrete job. It attempts to validate a user's login and returns the Boolean variable success as TRUE if the provided username and password are valid or as FALSE if the username and password do not match a record in the database. Notice that the fuse does not also display a login form or run a recursive query to pull all users and companies into a recordset. It is easy to describe this fuse's job.

Rule 2: A Fuse Is Reusable

A fuse's highest calling is to be reused by being called more than once in the same application. Maybe the fuse is called across fuseactions, or even better, across circuits. If you can write fuses that are reused, you can save development time. Often, however, fuses can be recycled instead of reused. Recycling fuses means writing the code once and copy-pasting it elsewhere with some modifications to its new environment and purpose. Either way, you save time.

To facilitate fuse reuse and recycling, fuses should not contain code that would better fit in another fuse. You might think the example in Rule 1 is too small, but according to that rule, fuses like being small. It might be tempting to change the second part of this fuse to this:

```
<cfif selectUser.recordcount is 1>
  <cfset client.userid=selectUser.userID>
  <cfset client.username=selectUser.username>
  <cf_location url="index.cfm?fuseaction=#xfa.success#">
<cfelse>
  <cflocation url="index.cfm?fuseaction=#xfa.fail#">
</cfif>
```

Although it might seem to make more sense to change it like this, you would most likely encounter problems later. What happens when your boss decides that the company intranet you built last month also needs to be accessible to consultants in the office? Consultants do not have usernames in the users table. Instead, they have a column, consultantID, which they use in place of an employee username. The first example of a fuse would not have to be changed to accommodate this requirement, but if you had included the second code snippet that sets client variables based on the users table, you would have to rewrite that fuse.

Rewriting fuses is not against any rules of Fusebox, however. If you wrote the qry_validateUser.cfm fuse to include the second code snippet also, you would just open it up in your code editor, make a couple lines of change, test it out for existing employees as well as consultants to make sure your changes did not create unforeseen bugs, and then you would be done. Not so bad, eh?

If you had to modify the fuse, you most likely would have no problems changing something so minor. However, we have a rule when we write code: If a fuse is bug free and in production, we do not want to touch it. We simply cannot be certain what will happen if we start modifying existing code. We also might forget something as simple as closing a tag or swapping a single quote for a double quote. If a fuse is golden, don't mess with it.

If we recommend that you do not modify existing fuses, how do you upgrade your code to accept the new requirement that consultants be able to log in?

The easiest way to accommodate such a requirement into your code is have two fuses—one that performs the database query and one that does the "action" based on the results of the database query. The first fuse, `qry_validateUser.cfm`, contains the code shown first, which just runs a query to look up a username and password combination. The second fuse, `act_processLogin.cfm` finishes the job by setting client variables and relocating based on the passed-in variable `success`.

Rule 3: A Fuse by Any Other Prefix Isn't a Fuse

Fuses get along much better than regular ColdFusion templates mostly due to their strict naming schemes. This well-defined yet extensible filenaming convention is used for every fuse (do not let any of them escape) and denotes the content of the file. You can tell what the code inside does just by looking at the file prefix.

Table 5.1   **File Prefixes and Descriptions for Fuse Types**

Fuse Prefix	Fuse Type	Description
dsp_	Display	Only fuse type that can contain display, be it HTML, WML, or SOAP headers. CFML is limited to only that which is required to output, including `<cfoutput>`, `<cfif>`, `<cfloop>`, and so on.
lay_	Layout	Specified in the `fbx_layouts.cfm` file, layout files assemble the request for presentation to the user by handling headers, footers, and embedded fuseactions.
qry_	Query	Only fuse type that can perform database interactions whether it be via `<cfquery>`, `<cfstoredproc>`, or any other tag that produces a recordset. Always returns a recordset. No display is allowed from this fuse type.
act_	Action	Any generic ColdFusion code that does not fall into the previous three fuse types. Used primarily for data manipulation, form validation, and external systems interaction, such as `<cfmail>` and `<cfpop>`. This fuse type cannot display output to the browser.
fbx_	Fusebox framework reserved fuse	The seven reserved Fusebox fuses use the `fbx_` prefix. No user-defined files should use this prefix.

Rule 4: A Fuse Can Be a Naming Rebel

The situation is indeed rare, but sometimes fuses beg to have a file prefix other than one of the five listed in Table 5.1. Fusebox, being the amicable framework that it is, allows any file prefix to be used that you see fit.

Here is an example: You get a few weeks into development of your application and you realize that you are making heavy use of the `<cfobject>` tag to access COM objects on your server. Up until now, you have been calling them in action files and using the `act_` prefix. But you are getting confused about some of the filenames. You find yourself staring at the file list wondering what the difference could be between `act_emailUser.cfm` and `act_userEmail.cfm`.

Although a better-named file might be a good answer, you know that one of those two files contains a large `<cfmail>` tag, and the other contains a COM object call to the domain's Exchange server to retrieve a list of emails for a `userID`. Which is which?

Sure, you could just open them both to figure it out and then jot it down on a sticky note, but we know plenty of developers who have too many sticky notes on their monitors already. It would have made much more sense if the files were instead named `act_emailUser.cfm` and `com_userEmail.cfm`. That way, the distinction would be obvious.

Of course, for every extension you make to the five defined prefixes, you move further away from what every other Fusebox developer is doing. Adding one or two well-needed prefixes to an especially complex application should be fine, but if you decide to resell the application later on, it might be deceiving if you were to label it "Fusebox" only to have to answer support questions about your unusual filenaming conventions.

So it boils down to a balance; use the established prefixes, and add your own only if you must.

If you poke around with existing Fusebox applications enough, you will probably encounter two non-standard prefixes: `url_` and `app_`.

The `url_` prefix was designed to handle URL redirection code—those fuses whose sole purpose is to redirect the user via `<cflocation>`, usually based on some variable. The benefit of this fuse is that the `fbx_switch.cfm` file can appear cleaner by removing `<cflocation>` tags from within the `<cfcase></cfcase>` blocks.

The `app_` prefix was used extensively in early versions of Fusebox and was meant to handle application-level code. Largely replaced by each circuit's `fbx_settings.cfm`, `app_`-prefixed fuses were commonly used to declare local and global-style variables as well as contain server-specific code, such as directory mappings and file system references.

If you encounter these prefixes, treat them like any other non-standard pre-fix. Maybe they can be renamed and reorganized to fit into one of the prede-fined prefixes, but maybe not. The previous developer thought these prefixes were necessary, and they might still be relevant to the application.

Rule 5: A Fuse Has a Sense of Self

Fuses are elitists in that a fuse of one type would never be caught dead with code inside it that should be in another type. A display fuse never contains database queries, a query fuse never contains HTML, and an action fuse does not contain HTML. The fbx_-prefixed fuses are reserved for use by the Fusebox framework. Consider this rule-breaking fuse, for example:

```
<cfquery name="selectUsers" datasource="#request.DSN#">
  select * from tblUsers where groupID=#attributes.groupID#
</cfquery>
<cfoutput>
<h2>Users in group #attributes.groupID#</h2>
<cfloop query="selectUsers">
#selectUsers.name#<br>
</cfloop>
</cfoutput>
```

This fuse is trying to be a query fuse by making a database query. However, query fuses cannot produce output, which is happening just after the query, in the <cfloop> section. This is not a well-coded fuse.

Following this rule encourages separation of display from action and frame-work files from application files, which makes debugging easier and development faster. Later in this chapter, we will cover code examples of each fuse type.

Rule 6: Fuse Types Congregate Together

Some developers like to store the different fuse types in separate folders. For example, an application child circuit would have subfolders called actions, queries, display, and layouts where those fuse types would be. The main circuit folder would only contain fbx_settings.cfm, fbx_switch.cfm, fbx_layouts.cfm, and the layout files (lay_default.cfm, for example). If this is something you do already, keep in mind that your <cfinclude> tags will now have to include the directory path like this:

```
<cfinclude template="queries/qry_validateUser.cfm">
```

The examples in this book do not use separate folders for fuse types, but doing so is a stylistic issue that is left up to you, the developer. If you think it makes sense to have a separate folder for queries, then go for it.

Rule 7: A Fuse Contains Fusedocs

We covered Fusedocs briefly in Chapter 1, "The Arrival of Fusebox," and we cover them in complete depth in Chapter 7, "Fusedocs." For our purposes right now, though, let's just say fuses contain Fusedocs, and leave the rest of the discussion for later.

Note that fuses with the `fbx_` prefix do not normally contain Fusedocs. However, the `<history>` section of the Fusedoc would be useful in these files. Whether you do so or not is up to you. Why should you not fully Fusedoc these files? There are a few reasons why you need not bother for each framework file.

First, these framework files tend to control or affect large portions of the application. Making a Fusedoc for the `fbx_switch.cfm`, for example, would be a nearly futile effort because, in reality, it `<cfinclude>`s every other fuse on the circuit. The number of variables used in the `fbx_switch.cfm` includes every variable used by every template.

Second, these files tend to be created once (or not at all as in the case of `fbx_savecontent.cfm` and `fbx_fusebox31_CFxx.cfm`).

Third, you do not need Fusedocs for `fbx_switch.cfm` because the control flow is self documented by the `<cfswitch>` statement in that file.

Fourth, `fbx_circuits.cfm` only creates the circuits structure which, if Fusedoc'ed, would simply be a copy of the structure in XML.

As for `fbx_layouts.cfm`, the only variable it should be creating is `fusebox.layoutFile`. Other variables can be created in that file, and as such, they should be Fusedoc'ed.

Using Fusedocs allows developers to write the fuse without knowledge of the rest of the application. Even if you are a one-man shop developer, this can be beneficial. How many times have you opened up a file that you wrote last year, last month, or even last week, and said to yourself, "What the heck was I thinking?" Fusedocs are designed to reduce the likelihood of this occurring again.

Rule 8: A Fuse Is Clueless

Despite the fact that fuses can accomplish some magnificent deeds (depending on the skill of the fusecoder), they generally are dummies when it comes to the big picture. Fuses cannot rely on anything that they are not explicitly told. Where do you tell a fuse what it can use? The Fusedoc defines the variables that are available and the variables that the fuse is responsible for creating.

Fuses also should not <cfinclude> other fuses. You can quickly get into a dependency nightmare if you break this rule, where a change in one fuse inadvertently (but gravely) affects another fuse.

What happens if, as you are coding a fuse, you realize that this fuse needs to reference the variable #application.versionName# and the Fusedoc does not declare it? Of course, you can reference that variable, but the Fusedoc needs to be updated to reflect that change. It is with this principal in mind that we think of fuses like black boxes. A fuse has to remain unaffiliated with the application. Otherwise, we get spaghetti code, which lacks structure.

Rule 9: A Fuse Should Watch Its Back

Similar to the way that fuses should not rely on the rest of the application, they also should be suspect of any variable that is supposed to be available. A Fusedoc might say that a variable userID in the attributes scope is incoming, but can we be certain? Take a look at the following code, taken from a fuse called qry_userDetails.cfm:

```
<cfquery name="userDetails" datasource="#request.DSN#">
  SELECT * FROM users WHERE userID=#attributes.userID#
</cfquery>
```

What will happen to this code if attributes.userID is not defined? What will happen if attributes.userID is a text string, not an integer like we assume it to be? If userID is passed on the URL string, it could be anything, including something like this:

```
?userID=14%3BDROP%20TABLE%20users
```

which would be outputted as this:

```
SELECT * FROM users WHERE userID14;DROP TABLE users
```

In SQL Server, this SQL statement would drop the users table, which would erase all the data stored inside.

The ways you can protect fuse code from malicious or unexpected errors are ColdFusion-based and fall outside the scope of this book and Fusebox in general. In the previous case, we suggest you check out the <cfqueryparam> tag and use <cfparam> or IsDefined() in your code. Fusebox does not create security holes that do not already exist in ColdFusion, so it is up to you to make sure that each fuse is thoroughly bug proof.

Rule 10: A Fuse Has a Good Name

Rules 3 and 4 cover filenaming prefixes, but it is also important that the rest of the fuse name is obvious. You might dismiss this rule as a stylistic issue especially if you do not like files with long, obvious names like `dsp_searchResults.cfm` and instead prefer `dsp_srt.cfm`. You might also insist that our pleas cannot sway you. However, please consider for a moment the benefits of a widely accepted naming scheme.

It is important to give files an obvious name, preferably free of abbreviations. One of the main benefits of using Fusebox (and clear filenaming) is that by using an established framework and methodology, developers can easily join your team or handle maintenance of your project without first having to learn the architecture employed. The same is the case for filenames. Obvious filenames are, well, obvious, making maintenance simpler than a cryptic naming scheme.

Another thing to keep in mind regarding filenaming is query fuses. Query fuses should always return the recordset named the same as that of the file, minus the prefix and extension. Take a look at this query fuse as an example:

```
<!--- qry_productDetail.cfm --->
<cfquery name="productDetail" datasource="#request.DSN#">
  SELECT * FROM product WHERE productID=#attributes.productID#
</cfquery>
```

Notice how the name of the file is `qry_productDetail.cfm`, and the recordset returned bears the same name, `productDetail`.

Now when you are assembling your fuses into fuseactions, and you know you need to `<cfinclude>` `qry_productDetail.cfm`, you also know that the next fuse can reference the recordset called `productDetail`. Following this practice will save you time in development.

Rule 11: Follow the Other 10 Rules

Upon first investigating Fusebox, many developers quickly notice the fuse rules of file prefix and content restrictions. In fact, many Fuseboxers note that prior to using Fusebox, they followed a similar naming scheme. Even though your previous naming scheme worked for you, other developers would still have to learn it. When we all use the same naming scheme, we all know what each of our applications is doing. Bug fixing is simplified, more team members can cooperate on a project, and most importantly, a developer does not need an encyclopedic understanding of the application to be efficient with updates or development.

Each fuse is broken into the smallest possible unit, and each of these units is not reliant on the other fuses to do its job. This way, fuses are reusable. Also, by following the Fusedoc standard of fuse documentation, these rules can be quantified in each fuse. Fuses' comments are thorough and complete.

Fuse Examples

Now that we have completed the lecture on fuse rules, you are probably masters of fuse use. However, you have not seen examples of each fuse type, so here we go.

Action Fuses in Use

Action files have one infallible rule: If a file uses the `act_` prefix, it cannot output. Whether the requesting client is a browser, a WAP phone, a web service, or a `<cfmodule>` tag, action fuses can only contain CFML logic and service calls. Use of `<cfoutput>` should be strictly limited to looping over query result-sets to perform manipulations of the data. We even prefer to use `<cfloop query="">` instead of `<cfoutput query="">` in action fuses. The `<cfoutput>` tag introduces extra whitespace, which, although harmless, is not pretty in action fuses.

In rare instances, an action fuse can perform database queries. For example, you might need to emulate the functionality of a stored procedure by running a query, looping through it, and performing subsequent queries based on the results of the first query.

Let's take a look at an example action file:

```
<cfset attributes.generatedpassword="">
<cfloop from="1" to="10" index="count">
  <cfset Randomize(randrange(1,1000))>
  <cfif randrange(0,1)>
    <cfset attributes.generatedpassword="#attributes.generatedpassword
    ➥##chr(randrange(65,90))#">
  <cfelse>
    <cfset attributes.generatedpassword="#attributes.generatedpassword
    ➥##randrange(1,10)#">
  </cfif>
</cfloop>
```

This code creates highly random alphanumeric passwords, but it does not output anything to the client. It also does not make database calls. This code is an ideal example of an action fuse, although it does not occur too often. Most ColdFusion code consists of querying a database and then displaying the returned data. Fusebox developers write a lot of query and display fuses; action fuses are less common.

Even though they are not as common as the other fuse types, action fuses play an important role in Fusebox applications. More than any other type, action fuses are the domain of the ColdFusion programmer. If you have some "data massaging" to perform, such as retrieving data from a few unrelated databases and looping through it, or running routines based on some kind of aggregate results, then that code would be best contained in an action fuse.

Here is another example action fuse:

```
<cftry>
  <cfloop list="#GetClientVariablesList()#" index="clientvar">
    <cfset temp=DeleteClientVariable(clientvar)>
  </cfloop>
  <cfcookie name="CFID" expires="NOW"><cfcookie name="CFToken"
  ⇒expires="NOW">
  <cfcatch type="Any"></cfcatch>
</cftry>
<cf_location url="index.cfm?fuseaction=#xfa.continue" addtoken="No">
```

> **Note**
> Jordan Clark's most excellent custom tag <cf_location> serves as a true replacement for
> ColdFusion's native <cflocation>, but it allows cookies to be set on the same request before
> redirecting. Find it on the Macromedia Developer's Exchange.

This action fuse logs out the current user. It has no database calls and outputs no display to the browser.

(Well, there we go contradicting ourselves—kind of. We used the <cf_location> custom tag (the native <cflocation> works the same way), which actually sends http header information to the browser, informing it that the requested page has moved somewhere else. So something did go to the browser, but nothing the user would ever see.)

Keep in mind that action fuses are used as something of a catch-all for whatever code we need to write that does not otherwise fit into another fuse type. Remember that it should "catch" only the code that does not fit elsewhere. It should contain no database calls and no output.

Query Fuses in Use

Like action fuses, query fuses that use the qry_ prefix cannot display HTML to the client. Query fuses should be as modular as possible to allow maximum reuse of the query. This means that the only code that should usually be contained in a query fuse is a <cfquery> or <cfstoredproc> tag, a few <cfparam> tags to create defaults for the query, and maybe some looping afterward to rearrange the data output if it could not be accomplished in the query.

Here is an example of a query fuse:

```
<cfparam name="attributes.userid" default="0">
<cfquery name="getUser" datasource="#request.DSN#">
SELECT username as name, email, phonenumber, password FROM users
WHERE userid=#attributes.userid#
</cfquery>
```

It is pretty obvious what this fuse does. Based on a passed-in variable `attributes.userid`, it retrieves user details.

Query fuses never generate output to the browser, and they are the only fuse type that interacts with databases. What else do they do?

One rule of query fuses is that they usually generate a recordset. Stored procedures and some SQL queries do not return resultsets, even though they are fine to use in query fuses. However, some tags produce "queries" (as ColdFusion calls them) that do not interact with a database. Tags like `<cfsearch>`, `<cfdirectory>`, and `<cfpop>` produce queries that are fully compliant with ColdFusion's query tags, such as `<cfoutput>` and `<cfloop>`, and the query functions like `QuerySetCell()`. Can these tags be in query fuses?

Remember that we just said that query fuses usually produce a recordset. Therefore, using those tags is fine in query files. However, we also mentioned that action fuses serve as a catch-all for whatever does not fit well into the other fuse types. That means that it is okay to use those query-producing tags in action fuses, too—the choice is up to you. Whatever you and your team members decide, be consistent across your application.

Who Writes Query Fuses?

If you are lucky enough to work with other developers, chances are that one of you is better at writing SQL than the others. That means that this person becomes the "database guru" and can easily be tasked with writing and optimizing queries. In fact, it is not important that this person even understand Fusebox or ColdFusion. Oftentimes, a decent-sized project will have an appointed database administrator (DBA). It could not get much easier than telling the DBA, "Optimize all the files in the application that start with the `qry_` prefix." If your DBA wants to convert the effective but crude SQL query that you wrote to a well-tuned database-side stored procedure, then that is up to her. All that matters to you is that you `<cfinclude>` a query fuse and it returns a recordset.

What if you do not have the luxury of a dedicated DBA for your application? Or what if you do have one, but that person is busy and cannot write the queries you need when you need them?

QuerySims

Hal Helms invented QuerySims (short for "query simulations") to get around this dependence on a DBA. In fact, QuerySims get around a dependence on a database altogether! Here is an example of the QuerySim syntax:

```
<cf_querysim>
allUsers
name,email,phonenumber,password
Stan Cox¦stancox@hotmail.com¦717-283-0000¦rockinhorse
Brody Scully¦brody@designonline.com¦¦honeybear
Janice MacKenzie¦janice@thirdwheelbikes.com¦800-twbikes¦builtfortwo
</cf_querysim>
```

This code would go in the query file named `qry_allUsers.cfm`. Instead of writing an SQL query using the `<cfquery>` tag, we can write a QuerySim. To the application and the fuse that is outputting this recordset, a QuerySim looks just like a real query. It returns a query recordset that can be looped over and has a `query.recordcount`, `query.columnlist`, and so on, but it does not connect to a database. If it does not connect to a database, where does the data come from?

You make up the data, and the `<cf_querySim>` tag uses the ColdFusion functions `QueryAddRow()` and `QueryAddColumn()` to create a dummy recordset. This works flawlessly while developing an application. After all, if you need to display a user's details on a profile page, do you really care about a person named Janice MacKenzie whose telephone number is 800-twbikes? Of course not—you just need realistic-looking data.

After the actual SQL query is written (by you or by the more skilled DBA), it can be substituted for the fake data that is produced by the QuerySim by swapping out the call to `<cf_querySim>` with a `<cfquery>` or `<cfstoredproc>` tag. The replacement is completely transparent to the application.

Although we have presented QuerySims as a development tool, some developers use these in place of true queries where the information being returned is pretty static, like a list of the states making up the United States. By storing this kind of data in plain text, QuerySims can save a lot of time if changes need to be made, like adding an abbreviation column to the states list. Rather than putting this information into a database and needing forms to manage it all (select, insert, update, delete), a simple QuerySim block can be maintained without the hazard of changing code files.

Finally, QuerySims allow us as developers to decide on the naming scheme for data. For some reason, it seems that many "database people" use the most cryptic naming schemes imaginable. Having a column named `username` is a lot more readable than `usr_fn` and `usr_ln`. Using QuerySims specifies how the data should be returned in the recordset without having to worry about exactly how the data is stored in the database. If the column names end up being different in the database from those that were specified in the QuerySim, the DBA can just use column aliases to rename the column outputs. You can get this great tag at www.halhelms.com.

Finally, remember Rule 10: "A fuse has a good name." Name your query fuses the same as the recordset names they produce. If your query is called qry_getUserDetails.cfm, name the recordset getUserDetails.

Display Fuses

Exactly what display fuses do and how they are used has some wiggle room. Some developers use multiple display files to create one fuseaction's worth of output. Some developers need to nest display fuses together to simplify massive display pages. The one unbreakable rule is that display fuses are the only type that allows output to the browser or any other client.

Because of the fact that these fuse types generate content, they contain a minimal amount of ColdFusion logic and should not contain code that would normally go in another fuse type. Common ColdFusion tags used in display fuses include <cfoutput>, <cfloop>, <cfset>, <cfparam>, and <cfif>. Tags like <cfquery>, <cflocation>, and <cfobject> are not desired. The tags should instead be quarantined into query or action files. Of course, you are free to use whatever tags are necessary to get the job done for a fuse, but if you find yourself writing blocks of ColdFusion code, it should probably be moved into an action fuse.

Embedded Display Fuses

Display fuses are almost always embedded in a layout file. What do we mean by that? Here is an example display file:

```
<cfoutput>
<div class="heading">5 Best Sellers</div>
<hr size="1" color="##339933">
<cfloop query="best5sellers">
<a href="#request.self#?fuseaction=#xfa.bestsellerlink#&productID=
➥#best5sellers.productID#">#best5sellers.displayName#</a>
<cfif len(best5sellers.salePrice) AND dateCompare
➥(best5sellers.saleEndingDate,now()) is 1>
<span class="line-through">(#dollarFormat(best5sellers.retailPrice))
➥</span> <span class="saleprice">(#dollarFormat
➥(best5sellers.salePrice))</span>
<cfelse>
(#dollarFormat(best5sellers.retailPrice))
</cfif><br><br>
</cfloop>
</cfoutput>
```

Even though this fuse presents output to the browser, notice how it does not contain <html> or <body> tags.

The fuse does not do all its own formatting because it becomes nested in the layout of the page by the layout file (discussed next). The layout file contains the opening and closing <html>, <head>, <title>, and <body> tags. In fact, this fuse is actually nested inside an HTML table.

None of that matters because this fuse is at its most basic level; it performs a small task without being concerned with the rest of the page. If you were to view this fuse by itself (ignoring the incorrectly formatted HTML), it would look quite boring. You would see one lone list surrounded by whitespace. When the fuse is nested into the final page, however, it looks like Figure 5.1 (the circled part in red).

Figure 5.1   Display fuse in final page.

The other portions of this page are display fuses from other fuseactions. The layout file assembles them all together. (Although you might be tempted to skip ahead to the layout file section coming up, just hold on—we are almost finished talking about display fuses!)

JavaScript in Display Fuses

How do you use JavaScript in display fuses when the page is embedded? Let's take a look at an example of that:

```
<script language="JavaScript">
  function checkEmail() {
    if (feedbackForm.email.value=='') {
      alert('Please enter your email.');
      return false;
    }
    else return true;
  }
</script>
<cfoutput>
<form action="index.cfm?fuseaction=#xfa.submit#" method=
➥"post" onsubmit="return checkEmail()" name="feedbackForm">
  <input type="Text" name="email">
  <input type="Submit" value="submit">
</form>
</cfoutput>
```

This display fuse contains some JavaScript that performs client-side validation of the feedback form. Display files are the place for JavaScript. By keeping the JavaScript that pertains to this fuse on this fuse's page, developers can easily write client-side code all in one place.

Early browsers did not correctly run JavaScript unless it was placed between the <head></head> tag at the top of the page. If you have to write applications with that compliancy in mind, you need to place the JavaScript in a variable and then output that variable in the layout file. This is because ColdFusion processes the layout file after the display fuse and because the layout file usually contains the <head></head> tag. Here is an example of storing JavaScript in a ColdFusion variable:

```
<cfparam name="page.javascript" default="">
<cfset page.javascript=ListAppend(page.javascript,"function
➥cancelOrder(){ sure=confirm(""Are you sure you want to cancel
➥this order?\nThere is no way to undo this action."");if (sure)
➥{ theForm.fuseaction='#xfa.cancelOrder#';
➥theForm.submit(); } }",chr(10))>
```

Notice how the JavaScript function cancelOrder() must be written all on one line. This code was first written with line breaks included to make sure it ran. Then it was concatenated into one line. By using the ColdFusion ListAppend() function along with <cfparam>ing the variable page.javascript, we can piece together as much JavaScript as is needed, without overwriting anything that was written previously.

Style Sheets in Display Fuses

In the first example (the "best sellers" one), you might have noticed the `class` attribute being used in some `<span>` and `<div>` tags. The `class` attribute applies a style to text. That means that a style sheet has to be included on this page. Where is it?

Remember how the core file processed the page request? The `fbx_switch.cfm` file is processed first, and then the result is embedded into the layout file. That means that the layout file is where the style sheet is. We set the style sheet once:

```
<link rel="stylesheet" href="thirdwheelbikesstyles.css"
➥type="text/css">
```

Then we can access the styles on any display fuse. Remember that ColdFusion and Fusebox finish all their processing before the result is sent to the browser. Those class attributes are never stranded—they always have the layout file to back them up.

That's it for display fuses. They present display to the browser or whatever client is requesting it (WAP phones, SOAP services, and so on), and they are embedded in a larger layout file. Display fuses are processed before the layout file, but they can use client-side technologies that are initialized in the layout file. Now it is time to piece the display fuses together. We're on to layout files!

Layout Fuses

We know that layout files are where the display fuse is embedded for presentation to the client. What does that mean? How do you "embed" a display fuse in a layout file?

Well, you do not exactly embed the display fuse. Instead, during the processing of the core file, the Fusebox framework traps the output of the fuse-action (from the `<cfcase></cfcase>` tags in `fbx_switch.cfm`) into a variable called `fusebox.layout`. Because the display fuse is processed during a fuse-action, the output of a display fuse is stored in `fusebox.layout`. This means that to embed a fuseaction (and any display fuse called from that fuseaction), we have to output the variable `fusebox.layout` in the correct place. That is what happens in a layout file.

Here is a simple example layout file:

```
<html>
<head>
  <title>Page Title</title>
</head>
<body>
```

```
<table border="2" bgcolor="#0000ff">
<tr>
  <td><cfoutput>#fusebox.layout#</cfoutput></td>
</tr>
</table>
</body>
</html>
```

The output that the requested fuseaction created is stored in the variable
`fusebox.layout`. The preceding layout file contains the entire HTML formatting for the page and outputs the fuseaction display in the correct place. By
doing this, our display fuses do not contain HTML formatting. They exist as
individual units, unaware of and not responsible for the layout of the page.
How do we embed multiple layouts on one page?

Calling Fuseactions from the Layout

The layout file is responsible for assembling the output for display to the
browser. It does this job primarily by outputting the variable `fusebox.layout`.
However, it can also output other fuseactions as well. Think about a portal
page for a moment. All on one page, it might contain a horoscope, the local
weather, top news stories, some products on sale, and maybe a login form.
Each of those elements would be a separate fuseaction, assembled together by
the layout file. Here is an example of a "portal-style" layout file:

```
<html>
<head>
  <title>Our Portal</title>
</head>
<body>
<table border="2" bgcolor="#0000ff">
<tr>
  <td valign="top"><cfmodule template="#request.self#" fuseaction=
  ➥"menus.leftNav"><br><br><cfmodule template="#request.self#"
  ➥fuseaction="horoscopes.top"></td>
  <td valign="top">
  <table>
    <tr>
      <td><cfoutput>#fusebox.layout#</cfoutput></td>
    </tr>
    <tr>
      <td><cfmodule template="#request.self#"
      ➥fuseaction="weather.top"></td>
    </tr>
  </table>
  </td>
  <td width="25%" valign="top"><cfmodule template="#request.self#"
  ➥fuseaction="users.loginForm"><br><cfmodule template=
  ➥"#request.self#" fuseaction="main.bestSellers"></td>
```

```
</tr>
<tr>
 <td><cfmodule template="#request.self#"
 ➥fuseaction="menus.bottom"></td>
</tr>
</table>
</body>
</html>
```

Are You a Web Programmer or a Web Designer?

Back when the web first started, many developers did it all—HTML, a little CGI, maybe a little graphics work. These days, programming for the web has become so specialized that it is difficult for many designers and artists to keep up. The same is true for programmers. We might know our way around graphics programs like Photoshop and Flash, but few of us are good at both fields.

It is with this in mind that we always let graphics and "HTML people" make layout and display files. Little ColdFusion is involved in creating layout files. In fact, with a short lesson on `<cfoutput>`, pound signs, and `<cfmodule>`, web designers can assemble their own complete pages based on the individual fuseactions you create. Each fuseaction can be treated as a "component."

This powerful nested layout model is discussed further in Chapter 9, "Nested Layouts." For now, just remember that the content of the fuseaction is trapped in the variable `fusebox.layout`, and the layout file controls where that content is displayed.

Fusebox Reserved Files

Only three Fusebox files with the `fbx_` prefix are modifiable. They include `fbx_settings.cfm`, `fbx_layouts.cfm`, and `fbx_circuits.cfm`. Those files were discussed in previous chapters, so there is nothing more that we will discuss here. Keep in mind, though, that the kind of code that goes in the other fuse types should not go in any Fusebox file.

One example of the interaction between Fusebox files and other fuse types is in the root `fbx_settings.cfm` file. A typical line in that file might read as follows:

```
<cfinclude template="qry_states.cfm">
```

Reviewing qry_states.cfm, we see that it runs a QuerySim to load the states in the U.S. into an application-scoped query:

```
<cflock scope="application" timeout="10" type="READONLY">
<cfif not IsDefined("application.states")>
    <cfset build=1>
```

```
<cfelse>
    <cfset build=0>
</cfif>
</cflock>
<cfif build>
<cf_querysim>
states
stateID,abbreviation,fullname
1|AL|Alabama
2|AK|Alaska
...
</cf_querysim>
</cfif>
```

The root `fbx_settings.cfm` file `<cfinclude>`d a query fuse; it did not contain the QuerySim itself. This separation is crucial to remember when dealing with the Fusebox framework files.

That's It for Fuses

Guided by the 10 (plus one) fuse rules, we can be assured that fuses we write will be correctly formatted and easily maintainable. Fuses also come in different types (query, display, and action), each having different purposes.

By following the same rules that other Fusebox developers adhere to, our application will be easy to interpret by other developers who are skilled with Fusebox. But even better, we will be able to tell what the code is without opening the file. As applications grow in size, clear and efficient filenaming conventions and management are an absolute must.

"If you're going to have centralization,
why not have it!"

—Frank Lloyd Wright

6

Exit Fuseactions

IN THE LEXICON OF FUSEBOX 3, exit fuseactions (XFAs) are one of the "power tools" that help improve the modularity of Fusebox applications and encourage code reuse. An XFA is an application of a well-respected programming principle (applying variables in place of hard-coded values) to a specific situation (carrying processing from one fuseaction to the next).

This chapter examines what fuseactions are, how they are used, and why they were adopted for Fusebox 3.

What Are XFAs?

The subject of XFAs generates a fair amount of conversation within the Fusebox community, particularly as new adopters are introduced to the methodology. There seems to be a conception that, because there is an official name for this "thing," it must be a development tool or a piece of software that can be incorporated into a Fusebox application.

But XFAs are not something to be downloaded. Rather, they represent an idea that allows Fusebox circuits to be flexible, modular, and portable. To help clarify, we'll first define the term and then look at exit points in action.

Definitions

Taken on its face, exit fuseaction is a phrase that doesn't convey a clear message. But if we look at the components of the phrase, we can get to the bottom of the idea.

As we've seen in the previous chapters, a fuseaction is something that a Fusebox circuit can do. The action is represented by a verb, such as showMenu.

An exit is the point at which processing leaves a fuseaction. The exits (also called *exit points*) of a fuseaction are generally found in the last fuse in a fuseaction's <cfcase> block.

An XFA is something that a Fusebox application can do when processing leaves a fuseaction. However, the concept of XFAs is a little more powerful than that basic idea; XFAs take exits one step further by dynamically indicating what the application will do next.

As an example, consider Figure 6.1. It represents a process that has two potential outcomes: success and failure. If the process succeeds, it calls a process named showMenu. If it fails, the process showError is called. These directives are hard-coded in the process; to see what's going to happen, we need to see inside the process box.

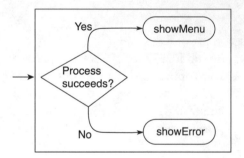

Figure 6.1   Process with hard-coded exits.

By comparison, Figure 6.2 shows the same process with one modification. Instead of having the directives for the next process inside myProcess, the calling process sets values for the onSuccess and onFailure events before calling myProcess. Using this method, we don't need to know what's inside myProcess to know how the program will change course based on its results.

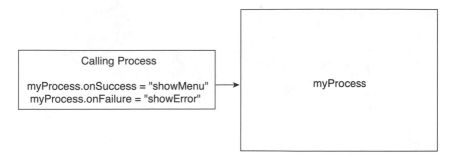

Figure 6.2   Process with variable exits.

This is how XFAs work. They replace hard-coded values in a fuseaction's exit points with variables. This opens the door to making use of a fuseaction's fuses in other fuseactions, other circuits, or other applications.

We'll talk about specific coding techniques for XFAs in the next part of this chapter, but first we need to look at the nature of exit points within fuses. This will help to identify places within applications where XFAs should be applied.

Identifying Exit Points

Exit points are the places at which the fuse can pass control to another fuse.

To make this idea clear, let's forget about Fusebox and ColdFusion for a moment and think strictly about HTML.

HTML Exit Points

When you write an HTML page, you can pass control from one page to another in three ways: links, form actions, and <meta> tag redirections. Figure 6.3 shows a page with each of these represented. Listing 6.1 shows the code for the same page.

Listing 6.1   **Code for Figure 6.3**

```
<html>
<head>
  <title>Exit Points</title>
  <meta http-equiv=refresh content=timeoutPage.html;60>
</head>
<body>
This document demonstrates HTML exit points.
<p>
An exit point can be either a <a href="otherPage.html">link</a>,
or a form action, as shown below:
</p>
```

continues

Listing 6.1 **Continued**

```html
<form action="mailto:webmaster@mysite.com">
  <input type="hidden" name="subject" value="Suggestion Card">
  Name: <input type="text" name="myName"><br>
  Suggestion: <input type="text" name="myMessage"><br>
  <input type="submit" value="Send Card">
</form>

</body>
</html>
```

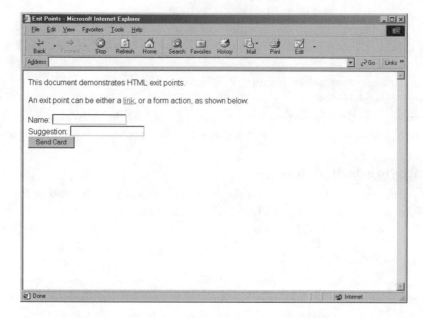

Figure 6.3 HTML exit points.

If the user clicks the link, the exit point is the link to otherPage.html; if the user fills out the form and clicks the Send Card button, the exit point is the form action, which generates an email message; if the user does nothing for 60 seconds, the <meta> tag invokes a redirect to timeoutPage.html.

Adding on to basic HTML, we can also exit a page through the use of a script.

JavaScript Exit Points

JavaScript adds the ability to use the window.location property to pass control to another page.

Figure 6.4 shows a sample page with an image button to allow an exit. Figure 6.5 shows the page to which it links with a JavaScript action to submit a form. Listing 6.2 shows the code for both pages.

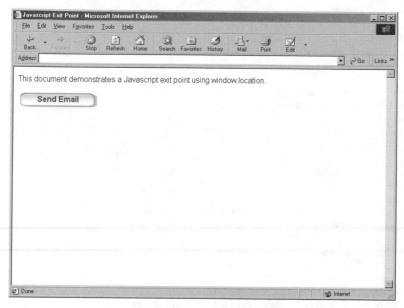

Figure 6.4   JavaScript `window.location` exit point.

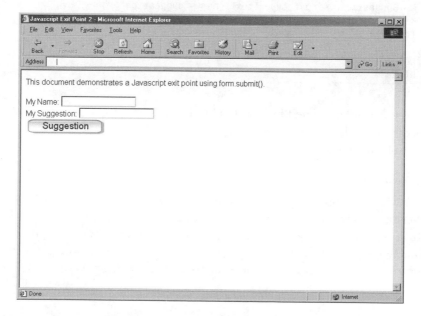

Figure 6.5   JavaScript `form.submit()` exit point.

Listing 6.2 **Code for Figures 6.4 and 6.5**

```
<!-- Figure 6.4 Code -->
<html>
<head>
  <title>Javascript Exit Point</title>
</head>
<body>
This document demonstrates a Javascript exit point using window.location.
<p>

<img src="btnSendEmail.jpg"
 onclick="window.location='sendEmail.html'">

</body>
</html>

<!-- Figure 6.5 Code -->
<html>
<head>
  <title>Javascript Exit Point 2</title>
</head>
<body>
This document demonstrates a Javascript exit point using form.submit().
<p>

<form action="mailto:webmaster@mysite.com">
  <input type="hidden" name="subject" value="Suggestion">
  My Name: <input type="text" name="customer"><br>
  My Suggestion: <input type="text" name="suggestion"><br>
  <img src="btnSuggest.jpg" onclick="form.submit()">
</form>

</body>
</html>
```

Exit points can be defined by simple HTML or JavaScript actions. Of course, most of the work we'll be doing will involve ColdFusion-based exit points, so we'll look there next.

ColdFusion Exit Points

When we move into a ColdFusion environment, we add to our HTML and JavaScript exits the ability to pass control to another page using the <cflocation> tag. Listing 6.3 shows an example of using <cflocation> to conditionally pass control to another page. (This example is not from a Fusebox application, so you don't see a reference to index.cfm or #self#.)

Listing 6.3 **ColdFusion Exit Point**

```
<cfif not loggedIn>
  <cflocation url="/login.cfm">
</cfif>
```

These sections have shown that, when working in a Fusebox environment, we have five ways to exit a fuse:

- Links
- Form actions
- `<meta>` tags
- JavaScript
- `<cflocation>` tags

Each type of exit has appropriate uses within each type of fuse.

Exit Points and Fuse Types

Because they involve interaction with the user, links and form actions are used in display fuses. JavaScript and `<cflocation>` can also be used in display fuses, if they are needed.

Action fuses can use JavaScript and `<cflocation>`, but generally don't use links or form actions. This is because action fuses don't provide interaction with the user. We have seen, however, cases in which a form construct filled with hidden inputs is triggered with a JavaScript `form.submit()` method to pass data out of an action fuse. This is perfectly legitimate.

Now that we understand the concept of an exit point, all we need to do is translate the hard-coded method of coding exit points into XFAs. To facilitate this transition, we'll look at examples of each of the four types of exit points, how they would have looked if hard-coded, and how they would be coded using an XFA. We'll also look at the `switch` statement from the Fusebox file to see the real impact of using XFAs.

Implementing XFAs

Essentially, the process of implementing XFAs involves two steps: changing hard-coded exit points to use XFA variables, and setting the values for the variables in the Fusebox file.

The next few sections will cover specific examples of XFA syntax compared with hard-coding. Then we'll take a quick look back at the overall technique.

Coding Techniques

These examples are illustrations of each type of exit point we discovered in the last section. Each example compares hard-coded syntax with the same job done using an XFA. Note that when an XFA is employed, its name is indicative of its related event. The reason for this becomes apparent when we look at the code used in the Fusebox file (`fbx_switch.cfm`) to call the fuseaction. We'll talk about each case as it is presented.

Link Example

This set of listings shows an example of using a link to call another fuseaction. Listings 6.4–6.7 are included:

Listing 6.4—Hard-coded link example

Listing 6.5—Fusebox file section for hard-coded link example

Listing 6.6—Link example with XFA

Listing 6.7—Fusebox file section for link example with XFA

The hard-coded link example shows how we can create a link to call the `showMenu` fuseaction from the `menu` circuit. This code appears in a fuse named `dsp_Links.cfm`.

Listing 6.4   **Hard-Coded Link Example**

```
<a href="#self#?fuseaction=menu.showMenu">My Menu</a>
```

The Fusebox file (`fbx_switch.cfm`) for the application that uses the `dsp_Links.cfm` fuse contains a case for a fuseaction named `showLinks`.

Listing 6.5   **Fusebox File Section for Hard-Coded Link Example**

```
<cfcase value="showLinks">
  <cfinclude template="dsp_Links.cfm">
</cfcase>
```

Note that no information in Listing 6.5 indicates anything about program flow; it only tells us that the fuseaction `showLinks` uses a fuse named `dsp_Links.cfm`.

Now we'll look at the same link, but this time we'll use an XFA in place of the hard-coded fuseaction.

Listing 6.6   **Link Example with XFA**

```
<a href="#self#?fuseaction=#XFA.lnkMyMenu#">My Menu</a>
```

The hard-coded fuseaction `menu.showMenu` has been replaced with the variable `#XFA.lnkMyMenu#`. It's easy to identify as an exit fuseaction because we use the prefix `XFA.` to indicate just that. We also use a name for the XFA that is indicative of its job; in this case, `lnkMyMenu` tells us that this is an XFA associated with a link whose text is `My Menu`. This sort of naming convention makes a world of difference when we look at the next listing, the Fusebox file section from Listing 6.5, modified to accommodate the XFA.

Listing 6.7   **Fusebox File Section for Link Example with XFA**

```
<cfcase value="showLinks">
  <cfset XFA.lnkMyMenu="menu.showMenu">
  <cfinclude template="dsp_Links.cfm">
</cfcase>
```

The fuseaction name we want to execute when using the link to `My Menu` has been moved into the Fusebox file and stored in the XFA variable `XFA.lnkMyMenu`, at the beginning of the case block for the `showLinks` fuseaction. This case block now tells us that the `showLinks` fuseaction uses the template `dsp_Links.cfm`, and that if the user clicks the `My Menu` link, the fuseaction `menu.showMenu` will be called.

Now we'll look at XFA handling for a form action.

Form Action Example

This set of listings shows an example of using a form action to call another fuseaction. Listings 6.8–6.11 are included:

Listing 6.8—Hard-coded form example

Listing 6.9—Fusebox file section for hard-coded form example

Listing 6.10—Form example with XFA

Listing 6.11—Fusebox file section for form example with XFA

The hard-coded form example shows how we can create a form to call the `showMenu` fuseaction from the `menu` circuit. This code appears in a fuse named `dsp_LoginForm.cfm`.

Listing 6.8 **Hard-Coded Form Example**

```
<form action="#self#">
  <input type="hidden" name="fuseaction" value="login.validateUser">
  User ID: <input type="text" name="userID"><br>
  Password: <input type="password" name="pword">
  <input type="submit" name="btnLogin" value="Login">
</form>
```

The Fusebox file (`fbx_switch.cfm`) for the application that uses the `dsp_LoginForm.cfm` fuse contains a case for a fuseaction named `showLogin`.

Listing 6.9 **Fusebox File Section for Hard-Coded Form Example**

```
<cfcase value="showLogin">
  <cfinclude template="dsp_LoginForm.cfm">
</cfcase>
```

Note that no information in Listing 6.5 indicates anything about program flow; it only tells us that the fuseaction `showLogin` uses a fuse named `dsp_LoginForm.cfm`.

Now we'll look at the same form, but this time we'll use an XFA in place of the hard-coded fuseaction.

Listing 6.10 **Form Example with XFA**

```
<form action="#self#">
  <input type="hidden" name="fuseaction" value="#XFA.btnLogin#">
  User ID: <input type="text" name="userID"><br>
  Password: <input type="password" name="pword"><br>
  <input type="submit" name="btnLogin" value="Login">
</form>
```

The hard-coded fuseaction `login.validateUser` has been replaced with the variable `#XFA.btnLogin#`. It's easy to identify as an exit fuseaction because we use the prefix `XFA.` to indicate just that. We also use a name for the XFA that is indicative of its job; in this case, `lnkMyMenu` tells us that this is an XFA associated with a form whose text is `My Menu`. This sort of naming convention makes a world of difference when we look at the next listing: the Fusebox file section from Listing 6.5, modified to accommodate the XFA.

Listing 6.11   **Fusebox File Section for Form Example with XFA**

```
<cfcase value="showLogin">
  <cfset XFA.btnLogin="login.validateUser">
  <cfinclude template="dsp_LoginForm.cfm">
</cfcase>
```

The fuseaction name we want to execute when using the form to log in has been moved into the Fusebox file and stored in the XFA variable `XFA.btnLogin`, at the beginning of the case block for the `showLogin` fuseaction. This case block now tells us that the `showLogin` fuseaction uses the template `dsp_LoginForm.cfm`, and that if the user clicks the Login button, the fuseaction `login.validateUser` will be called.

Now we'll look at XFA handling for a `<meta>` tag redirection.

`<meta>` Example

This set of listings shows an example of using a `<meta>` tag to redirect to another fuseaction. Listings 6.12–6.15 are included:

Listing 6.12—Hard-coded `<meta>` example

Listing 6.13—Fusebox file section for hard-coded `<meta>` example

Listing 6.14—`<meta>` example with XFA

Listing 6.15—Fusebox file section for `<meta>` example with XFA

The hard-coded `<meta>` example shows how we can create a `<meta>` tag to call the `showIntro` fuseaction from the `info` circuit. This code appears in a fuse named `dsp_Register.cfm`. If the user doesn't complete a registration form within 60 seconds, we want to return to the site's intro page.

Listing 6.12   **Hard-Coded `<meta>` Example**

```
<meta http-equiv="refresh"
content="#self#?fuseaction=info.showIntro;60">
```

The Fusebox file (`fbx_switch.cfm`) for the application that uses the `dsp_Register.cfm` fuse contains a case for a fuseaction named `showRegForm`.

Listing 6.13   **Fusebox File Section for Hard-Coded `<meta>` Example**

```
<cfcase value="showRegForm">
  <cfinclude template="dsp_Register.cfm">
</cfcase>
```

Note that no information in Listing 6.13 indicates anything about program flow; it only tells us that the fuseaction `showRegForm` uses a fuse named `dsp_Register.cfm`.

Now we'll look at the same `<meta>` tag, but this time we'll use an XFA in place of the hard-coded fuseaction.

Listing 6.14   *<meta>* **Example with XFA**

```
<meta http-equiv="refresh"
content="#self#?fuseaction=#XFA.metaRefresh#;60">
```

The hard-coded fuseaction `login.validateUser` has been replaced with the variable `#XFA.metaRefresh#`. It's easy to identify as an exit fuseaction because we use the prefix `XFA.` to indicate just that. We also use a name for the XFA that is indicative of its job; in this case, `metaRefresh` tells us that this is an XFA associated with a `<meta>` tag whose job is to refresh the page request. This sort of naming convention makes a world of difference when we look at the next listing: the Fusebox file section from Listing 6.5, modified to accommodate the XFA.

Listing 6.15   **Fusebox File Section for *<meta>* Example with XFA**

```
<cfcase value="showRegForm">
  <cfset XFA.metaRefresh="info.showIntro">
  <cfinclude template="dsp_Register.cfm">
</cfcase>
```

The fuseaction name we want to execute when using the `<meta>` tag to refresh the page has been moved into the Fusebox file and stored in the XFA variable `XFA.metaRefresh`, at the beginning of the case block for the `showRegForm` fuseaction. This case block now tells us that the `showRegForm` fuseaction uses the template `dsp_Register.cfm`, and that there is a `<meta>` tag that will refresh the page to the fuseaction `login.validateUser`.

Now we'll look at XFA handling for JavaScript exit points.

JavaScript Examples

This set of listings shows an example of using JavaScript to redirect to another fuseaction. The two examples we'll use are the `window.location` property and the `form.submit()` method. Listings 6.16–6.19 are included:

Listing 6.16—Hard-coded JavaScript example

Listing 6.17—Fusebox file section for hard-coded JavaScript example

Listing 6.18—JavaScript example with XFA

Listing 6.19—Fusebox file section for JavaScript example with XFA

The hard-coded JavaScript example shows how we can use JavaScript to call the `showIntro` fuseaction from the `info` circuit. This code appears in a fuse named `dsp_UserActionForm.cfm`. If the user doesn't complete a registration form within 60 seconds, we want to return to the site's intro page.

Listing 6.16   **Hard-Coded JavaScript Example**

```
<form action="#self#">
  User ID: <input type="text" name="userID"><br>
  <img src="editButton.jpg"
  onclick="this.form.action=#self#?fuseaction=users.userEditForm;
  ↦form.submit()"><br>
  <img src="viewButton.jpg"
   onclick="this.form.action=#self#?fuseaction=users.userViewForm;
   ↦form.submit()"><br>
</form>
<img src="cancelButton.jpg"
 onclick="window.location='#self#?fuseaction=main.showMenu'">
```

The two `<img>` tags inside the form in this example demonstrate using the `this.form.action` property to change the form's action attribute, and the `form.submit()` method to submit the form. With this technique, we can use a single form as the front end for multiple destinations.

The `<img>` tag below the form provides a Cancel button that uses the `window.location` property to send the browser back to a menu.

The Fusebox file (`fbx_switch.cfm`) for the application that uses the `dsp_UserActionForm.cfm` fuse contains a case for a fuseaction named `showUserActForm`.

Listing 6.17   **Fusebox File Section for Hard-Coded JavaScript Example**

```
<cfcase value="showUserActForm">
  <cfinclude template="dsp_UserActionForm.cfm">
</cfcase>
```

Note that no information in Listing 6.17 indicates anything about program flow; it only tells us that the fuseaction `showRegForm` uses a fuse named `dsp_UserActionForm.cfm`.

Now we'll look at the same example, but this time we'll use XFAs in place of the hard-coded fuseactions.

Listing 6.18 **JavaScript Example with XFAs**

```
<form action="#self#">
  User ID: <input type="text" name="userID"><br>
  <img src="editButton.jpg"
   onclick="this.action="#self#?fuseaction=#XFA.btnEdit#"><br>
  <img src="viewButton.jpg"
   onclick="this.action="#self#?fuseaction=#XFA.btnView#"><br>
</form>
<img src="cancelButton.jpg"
 onclick="window.location='#self#?fuseaction=#XFA.btnCancel#'">
```

The hard-coded fuseactions have been replaced with the variables
#XFA.btnEdit#, #XFA.btnView#, and #XFA.btnCancel#. They're easy to identify as
exit fuseactions because we use the prefix XFA.. We also use a name for the
XFA that is indicative of its job; in this case, btnEdit tells us that this is an
XFA associated with a button whose job is to send the user somewhere related
with editing. The btnView and btnCancel XFAs are named in similar fashion.
This sort of naming convention makes a world of difference when we look at
the next listing: the Fusebox file section from Listing 6.17, modified to accommodate the XFA.

Listing 6.19 **Fusebox File Section for JavaScript Example with XFA**

```
<cfcase value="showUserActForm">
  <cfset XFA.btnEdit="users.userEditForm">
  <cfset XFA.btnView="users.userViewForm">
  <cfset XFA.btnCancel="main.showMenu">
  <cfinclude template="dsp_UserActionForm.cfm">
</cfcase>
```

The fuseaction names we want to execute when clicking the various buttons
have been moved into the Fusebox file and stored in the XFA variables
XFA.btnEdit, XFA.btnView, and XFA.btnCancel at the beginning of the case
block for the showUserActForm fuseaction. This case block now tells us that the
showUserActForm fuseaction uses the template dsp_UserActionForm.cfm, and
that three buttons will call the fuseactions: users.userEditForm,
users.userViewForm, and main.showMenu, respectively.

Now we'll look at XFA handling for <cflocation> exit points.

<cflocation> Example

This set of listings shows an example of using a <cflocation> tag to redirect to
another fuseaction. Listings 6.20–6.23 are included:

The hard-coded `<cflocation>` example shows how we could use a `<cflocation>` tag to call the showWelcome fuseaction from the info circuit. This code appears in a fuse named act_Register.cfm. When processing reaches the point where the `<cflocation>` tag is placed, we want to take the user to the site's welcome page.

Listing 6.20 **Hard-Coded** *<cflocation>* **Example**

```
<cflocation url="#self#?fuseaction=info.showWelcome">
```

The Fusebox file (fbx_switch.cfm) for the application that uses the act_Register.cfm fuse contains a case for a fuseaction named saveRegistration.

Listing 6.21 **Fusebox File Section for Hard-Coded** *<cflocation>* **Example**

```
<cfcase value="saveRegistration">
  <cfinclude template="act_Register.cfm">
</cfcase>
```

Note that no information in Listing 6.21 indicates anything about program flow; it only tells us that the fuseaction saveRegistration uses a fuse named act_Register.cfm.

Now we'll look at the same `<cflocation>` tag, but this time we'll use an XFA in place of the hard-coded fuseaction.

Listing 6.22 *<cflocation>* **Example with XFA**

```
<cflocation url="#self#?fuseaction=#XFA.continue#">
```

The hard-coded fuseaction login.validateUser has been replaced with the variable #XFA.motaRofrooh#. It's easy to identify as an exit fuseaction because we use the prefix XFA.. We also use a name for the XFA that is indicative of its job; in this case, continue gives an indication that this is an XFA associated with a `<cflocation>` tag whose job is to refresh the page request. Although no part of the name directly specifies a `<cflocation>`, this sort of name is common when no user interface element is available with which to associate the action, as is the case within action fuses. Similar XFA names used with <cflocation> include XFA.onSuccess, XFA.onFailure, and so on. This sort of naming convention makes a world of difference when we look at the next listing: the Fusebox file section from Listing 6.21, modified to accommodate the XFA.

Listing 6.23   **Fusebox File Section for *<cflocation>* Example with XFA**

```
<cfcase value="saveRegistration">
  <cfset XFA.continue="info.showWelcome">
  <cfinclude template="act_Register.cfm">
</cfcase>
```

The fuseaction name we want to execute when using the <cflocation> tag to refresh the page has been moved into the Fusebox file and stored in the XFA variable XFA.continue, at the beginning of the case block for the saveRegistration fuseaction. This case block now tells us that the saveRegistration fuseaction uses the template act_Register.cfm, and that an exit point will refresh the page to the fuseaction info.showWelcome.

That's the end of the specific examples for XFA usage. Now we'll take a quick look back over the general concepts illustrated in the specific examples in this section.

General Concepts

As each of the examples in this section has illustrated, the basic approach of using Exit Fuseactions involves two techniques:

1. Set XFA variables in the case blocks of the Fusebox file's switch construct.
2. Read XFA values from the variables within fuses.

This approach to handling fuseactions offers benefits for both architects and coders, as we'll see in the next section.

Why Use XFAs?

Fusebox is about modularity, maintainability, and focusing the talents of team members. Exit fuseactions contribute to each of these areas. This section looks at each of these areas to see how.

Modularity

When we think about modularity, we think in terms of the ability to take circuits from one application and "plug" them into another application with a minimum of modification. Exit fuseactions add to the modularity of an application by removing the need to edit fuses when a circuit is moved to a new application.

If we've properly designed our Fusebox 3 application, when we move a new circuit into it, the only thing we'll need to edit is the application's circuit definition file (fbx_circuits.cfm) and perhaps the new circuit's Fusebox file (fbx_switch.cfm). For example, look at the circuit definition file in Listing 6.24.

Listing 6.24   **Circuit Definition File (*fbx_circuits.cfm*)**

```
<cfset fusebox.circuits.main = "ourLibrary">
<cfset fusebox.circuits.branches = "ourLibrary/branches">
```

To add a new circuit, all we need to do is add a line to the circuit definition file. Listing 6.25 shows this addition.

Listing 6.25   **Adding a New Circuit (*fbx_circuits.cfm*)**

```
<cfset fusebox.circuits.main = "ourLibrary">
<cfset fusebox.circuits.branches = "ourLibrary/branches">
<cfset fusebox.circuits.login = "ourLibrary/login">
```

As long as we use the same alias for the new circuit that we used in the original application (in this case, "Login"), we don't need to make edits to the circuit's Fusebox file.

The other place we'll need to look when moving a circuit to a new application is the circuit's Fusebox file. Modifications probably will be needed in some of the circuit's process logic. Fortunately, the "roadmap" quality of the Fusebox file makes this bit of editing easy.

The Circuit's Roadmap

We often call the Fusebox file (fbx_switch.cfm) a circuit's roadmap. This is because the <cfswitch> block in the Fusebox file clearly documents all the fuseactions in the circuit. With XFAs in place, the roadmap becomes even more detailed; in addition to a list of fuseactions, the Fusebox file contains information about which fuseaction will be fired in response to various events in the application.

When moving a circuit to a new application (sometimes referred to as *repurposing* a circuit), exit fuseactions probably will need to be modified to get the desired result. For example, if the original application took the user to the fuseaction "menu.showMain" following successful login, the case block for the doLogin fuseaction might look like this:

```
<cfcase value="login.doLogin">
  <cfset XFA.success="menu.showMain">
  <cfset XFA.failure="login.showLoginForm">
  <cfinclude template="act_validateUser.cfm">
</cfcase>
```

If, in the new application, we want a successful login to take the user to the fuseaction "catalog.showDepts", we would change the case block to look like this:

```
<cfcase value="login.doLogin">
  <cfset XFA.success="catalog.showDepts">
  <cfset XFA.failure="login.showLoginForm">
  <cfinclude template="act_validateUser.cfm">
</cfcase>
```

That's all there is to it. We no longer worry about editing fuses or mucking about in the circuit. Just a quick change to the Fusebox file is all that's needed.

This roadmap characteristic of the Fusebox file aids the architect both in development and maintenance. During the development of the application, the architect can check the program's logical flow through the Fusebox file, ensuring that all the required actions are represented.

After the application has gone through its initial development and is in production, an architect can get up to speed on how the application works by simply reading the Fusebox files. This greatly increases an architect's ability to examine a project created by a different architect and make good design recommendations in a short amount of time.

Exit fuseactions also benefit the coders who are tasked with writing the individual fuses. XFAs reduce the number of decisions the coder has to make, allowing focus on the important job of writing great code.

Streamline Coding

Consider the job that a fusecoder has without XFAs. Whenever an exit point is encountered in a fuse, the fusecoder must know what circuit and fuseaction to use for it. This means the architect has to communicate the information to the fusecoder. This information isn't communicated easily. The Fusedoc isn't a good solution, although the architect could use a <note> element to do the job. (We'll get into this in detail in Chapter 7, "Fusedocs.") If the fuse is copied to another circuit or the circuit to another application, both the Fusedoc and the fuse's code must be updated to reflect the changes.

XFAs solve these problems by removing the process flow information from the fuse and placing it into the Fusebox file. In other words, the issue is moved from the fusecoder's sphere of responsibility to the architect's. Consequently, the fusecoder no longer needs the broader knowledge of the application. The architect communicates the XFAs as variables in the Fusedoc's `<in>` section—the place designed to communicate input variables. When the fuse or its circuit moves, changes are not required in the fuse. The architect who is using the fuse or circuit simply makes the changes to the circuit's Fusebox file.

In addition, the fusecoder's job is greatly streamlined where XFAs are involved. Instead of needing specific process information to code an exit point, the fusecoder only needs the name of the XFA as communicated in the Fusedoc. In most development shops, naming conventions make the names of XFAs reasonably predictable. These factors mean that the fusecoder doesn't need to waste time hunting unnecessary process information. Instead, time can be spent focusing on doing the more important work of creating effective fuses.

Filling the Toolbox

We've seen in this chapter that exit fuseactions (XFAs) are a tool for creating better application structure. The use of variables to contain fuseaction values increases modularity, maintainability, and job focus when building Fusebox applications.

XFAs are a benefit to both the architect and the fusecoder, providing better self-documenting features, better information distribution for application design and planning, and streamlined coding. The use of XFAs in place of hard-coded fuseactions makes fuses and circuits more portable, increasing the ability to reuse code.

All in all, XFAs are one of the "power tools" of Fusebox 3. They provide a wealth of power in trade for a simple change in coding practice. We'll be looking at another powerful tool next, which also provides a great deal of power in exchange for a change in practices. That tool is the "new and improved" Fusedoc, the subject of the next chapter.

7

*"The things I assert most vigorously are
those that I resisted long and
accepted late."*

—C.S. Lewis

Fusedocs

The Essence of Fusedoc

Sitting at his desk considering his thoughts for the next chapter of a book,
Stan struggled to get his head around the idea of Fusedocs and their relevance
to the whole Fusebox concept. Just one good metaphor would do the trick,
but even one failed to appear.

Just when he thought he would never come up with a clear understanding
of the whole thing, Stan turned his chair around for a look out the window.
(For a proper introduction to Stan and his counterparts, see this book's
Introduction.) Things were getting interesting on the construction site next
door. "I wonder what's going in over there," he thought, not for the first time.
The foundation hole was getting bigger every day, and rumors made the
rounds of the office about what was being built. "Sure wish I could see the
blueprints for whatever they're building over there…" The thought wasn't
even complete in his head when the light bulb went off—blueprints and parts
lists are the Fusedocs of the construction world!

Actually, it's more the case that Fusedocs are the blueprints and parts lists of
the Fusebox world, but we won't worry about splitting hairs. We *will* worry
about what Fusedocs are, how to create them, and the enormous power they
offer to our development projects.

Fusedocs bring the power of communication and documentation to Fusebox. Through their use, we'll see that applications can carry a wealth of information that is available both to humans who are working on the project and to programs that are designed to read the standard Fusedoc format. There is much to see and do in this chapter, so we'll get right to it.

What Is Fusedoc?

Fusedoc is a documentation standard developed by Hal Helms and patterned originally after the JavaDoc concept. Since its inception, it has grown into the current Fusedoc 2.0 standard, which is an XML vocabulary. Fusedocs appear at the top of every fuse file, providing detailed information about the fuse and its input-output requirements.

For architects, Fusedocs represent a blueprint concept, allowing careful planning of every fuse in an application. For coders, who might not get to see the entire application, Fusedocs represent more of a builder's parts list, providing detailed instructions on what the fuse needs to do. Note, however, that Fusedocs do *not* tell the coder *how* the fuse should work, only *what* it should do.

Much discussion has taken place about what Fusedoc is and why it should be used. Some developers feel that Fusedoc represents too much overhead work. In reality, well-constructed Fusedocs represent the potential for decreased workload overall, and a much more robust system. This is because Fusedocs are part of the planning process for a Fusebox application. Their power is based on initial creation by the architect and a consistent understanding by everyone on the project that the Fusedocs are the technical definition of the application. Consequently, the practice of using Fusedocs is structured and flows through every aspect of the development process.

The Tao of Fusedoc

When using Fusedocs, we have expectations about how they will be used. Consistency is the key to successful Fusedocs. Fusedoc is a standard for embedded program documentation. That is, every fuse in a Fusebox application should have a Fusedoc embedded at the top of the file. This ensures the ability to easily examine the documentation for any fuse. Listing 7.1 shows a sample Fusedoc as it might appear in a typical fuse.

Listing 7.1 **Typical Fusedoc**

```
<!---
<fusedoc fuse="act_Login.cfm" language="ColdFusion" specification="2.0">
  <responsibilities>
    I validate a user's login information.
  </responsibilities>
  <properties>
    <property name="Date" value="01 Jan 02" comments="Sample for book"/>
  </properties>
  <note>
    Notes can be used to capture information that doesn't have a
    ↪specific Fusedoc element.
  </note>
  <io>
    <in>
      <string name="XFA.onSuccess" optional="No" comments="Use if
      ↪process succeeds"/>
      <string name="XFA.onFailure" optional="No" comments="Use if
      ↪process fails"/>
      <string name="userID" optional="No"/>
      <string name="password" optional="No" comments="Hash() this
      ↪string before comparing to password in database"/>
    </in>
    <out>
      <string name="userID" scope="client" oncondition="User is valid"/>
      <string name="firstName" scope="client" oncondition="User is valid"/>
<string name="email" scope="client" oncondition="User is valid"/>
    </out>
  </io>
</fusedoc>
--->
```

Fusedocs are written before the application's code is written. We'll get into this in great detail shortly; the important idea is that the emphasis on Fusedoc comes during the architectural design stage of the development project, as opposed to the more traditional approach of documenting code as it is written.

The process of writing Fusedocs is an analytic and creative one. The objective is to create a blueprint for the application that coders can then pick up and work from. In truth, Fusedocs are more like a parts list that a contractor gives a builder. Fusedocs tell builders exactly what parts will be needed to successfully complete the job in question. That's what Fusedocs do—detail the variables and data that are available to the coder, along with some explanation of what's expected from the fuse in question. Armed with this information, the coder is then able to build the fuse without the need to consult outside resources.

If the coder is supposed to be able to write the fuse without consulting outside resources, it's clear that a Fusedoc needs to be explicit about what the architect expects from the fuse. Fusedocs are about *what* the fuse is to do, not about *how* to do it. This is a fine line to walk, but it is important.

For example, the Fusedoc in Listing 7.1 tells the fusecoder to validate the user according to the userID and password. The fusecoder might choose to run a SQL query against the database that asks for records matching the userID and password, and check the output for records. Another possibility would be to loop over a recordset of userIDs and passwords, looking for a match. The approach that works best is up to the fusecoder.

The creation of good Fusedocs is a skill learned only through the experience of having others write code according to your Fusedocs. In this regard, writing Fusedocs can be considered an art.

The Art of Writing Good Fusedocs

Although software development is generally recognized as a technical discipline, writing good Fusedocs can be an elusive pursuit. Success depends on experience, on the refinement that comes only through trial and error. This is what we mean by "art"; writing good Fusedocs is a skill that cannot be communicated through technical instruction alone. Every Fuseboxer to whom we've spoken has agreed with the observation that the first Fusedocs we write are far from adequate for the job. Hal Helms describes the first time he sent Fusedocs to an outsource for coding this way:

"A week later I got the coded fuses back, and when I looked at them, I immediately wanted to know what idiot had been messing with my Fusedocs. It just wasn't possible that what came back to me was what I sent out. Of course it was; I just didn't realize how many assumptions I had made when I wrote the Fusedocs."

If the creator of the system has this sort of experience on his first time out, it's no surprise that the rest of us have experienced a similar situation. We all make assumptions about the systems we're building. For that reason, a sort of motto for writing good Fusedocs has come to be, "When in doubt, put it in." A word of caution, though; this does *not* mean that we should include every variable imaginable in every fuse's Fusedoc. In fact, we want to do exactly the opposite. We want to include everything the coder needs to write the fuse, and *nothing more*. We state this as the first rule of Fusedocs:

Include everything a coder needs to write the fuse, and nothing more.

Again, the artistic aspect of writing Fusedocs becomes apparent as we consider the fine distinction between "everything the coder needs" and "nothing more."

Everything the Coder Needs

We have habits about the way we work that we might not realize we have. For instance, we sometimes use a variable named `request.dsn` to store the name of the ODBC datasource that our system is using. Similarly, we use a variable named `request.dbt` to store the dbtype; in the case of an ODBC datasource, its value would be "ODBC." This makes it easy to transport a query fuse from one application to another.

The use of these variables makes sense, but it can cause a problem when we start writing Fusedocs. The fact that we use these variables as part of every query we write means that they become a sort of background noise in our coding environment. They're always there, and we can easily forget about their importance. If we forget to include them in a Fusedoc that we write for someone in-house, there's not much impact. The in-house coder knows our local conventions and will probably write the query after that fashion, so no harm is done. On the other hand, if we send the fuse to an outsource for coding, the coder has no idea about the common use of those two variables in our shop, and he cannot successfully complete the fuse without them. A Fusedoc must include everything the coder needs to successfully write the fuse.

The art of writing Fusedocs includes the decision about what the coder needs to write the fuse. Our example with `request.dsn` and `request.dbt` is a good illustration of this principle. If we're writing Fusedocs for in-house coders, we probably won't include those two variables. If we're writing Fusedocs for outsourcing, though, we had better put them in or we'll risk delaying the project while we clarify these issues with our coders.

This is where the "when in doubt..." motto comes in. While you're writing a Fusedoc, if you find yourself wondering whether to put in a particular piece of information, go ahead and put it in. In the case of our datasource and dbtype example, including them makes the Fusedoc accessible to both in-house and out-sourced coders—the sign of a good Fusedoc. Again, we resist the urge to throw in everything that comes to mind, needed or not.

To be effective Fusebox architects, we need to be familiar with the elements that comprise the Fusedoc vocabulary. These elements can be found in the Fusedoc document type definition (DTD), available at `www.fusebox.org`. The next sections cover the details of each Fusedoc element and how to use it.

Elements of Fusedoc

When you get right down to it, Fusedocs are really basic collections of information. They describe what a fuse is going to do (its Responsibilities); who created it, when, and why (its Properties); what variables are present when it runs and are to be created by it (its Input-Output, or IO); and what kinds of situations it expects (its Assertions).

Of these areas, only Responsibilities is a required section in any Fusedoc. The others can be used at your discretion. Keep in mind, though, the first rule of Fusedocs.

Responsibilities, Properties, and IO sections are commonly found in most Fusedocs, whereas an Assertions section is a bit more esoteric. In this section, we'll look at Responsibilities, Properties, and Assertions. Because the IO portion of a Fusedoc is the meat of it, we'll save it for the next section.

Responsibilities

The Responsibilities element of a Fusedoc is the most loosely defined portion of the Fusedoc and, at the same time, its most important. It is a plain-language description of what the fuse is expected to do.

Responsibilities should be written in first-person active voice. This style is not required, but we strongly recommend it. There is something about framing tasks in first-person language that makes them seem more real. By placing yourself in the metaphorical shoes of the fuse, it becomes much easier to examine what jobs you need to do and what information you'll need to do them. The first-person point of view also tends to result in descriptions of what must be done, rather than how to do it.

Listing 7.2 shows an example of a very descriptive Responsibilities section.

Listing 7.2   **Fusedoc Responsibilities (Long)**

```
<responsibilities>
  I display a form for the user to create a new account.  I have
  fields for userID, firstName, lastName, email, and password.  If
  the user clicks the Create button, I return XFA.btnCreate.
</responsibilities>]
```

Listing 7.3 shows an example of a more terse Responsibilities section.

Listing 7.3 **Fusedoc Responsibilities (Short)**

```
<responsibilities>
  I display a form for the user to create a new account.
</responsibilities>
```

Notice the difference between the two listings. Whereas the first one is detailed in its narrative, the second is terse. This is indicative of the artistic nature of writing Responsibilities sections.

Under the original Fusedoc specification, the data-related sections were not as tightly defined as they were in Fusedoc 2.0. As a result, more emphasis was placed on the Responsibilities section to carry the weight of describing what the fuse was about. Architects who have used Fusedocs under both systems tend to write more verbose Responsibilities sections, like the one in Listing 7.2.

Under Fusedoc 2.0's XML definition, the `<io>` section of the Fusedoc carries much more well-defined information than the equivalent Attributes section under Fusedoc 1.0 would have. As a result, the Responsibilities section does not need to be as narrative under the new version. Architects who have been introduced to Fusedocs after the creation of version 2.0 tend to write more terse Responsibilities sections like the one in Listing 7.3, because the information about form fields, variables, and so on is detailed in the `<io>` section of the Fusedoc. This approach is preferable because the technical details are structured in a much more standardized fashion, and the Responsibilities section contains only the information that is not communicated elsewhere in the Fusedoc.

After we've described what the fuse is expected to do, we might want to include some information about who designed the fuse, when it was designed, and so on. This is the purview of the Properties section.

Properties Element

Properties are simply the characteristics of an object. For example, as a person, you have some characteristics such as height, eye color, and age. The optional `<properties>` element in a Fusedoc uses the elements `<history>`, `<property>`, and `<note>` to capture this type of information.

Web developers are often exposed to the idea of objects and properties without being formally aware of it. JavaScript, as a language based on Java, uses an object-oriented style of notation. You can refer to properties of the window, for example. Most of us web developers are familiar with the location property of the window object because we can use it to redirect to a new URL:

```
<script language="Javascript">
  window.location='myPage.cfm';
</script>
```

In similar fashion, a Fusedoc can store a set of properties for its fuse. These can be described using the history, property, and note elements.

History Elements

Purpose: Specifies a milestone in the lifecycle of the fuse.
Attributes:

        author—The author of the milestone.
        email—The author's e-mail address.
        type—The type of the milestone.
                Values—Create (default)
                        Update
        date—The date of the milestone.
        role—The role of the author.
                Values—Architect
                        DBA
                        FuseCoder
                        TextEditor
                        Graphics
                        Any text
        comments—Any comments you want to add

The history element is useful for recording the life of a fuse's code with brief comments. For example, when an architect creates the Fusedoc, a history element exists with a type of Create. If the Fusedoc is subsequently modified for some reason, a second history element is added with a type of Update. You can insert a history element any time you want to record a milestone for the Fusedoc. Listing 7.4 shows a set of history elements.

Listing 7.4   **History Elements**

```
<history author="Jeff Peters"
         email="jeff@grokfusebox.com"
         date="01/22/02"
         role="Architect"
         type="Create" />

<history author="Stan Cox"
         role="FuseCoder"
         date="01/23/02"
         type="Update"
       comments="Started coding" />

<history author="Stan Cox"
         role="FuseCoder"
```

```
        date="01/24/02"
        type="Update"
    comments="Finished coding">
This fuse should be retested after next week's DB upgrade.
</history>
```

The purposes for which you might use history elements have few restrictions. You can use them in whatever fashion will satisfy local requirements. If you need longer comments, you can employ an end tag like the third example shown earlier, instead of trying to put a lot of text in the `comments` attribute. History and note elements are also among the few elements that are added after coding of the fuse begins.

Because the creation of Fusedocs should be a planning exercise, it's important to avoid the mindset that says you can update your Fusedocs whenever the fuse's code requires you to. Although it's important that the Fusedoc and the code agree, it's much more important to the discipline of good planning that Fusedocs be as complete as possible from the outset, rather than being changed to suit shifting coding needs as the project progresses.

Property Elements

Purpose: Specifies a property of the fuse.
Attributes:

> name—The name of the property.
> value—The value of the property.
> comments—Any comments you want to add.

Property elements are the most flexible of all Fusedoc elements. Note that property elements are *not* the same as the properties element that encloses them. A Fusedoc has only one properties element; any number of property elements can exist within a Fusedoc.

You can capture almost any property you can imagine with a property element. Its attributes—name, value, and comments—work in much the same way as Windows INI files or registry entries. The name attribute specifies what the property is, and the value attribute specifies the value that is assigned to the property. The optional comments attribute offers the ability to add any detail that is not made clear in the name and value. Listing 7.5 has sample properties elements.

Listing 7.5 **Property Elements**

```
<property name="client" value="ThirdWheelBikes" />

<property name="copyright"
         value="2002, ThirdWheelBikes"
      comments="Reverts to GrokFusebox.com in 2004" />

<property name="clientsFavoriteColor"
         value="Cornflower Blue" />
```

The last element in Listing 7.5 serves to show how open-ended the property element can be. Sure, it doesn't make much sense, but it's perfectly allowable.

For slightly more formal comments on the fuse, note elements do a good job.

Note Elements

Purpose: Specifies a note for the fuse.
Attributes:
>   author—The author of the milestone.
>   date—The date of the milestone.

Note elements are an easy way to toss quick comments into a Fusedoc. Some authors use them in much the same way that you might use a history element; however, whereas history elements are much more specific in the attributes they capture, note elements are much more free-form. Note elements capture text between opening and closing tags, so they allow much more text to be included than the limited comment attribute in a history element. Listing 7.6 shows some sample note elements.

Listing 7.6 **Note Elements**

```
<note author="jeff@grokfusebox.com" date="01/22/02">
  Stan, make sure you get the spelling of the Wryxizschokville office
  right.  Mr. Wryxizschok is very sensitive about that particular
  town.
</note>

<note author="stancox@fusebox.org" date="01/23/02">
  When making tables, use blinking green background only.
  This is very important to the success of this project.
</note>

<note author="brody@fusebox.org" date="01/23/02">
  Blinking backgrounds are out.  I helped Janice come to her senses.
</note>
```

Notes are a good way to encourage communication between coders. They are also useful for recording local conventions that might not be well known, or might be easily forgotten if the project is set aside for a while.

For example, if an application is concerned with measurements that are governed by a standards committee, you could record the source for the standards in a note. If the fuse has to be changed to accommodate future changes in the standard, the information could make the fix much easier.

Properties are useful throughout the life of the fuse, and can be used to document a wide variety of information. Assertions, on the other hand, are specific pieces of data that communicate information about the fuse's expected environment.

<assertions> Element

The <assertions> element is used to contain <assert> elements. These elements allow you to specify conditions that are expected to exist when the fuse is run. The <assert> elements can specify what should be done by the fuse if the condition is true or if it is false. Listing 7.7 shows the Fusedoc for a single assertion. More than one <assert> element may be contained within the <assertions> element.

<assert> Element

Purpose: Specifies a condition that is expected when the fuse is run. One course of action is given if the condition is true, and an alternate course of action is given if the condition is false.

Attributes:

        that—The expression to be evaluated.

        on—Where the condition is expected to exist.

            Values—Client

                Server (default)

        else—The action to perform if the expression is false.

        comments—Any comments you want to include.

        onCondition—The action to perform if the expression is true.

Listing 7.7   **Assertions and Assert Elements**

```
<assertions>
  <assert that="battingAvg GT .300"
  oncondition="inLineup EQ True"
         else="XFA.pickLineup" />
</assertions>
```

The next section is where we'll really get into the meat of the Fusedoc specification—the `<io>` element. This element is used to encapsulate all the input and output elements that are used for a Fusedoc. The collection of elements that is available within the Fusedoc 2.0 specification is capable of describing any data needs you might have within a fuse. Understanding the elements and their use is one of the keys to the art of writing Fusedocs.

IO Element

Most of the Fusedoc elements are fairly easy to decipher from their names, and the `<io>` element is no exception. Its job is to contain the elements that describe the input to the fuse (the `<in>` element) and the output the fuse is expected to create (the `<out>` element). In similar fashion, variables that are available as input to the fuse but should not be altered in any way by the fuse can be specified in a `<passthrough>` element.

In Element

The `<in>` element is another one of those almost self-explanatory Fusedoc elements. It contains elements to describe variables that are available for the fuse to use. An `<in>` element can contain any of the following elements for describing data:

- String
- Number
- Boolean
- Datetime
- Array
- Structure
- Recordset
- List
- Cookie
- File

Each of these elements falls into one of two categories: simple or complex. `Cookie` and `file` elements are an exception to this, but we'll get to that later. Simple datatypes are those that represent a single value. `string`, `number`, `boolean`, `datetime`, and `list` are all simple datatypes. Complex datatypes are those that can contain multiple values, such as `arrays`, `structures`, and `recordsets`. (Lists can store multiple values, but because they are actually strings, they are categorized with the simple datatypes). Table 7.1 shows each category and the datatypes within them.

Table 7.1 **Datatypes**

Simple	Complex	Other
String	Array	Cookie
Number	Structure	File
Boolean	Recordset	
Datetime		
List		

The elements `<cookie>` and `<file>` are a bit different from other Fusedoc elements. Although they are essentially simple, they are not really datatypes per se. We'll look at each of the elements we can use within the `<in>` element. Following the specifications for each element, we'll look at some examples to help clarify the definition.

<out> Element

The `<out>` element is used to contain elements for any variables with values that are created by the fuse for use in the next fuseaction. It is formed in exactly the same manner as the `<in>` element, and might contain any of the elements specified in the detailed discussion earlier. The `<out>` element is optional.

<passthrough> Element

The `<passthrough>` element is used to contain elements for any variables that are available as input to the fuse, and are passed along unchanged for use in the next fuseaction. The `<passthrough>` element is formed in the same manner as the `<in>` element, and it might contain any of the elements specified in the detailed discussion earlier. The `<passthrough>` element is optional.

Simple Datatype Elements

The simple datatype elements are `<string>`, `<number>`, `<boolean>`, `<datetime>`, and `<list>`.

String Element

Purpose: Specifies a variable that stores a string value.

Attributes:

      name—The name of the variable (required).

      scope—The scope of the variable (optional).

            Values—Application

                    Attributes

                    Caller

                    Cgi

                    Client

                    Form

                    FormOrUrl

                    Request

                    Server

                    Session

                    Url

                    Variables (default)

      comments—Any comments you want to include.

      mask—Details for expected format of the string. No standard exists for creating masks as of Version 2.0 of Fusedoc; ColdFusion string masks are common practice.

      onCondition—The condition that causes the variable to exist. For example, a `state` variable might only exist if the `country` variable represents a country that has states. Used in conjunction with the optional attribute.

      format—The format in which the variable is encoded.

            Values—CFML (default)

                    WDDX

      optional—Whether the variable is optional.

            Values—True

                    False (default)

      default—The default value taken by the variable. For example, a variable named `homeTown` might have a default value of "Springfield."

Listing 7.8 gives examples of Fusedoc elements for several string variables.

Listing 7.8   **String Elements**

```
<string name="XFA.onSuccess"
    optional="No"
    comments="Use when login succeeds" />
```

```
<string name="XFA.onFailure"
    optional="No"
    comments="Use when login fails" />

<string name="userID" optional="No" scope="formOrUrl" />

<string name="password"
    optional="No"
        scope="form"
    comments="hash this value to check against database" />

<string name="homeTown"
    optional="Yes"
        scope="attributes"
 onCondition="user chooses to omit" />
```

Number Element

Purpose: Specifies a variable that stores a numeric value.

Attributes:

> name—The name of the variable (required).
>
> scope—The scope of the variable (optional).
>
>> Values—Application
>>> Attributes
>>> Caller
>>> Cgi
>>> Client
>>> Form
>>> FormOrUrl
>>> Request
>>> Server
>>> Session
>>> Url
>>> Variables (default)
>
> comments—Any comments you want to include.
>
> precision—Numeric precision of the variable.
>
>> Values—Integer
>>> Decimal
>
> onCondition—The condition that causes the variable to exist. For example, a `taxRate` variable might only exist if the `taxableIncome` variable is over a certain amount. Used in conjunction with the optional attribute.

optional—Whether the variable is optional.

Values—True

False (default)

default—The default value taken by the variable. For example, a variable named averageAge might have a default value of "25."

format—The format in which the variable is encoded.

Values—CFML (default)

WDDX

Listing 7.9 gives examples of Fusedoc elements for several numeric variables.

Listing 7.9 **Number Elements**

```
<number name="growthRate" precision="Decimal" default="0.13" />

<number name="ageInYears" precision="Integer" />

<number name="quantity" scope="attributes" precision="Integer" />

<number name="currentMileage"
      scope="attributes"
   precision="Decimal"
    comments="to the tenth of a mile" />

<number name="gears"
    optional="True"
    precision="Integer"
 onCondition="bike has multiple gears" />
```

Boolean Element

Purpose: Specifies a variable that stores a Boolean (true or false) value.

Attributes:

name—The name of the variable (required).

scope—The scope of the variable (optional).

Values—Application

Attributes

Caller

Cgi

Client

Form

FormOrUrl

Request

Server

> Session
> Url
> Variables (default)

comments—Any comments you want to include.

onCondition—The condition that causes the variable to exist. For example, an `isPregnant` variable might only exist if the `patientGender` variable is "female". Used in conjunction with the optional attribute.

optional—Whether the variable is optional.

> Values—True
> False (default)

default—The default value taken by the variable. For example, a variable named `isDeceased` might have a default value of "false."

format—The format in which the variable is encoded.

> Values—CFML (default)
> WDDX

Listing 7.10 gives examples of Fusedoc elements for several Boolean variables.

Listing 7.10   **Boolean Elements**

```
<boolean name="isUnionMember"
    default="Yes"
    optional="Yes"
  oncondition="workerAlive EQ True" />

<boolean name="isMudHensFan" default="False" />

<boolean name="isLoggedIn" scope="request" default="False" />

<boolean name="useScreenReader" scope="client" default="False" />

<boolean name="ccApproved" scope="request" />
```

Datetime Element

Purpose: Specifies a variable that stores a date/time value. Date/time values can store a date, a time, or both.

Attributes:

> name—The name of the variable (required).
> scope—The scope of the variable (optional).
>> Values—Application
>> Attributes
>> Caller
>> Cgi

Client
Form
FormOrUrl
Request
Server
Session
Url
Variables (default)

mask—The format of the date variable. Default is "m/d/yy." There is no standard for creating masks as of version 2.0 of Fusedoc; ColdFusion numeric masks are common practice.

comments—Any comments you want to include.

onCondition—The condition that causes the variable to exist. For example, an `anniversaryDate` variable might only exist if the `maritalStatus` variable is a certain value. Used in conjunction with the optional attribute.

optional—Whether the variable is optional.

Values—True
False (default)

default—The default value taken by the variable. For example, a variable named `taxesDueDate` might have a default value of "04/15/2003."

format—The format in which the variable is encoded.

Values—CFML (default)
WDDX

Listing 7.11 gives examples of Fusedoc elements for several datetime variables.

Listing 7.11   **Datetime Elements**

```
<datetime name="birthDate" mask="mm/dd/yyyy" />

<datetime name="startTime" mask="hh:nn" />

<datetime name="hireDate" scope="client" mask="mm/dd" />

<datetime name="gateOpened" mask="hh:nn:ss" optional="True" />

<datetime name="gateClosed" mask="hh:nn:ss" optional="True"
↪onCondition="gateOpened exists" />
```

List Element

Purpose: Specifies a variable that stores a list of values.
Attributes:

> name—The name of the variable (required).
> delims—The delimiters that are used to separate values in the list.

Default is comma.

> scope—The scope of the variable (optional).
>> Values—Application
>> Attributes
>> Caller
>> Cgi
>> Client
>> Form
>> FormOrUrl
>> Request
>> Server
>> Session
>> Url
>> Variables (default)
>
> comments—Any comments you want to include.
> onCondition—The condition that causes the variable to exist. For example, a `lstDegrees` variable might only exist if the `isHSGrad` variable is True. Used in conjunction with the optional attribute.
> format—The format in which the variable is encoded.
>> Values—CFML (default)
>> WDDX
> optional—Whether the variable is optional.
>> Values—True
>> False (default)
> default—The default value taken by the variable. For example, a variable named `schoolColors` might have a default value of "maroon,silver,white."

Listing 7.12 gives examples of Fusedoc elements for several lists.

Listing 7.12 **List Elements**

```
<list name="lstMonths"
   default="Jan,Feb,Mar,Apr,May,Jun,Jul,Aug,Sep,Oct,Nov,Dec" />

<list name="lstFields" delimeters="¦" />
```

continues

Listing 7.12   **Continued**

```
<list name="formfields" scope="form" />

 <list name="lstDegrees"
       scope="form"
    optional="True"
onCondition="IsParameter('isHSGrad') " />

 <list name="schoolColors" scope="attributes" default="blue,gold" />
```

Complex Datatype Elements

Complex datatypes have the ability within them to combine more than one simple datatype. The complex datatypes are array, structure, and recordset. Each of these has an element in the Fusedoc specification.

Array Element

Purpose: Specifies a variable that stores an array of values. An array element can contain any of the simple or complex datatype elements. For multi-dimensional arrays, use nested array elements in the Fusedoc.
Attributes:

        name—The name of the variable (required).

        scope—The scope of the variable (optional).

                Values—Application

                        Attributes

                        Caller

                        Cgi

                        Client

                        Form

                        FormOrUrl

                        Request

                        Server

                        Session

                        Url

                        Variables (default)

      comments—Any comments you want to include.

      onCondition—The condition that causes the variable to exist. For example, a shopping cart variable might only exist if the user has selected items for purchase. Used in conjunction with the optional attribute.

format—The format in which the variable is encoded.

        Values—CFML (default)

                WDDX

optional—Whether the variable is optional.

        Values—True

                False (default)

Listing 7.13 gives examples of Fusedoc elements for several arrays.

Listing 7.13   **Array Elements**

```
<!--- An array of numbers --->
<array name="aryLegalFreqs" comments="allowed frequencies">
  <number precision="Decimal" comments="frequency in kHz" />
</array>

<!--- An array of strings --->
<array name="aryParts" scope="form" format="WDDX">
  <string comments="part number" />
</array>

<!--- An array of lists --->
<array name="aryCart" comments="stores shopping cart items">
  <list comments="ItemNumber,Quantity" />
</array>

<!--- An array of structures --->
<array name="aryCart" comments="stores shopping cart items">
  <structure name="stuItems">
    <string comments="ItemNumber" />
    <number precision="Integer" comments="Quantity" />
  </structure>
</array>

<!--- A two-dimensional array --->
<array name="aryInvLines" comments="stores invoice rows; first row
⇒is field names">
  <array comments="stores invoice columns>
    <string />
  </array>
</array>
```

Structure Element

Purpose: Specifies a variable that stores an array of values that are addressed by index names. A structure element can contain any of the simple or complex datatype elements. ColdFusion structures are also known as *associative arrays*; this accounts for the similarity in the definition of array elements and structure elements.

Attributes:

      name—The name of the variable (required).

      scope—The scope of the variable (optional).

            Values—Application

                    Attributes

                    Caller

                    Cgi

                    Client

                    Form

                    FormOrUrl

                    Request

                    Server

                    Session

                    Url

                    Variables (default)

      comments—Any comments you want to include.

      onCondition—The condition that causes the variable to exist. For example, a shopping cart variable might only exist if the user has selected items for purchase. Used in conjunction with the optional attribute.

      format—The format in which the variable is encoded.

            Values—CFML (default)

                    WDDX

      optional—Whether the variable is optional.

            Values—True

                    False (default)

Listing 7.14 gives examples of Fusedoc elements for several structures.

Listing 7.14   **Structure Elements**

```
<structure name="stuCart" comments="stores shopping cart items" >
  <string comments="ItemNumber" />
  <number comments="Quantity" precision="Integer" />
</structure>
```

```
<structure name="stuStates" comments="state names by abbreviation">
  <string comments="stateAbbreviation" />
  <string comments="full state name" />
</structure>

<structure name="stuStates"
       comments="state information by abbreviation">
  <string comments="stateAbbreviation" />
  <structure comments="state information">
    <string comments="bird¦flower¦song¦tree" />
    <string comments="data" />
  </structure>
</structure>

<structure name="stuZipCodes" comments="zip codes and cities">
  <string comments="zipCode" />
  <string comments="City" />
</structure>

<structure name="stuStormWarnings" scope="request">
  <number comments="warning level" />
  <string comments="Description" />
</structure>
```

Recordset Element

Purpose: Specifies a variable that stores a query recordset. A recordset element can contain any of the simple datatype elements or any of the complex datatypes that are stored in WDDX format.

Attributes:

> name—The name of the variable (required).
>
> scope—The scope of the variable (optional).
>
>> Values—Application
>>> Attributes
>>> Caller
>>> Cgi
>>> Client
>>> Form
>>> FormOrUrl
>>> Request
>>> Server
>>> Session
>>> Url
>>> Variables (default)

primarykeys—The elements of the recordset that make up its primary key. Multiple elements can be specified as a comma-delimited list.

comments—Any comments you want to include.

onCondition—The condition that causes the variable to exist. For example, a user's recordset might only exist if he successfully logs in. Used in conjunction with the optional attribute.

format—The format in which the variable is encoded.

> Values—CFML (default)
>
> > WDDX

optional—Whether the variable is optional.

> Values—True
>
> > False (default)

Listing 7.15 gives examples of Fusedoc elements for several recordsets.

Listing 7.15   **Recordset Elements**

```
<recordset name="qryGetUser">
  <string name="userID" />
  <string name="firstName" />
  <string name="lastName" />
  <string name="email" />
  <number name="battingAverage" precision="Decimal" />
</recordset>

<recordset name="qryGetState">
  <string name="stateName" />
  <string name="capital" />  <string name="flower" />
  <string name="bird" />
  <string name="song" />
  <string name="tree" />
</recordset>

<recordset name="qryTeamStats">
  <string name="teamName" />
  <number name="wins" precision="Integer" />
  <number name="losses" precision="Integer" />
  <number name="ties" precision="Integer" />
  <number name="forfeits" precision="Integer" />
</recordset>
```

Other Elements

The `<cookie>` and `<file>` elements in Fusedoc don't really belong to either the simple datatype elements or the complex datatype elements. They are specialized elements that help document the behavior of cookies and files, respectively. Because of their unique natures, we'll look at them separately from the other IO-related elements.

Cookie Element

Purpose: Specifies a variable that is stored on the user's computer as a cookie.
Attributes:

> name—The name of the variable (required).
> expires—When the cookie expires.
>> Values—Now
>>> Never
>>> A valid datetime value.
> secure—Whether the server uses SSL when writing the cookie. (See `<cfcookie>` in ColdFusion documentation.)
>> Values—True
>>> False (default)
> comments—Any comments you want to include.
> mask—Details for expected format of the string. No standard exists for creating masks as of version 2.0 of Fusedoc; ColdFusion string masks are common practice.
> onCondition—The condition that causes the variable to exist. For example, a `taxRate` variable might only exist if the `taxableIncome` variable is over a certain amount. Used in conjunction with the optional attribute.
> format—The format in which the variable is encoded.
>> Values—CFML (default)
>>> WDDX
> optional—Whether the variable is optional.
>> Values—True
>>> False (default)
> default—The default value taken by the variable. For example, a variable named `homeTown` might have a default value of "Springfield."

Listing 7.16 gives examples of Fusedoc elements for several cookies.

Listing 7.16   **Cookie Elements**

```
<cookie name="lastLoggedIn" expires="never" />
<cookie name="userID"expires="now"/>
<cookie name="userOrganization" expires="now" />
```

File Element

Purpose: Specifies a file to be used in the fuse, such as to be read using the
`<cffile>` tag. This is used to document files on the server.
Attributes:

> path—The full path of the file (required).
> action—The action to be performed with the file.
>> Values—Read
>>> Write
>>> Append
>>> Overwrite
>>> Delete
>>> Available (default)
> comments—Any comments you want to include.
> onCondition—The condition that causes the variable to exist. For
> example, an output file might only be available if the user requested
> downloadable output. Used in conjunction with the optional
> attribute.
> optional—Whether the variable is optional.
>> Values—True
>>> False (default)

Listing 7.17 gives examples of Fusedoc elements for several files.

Listing 7.17   **File Element**

```
<!--- To document a date-named text file for read access --->
<file path="c:\datastuff\output\%yyyy%-%mm%Dump.txt"
    action="read"
   comments="%yyyy% and %mm% are year and month, respectively" />

<!--- To document a file uploaded by the user --->
<file path="c:\userdata\%fileName%"
    action="available"
   comments="%fileName% is the name of a file uploaded by the user." />

<!--- To document a file that serves as a flag.  We don't care
➥what's in the file, just that it exists. --->
```

```
<file path="c:\processFlags\HoldPending.txt"
   action="available"
   comments="If this file doesn't exist, throw an error." />

<!--- To document a log file for writing entries --->
<file path="c:\myLogs\%yyyy%-%mm%-%dd%.log"
   action="append"
   comments="%yyyy%, %mm%, and %dd% are year, month, and day, respectively"
/>

<!--- To document a file to be deleted --->
 <file path="c:\processflags\HoldPending.txt"
    action="delete"
onCondition="processCompleted" />

<!--- To document a file to be written.  If the file exists, there
➥should be an error. --->
<file path="c:\data\lastUpdate.txt" action="write" />

<!--- To document a file to be written.  If the file exists, there
➥should NOT be an error. --->
<file path="c:\data\lastUpdate.txt" action="overwrite" />
```

Elements to Tools

After we've mastered the elements of Fusedoc, we're ready to move on and take a look at some of the tools that exist based on Fusedoc. Some of these tools assist in the creation of Fusedocs, and others take advantage of the Fusedoc standard to help in the application-development process.

Tools for Fusedoc

The current specification for Fusedoc (2.0) defines Fusedoc as an XML vocabulary. Previous versions were written in a proprietary format described by an Extended Backus-Naur Form (EBNF) notation; you'll sometimes see it referred to as Fusedoc 1 or (incorrectly) EBNF Fusedoc. This volume is only concerned with the current version, which is an XML vocabulary.

Note that whereas Fusebox is currently in version 3, Fusedoc is in version 2. This is because Fusedoc is a standard that is independent of the Fusebox standard. The Fusedoc standard is only concerned with the creation of code documentation blocks known as Fusedocs.

Fusedoc Creation Tools

Fusedoc 2.0 is based on open standards. This means it's much easier to build tools to assist in the creation of Fusedocs than it was when the standard was proprietary. The first of these tools is the set of Fusedoc VTML extensions created by Steve Nelson and Hal Helms.

The Fusedoc VTML extensions provide tag completion tips and Fusedoc help for ColdFusion Studio. They are available at `fusebox.org`.

The installation for the VTML extensions is fairly straightforward; if you follow the readme files, you shouldn't have trouble. You must unpack a zipped archive to specific locations within the CF Studio directory structure and edit a couple of Studio's configuration files. After the extensions are installed, you'll get tag completion and help for Fusedocs. Figure 7.1 shows tag completion for Fusedocs in action.

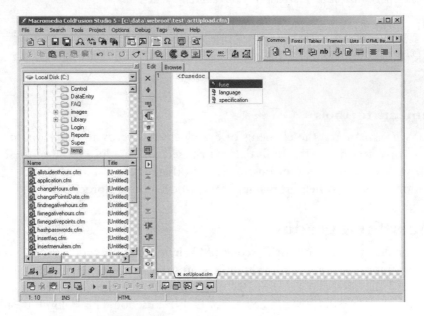

Figure 7.1   Fusedoc tag completion.

Figure 7.2 shows the help file for Fusedocs in action.

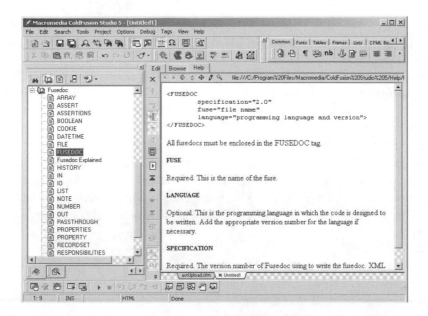

Figure 7.2   Help for Fusedocs.

One small caveat exists when using the tag completion for Fusedocs. The Fusedoc VTML extensions cannot check for trailing slashes on tags that lack closing tags. It's easy to write variable definition tags such as string, number, boolean, and so on without the trailing slash required for XML well formed-ness. Keep your eyes open, and make sure you put them in.

Thanks to Fusedoc's tag basis and ColdFusion Studio's extensibility, the potential exists for more sophisticated tools to assist in creating Fusedocs. There should be non-ColdFusion Studio-based tools appearing as well.

Fusedoc's XML-based design makes it amenable to far more than just creation tools, though. The real power of Fusedocs starts to show when their standard nature is tapped within the scope of the application development.

Fusedoc-Based Tools

The XML specification provides a way to create custom tag-based vocabularies for the purpose of communicating rich data. Because this is precisely the purpose of Fusedoc, XML is a good fit.

XML vocabularies can be defined in a couple of ways. The first way is through the use of a DTD. The second way is through the use of a schema, which is an XML vocabulary of its own that is designed to describe XML vocabularies. Although schemas are gaining in popularity, few real-world tools exist for the validation of schema-based vocabularies; therefore, Fusedoc 2.0 relies on a DTD.

You can download the Fusedoc DTD from `http://www.fusebox.org`. You can also find a reference copy in Appendix C, "Fusebox Data Type Definition." The DTD details all the tags that are allowed within a Fusedoc and the other tags or attributes that each tag might contain.

The purpose of having a DTD is to provide the ability to validate a Fusedoc. The XML world refers to any given XML dataset with two qualities: well formedness and validity. An XML dataset is said to be well formed if its tags meet the requirements of XML. For example, all tags must be closed, either by a closing tag or an ending slash. These tags are well formed:

```
<mytag />
<mytag></mytag>
```

This one is not:

```
<mytag>
```

The preceding tag is not well formed because it is not closed. (Note the lack of a closing tag or ending slash.) Well formedness has nothing to do with the particular vocabulary, only with how the tags are formed.

Validity, however, is concerned with the specific vocabulary. To be valid, an XML dataset must contain only those tags and attributes that are allowed for its vocabulary. This is where the DTD comes in. The XML dataset has an attribute that references the DTD for its vocabulary. A validating parser can then check the contents of the dataset against the DTD to ensure that only allowable elements are used.

Most users of Fusedoc will not concern themselves with actually parsing the Fusedoc or validating its XML. Validity will be a concern only for those who are interested in taking advantage of Fusedoc through the use of utilities that read and interpret Fusedocs. Every writer of Fusedocs needs to be concerned with well formedness, though; if a Fusedoc is not well formed, these same utilities cannot use it.

With well-formed Fusedocs available as XML data, we are open to a whole new world of tools based on the wealth of information that is available through them. The next sections discuss Harness—a tool for generating test harnesses from Fusedocs—and other tools that take advantage of the existence of Fusedocs.

Harness

The first tool to take advantage of Fusedoc as a standard was Harness, by Jeff Peters (http://www.grokfusebox.com). Harness was able to generate test harnesses for every fuse that had a Fusedoc. It could recurse (travel through every branch of) an application's directory tree to make sure every fuse got a test harness. The details of unit testing with test harnesses can be found in Chapter 15, "Unit Testing."

Harness was a nice idea, but it had some limitations imposed by the original Fusedoc format. For example, Harness was not capable of building arrays or structures for test harnesses.

Harness 2.0 is constructed to read 2.0-compliant Fusedocs. It is much more robust than the original. It is a custom tag that uses the SOXML parser to handle the XML chores. If you have SOXML installed, all you do to install Harness is copy it to your CustomTags directory.

After Harness is on your machine, all you need to run it is a simple calling file, usually named `HarCall.cfm`, as shown in Listing 7.18.

Listing 7.18   *HarCall.cfm*

```
<cf_harness verbose="yes"
rootDir="#GetDirectoryFromPath(GetCurrentTemplatePath())#">
```

The output from running Harness in verbose mode prints a line for each test harness that is written and is organized according to the directory structure. It makes a good checklist for unit testing as well; as you run the test harness for each fuse and verify its capability, you can check it off on the printed output from Harness.

Future Tools

Considering the recursive nature of Harness, other Fusedoc-reading utilities are easy to imagine. For instance, consider a tool that would read all the Fusedocs in a project and return a report with all the <history> and <note> elements interpreted as a development progress report, with metrics for percentage of fuses waiting to be coded, in coding, and completed.

How about a tool to read Fusedocs and find out which query fuses have a <recordset> element in their <out> sections?

Perhaps we need to know which fuses were missed when some new circuits were brought in and the local standard variables were added to their fuses. A quick cruise of the Fusedocs by an automated tool could give us this information.

These tasks are not only possible, they are also comparatively simple with the XML-based power of Fusedoc 2.0. We strongly encourage you to become familiar with Fusedoc and then start thinking about how you could improve your own development processes by leveraging XML and Fusedoc. You can get started with XML parsers like Site Objects' SOXML ColdFusion tags (`www.siteobjects.com`) and the Torchbox effort (`www.torchbox.com`), which are good launching points for working with Fusedoc XML. You can also use Microsoft's MSXML library (`http://msdn.microsoft.com`) if you need to use a COM object, or CFDev.com's Java-based XML parser (`www.cfdev.com`).

Our final section in this chapter will look at how we go about using Fusedocs in the application-development process.

Fusedoc in Applications

It's worth mentioning yet again that the purpose of Fusedoc is to communicate information between members of a development team, even if the members are "me," "myself," and "I." We'll start with the point at which the architect hands information to a fusecoder in the form of a fuse stub.

Fuse Stubs

A *fuse stub* is the combination of a Fusedoc and any HTML from the prototype that belongs to the fuse. This is the means by which the architect tells the fusecoder about two vital areas: the development environment (in the Fusedoc) and the presentation (in the HTML).

Figure 7.3 shows a simple fuse stub for a login form. The top part of the form shows the Fusedoc, and the bottom has the HTML that was pulled from the prototype.

The fusecoder's job is to turn the fuse stub into a finished fuse by writing any code that is necessary to achieve the objectives described in the Requirements section of the Fusedoc. This includes making any outputs from the fuse conform to the Fusedoc.

A common misconception exists about Fusedocs and what information they are intended to convey. Some Fuseboxers are intent on finding ways to communicate presentation information, such as style names, through Fusedocs. Fusedocs are not intended to communicate anything about presentation or visual design. Fusedocs are only intended to contain information about the ColdFusion development environment. They are a communication conduit between the application architect and the fusecoder. If you are tempted to include design-related information in a Fusedoc, stop yourself and make a mental note about to whom the Fusedoc is talking.

Design information, on the other hand, must be included in the fuse some-how; otherwise, the fusecoder would have no way of knowing what a display fuse is supposed to look like. This is where the world of the designer collides with the world of the developer. To prevent the collision from being cata-strophic, we make use of a fuse stub.

Figure 7.3   Fuse stub for login form fuse.

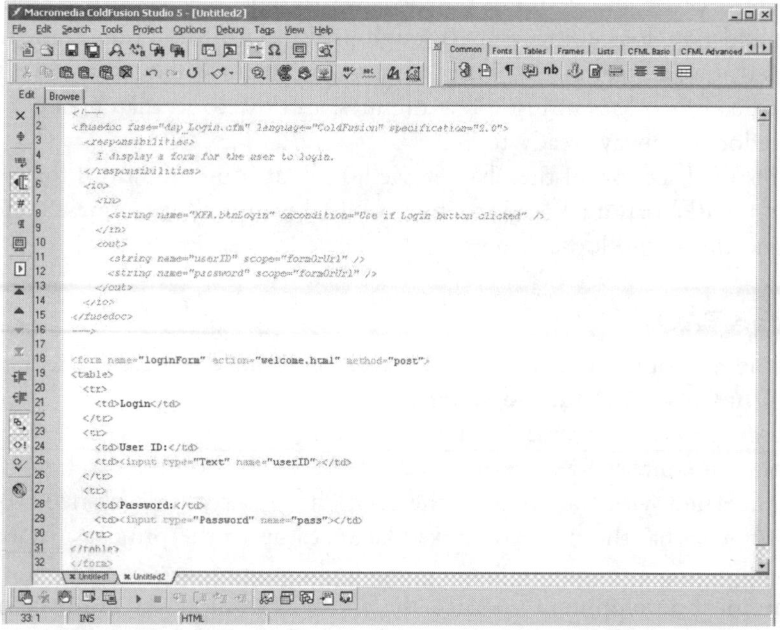

Fusedocs During Coding

As the coding process continues, the only alterations that should be made to Fusedocs, ideally, are the addition of `<history>` and `<note>` elements to help track progress.

Of course, this assumes that the architect is perfect and has missed nothing in the creation of the Fusedocs for the entire system. This is seldom the case. In reality, oversights must be adjusted, and the Fusedoc for a fuse should always reflect the correct state of the fuse. However, this does not mean that team members should run up and change the Fusedoc at every whim. The desire to change a Fusedoc should prompt a discussion between members of the team to determine if the change is appropriate, and whether it has a broader implication in the overall project. Fusedoc reinforces Fusebox's overall emphasis on structure and consistency.

This has been a long and detailed chapter. Questions about Fusedoc are asked regularly within the Fusebox community, so it's worth taking some time to look at some of the more common ones, and reviewing what we've covered.

Wrapping Up

You can't become an overnight Fusedoc wizard. The skill that is necessary to write good Fusedocs comes only through practice. On the other hand, the benefits to be had from using Fusedocs are almost immediate. Fusecoders can learn to read Fusedocs in just a few minutes, and the tools that already exist for Fusedoc are always ready to go.

In this final section of the chapter, we'll look at some questions that are commonly asked about Fusedoc. Then we'll take a quick look back at everything and tie up the loose strings.

Fusedoc FAQs

Following are some frequently asked questions about the use of Fusedocs:

Q: What about database schemas for qry files?

A: In the Fusedoc world, we aren't concerned with database schemas. Fusedocs are concerned with the needs of the application architect, who is in turn concerned with the needs of the user. The architect doesn't need to worry about what the database looks like; that's up to the project's database expert.

In an ideal development scenario, the database wouldn't be constructed until the last part of the development lifecycle. Through the use of querysims, we can build fully functional applications without messing with a database behind them. This means that the database pros can wait until we've ironed out all the application details before they have to create a database schema to satisfy the application requirements.

If we start specifying database details in the Fusedocs, we take away the ability of the database pros to build a database that is tuned to the needs of the application.

In small or one-person shops, it is tempting to put database details in the query fuses' Fusedocs because you'll be building it anyway. Try to resist the temptation, though. When you have the opportunity to build the database all in one shot based on the qry fuse definitions, you'll appreciate the ability to focus on it exclusively.

Q: What about global variables? Should they be put in the Fusedoc for every fuse?

A: This is a judgment call, but remember the first rule: "Include everything a coder needs to write the fuse, and nothing more." Many frequently used variables are such common practice in a development shop that it's not necessary to include them in every Fusedoc. The variable `fusebox.fuseaction` is a good example of this. Few architects put `fusebox.fuseaction` in their Fusedocs, because it's common knowledge that this variable exists in Fusebox 3.0 applications.

That said, keep in mind that the more complete your Fusedocs are, the easier it will be to maintain the application in the future.

Q: Should I document external resources such as component APIs in my Fusedocs?

A: As with the previous question, see the first rule. If there is a portion of an API (for example, a component API to be called with `<cfobject>`) that the coder needs to know about, it is appropriate to include information about it, perhaps in a note element.

Q: Should I document file dependence, and thus Fusedoc dependence?

A: This is an area that calls for some careful attention to detail. As with other questions about Fusedocs, we encourage an emphasis on the first rule. However, it is possible to get carried away. The goal is to include what the fusecoder needs to write this fuse. Although it might seem nice for the fusecoder to know all about other fuses with which this one will interact, the end result will most likely be confusion resulting from information overload. Another objective of Fusebox is to achieve simplified code re-use; if specific fuse dependencies are documented in the Fusedoc, confusion will result when the fuse is reused in another application.

Q: Should a fuse have only one Fusedoc?

A: Yes. The Fusedoc appears at the top of the fuse, and it provides a single coherent set of data for the fuse. Fusedocs are not used for inserting programmer's comments throughout the fuse file.

These questions and their answers provide a good overview of daily Fusedoc concerns. Fuseboxers everywhere are taking advantage of this powerful standard to improve their success rates in application development.

Fusedoc for Success

Fusedoc is essentially a meta-language (a language about language) whose subject is fuses. Some programming disciplines introduce the concept of a *program
definition language*, or PDL. These are simply formalized ways of describing
programs.

Fusedoc's two goals are simple: to force the architect to carefully consider
the needs of the system, and to provide carefully constructed information to
the rest of the team.

In achieving these two objectives, Fusedoc also provides secondary rewards.
An application that has effective Fusedocs is inherently well documented.
Because the Fusedoc is an integral part of the fuse's code, it travels with the
fuse as part of the program code; therefore, it's not necessary to look up entries
in an external form of documentation to get at important program information. This also means that, if we construct an application from a collection of
fuses that was originally built in other applications, each fuse retains its original
documentation; we aren't forced to cobble together bits and pieces of documentation from each of the donor systems.

Fusedocs convey all the information that a coder needs to write a fuse, and
nothing more. For display fuses, HTML from the prototype is joined with the
Fusedoc to provide a fuse stub for the coder. The Fusedoc carries the programming environment information, whereas the HTML carries the presentation information.

With a way to easily document hierarchies of circuit directories well in
hand, we can move on to look at one of most powerful ideas represented by
Fusebox 3: nesting.

8

"Everything should be made as simple as possible, but not simpler."

—Albert Einstein

Nesting Circuits

THE SINGLE MOST POWERFUL FEATURE OF FUSEBOX 3, when compared with Fusebox 2, is its ability to easily nest circuits into a cohesive application. Whereas Fusebox 2 was aimed at creating a collection of circuits that were related only by explicit interaction in the program code, Fusebox 3 is designed to allow circuits to be arranged into a more integrated hierarchical design, with each circuit inheriting the characteristics of its parent and contributing to the parent's output. Fusebox 3 applications reflect their design in the layout of their circuit directories as well as the explicit behavior of their program code.

Nesting furthers the organizational power of Fusebox. Whereas Fusebox has always helped organize applications by separating code into fuses according to purpose, Fusebox 3 helps organize on a larger scale by arranging circuits according to a broader purpose. Just as the fuses in a circuit share a common purpose, the circuits in a nested branch share common factors. The commonality might be based on function, on site organization, or on whatever criteria the architect establishes. Nesting is the key to this powerful flexibility.

Throughout this chapter, we'll look at how Fusebox 3 enables nesting, how nesting adds functionality to Fusebox applications, how Fusebox 3 applications are structured, and what the performance considerations are surrounding nested applications. The functionality that nesting brings to Fusebox adds new power for the application architect, allowing the ability to build component-like circuits. This, in turn, can lead to a more modular approach to application design. Of course, increased modularity leads to the creation of circuits that have the potential to work together, even if they weren't designed as part of the same application.

We'll also spend some time looking at the performance considerations of nested Fusebox applications. Most developers who are new to Fusebox are concerned about the potential impact of deeply nested code on the performance of their applications. We'll take some time to address this concern.

The place to get started is a look at why we're interested in nesting in the first place. What power do nested applications offer over non-hiearchical designs?

The Power of Nesting

The power of nesting lies in the additional functionality it allows. The idea is to allow circuits to be added to an application without going to great lengths to customize the circuit. This is done by constructing Fusebox circuits as homogeneous modules. To easily allow the desired functionality, Fusebox 3 focuses on modular design.

Modular design, in turn, means that Fusebox circuits can for the first time offer the prospect of working as a standalone application or as part of a larger application. This points toward the future potential of having Fusebox plug-in components that can be "snapped" together to create custom solutions.

For example, nearly every web application involves a login feature of some kind. Most of these login processes are similar, so if we build a Login circuit, we can easily copy it into a new application instead of writing the login feature from scratch. In similar fashion, we can consider commonly used features such as scheduling, email processing, and mail list subscription as components that can be used in a variety of applications.

These plug-in components also offer a new market for third-party application development. Just as a market for custom tags within the ColdFusion development world is currently available, soon a market might exist for Fusebox custom circuits. Certainly, every Fusebox shop tends to develop its own library of circuits that can be tapped for new development efforts.

In addition, the organization of an application into a sensible hierarchy increases the leverage that can be applied in team development situations. Whereas Fusebox has always allowed team members to focus on display code versus process code, nested circuits encourage focus based on functional similarities. A large development team might have one group that specializes in commerce components, another that specializes in content management components, and a third that specializes in advertising and promotion management.

All of these advanced ideas about circuit management, component use and re-use, and parallel development begin with the simple jumping-off point of modular design.

Modular Design

Generically speaking, something is modular when it is made up of standardized pieces for easy assembly or flexible arrangement. The concept of modular design has been applied to everything from furniture to housing.

As any modular design illustrates, the ability to add and remove modules from a system greatly improves the flexibility of the system. One of the great examples of modularity that most children are familiar with is interlocking building blocks, as shown in Figure 8.1.

Figure 8.1   Building block modules.

The pieces might vary by size, color, and job, but they all have one thing in common—their universal interlocking design. Regardless of the age of the piece or its designed purpose, a child knows without hesitation that one such block will function properly with another one.

This interoperability is the same objective that Fusebox 3 is moving toward—the ability to create standardized components that can be easily assembled in a variety of ways, just like the building blocks.

To turn circuits into modules of this nature, it is necessary to recognize the interfaces of circuits in general. In other words, circuits have a handful of characteristics in common. These characteristics become the interlocking aspects that allow us to connect circuits one to the next, just as the cylinders on the top and spaces on the bottom of the blocks allow them to interface.

Where circuits are concerned, the interface characteristics include the input data that the circuit requires, the output that the circuit generates, and any database interaction that the circuit might perform.

Circuit Input

A circuit might require data to be input to it from an external source. Where interfacing with an application is concerned, we only need to worry about those inputs that the user won't provide. Numeric and date conventions are examples of this type of input. If the child circuit is used within an application in Europe, it should use different conventions than it would if used in the U.S. We'll get into the details of how these circuits work in the section of this chapter titled "Understanding the Application's Structure." These techniques allow us to create components that can practically be plugged together into an application.

Plug-In Components

The design perspective that led to Fusebox 3.0 is centered around the ideal of creating circuits that can be plugged together much like building blocks, with a minimum of modification to the existing program code. Although this might seem like an unrealistic goal, the differences between Fusebox 2 and Fusebox 3 illustrate how far we've progressed toward homogenizing the overall design of a circuit.

However, standardizing design doesn't magically take away all the barriers to plug-n-play circuits. Any circuit that is designed to be a portable unit will have its share of baggage that the developer must take into account when using it. For example, a circuit's fuseactions need to be well documented so that the developer can easily understand what the circuit is designed to do. The circuit's expected inputs must also be well documented. When adopting a new circuit, the developer needs to take these factors into account and adjust accordingly.

Fusebox 3 doesn't make these adjustments automatically. However, it does bring us much closer to such a possibility by shaping circuits in a similar fashion, allowing the developer to easily examine its characteristics. This is entirely due to the fact that Fusebox 3 circuits are constructed in a predictable manner.

With the current specification, it is possible to create circuits that are designed to be plugged into other applications. In the near future, we expect to see developers take advantage of this capability, creating collections of circuits that are trafficked on the web in much the same way that custom tags are today.

If enough such plug-in components begin to surface, it would be completely reasonable to expect a market for third-party applications to appear. After all, if you build it, will they not come?

Third-Party Applications

The Fusebox community is full of developers who have created a genuine treasure trove of custom tags, UDFs, and specialized CFML. Most of these tools are available for the cost of a download.

We all know, though, that the primary objective of our vocation is to put food on the table. Most of us get a great deal of enjoyment and satisfaction out of the creative work we do, but the bottom line for most is still making a living.

To that end, Fusebox provides a standard framework within which a developer like Stan can create a circuit application with market potential. (For more on Stan, see this book's Introduction.) He has two potential customers for such a circuit: second parties who purchase the circuit for use in a project at their company, and third parties who purchase the circuit for use in an application they're developing for someone else.

The second-party scenario is fairly straightforward because the developer of the application is the owner of the application, and he will know where to find Stan if problems arise. The third-party scenario is a bit different, though.

When a developer buys components for use in an application to be sold to a client, there must be a high level of assurance that the component works as advertised and will be reliable as the application is deployed. The end user has no idea that components are involved that were created by someone other than the solution provider. For this reason, developers of third-party solutions need to exercise great care in building circuits and applications. Fusebox 3 provides the ability to create robust circuits that are suitable for use in third-party applications by providing a consistent development framework.

Of course, using Fusebox 3 is no guarantee that everything you build will be bulletproof, but it will make it much easier to stop the bleeding, so to speak. We've come a long way from the early days of custom tags.

Custom Tags to Custom Application

From its beginnings, Fusebox has progressed from a collection of ideas to a cohesive concept. The nature of the code that is underlying Fusebox has undergone a similar progression, going from a collection of coding practices to a development concept paired with some creative custom tags and finally coming to the application framework that is Fusebox 3.

The fundamental idea that started Fusebox was the concept of treating a central file (Fusebox) as the control center for an application. The Fusebox was allowed to control which files (fuses) should be used for any given page request (fuseaction). This resulted in the ability to separate display logic from process logic—a fundamental stepping stone to code reuse.

Building on the original concept, custom tags were created to help streamline the logic of building an application. The foremost of these early tags was Steve Nelson's `<cf_formURL2attributes>`, which allowed a circuit to be called as a standalone application or as a custom tag by the simple expedient of copying all URL and form-scoped variables into the attributes scope. Later, custom tags further contributed to the modularity of the Fusebox concept, like `<cf_bodycontent>`, another Nelson tag that collected all the generated output of a circuit into a variable, allowing great flexibility in producing output. BodyContent was such a hit that it inspired the `<cfsavecontent>` tag in ColdFusion 5.

As the Fusebox concept grew and the use of custom tags expanded, the creation of circuits became more complex. The number of factors that the developer had to check increased with every new custom-tag-based feature. Eventually, it was decided that a simpler approach was needed. This resulted in the Fusebox 3 custom application, often referred to as the Fusebox core file.

The Fusebox core file, put simply, is a standardization and aggregation of the functionality that the collection of Fusebox custom tags performed previously. The core file is also the engine that regulates and interprets the application's structure.

Understanding the Application's Structure

The key to successful Fuseboxing is understanding how the application's circuits are related to one another. This structure is the underlying basis for how the Fusebox core file operates, nesting circuits' functionality and display layouts.

The basic structure of a Fusebox application is a simple hierarchy. Like a traditional organization chart, the Fusebox application branches out from a single top-level node. This node is known as the *main circuit*. Subcircuits are arranged below the main circuit just as lower levels of an organization are arranged below higher levels in the organization chart. Figure 8.2 compares the organization chart with a Fusebox application.

Hierarchies

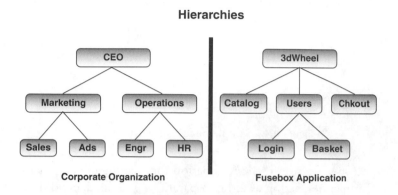

Figure 8.2   Organization and Fusebox hierarchies.

Although it might not be obvious, the most simple Fusebox application is a single standalone circuit. In a case like this, the single circuit is, by default, the main circuit. But take that single circuit and combine it with other circuits, and it's possible to create a larger application.

It's important to recognize that the single circuit could be the main circuit in the new application, or it could be plugged in as a subcircuit. The relationship depends only on how the architect chooses to use the circuit. For example, Figure 8.3 shows the structure of a Fusebox application in which a circuit called Calendar acts as a subcircuit of the main circuit, StaffSchedules. Figure 8.4 shows the same Calendar circuit acting as the main circuit of a different application, with a subcircuit called Tournaments.

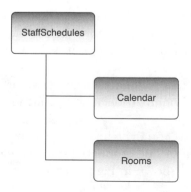

Figure 8.3   Sample circuit structure I.

Figure 8.4 Sample circuit structure II.

The Fusebox 3 specification is the foundation for creating circuits that can be retasked in this manner, acting as either a parent or a child, depending on the situation. To take advantage of these relationships, we need to look at how inheritance works between parent and child.

Inheritance Down the Tree

We've noted the similarities between a Fusebox application's structure and a traditional organization chart. The genealogists among us also recognize this model as a basic family tree. The lexicon of family relationships is often applied to hierarchical models. It makes sense because we all have family relationships.

A Fusebox circuit can have a parent and children. It can behave as a parent or as a child, depending on the application where it's used. It should even be able to change roles with a minimum of effort on the part of the architect and developer. These are goals of Fusebox 3.

Just as children inherit things from their parents, subcircuits inherit things from their parent. In the case of Fusebox, the child inherits variables and layouts from its parent. Absent variables from the parent, the child can set its own values for variables. This allows the circuit to behave and look differently depending on its role in the application.

Although the family tree metaphor makes sense for understanding the entire application model, another metaphor is much more useful for examining specific fuseactions.

A fuseaction represents a straight-line set of parent-child circuit relationships. It's essentially a direct line of inheritance. The line of circuits used by each fuseaction differs, as shown in Figure 8.5.

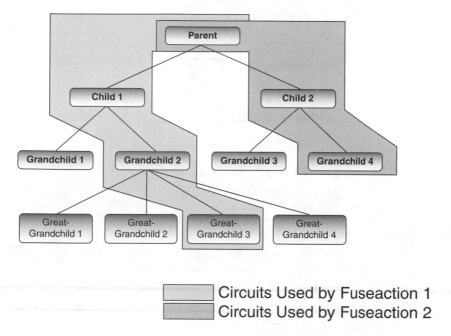

Circuits Used by Fuseaction 1
Circuits Used by Fuseaction 2

Figure 8.5   Structure of a fuseaction.

Recognizing this relationship, we can think of the behavior of Fusebox within the process of a fuseaction in terms of an elevator. As the elevator descends from the main circuit to the target circuit of the fuseaction, inheritance of variables takes place. As the elevator ascends from the target circuit back to the main circuit, it inherits screen displays or *layouts*. Layouts are discussed in Chapter 9, "Nested Layouts." Each fuseaction can be represented as a round trip of the elevator from the main circuit to the target circuit and back (see Figure 8.6).

If the elevator represents a fuseaction, the people in it are variables. Specifically, the people are the Fusebox API. When the fuseaction is first called, the elevator is filled with its collection of passengers at the top floor (home circuit). As the elevator descends to the target circuit, the passengers are given new values to carry. Each variable inherits its value according to specific rules, so we'll take a closer look at them next.

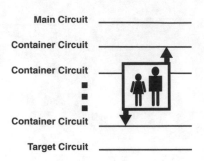

Main Circuit

Container Circuit

Container Circuit

Container Circuit

Target Circuit

Figure 8.6   Fuseaction behavior.

Inheritance and Fusebox Variables

Each Fusebox API variable has a distinct purpose, and consequently its own inheritance characteristics. Here's a quick look at how each variable behaves as the fuseaction elevator travels down:

- **fusebox.isCustomTag**—This variable is set to True if the fuseaction is called as a custom tag (that is, using <cfmodule>). Because the calling method throughout the fuseaction doesn't change, its value doesn't change through inheritance.

- **fusebox.isHomeCircuit**—This variable is set to True if the fuseaction that is being called belongs to the home circuit. As the elevator makes its trip from the home circuit to the target circuit and back, the variable's value changes for each circuit. It is True only at the beginning and the end of the round trip.

- **fusebox.isTargetCircuit**—This variable is set to True if the fuseaction that is being called belongs to the target circuit. As the elevator makes its trip from the home circuit to the target circuit and back, the variable's value changes for each circuit. It is True only at the middle of the round trip, when the target circuit is being dealt with.

- **fusebox.circuit**—This variable is set to the first part of the dot-delimited fuseaction that is passed as attributes.fuseaction. Its value does not change as the fuseaction is processed.

- **fusebox.fuseaction**—This variable is set to the second part of the dot-delimited fuseaction that is passed as attributes.fuseaction. Its value does not change as the fuseaction is processed.

- **fusebox.homeCircuit**—This variable is set to the root-level circuit as defined in the `fusebox.circuits` strucure. Its value does not change as the fuseaction is processed.

- **fusebox.targetCircuit**—This variable is set to the circuit in which the requested fuseaction is designed to run. The difference between this variable and `fusebox.circuit` is that this variable is the circuit *alias* that was found in the `fusebox.circuits` file as opposed to the circuit that was specified in the fuseaction. In all non-error situations, `fusebox.targetCircuit` and `fusebox.Circuit` will be the same. The value of `fusebox.targetCircuit` does not change as the fuseaction is processed.

- **fusebox.thisCircuit**—This variable is set to the alias of the circuit where processing is currently occurring. As the elevator makes its trip from the home circuit to the target circuit and back, the variable's value changes for each circuit.

- **fusebox.thisLayoutPath**—This variable is set to the directory path that the layout file being used is called from. As the elevator makes its trip from the home circuit to the target circuit and back, the variable's value changes for each circuit *on the way back up*, when layouts are processed. It does not change on the way down.

- **fusebox.circuits**—This variable is a structure whose keys are the circuit aliases created in `fbx_circuits.cfm` and whose values are the directory paths to those circuits. It does not change as the fuseaction is processed.

- **fusebox.currentPath**—This variable is set to the relative path from the root circuit to the circuit where processing is taking place. For example, if the root circuit is located at `/intranet/hrApp` and the current circuit is located at `/intranet/hrApp/Directory/archive`, then `fusebox.currentPath` will be `Directory/archive`. As the elevator makes its trip from the home circuit to the target circuit and back, the variable's value changes for each circuit.

- **fusebox.rootPath**—This variable is set to the relative path from the circuit where processing is taking place to the root circuit. For example, if the root circuit is located at `/intranet/hrApp` and the current circuit is located at `/intranet/hrApp/Directory/archive`, then `fusebox.currentPath` will be `"../.."`.

- **fusebox.defaultFuseactionString**—This variable is set to the string that the core file will use for `fusebox.fuseaction` if no fuseaction is specified in the page call. It is set to `fusebox.defaultfuseaction` and can only be altered by modifying the Fusebox core file.

These API variables provide the "common ground" on which Fusebox applications operate. Once familiar with them, a developer can find the way around any Fusebox application's behavior.

But variables aren't the only consideration when nesting circuits. We also need to understand Fusebox's treatment of folders between the main circuit and the target circuit.

Nesting and Inheritance

There is a subtle difference between nesting Fusebox circuits and the inheritance that occurs among nested circuits. Although it appears that the processing of each circuit is nested within the processing of the circuit above it, that's not entirely true.

Nested circuits don't inherit the behavior of their ancestors in linear fashion. Returning to the elevator illustration, we can say that settings and layouts are inherited through all circuits between the main and target circuits, but actual processing is inherited by the target circuit directly from the main circuit.

In other words, Fusebox is concerned with the environment of each circuit going down the directory tree (inheritance of settings) and the nature of the display of each circuit on the way back up the directory tree (inheritance of layouts), but the actual processing of a fuseaction is only concerned with the target circuit (see Figure 8.7).

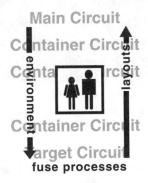

Figure 8.7   Inheritance versus processing.

To make all this processing possible in a manageable environment, we need a way to identify circuits within the application and the relationships between them. Circuit definitions make it all possible.

Circuit Definitions

A circuit definition in Fusebox is simply a way to define a reference, or alias, to a circuit within the current application. Circuit definitions are contained in the circuits definition (fbx_circuits.cfm) file.

The circuits definition file establishes a structure named fusebox.circuits to act as a container for the application's circuit definitions. Each key-value pair in this structure defines one circuit's alias and location within the application.

Each circuit must have a unique alias within the application. Aliases are completely arbitrary; their only constraint is uniqueness within the application. If a circuit is copied into a different application, a completely different alias can be used. This makes reusing circuits simple; if two circuits from separate applications exist that were originally designed with the same alias, the architect can simply give one of them a new alias to use both in a single application.

Listing 8.1 shows a sample circuits definition file. The left side of each line describes the circuit's alias, and the right side defines the circuit's path relative to the main circuit.

Listing 8.1 **Circuits Definition File**

```
<!---
<fusedoc fuse="FBX_Circuits.cfm">
  <responsibilities>
    I define the Circuits structure used with Fusebox 3.0
  </responsibilities>
  <io>
    <out>
      <string name="fusebox.circuits.*"
          comments="set a variable for each circuit name" />
    </out>
  </io>
</fusedoc>
--->

<cfset fusebox.circuits.home="home">
<cfset fusebox.circuits.child="home/child">
<cfset fusebox.circuits.baby="home/child/baby">
```

The first <cfset> line defines the alias for the main circuit. Like all aliases, this alias is arbitrary; our samples use "home" just to make them easier to interpret. The value assigned to the main circuit is also arbitrary. Its use is as a placeholder to define the relative paths to other circuits.

Subsequent lines define aliases for each circuit in the application, with the paths to them defined relative to the main circuit. The definition for the circuit "child" says that the circuit is located in a directory named "child" immediately beneath the main circuit's directory.

The circuit's alias and its directory name do *not* need to match. It is often a simple expedient to make them the same, but the definitions in Listing 8.2 are as valid as those in Listing 8.1.

Listing 8.2   **More Circuits Definitions**

```
<!---
<fusedoc fuse="FBX_Circuits.cfm">
  <responsibilities>
    I define the Circuits structure used with Fusebox 3.0
  </responsibilities>
  <io>
    <out>
      <string name="fusebox.circuits.*"
          comments="set a variable for each circuit name" />
    </out>
  </io>
</fusedoc>
--->

<cfset fusebox.circuits.thirdWheel="TWB">
<cfset fusebox.circuits.cat="TWB/Catalog">
<cfset fusebox.circuits.kudos="TWB/Catalog/Testimonials">
```

The only real restriction on a circuit alias is that it must be unique within the application. In other words, no matter how many circuits or levels are in the application, only one circuit can exist with any given alias. This is what enables the use of the two-part fuseaction, such as `cat.showSearchForm`. The first half of the fuseaction, the circuit alias, gives Fusebox a reference to the circuit where the fuseaction `showSearchForm` will be found. Fusebox refers to the `fusebox.circuits` structure to find that the circuit aliased as `cat` can be found in the directory `Catalog` beneath the main circuit.

The circuits definition file is only required at the main circuit level; files named `fbx_circuits.cfm` in circuit directories below the main level are ignored. It is considered good form to provide a circuits definition file for each circuit, though, to improve portability of the circuit. If the circuit is ever copied out of the application to become the main circuit of another application, then `fbx_circuits.cfm` is already in place, ready to go to work.

The circuits definition file is not the only thing that gets a different treatment depending on whether it's in the main circuit or a subcircuit. The circuit folders between the main circuit and the target circuit are called *container folders*.

Container Folders

Container folders play a critical role in Fusebox applications, but their role is easy to misunderstand. When a folder is neither the main circuit nor the target circuit, it contributes only its settings and layout to the fuseaction that is being processed.

Because the target circuit changes with every fuseaction, a circuit might be called upon to be the target or a container at any time. Regardless of whether it's the target or just a container, the circuit contributes its settings to the fuseaction on the trip "down" to the target circuit, and contributes its layout to the overall layout on the trip back "up" to the main circuit.

The fuses in container folders for a fuseaction, however, are ignored. Fusebox is only interested in the *settings* and *layouts* that are involved in container folders, not their fuses.

All this running up and down the folder tree might seem a bit confusing, so here are the main points:

- Settings are collected on the way from the main circuit to the target circuit.
- Layouts are collected on the way back from the target circuit to the main circuit.
- Container folders' settings and layouts are used in the fuseaction process.
- Container folders' fuses are not used in the fuseaction process.
- Any folder can behave as either a container or the target, depending on the fuseaction.

With all this running up and down the folder tree, inheriting settings and layouts, it might seem that using Fusebox has serious performance consequences. Although the consequences are by no means application threatening, they should be considered carefully.

Performance Considerations

Fusebox is an inherently organized framework. As this chapter has detailed, the ability to organize application behavior into a hierarchy of circuits offers a great deal of power for the development of complex systems.

To offer this well-organized modularity, though, Fusebox makes extensive use of `<cfinclude>` to build the code that will be executed for any given fuse-action. For each circuit that Fusebox involves in a fuseaction's inheritance, it pulls in code from `fbx_settings.cfm`, `fbx_layouts.cfm`, and any additional layout files specified in `fbx_layouts.cfm`. From the main circuit, code from `fbx_circuits.cfm` is also included. In addition, code from the target circuit's fuse files is brought into the page request.

This code assembly can impact performance in two primary ways: as application depth increases, and as the number of users hitting the system (load) increases.

Performance Versus Depth

Depth refers to the number of levels involved in a fuseaction, or how deeply nested a circuit is. The more deeply a circuit is nested, the more container folders Fusebox must work through in the course of processing a fuseaction.

Although depth of nesting has a minor impact on performance, we have seen few applications that warrant nesting more than four or five levels deep. If an application is so complex that it seems to call for nesting much deeper than this, it would be a good idea to carefully consider how the circuits could be designed to flatten the hierarchy a bit.

Applications can be deeply nested if necessary, though, so we'll take a look at what to expect if such a case arises. The performance impact caused by deeply nesting circuits depends on the complexity of the settings and layouts in the container folders.

Settings tend to be quite straightforward compared to layouts. Essentially, each `fbx_settings.cfm` file either leaves a variable alone or sets its own value for the variable. This is not server-intensive processing, so the performance impact remains negligible.

Layouts, however, can vary widely throughout an application and might involve conditional logic that generates a substantial amount of processing while building the output that results from a fuseaction. The impact of nested layouts on performance can vary vastly, from little in the case of simple layout wrapping to considerable in the case of extensive conditional logic.

The processing that occurs within fuse files is not impacted at all by nesting; a fuse takes the same amount of processing to run regardless of whether it is executed in a first-level or a fifth-level circuit. A problem with performance in a deeply nested application typically has more to do with a poorly performing fuse than it does with the overhead of nesting. Be careful not to blame performance woes on nesting without investigating the situation first.

If performance becomes a problem and no bottlenecks have been discovered in the fuses, then the place to start looking is in layout construction and the logic that is being performed there.

Performance Versus Load

As with all web-based applications, Fusebox applications are subject to potential problems when placed under a high user load. However, the techniques for making a Fusebox application behave well in a large-scale environment do not differ from the techniques for making a ColdFusion application scale well.

Although we don't have nearly enough space to devote to the subject of large-scale application considerations, we can hit a few highlights. For example, query-tuning techniques that work for run-of-the-mill ColdFusion applications work for Fusebox as well. Putting as much processing on the database server as possible will help performance. If the application uses <cfmail>, a dedicated SMTP server will help. All the little performance coding tips that are available from ColdFusion listservs and CFUG web sites are just as valid in Fusebox applications as they are elsewhere.

In other words, there's nothing really mysterious about Fusebox application performance relative to load. The things to be considered under Fusebox are the same things that any ColdFusion application must face. The nice thing about Fusebox, though, is the ease of using the server's debug information to see exactly which pieces of a process are using the most processing time. Fusebox's highly modular nature results in a fine level of granularity when the server reports processing times for each file in a page request. This is a clear advantage that Fusebox has over methodologies that are less modular.

Although Fusebox adds the considerations of processing settings and layouts to the concept of performance tuning, in general, Fusebox applications are not much different from other ColdFusion applications from a tuning point of view.

Nested Circuits Allow Nested Layouts

After all is said and done, Fusebox applications are just specialized ColdFusion applications. The factors we think about when making them work well, quickly, and smoothly are the same factors we apply to any ColdFusion application. Fusebox's modular nature, however, tends to make Fusebox applications much easier to deal with from a maintenance and tuning perspective.

As a fuseaction is executed in Fusebox, it follows an "elevator ride" from the main circuit to the target circuit, inheriting settings from each container circuit on the way down.

After the fuse files are at the target circuit, they are processed. Then their output is placed on the elevator for the trip back to the main circuit.

On the way back up to the main circuit, each container circuit's layout is processed and wrapped around the existing output so that the final presentation to the user is the aggregate contribution of a collection of nested circuits. Layouts and the process by which they are assembled get our attention next. "Ninth floor: nested layouts, lawn furniture, and sporting goods…"

"You ought to have seen how it looked in the rain,/ The fruit mixed with water in layers of leaves,/ Like two kinds of jewels, a vision for thieves."

—Robert Frost, "Blueberries"

9

Nested Layouts

DEVELOPERS WHO HAVE WORKED WITH FUSEBOX 2 are familiar with using a header file (usually called `app_header.cfm`) and a footer file (usually called `app_footer.cfm`) to establish a uniform layout for a web site. The Fusebox file would process the fuseaction's output into the variable `bodycontent`, include the header file, output the `bodycontent` variable, and include the footer file. This method was flexible and easily understood. It also was not terribly well suited to objectives of modular design. The use of header and footer files called from within the Fusebox file didn't provide the capability to gracefully nest circuits.

With the advent of Fusebox 3, the method for creating layouts changed to accommodate modular design. This change meant that Fusebox 3 had a great deal more versatility than Fusebox 2, but it also meant that it was necessary to put a little time into understanding the new model.

In this chapter we'll start with a look at how nested layouts work, exploring the interaction of layout files within the circuits that are involved in a fuseaction. Then we'll discuss designing a site with nested layouts in mind. We'll wrap up with a look at a couple of alternative interface concepts that are relative to nested layouts: Flash and web services. When it's all over, we'll be ready to move on to Chapter 10, "Nested Coding Concepts," for a look at coding practices in the nested environment. Let's start by looking at why nested layouts work in the first place.

Why Nested Layouts Work

We field questions regularly about why Fusebox moved to a nested layout model. After all, the old model seemed to work quite well. The answer to the "why" question has to do with the goal of creating a model that would allow circuits to behave as either parent or child, acting either alone or in concert with other circuits. To achieve that goal, circuits must be able to easily absorb the layouts of their potential children, and also allow their layouts to be easily absorbed by their potential parents. All this is accomplished through the use of nested layouts.

To begin our look at nested layouts, we'll turn to another analogy. This time, the academic and business worlds are the source of our example. In a way, nested layouts are a bit like the transparencies often used in these worlds. The next sections look at how we can assemble a layout like a stack of transparencies, one for each circuit from the target level back up to the main level.

Layered Transparencies

Before the advent of data projectors, nearly every classroom and conference room had an overhead projector that was capable of projecting images from transparencies. Remember the one Mrs. Byrd had in the back of your class—the one that never quite completely focused?

This type of projector could be used to build an image one layer at a time by adding successive transparent sheets to the projector's table. Figure 9.1 shows sample images and the result of combining them in this fashion.

This is much the way that layouts are constructed, one layer at a time, in a Fusebox 3 application. Except in the case of Fusebox, we use the Fusebox API variable `fusebox.layout` in place of sheets of transparent plastic.

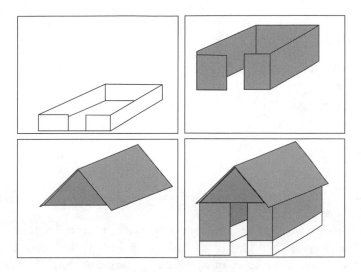

Figure 9.1   Transparencies.

Using *fusebox.layout*

Just as the sheets on a transparency projector are used to contain meaningful information that contributes to an overall concept, the variable `fusebox.layout` is used to contain data that contributes to the application's final layout.

Fusebox 2 developers are familiar with the use of the `<cf_bodycontent>` tag. This tag's functionality has been duplicated in the `<cfsavecontent>` tag starting with ColdFusion 5. When CFML is wrapped in the tag, the HTML that the CFML produces is not sent to the browser. Instead, it is stored in a variable that is specified in the tag. Listing 9.1 is a sample of using `<cf_bodycontent>` to store a section of content to a variable named `welcomeMessage`.

Listing 9.1   **Using <cf_bodycontent>**

```
<cf_bodycontent variable="welcomeMessage">
  <cfoutput query="qryGetUserInfo">
    <span class="headline">Welcome to ThirdWheel, #firstName#.</span>
  </cfoutput>
</cf_bodycontent>
```

At any point after this code is executed, you can insert the HTML that it produces into a template simply by referring to the variable `welcomeMessage`, as in Listing 9.2.

Listing 9.2   **Output from <cf_bodycontent>**

```
<html>
<head>
  <title>#pageTitle#</title>
</head>
<body>
  <table width="400" align="center">
    <tr>
      <td>#welcomeMessage#</td>
    </tr>
  </table>
</body>
</html>
```

With `<cf_bodycontent>` (or `<cfsavecontent>`), we can create content in one place and use it in another. This is the basis of creating nested layouts in Fusebox. A Fusebox circuit uses this technique to store its fuses' output to the variable `fusebox.layout`, allowing its layout files to generate output to that variable.

The real power of nested layouts is realized when we start looking at how nested circuits interact with one another as a fuseaction is processed.

Aggregation Up the Tree

In Chapter 8, "Nesting Circuits," we compared processing a fuseaction to riding an elevator from the main circuit down to the target circuit. The return trip from the target circuit to the main circuit is where layouts are processed. Each circuit from bottom to top participates in building the layout that is displayed to the user.

After the fuses for a fuseaction have been processed, their output is stored in the `fusebox.layout` variable. Then the Fusebox core goes back to work to put the output together. For each circuit, starting with the target, the `fbx_Layouts.cfm` file is read to find out which layout file(s) to use for the fuseaction. These files are included in the request, and here's where the tricky part happens. A layout file can reference `fusebox.layout` to include the fuses' output. Then when the layout files have been processed for the circuit, Fusebox stores the results back into `fusebox.layout`.

After that, the layout for the parent circuit is processed, following the same procedure. The difference this time, though, is that there are no fuses to process; therefore, the content that is contained in `fusebox.layout` is just the output from the child circuit. In this manner, Fusebox wraps each circuit's layout in the layout of its parent, all the way back up to the main circuit. Going back to the transparency metaphor, the end result is the whole picture, with each layer's content contributing to the overall appearance.

Figure 9.2 is a diagram of output from nested circuits outlined so that you can see how they contribute to the finished layout.

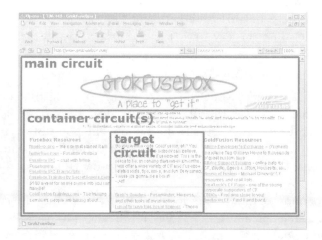

Figure 9.2   Nested layouts.

The nested layouts model makes it easy to assume that Fusebox layouts must always be concentric layers of content, with each layer subsuming one layer below it. Although this is the easiest way to approach layouts in Fusebox, it is by no means the only way. The ability to call circuits using the <cfmodule> tag allows one layout to include layouts from two or more other circuits directly. We'll explore this technique a little later, in the section titled "Designing for Layout." For now, the next step is to look at how the fbx_Layouts.cfm file and the individual layout files interact.

fbx_Layouts.cfm and Layout Files

Each Fusebox 3 circuit has an fbx_Layouts.cfm file. This file specifies the location of files that will produce the final output for the circuit. It's easy at first glance to confuse the job that layout files perform with the job that display fuses perform. Both are tasked with producing output for the circuit.

The difference between the two categories of file is twofold. First, display fuses *generate* specific output to be presented, but layout files actually *present* the output in context. This is because of the way the Fusebox core wraps the fuses' output into the `fusebox.layout` variable. Unless a layout file can reference this variable, the user will never see the output that the fuse generated. Second, the HTML that a display fuse generates is specific to a particular task, but the HTML that a layout file generates is generalized to the purpose of outputting the content that its fuses create.

To understand the generalized job performed by the layout files, we'll go through the process that `fbx_Layout.cfm` and its related layout files perform.

Referring to Layout Files

When processing a circuit's layout, the Fusebox core file calls the circuit's `fbx_layout.cfm` file. However, this file doesn't produce the circuit's layout. Rather, it calls layout files that actually do the job. The point of having `fbx_layout.cfm` is to allow flexible specification of layout files, including processing conditional logic to provide varying layouts depending on the circuit's situation.

The most common of these conditional situations is whether the circuit is the main circuit or a child circuit. In most cases, it is desirable to have the circuit's layout as a child be different from its layout as a main circuit. Listing 9.3 shows a simple logic block that activates a different layout based on this condition.

Listing 9.3   **Conditional *fbx_layout.cfm* for News Circuit**

```
<cfif fusebox.IsHomeCircuit>
  <cfset fusebox.layoutDir="">
  <cfset fusebox.layoutFile = "lay_asMain.cfm">
<cfelse>
  <cfset fusebox.layoutDir="">
  <cfset fusebox.layoutFile = "lay_asChild.cfm">
</cfif>
```

If the circuit is the main circuit, as would be the case if it were run as a standalone application, the layout file `lay_asMain.cfm` would be used. If the circuit is a child participating in a larger application, the layout file `lay_asChild.cfm` would be used. Note that the names of layout files, including the `lay_` prefix we use, are completely arbitrary and not controlled by the Fusebox 3 specification. Listing 9.4 has the code found in `lay_asMain.cfm`, and Listing 9.5 has the code found in `lay_asChild.cfm`.

Listing 9.4   *lay_asMain.cfm* **for News Circuit**

```
<cfoutput>
  <table width="580" align="center" border="1">
    <tr>
      <td align="center">
        <h3>Today's Headlines #DateFormat(Now(),"mmm dd, yyyy")#</h3>
      </td>
    </tr>
    <tr bgcolor="##EEEEEE">
      <td align="left">
        #fusebox.layout#
      </td>
    </tr>
  </table>
</cfoutput>
```

Listing 9.4 creates a table for the news items to be displayed within, sets a header line on the page including the current date, and uses the `fusebox.layout` variable to output the actual news items. Listing 9.5 simply references the `fusebox.layout` variable. This makes the output of the headlines circuit available to the circuit's parent, allowing it to be displayed according to the layout established at that level.

Listing 9.5   *lay_asChild.cfm* **for News Circuit**

```
<cfoutput>
  #fusebox.layout#
</cfoutput>
```

The two different layouts produced by this code are shown in Figure 9.3, which presents the circuit performing as a standalone application (main circuit) and Figure 9.4, which presents it performing as the child of another circuit. The parent circuit provides the layout shown in Figure 9.4.

Although the content of the headlines circuit is the same in Figures 9.3 and 9.4, the layout file that is processed determines the way that the content is displayed.

With `fbx_layout.cfm` providing a way to incorporate various layout schemes on a conditional basis, the sky's the limit with respect to options for presenting a circuit's content to the user. Taking advantage of `fusebox.layout` within the layout files is the key.

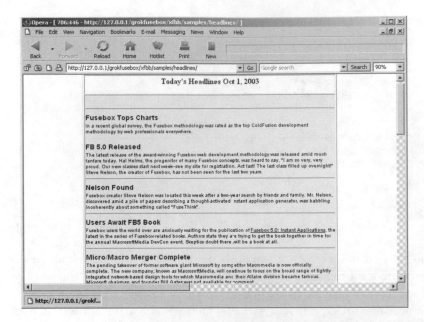

Figure 9.3   News circuit as standalone.

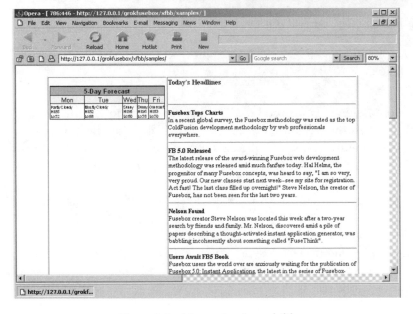

Figure 9.4   News circuit as child.

Layout Files and *fusebox.layout*

As the code in Figures 9.3 and 9.4 illustrates, layout files are concerned with how to present the circuit's content to the user. The circuit's content is always contained within the `fusebox.layout` variable.

This might seem at first to be a limiting situation because the layout simply incorporates the content from `fusebox.layout`. With that content already set, it doesn't seem that much can be done to change it after the fact. However, two techniques can go a long way to overcome this first impression.

The first technique is the use of style sheets within the layout files. This is the way the appearance of the News circuit is changed in Figures 9.3 and 9.4. When the circuit is the child of a larger application, the layout file doesn't apply a style sheet. This allows the parent application the opportunity to employ styles of its own. When the News circuit operates as a standalone application, its layout file applies a style sheet, resulting in a specific appearance.

When using style sheets in these examples, the class names used are the focus of the technique. If custom classes are used, the same classes must be defined in any style sheet that is to affect the circuit. When moving the circuit to a different application, the custom class names must be communicated to the architect of the new application. On the other hand, if styles are used to modify standard HTML tags, the circuit can easily inherit its parent's settings, assuming the parent also modifies standard tags through the use of styles.

The second technique to remember for layout processing is to use conditional logic within `fbx_switch.cfm` or the display fuses.

Conditional Layout Logic

Using conditional logic within `fbx_switch.cfm` or fuse files is less desirable than changing layout based on the parent/child role within `fbx_layout.cfm`, but it is valid nonetheless, and sometimes it is the only way to create the desired behavior. For example, a fuseaction's job might be to retrieve a recordset from the database and then either present the data in a table (if the circuit is the main circuit) or return a WDDX packet of the recordset (if the circuit is a child). This task could be performed in a couple of different ways.

Incorporating the conditional logic into `fbx_switch.cfm`, the fuseaction's <cfcase> block would look like Listing 9.6. Using this method, we create two different fuses: one that builds a table, and one that creates a WDDX packet. Because the latter doesn't generate HTML, it's an action fuse instead of a display fuse.

Listing 9.6   **CFCASE Block for Conditional Output**

```
<cfcase value="showOutput">
  <cfinclude template="qryGetMembers.cfm">
  <cfif fusebox.IsHomeCircuit>
    <cfset XFA.btnOK = "main.showMenu">
    <cfinclude template = "dsp_MemberTable.cfm">
  <cfelse>
    <cfset XFA.continue = "xmit.sendToPersonnel">
    <cfinclude template = "act_BuildMemberWDDX.cfm">
  </cfif>
</cfcase>
```

On the other hand, we could also incorporate the conditional logic into the display fuse. In this case, the fuse would generate either an output table or a WDDX dataset, depending on whether the fuse is participating in a child circuit. Listing 9.7 shows how the logic would be incorporated into the display fuse.

Listing 9.7   **Display Fuse with Conditional Output**

```
<cfoutput>
  <cfif fusebox.IsHomeCircuit>
      <table width="580" align="center" border="1">
        <tr>
          <td class="pageTitle">
            Today's Headlines #DateFormat(Now(),"mmm dd, yyyy")#
          </td>
        </tr>
        <cfloop query="qryGetNews">
        <tr bgcolor="##EEEEEE">
          <td class="headline">
            #headline#
          </td>
          <td class="story">
            #story#
          </td>
        </tr>
        </cfloop>
      </table>
  <cfelse>
      <cfwddx action="CFML2WDDX"
              input="#qryGetNews#"
              output="newsPacket">
  </cfif>
</cfoutput>
```

The more conditional logic that a fuse contains, the less portable it becomes. Because one of the objectives of Fusebox is to create small, tight, portable code, this last approach to conditional layouts should be considered carefully before it is employed. Our point here is not to recommend the technique, but to clarify the idea that "there's more than one way to skin a cat."

Regardless of where the code is placed to enable conditional layouts, the concept of nested layouts should be taken into account from the beginning of the project's architectural design.

Designing for Layout

At the point that the prototype is approved, the application's architect must begin to consider appropriate ways to group the application's activities into circuits. Part of this organizational process is deciding how nested circuits might provide solutions to the project's requirements. To get this process rolling, the architect takes screenshots of the prototype and examines the output presented on each one.

Considering Hierarchy

When designing an application's circuit structure, Fusebox's potential for nested circuits adds a dimension to the architect's conceptualization of the model. Simply put, rather than the simple one- or two-tier circuit model popularized in Fusebox 2, the architect can construct an n-tier model based on the needs of the application.

Figure 9.5 is a screenshot from `ThirdWheelBikes.com`, showing how various circuits might contribute to the final layout. Notice that sometimes one circuit's layout incorporates the layout from more than one other circuit. For example, the `twb` (main) circuit includes content from the `sidebars`, `content`, and `menu` circuits.

Under Fusebox 2, the design would probably have followed one of two models: either the twb circuit would have been the main circuit, with sidebars, content, menu, and breadcrumbs all circuits beneath it, or all the circuits would have been defined at the same level—the original "flat" Fusebox design.

Although either of these designs could be made to work, neither is particularly intuitive when it comes to the behavior of the application. For example, Janice has determined that a set of "breadcrumb" links should be part of the main menu. As the architect, Stan realizes that breadcrumbs are a useful and reusable sort of concept, so he wants them in a circuit of their own, separate from the menu circuit. (For a formal introduction to Stan and Janice, see this book's Introduction.) In either of the Fusebox 2 models, there is no indication other than the code that this relationship exists. The two circuits simply exist as equal players in the collection of circuits.

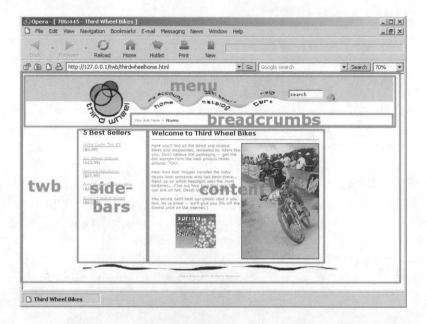

Figure 9.5   Nested layouts from `ThirdWheelBikes.com`.

Under a Fusebox 3 model, though, the relationship can be clearly defined by making the breadcrumbs circuit a child of the menu circuit. It then becomes readily apparent from the application's directory structure that something hierarchical is occuring.

Also available in Fusebox 3, thanks to the original Fusebox design goal of allowing circuits to be referenced via `<cfmodule>`, is the ability to incorporate more than one child circuit into a parent circuit's layout. This is precisely what is going on in Figure 9.5 with the twb circuit. Rather than having a single inheritance chain descending through a line of circuits, the twb circuit takes advantage of `<cfmodule>` to make calls to the menu, sidebars, and content circuits.

Figure 9.5 illustrates only one of the many ways that the Third Wheel application might be designed. Categorizing the activities required by an application into circuits is an art. As with most arts, it is refined over time through trial and error. We often look back on applications done in the past, shake our heads, and mutter, "What were we thinking?"

Indeed, sometimes the need to even use nested layouts comes into question.

Must I Use Nested Layouts?

Nested layouts are one of the most powerful features of Fusebox 3. They can also carry a bit of a pitfall, though. We sometimes get so caught up in the "gee-whiz" concept of nesting circuits that we feel as though we *must* apply a certain degree of nesting to an application. Otherwise, it might not be cool. This is a clear indication of the need for some fresh air.

The requirements for any application are never the same as those for any other application. In addition, the design of our latest application need not be cooler, more exotic, or more sophisticated than the previous one we did. It must, however, be right for the job at hand. Sometimes that job calls for a simple, flat circuit design, much like we might have done with Fusebox 2. There is nothing wrong with such a design if the project warrants it. Some projects by all measures should be single-circuit designs. If the desire to produce a nested design outweighs the requirements of the project, the end result will not be as good as it might have been.

As a last note on layout design, we'll take a look at some ways Fusebox can be used to produce output for applications that have different layout goals than the typical user interface.

Fusebox with Different Layout Goals

Although the majority of sites and applications designed under Fusebox will involve a typical HTML-based interface, an increasing number of applications calls for alternative output styles. For example, incorporating Flash as a front end to a Fusebox application or creating a web service both call for a different approach to layout design. Fortunately, the flexibility of the Fusebox layout concept easily accommodates both of these tasks.

Flash

When designing an application to use a Flash-based interface, the layout requirements for a circuit are much different from what they would be for an HTML front end. For starters, the user isn't presented with an HTML layout. The entire goal is to provide data to the Flash interface, where it will be used to generate the user interface.

To provide data to Flash, results of fuseactions must be formatted specifically, including the elimination of whitespace from the layout. Fusebox 3 handles this requirement quite nicely, allowing the creation of datasets with no whitespace whatsoever.

A more detailed discussion of Flash applications can be found in Chapter 18, "Fusebox Exotica."

Web Services

Web services are another area in which Fusebox's layout processing can help
manage the required output. As with an application using a Flash interface, a
web service does not provide data directly to the user. Rather, it provides data
to be used as part of another application. Consequently, the output must be
generated based on the needs of the server and the protocol of the web service, rather than the needs of a set of users. In effect, the users of the application are the other programs that will employ the web service.

As with Flash interfaces, the layouts generated for a web service must be
formatted specifically, including elimination of whitespace.

More details on web services can be found in Chapter 18.

Bringing Nested Layouts Home to Roost

Nested layouts are one of the most powerful developments in Fusebox 3. They
offer the architect the ability to arrange circuits into meaningful hierarchies for
presentation to the user, and to allow circuits to modify their appearance with
respect to position in the hierarchy.

When processing a fuseaction, Fusebox builds the layout that is presented to
the user by interpreting the `fbx_layout.cfm` and individual layout files of each
circuit in the line of descendence from the target circuit back up to the main
circuit. The `fusebox.layout` variable is constructed in layers, with each circuit's
layout being wrapped around its child's before being stored back to
`fusebox.layout`.

Although nested layouts offer a great deal of power and flexibility, not every
application calls for a highly nested design. Sometimes simpler is better. In
practice, we've rarely seen an application that needs to use more than three
or four levels of nesting. A site like Third Wheel Bikes is typical of most
e-commerce applications—straightforward, without a great deal of nesting.
However, the power is available if you need it.

Fusebox layouts are also capable of creating layouts that are targeted at more
exotic environments than the typical HTML user interface. Flash interfaces
and web services are examples of these exciting alternative environments.

To put a cap on these chapters about nesting circuits in Fusebox, we need
to talk a bit about how ColdFusion code behaves in a nested environment,
and where to place code in a Fusebox application to get the effect we want.
All that's coming up in the next chapter.

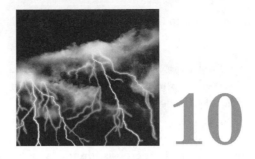

"It is a riddle wrapped in a mystery inside an enigma."

—Winston Churchill

Nested Coding Concepts

10

Having finished our discussion of Fusebox-specific nesting, we now turn our attention to some of the ColdFusion-related issues that accompany Fusebox nesting. Because a page request (fuseaction) can be constructed out of a variety of code included from various levels within the application hierarchy and its directory tree, it's important to understand what happens when operations like <cfinclude> are executed.

This chapter examines coding with portions of CFML that are location sensitive, such as <cfinclude> and directory functions; where to position your code within a Fusebox application to have the desired effect; and placing user-defined function (UDF) libraries. These concepts are useful when considering where in a Fusebox application you might place some code to achieve a given result.

Relativity

To understand how code is interpreted within the framework of a Fusebox application, we need to look at where ColdFusion is looking when various requests are made.

We'll start off with <cfinclude> because that's a commonly used directive in Fusebox applications. Then we'll look at some of ColdFusion's directory-related functions and how they work with respect to location. Finally, a quick look at UDFs will round out the discussion.

All of these discussions about nested coding are based on the basic framework of a Fusebox circuit, which is constructed through a series of <cfinclude> statements. Figure 10.1 illustrates the structure of a fuseaction in terms of the order in which the various <cfinclude> statements are processed.

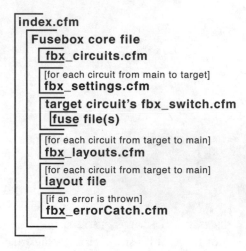

Figure 10.1   Fuseaction <cfinclude>s.

The next couple of sections are a bit easier to follow with this figure available as a reference. We begin with <cfinclude> and its behavior.

<cfinclude>

Most ColdFusion programmers are familiar with the <cfinclude> tag. This tag allows one template to be inserted into another one as though the code in the inserted template were part of the including template. <cfinclude> is important to us because it makes reuse of code a simple proposition. Code reuse is one of the hallmarks of Fusebox.

In most cases outside of Fusebox, programmers only include files in a single tier. That is, the included file doesn't include another file. Fusebox, on the other hand, not only has files including other files, but it also has files in a directory hierarchy, including files down and back up that hierarchy. As a result, it can be a bit confusing when trying to sort out where ColdFusion is looking for all these files.

A simple `<cfinclude>` can use an absolute or relative path to describe where the included template is located. If the tag `<cfinclude template="myfile.cfm">` is run, ColdFusion will look in the same directory with the calling template for the file named `myfile.cfm`. What happens if `myfile.cfm` is in another directory and also has a `<cfinclude>` tag in it?

Fortunately, the designers of ColdFusion constructed the parsing of `<cfinclude>` statements in a logical way. Rather than forcing us to consider the base location of a nested series of includes, `<cfinclude>` always considers relative paths to be in relation to the directory of the file that contains the tag. In other words, if `file1.cfm` includes `file2.cfm` from a subdirectory:

```
<cfinclude template="tests/file2.cfm">
```

and `file2.cfm` includes `file3.cfm`:

```
<cfinclude template="file3.cfm">
```

then ColdFusion will look for `file3.cfm` in the same directory with `file2.cfm`, not in the same directory with the originating template, `file1.cfm`.

For Fusebox developers, this behavior makes writing the various components of our applications much easier than it might be otherwise. We simply consider relative paths for `<cfinclude>`s in the same way we would consider them if we weren't doing all the nesting.

With a sense of security established around `<cfinclude>`, we can move on and look at ColdFusion's directory functions and how they behave in the Fusebox hierarchy.

Directory Functions

ColdFusion has a set of functions designed to provide information about a template's location on the web server. All these functions return filesystem paths on the web server, *not* web paths (URLs). We refer to these as directory functions. The next few sections provide some quick information on how these functions behave in nested and non-nested templates.

DirectoryExists()

The `DirectoryExists()` function is one of the lesser-used directory functions. It takes as its argument the fully qualified name of a directory. If the directory exists on the web server, the function returns `True`; otherwise, it returns `False`.

It is possible to use `DirectoryExists()` in a dynamic fashion, even though the directory name must be fully qualified (no relative paths allowed). To do this, another directory function must be used to construct the path argument.

For example, if you need to determine whether an image's directory exists below the current directory, you could use the following code:

```
<cfscript>
  thisPath = GetDirectoryFromPath(GetCurrentTemplatePath());
  imagesDir = "#thisPath#\images";
  okToCopy = DirectoryExists(imagesDir);
</cfscript>
```

Because `DirectoryExists()` makes no inferences about location, there is no difference in how it behaves between nested and non-nested templates.

ExpandPath()

The `ExpandPath()` function converts a relative path reference into an absolute path reference. It is the functional equivalent of using something like the following piece of code:

```
<cfscript>
  relPath = "images";
  thisPath = GetDirectoryFromPath(GetCurrentTemplatePath());
  expandedPath = "#thisPath#\#relPath#"
</cfscript>
```

The advantage of using `ExpandPath()` is that you can use any manner of relative path. For example, to find the absolute path to a directory that exists on the same level as the current directory, you could use the following code:

```
<cfset pathToFind = ExpandPath("..\siblingDir")>
```

You could use this technique along with `DirectoryExists()` to write a test to see whether the expected circuit directories within a Fusebox application exist.

GetCurrentTemplatePath()

The `GetCurrentTemplatePath()` function returns the absolute path of the template where the function is called. The path includes the name of the template, so it is common to use this function in conjunction with the `GetDirectoryFromPath()` function to return the path without the template name.

With respect to nested includes, this function can be useful. It always returns the path to the directory where the template is located, regardless of whether the template is included in another template in a different directory. Figure 10.2 shows the locations of two templates—one included in the other—and the values returned by `GetCurrentTemplatePath()` for each one.

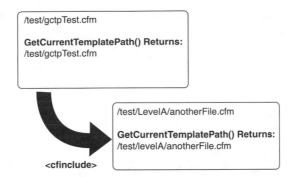

Figure 10.2 `GetCurrentTemplatePath()` results.

Whereas `GetCurrentTemplatePath()` provides a look at where the template is located on the server, another function is required to find out where it might have been called. For this purpose, ColdFusion gives us `GetBaseTemplatePath()`.

GetBaseTemplatePath()

The `GetBaseTemplatePath()` function returns the absolute path of the template from which the template containing the function was called. The base template is the first template in any nest of includes, custom tag calls, or `<cfmodule>` calls. Listings 10.1 through 10.3 show three templates, each included in the one before it, that retrieve the value of `GetBaseTemplatePath()`.

Listing 10.1   */test/baseTest.cfm*

```
<hr>
<cfoutput>
I am in #GetCurrentTemplatePath()#<br>
I was called from #GetBaseTemplatePath()#<br>
</cfoutput>
<cfinclude template="levelA/bt2Test.cfm">
```

Listing 10.1 includes the code in Listing 10.2, which is located one directory level down from Listing 10.1 (`/test/levelA`).

Listing 10.2   */test/levelA/bt2Test.cfm*

```
<hr>
<cfoutput>
I am in #GetCurrentTemplatePath()#<br>
I was called from #GetBaseTemplatePath()#<br>
</cfoutput>
<cfinclude template="levelB/bt3Test.cfm">
```

Listing 10.2 includes the code in Listing 10.3, which is located two directory levels down from Listing 10.1 (/test/levelA/LevelB).

Listing 10.3 */test/levelA/LevelB/bt3Test.cfm*

```
<hr>
<cfoutput>
I am in #GetCurrentTemplatePath()#<br>
I was called from #GetBaseTemplatePath()#<br>
</cfoutput>
```

Figure 10.3 shows the output from running baseTest.cfm as in Listing 10.1. Each of the templates from Listings 10.1 through 10.3 displays the path to its location (GetCurrentTemplatePath()) and the path to the location of the base-level calling file (GetBaseTemplatePath()).

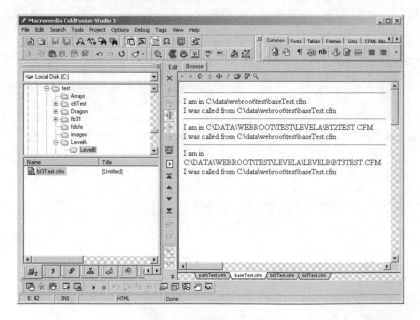

Figure 10.3   GetBaseTemplatePath() results.

GetBaseTemplatePath() can be used for error checking in Fusebox. It should always evaluate to the same file (usually index.cfm).

You might also be familiar with the `GetTemplatePath()` function. `GetTemplatePath()` is a deprecated function; although it is still supported in ColdFusion 5, you should use `GetBaseTemplatePath()` instead. The later function makes the intent of your code much clearer.

GetDirectoryFromPath()

The `GetDirectoryFromPath()` function returns the path portion of its argument, with any file information stripped from it. The following code returns the same value for both cases:

```
<!--- Case 1 --->
<cfset myPath = "c:\inetpub\wwwroot\test\pathTest.cfm">
<cfoutput>#GetDirectoryFromPath(myPath)#</cfoutput>
<br>
<!--- Case 2 --->
<cfset myPath = "c:\inetpub\wwwroot\test\">
<cfoutput>#GetDirectoryFromPath(myPath)#</cfoutput>
```

The result of this code is shown in Figure 10.4.

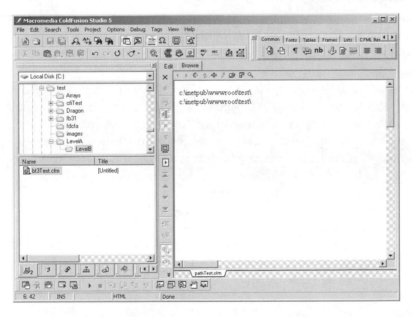

Figure 10.4 `GetDirectoryFromPath()` results.

It's important to note the trailing slash at the end of the `<cfset>` statement in Case 2. Without the slash, ColdFusion assumes that the last part of the path, `test`, refers to a file and strips it off.

`GetDirectoryFromPath()` is frequently used in conjunction with `GetCurrentTemplatePath()` or `GetBaseTemplatePath()` to return to the location of a template without the template's name.

Another aspect of coding for Fusebox's nested environment is sorting out where to insert your own custom code to affect various parts of the application. We'll explore these possibilities in the next section.

Placing Code in a Fusebox Application

Going back for a moment to Figure 10.1, it's clear that some confusion might arise when figuring out exactly where to place code to achieve a desired effect relative to selected portions of a Fusebox application. Placement of code will vary depending on whether the effect is intended to be applicable to a single fuse, a fuseaction, a whole circuit, or the entire application. Let's take a brief look at each of these cases in the context of setting a variable.

To Affect a Fuse

The simplest decision to make is where to place code that will impact a single fuse. On the face of it, the answer to this situation is to drop some code in the fuse and be done with it. We need to consider some things before we move on, though.

Decisions about adding code to an application should be made keeping in mind the structure of the overall page request. Just as with a single template, code that appears earlier in the assembled "template" of a fuseaction can impact code that appears later in the same fuseaction. When a change is made to a single fuse, the impact on any fuses that follow in the same fuseaction must be considered. If a variable is set in the second fuse included in a fuseaction, it will exist for all the fuses in the same fuseaction except for the first. It's important to remember that variables that are to be used by subsequent fuses should be documented in the <out> section of the setting fuse's Fusedoc.

In a similar fashion, if you want to set a variable that is intended to affect an entire fuseaction, but doesn't really pertain to any of the fuses in the fuseaction, the appropriate place to consider is a bit higher up than inside a fuse.

To Affect a Fuseaction

The code that includes the content for a fuseaction falls within a `<cfcase>` block in the `fbx_switch.cfm` file. Consequently, it makes perfect sense to place code that will affect all the fuses in the fuseaction at the beginning of the `<cfcase>` block for the fuseaction.

Exit fuseactions are perfect examples of this particular situation. They are typically set at the beginning of a fuseaction's <cfcase> block, and they are available through the entire fuseaction. In most instances, an XFA isn't used until the last fuse in the fuseaction, so it's clear that XFAs exist for all the fuses in that fuseaction.

At times, the temptation to add a lot of code to the <cfcase> block for a fuseaction might arise. We urge you to resist the temptation. Before you decide to add more than the simplest code at this point, consider whether it would be more logical to create a new fuse to be inserted into the fuseaction instead. This helps preserve the organization of the application and maintains a modular approach to construction.

This same logic continues to hold as we once again move up the hierarchy to look at modifications to circuits.

To Affect a Circuit

When the discussion turns from a fuseaction to a circuit, the scope changes a bit. We've now moved to the outer edges of the diagram in Figure 10.1. The only place within that diagram that code could be placed to affect the entire circuit would be at the top of index.cfm, somewhere before the core file is included. This is a legitimate approach if we're dealing with a main circuit (where index.cfm comes into play), but there are other ways to affect a circuit as well.

For our example of setting a variable, the preferred place to turn is fbx_settings.cfm. Because this file is designed to establish variables and other settings for the circuit, it's a natural container for our circuit-wide variable's <cfset> to be placed. The settings file can also contain conditional logic to include any of a set of smaller settings files, depending on whatever condition you care to set.

For example, we might have a site-hosting application that provides each customer with the option of using any of a dozen design schemes. Based on a value stored in their site's profile, we want to use the corresponding collection of settings for the customer's scheme. A conditional <cfinclude> inside the settings file would solve this need quite nicely.

To Affect a Child Circuit

When a variable is set within the scope of a circuit, it is by design available down through the hierarchy of that circuit's descendants. Remember that settings are constructed from the top down, processing each circuit's settings file in turn. Therefore, a variable named lstStates that is set in the main circuit will remain set for all the main circuit's descendants, unless an intervening parent deletes it.

Although it is possible to place your own code anywhere you like within a circuit's files, even the `fbx_` files, it's wise to give careful thought to the impact of doing so. Particularly from a maintenance point of view, the sanity you save could be your own!

The last level on the hierarchy is the entire application, which is really just a subtle variation on a circuit.

To Affect the Entire Application

At several points in this book, we've mentioned that a Fusebox application is a collection of one or more circuits, and that a circuit can behave as a standalone application in itself or as part of a larger application.

A circuit's ability to stand as an application in its own right is the clue we need to gain some insight into the placement of code that affects the entire application. The logic that governs this is no different from the logic that governs placement of code to affect a circuit. The only difference is that the circuit in question in this case is the main circuit.

Any settings that are applied in the main circuit's settings file or in the main circuit's `index.cfm` file will be available to any circuit, fuseactions, and fuses in the application. Clearly, a good deal of discretion should be exercised when considering such a modification.

The final place where code could be positioned to affect the entire application is in `Application.cfm` or `OnRequestEnd.cfm`. Although using these two files has the rough equivalence of placing code at the beginning or end of `index.cfm`, respectively, it is crucial to remember that `Application.cfm` is not called in the case of a custom tag syntax. In other words, if you use `<cfmodule>` to call your application or some of its circuits, the `Application.cfm` file in the called circuit's directory will not run, and neither will `OnRequestEnd.cfm`.

Knowing where to place code in general to achieve a desired result in Fusebox is vital, but users of ColdFusion 5 and later have one specific concern: where to put calls for UDF libraries.

UDF Positioning

Every ColdFusion developer is familiar with the use of functions. We use them regularly to do things like changing the case of a string with `LCase()` or `UCase()` and performing regular expression replacements with `REReplace()`.

ColdFusion 5 introduced UDFs to CFML. A UDF is simply a piece of CFScript that establishes a function that doesn't exist in the collection of ColdFusion functions. The new function can then be used within other CFScript blocks. This is a powerful extension to ColdFusion, but it's not without its pitfalls. We can create a proper UDF only to get an error when we try to use it. To make successful use of UDFs, we need to understand how to make them available to our code.

When UDFs Are Available

UDFs are typically placed in a library file that is separate from other code. This allows them to be used much more broadly than they would be if they were embedded directly into the template where the function is to be used. When placed in a library, a UDF is not available for use until its library (the template where its code is) has been made available to the template where the function is to be used. This is done through the use of our old friend <cfinclude>.

For example, the code in Listings 10.4 and 10.5 shows a simple UDF library and a template that includes the library and calls a function from it, respectively. Listing 10.4 is the library file, Ch10Lib.cfm. It contains a function called makeUserID(), which builds a user ID from a first name and last name.

Listing 10.4   *Ch10Lib.cfm*

```
<cfscript>
function makeUserID(firstName, lastName) {
  myUserID = Left(UCase(firstName),1);
  myUserID = myUserID & Left(lastName,8);
  return myUserID;
}
</cfscript>
```

Listing 10.5 is a file, udfTest.cfm, that uses <cfinclude> to make the Ch10Lib.cfm library available. It then uses the makeUserID() function in a <cfscript> block.

Listing 10.5   *udfTest.cfm*

```
<cfinclude template="ch10lib.cfm">

<cfscript>
  lName = 'Mertz';
  fName = 'Ethel';
  userID = makeUserID(fName, lName);
</cfscript>

<cfoutput>#fName# #lName#'s user ID is #userID#.</cfoutput>
```

The sequence of events for a UDF states that the function's library must be included before any ColdFusion code that uses the function. This factor reflects on how UDFs might be used within a Fusebox application. We need to consider placing not only the code to use the function, but also the code that pulls in the library.

Availability Versus Processing

When using UDFs in Fusebox, we need to think about two issues that are related to the location of code. First, the location of the call to the UDF library is important. Second, the location of code that uses the UDF must be considered. We call these locations the points of availability and points of processing, respectively.

Availability and processing are subtle shades of the same concept when designing UDFs for Fusebox. The *point of availability* refers to where the library's `<cfinclude>` directive should be placed so that its functions will be available as needed in the application. The *point of processing* refers to a place within the application where the function will be used.

The availability of the function library directly governs the options that are available for processing. For example, if a function library is included in the settings for one circuit, and a script that uses the function is placed in a fuse file from a different circuit, the function will not run. However, if the library is included at the main circuit, or application level, the function will be available for all circuits within the application.

This does not mean, however, that you should drop a `<cfinclude>` for every UDF library you can imagine using into the main circuit's settings file. As with every aspect of program execution, tradeoffs between performance and code size are involved. If every UDF you can imagine is included in the application for every page call, there will be a bloat-related performance impact. For that reason, use that same logic we went through about adding code to the application to determine the best place to drop a `<cfinclude>` tag for your UDF library.

A Place for Everything

Fusebox applications are hierarchical creations by design. This design characteristic improves modularity, eases maintenance, and generally improves development habits. However, to take best advantage of the hierarchy, it is imperative to understand how the various files of a circuit are interrelated, and how circuits relate to one another.

Choosing where to place code to affect various portions of an application is not a complex task as long as you take a bit of time to really understand the nested nature that is inherent to Fusebox. Fuses, fuseactions, circuits, and entire applications can be modified with appropriate placement of modifications. Finally, ColdFusion 5's UDFs can also be readily incorporated into Fusebox applications, using much the same logic that is applied to "regular" code.

This chapter wraps up our three-chapter romp through nesting in Fusebox, and is the end of Part 2, "Fusebox Coding." Now we're going to turn our attention to the less code-centered aspects of Fusebox. The methodology we have developed in the Fusebox community to create successful web applications is called the Fusebox Lifecycle Process (FLiP). Part 3 covers the process from beginning to end.

3

Fusebox Lifecycle Process (FLiP)

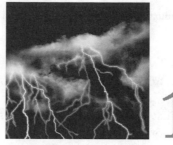

*"It isn't that they can't see the solution.
It is that they can't see the problem."*

—G. K. Chesterton

11

Introduction to Development Methodologies and FLiP

Stan hadn't been in Hal Helms' "Developing Applications with ColdFusion" class for more than five minutes before he heard about the "70% Failure Problem." This refers to a study that revealed that 70% of all system development efforts fail. That is, they are either never completed, or after they're completed, they fail to satisfy the needs they were intended to meet. (For more on Stan and friends, see this book's Introduction.)

Nodding his head in sympathy, Stan could easily remember a string of projects where nothing seemed to go right. He became keenly interested in the prospect of some tools and ideas that could prevent such problems on future projects.

What Stan was interested in, without being able to say so, was the idea of development methodologies. One of the best ways to avoid failure in developing a system is to apply a methodology to the process. This chapter introduces the general idea of development methodologies, and then gets into the specifics of the Fusebox methodology, known as the Fusebox Lifecycle Process (FLiP).

Methodologies as a general concept provide structure and consistency to development efforts. A methodology removes the concerns about how to do something, allowing us to focus on what to do. This distinction between "how" and "what" should be quite familiar by now—we've pointed it out in every topic from wireframes to Fusedocs. It keeps recurring because it is critical. After the method is determined, the objective becomes the focus. When we know that we will perform the steps in FLiP to develop an application, we are free to concentrate on the details of the particular application. Our strong methodology makes it all possible.

Methods and Methodologies

To paraphrase the old joke, if you ask three different developers to define the phrase "development methodology," you'll get at least six different answers. Most developers have some concept of using a methodology, whether they actually use one or not.

Boiled down to its simplest definition, a *methodology* is the formalization of how to do something. It's not the actual doing, but rather the process we follow to do it.

There is a subtle difference between a method and a methodology. A *method* is something you do in a particular fashion.

A *methodology*, on the other hand, involves some understanding. That Greek "ology" stuck on the end of the word implies a level of study or knowledge. Using a methodology means going through a process that we understand. Understanding means we've gone to at least some amount of effort to think about what we're doing.

Adopting a methodology results in what we often refer to as "best practices." You'll be hearing more about these in Chapter 17, "Best Practices."

The desire to use a methodology means we want to use methods that are familiar or understood. By doing so, whenever we do similar tasks, we'll do them in a similar way. That way, each time we do the task, we can do it more efficiently or with more quality, rather than reinventing the process every time.

Writing program code is a great place to employ a methodology, whether it's of your own invention or not. Programs tend to use the same kinds of logic over and over again, so you have many opportunities to standardize the way your code is written and organized.

Standardized coding can start as modestly as using naming conventions for variables or objects, and progress through tightly structured means of organizing program segments, libraries, code blocks, and even program flow structures.

For most Fusebox developers, the big advantage of using Fusebox is simply in getting a handle on where everything is located within their applications. After all, if you use a consistent style every time you build an application, it makes life much easier when trying to find individual pieces of code.

Every experienced Fuseboxer has had the experience of revisiting an old application after they've been away from it for a while. This is often a rather disheartening experience because your first tendency is to see all the things you could have done better in your code. If you've had this experience, be of good cheer—it simply means you're continuing to grow in your wisdom as a developer.

The second thing an experienced Fuseboxer notices in visiting that old Fusebox application is how easy it is to grasp the overall function of the program. Because Fusebox is so well organized, visiting old applications is not nearly as aggravating as it would be without such nice organization. We can jump right into the Fusebox file, read the applicaton's "roadmap," and then cruise through the dsp files to see how the screens look, and so on. The simple fact that Fusebox forces us to break code into meaningful modules brings focus to each part of the application.

Unfortunately, great code isn't the only objective of great application development.

Great application development must include great planning. Otherwise, we're just running around in the dark, swinging our keyboards in the hope of hitting a solution.

Planning

Planning seems to be an overlooked art within the application development community. It is absolutely critical to the success of a development project, yet it gets comparatively little press compared to programming issues. This might be because most of us programmers aren't interested in what we think of as "management issues," or it might be the result of focusing too intently on the practice of programming as opposed to overall application development.

Applications aren't about programming, they aren't about cool code, and they aren't even about what great programmers we all are. Applications are about getting a job done for the user, whoever that might be. The key to finding out what the job is and how we can help the user do the job better lies in planning.

You've probably been introduced to some form of planning an application, ranging from basic flowcharting to other more complex approaches. Let's take a look at some of the issues involved in planning, and then we'll move on to a Fusebox approach to those issues.

Planning Isn't Just Flowcharting

Back in the days of Computer Science 101—BASIC, programming instructors tended to equate flowcharting with planning a program. Some poor victims spent weeks being tortured over the art of flowcharts and how proper flow-charting was the foundation for successful programs. The sad part of it all is that, although quite useful, the overemphasis on flowcharting tended to blind students to the greater concepts of program planning and design.

Of course, flowcharts can still be useful, but it's important to understand *where* they're useful. A *flowchart* is simply a course plot for the program logic—a roadmap for the code, if you will. It is not a roadmap for the entire application. For information like that, we must begin to ask some very basic questions that have nothing to do with writing code. We have to ask, for example, the following questions:

- What should the program do?
- For whom should the program work?
- What does the client really want out of the program?
- In what environment will the program have to run?
- In what environment will we have to develop the program?
- What happens if the program doesn't work?
- Who has the final authority to make program decisions?

These and a thousand other questions must be answered before coding can begin. This is where the Fusebox methodologies that are not specifically related to coding come in.

Coding Without Planning: How to Kill an Application

One can cause failure on a given development project in many ways, but we can guarantee a formula that will work every time. It's really quite simple, and it consists of two easy steps:

1. Get a great idea.
2. Start coding.

Sounds pretty foolish, right? More likely, it sounds like something you've experienced. Most of us have. After all, coding in ColdFusion is straightfor-ward. That's one of the great things about ColdFusion—you can create some really cool stuff in short order. This is also one of the great weaknesses of ColdFusion—it's tremendously tempting to bolt out of the gate and start writing code before you've thoroughly developed the application concept.

Off you go, charging down Code Road, banging out ColdFusion as fast as you can think. You've got Studio humming, you're barely looking at those tag completion cues, and it's going to be a really great application.

Then your boss (or client, or both) jumps in with the first of the "Can we also do…" questions. It changes your whole vision of the project. Wanting to keep your job, you accept the new requirement, knowing you can incorporate into your ultimately flexible application.

As time passes, the boss or client is full of more requirements. The project is starting to spin out of control. You're not sure what to do, but you keep saying, "Sure, we can do that!" purely out of a sense of self preservation bordering on career-threatening panic. The launch date is approaching, so you keep at it, hoping beyond hope that all will be well if you just keep banging code.

The launch date arrives, and you watch in horrible dismay as error after error presents itself in the browser window. A small, dark cloud gathers over your cubicle…

Of course, we don't like projects to fail. We'd like to develop some habits for application development that cause you to react to a new project proposal in a radically different way. We'd like you to step back; say, "Wow. That sounds like a really cool idea. Let's talk about it some more"; and automatically start at the beginning of a well-organized planning process.

We refer to that planning process as the Fusebox Lifecycle Process (FLiP).

FLiP

We return for a moment to the question "What is Fusebox?" We've already seen how organizing an application's code under the Fusebox specification brings organization and simplicity. As we'll see in the following chapters, Fusebox covers a great deal more territory than just writing well-organized code. It's also about how to organize application-development projects from the beginning.

FLiP is the result of years of experience on the part of Hal Helms and the other members of the Fusebox Council, as influenced by an amazing assortment of folks from incredibly diverse disciplines. The Fusebox community has developers who are, in their "other lives," everything from accountants to surgeons. This means the process has had feedback from a broad range of experience.

FLiP consists of individual steps in a larger process. You don't have to adopt a monolithic Fusebox methodology to benefit from these ideas. Consider each idea and decide whether to adopt it, reject it, or modify it to suit local needs. Spend some time understanding the purpose behind each step; a great deal of time and effort has gone into their refinement as effective tools for application development.

The key to success in application development (web-based or otherwise) is to begin the development process long before you begin coding. Most well-designed applications have about an 80:20 ratio of planning time to coding time. This has two important implications:

- Planning *must* be the major emphasis in application development.
- By implementing strong planning procedures, we can increase the amount of time we spend inventing things and greatly reduce the amount of time we spend writing the code to implement them.

The following sections and chapters introduce FLiP and the steps it recommends for developing applications. The chapters follow the process, starting with wireframes and proceeding through prototypes, DevNotes, code planning, unit testing, and implementation. These are not trivial topics, and the time spent will be worthwhile.

Step 1: Wireframes

The idea of wireframing in the sense that we use it comes from the world of 3D modeling. In that world, a wireframe is a model of an object without surfaces, lighting, or final details applied. Figure 11.1 shows a wireframe model in action. In our world, a *wireframe* is an initial model of the business process for which the application is being built. Figure 11.2 is a screenshot of the Fusebox Wireframe tool in action.

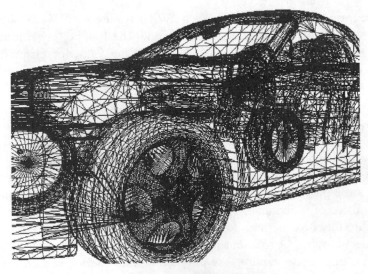

Figure 11.1   3D wireframe model.

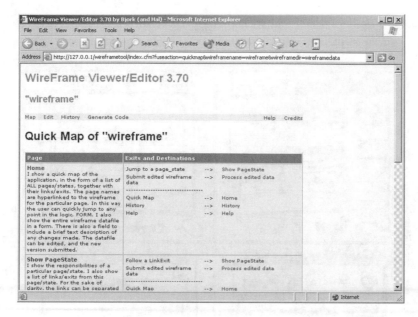

Figure 11.2   Fusebox Wireframe tool.

The important thing to realize about wireframes is that they are aimed at discovering the business process, not the web design. One way to keep this in mind is to imagine you're trying to design a system to be performed on paper. Forget about computers, web pages, ColdFusion, and so on. The point is to figure out *what* needs to be done, as opposed to *how* you're going to do it. The actual implementation will be addressed in the later steps of FLiP.

Step 1a: Storyboards

If you've ever seen a "making of" documentary about one of your favorite movies, you've probably been introduced to the idea of storyboards. This is the newest step in FLiP; some developers really like it and some don't. Often, you can move straight from wireframing an application to prototyping it. Some clients, though, respond well to informal illustrations of a concept. This is where storyboarding comes in.

Storyboards are intended to start the creative process for the application. They are simply drawings of the pages to be included in the prototype. Storyboards can be a rapid way to kick off the prototyping process in a comfortable and low-tech setting. Most people really enjoy being part of a group that gets to draw pictures and stick them to the wall! Figure 11.3 shows a storyboard concept for a sample application.

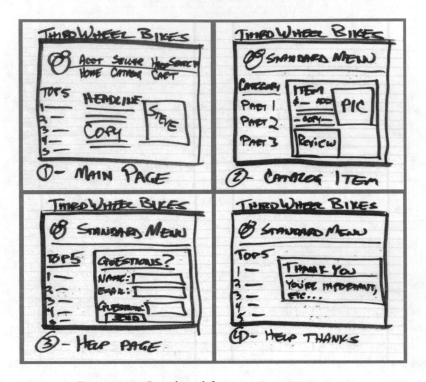

Figure 11.3   Storyboard for ThirdWheelBikes.com.

Not much time has been spent on developing techniques with storyboarding, so this book does not have a separate chapter on them. However, you should explore the use of storyboards or any other techniques you might find useful in developing a prototype. The goal is to get the client talking about what they need and what they want.

As the client's ideas begin to be defined, it's time to start formalizing the presentation of what will be built. We want to make sure that we understand what our client wants, and that she realizes that we understand. Prototyping the application serves these purposes.

Step 2: Prototypes and DevNotes

The prototype is perhaps the most critical step in FLiP. This is where one creates an HTML representation of the final application, complete with the colors, graphics, and so forth that the client would like to have. Figures 11.4 and 11.5 show a prototype page and a final page for our sample application.

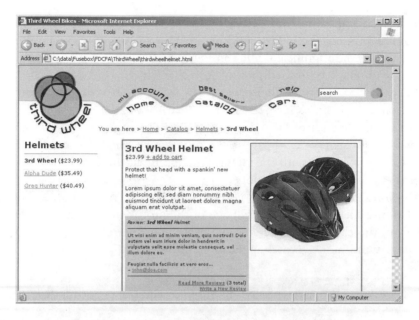

Figure 11.4   ThirdWheelBikes.com prototype page.

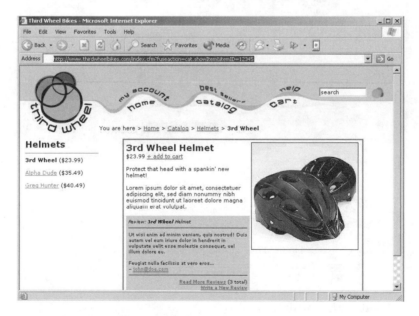

Figure 11.5   ThirdWheelBikes.com actual page.

Note that the only difference between the two is the URL, where you can see that Figure 11.4 is static HTML and Figure 11.5 is a ColdFusion application. This might seem insignificant, but consider what it means. If the prototype looks exactly like the finished product, the client won't be surprised by the result. You'll never have another project where the client sees the finished product and says, "That's nice, but it's not what I wanted."

You can use any set of HTML generation tools you care to use during the prototyping phase. The key is to use the prototype as the focus point for an extended conversation with the client, ironing out all the details of what the client is expecting to have developed.

DevNotes is a tool that allows you to easily place a small threaded Notes application at the bottom of every page of the prototype, encouraging feedback from the client while viewing the prototype. Figure 11.6 shows a prototype page with the DevNotes application at the bottom.

Figure 11.6   DevNotes in action.

Step 3: Code Planning

After you've agreed on the final form of the prototype, you're ready to start planning the code. This is the point at which a skilled application architect sits down with the prototype and organizes its requirements into circuits, fuseactions, and fuses, and then writes the Fusedocs for each fuse. Figure 11.7 shows a printout from the `ThirdWheelBikes.com` prototype with some of the markup that's typical of the code planning step.

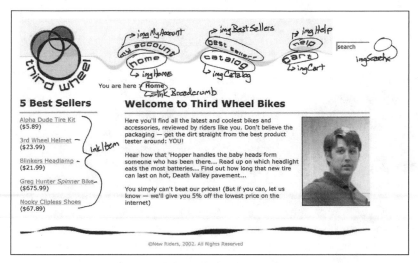

Figure 11.7 Code planning markup.

Step 4: Coding

In Fusebox, the actual writing of code is probably the least exciting aspect. By the time you get to this point in the project, the fuses are so well defined that coding is just a matter of having skilled coders interpret the language of the Fusedocs in CFML.

Don't let that last statement make you think coders are unimportant in Fusebox. They're quite the opposite: Fusebox is intended to allow coders to do what they do best—write great code. Although many attempts have been made over the years to build code generators, an experienced developer behind the keyboard has no substitute.

Step 5: Unit Testing

As Steve Nelson might say, "The beautiful thing about Fusebox is the way it helps you test fuses before you throw them into interaction with other code." (If you get to know Steve, you'll soon realize that many features qualify as "the beautiful thing about Fusebox.")

If you've ever spent time trying to find a bug in a substantial chunk of CFML you've written, you'll really appreciate the idea of unit testing.

A unit test in Fusebox is simply a test run on a single fuse. This is made possible through the use of test harnesses, which are specialized test-time-only files that establish the Fusebox environment just for the purpose of testing.

Step 6: Deployment and Integration

If we've done everything else correctly, this step in the process should be completely anti-climactic. In fact, deployment of a Fusebox application should carry no unexpected events (knock on wood). But, of course, you do need to watch out for some things in preparation for this major non-event. As with the other steps in FLiP, it's all about planning ahead and keeping your eyes open.

FLiP for Better Applications

Developing without a methodology is tantamount to dooming a project to failure before the first template is written. The steps of FLiP provide a strong methodology for *all* our web-development projects.

Even if the project seems too small to bother with all this preparation, prepare anyway. While working on this book, we needed an application to help track our progress and assignments. It was only a single circuit with 10 fuseactions. However, we went through the entire process, from wireframe to finished product, in about 10 hours. The result is a complete, well-documented little application. Although we could have thrown something together in less time, it wouldn't have been documented, well designed, or robust. The benefits of FLiP can be had on even the smallest efforts.

The steps in the FLiP progression are by no means restricted to the creation of Fusebox applications. We have found through the process of trying a wide variety of techniques that they work well as a start-to-finish process regardless of the architecture of the final application.

In fact, FLiP even works for projects where you won't have the luxury of using Fusebox. You don't even need to be working in ColdFusion for the techniques in FLiP to provide a strong foundation for the development effort.

The remainder of this part of the book explores each of the FLiP steps in detail, taking you through our sample bike shop application's development process as we go. As the chapters progress, we'll see how FLiP takes our minds off the worries about how to approach the project, and gets us into the work that contributes directly to successful completion. We'll start, as always, with a wireframe, and then move into prototyping the application, planning the code, coding, unit testing, application testing, and deployment. That's a lot to cover, so let's get started!

12

Wireframing

RECENTLY, STAN BOUGHT A NEW CAR. He spent a long time researching the different models in his price range that met his baseline criteria. He spent hours poring over consumer review web sites deciphering all the details of each model—engine size, available option packages, safety ratings, and maintenance reports. He went to the bookstore night after night and read the latest reports of new cars, trying to crop the list. Eventually, he had narrowed the field from hundreds of models to a small handful. Finally, he test-drove the candidates. The winner was determined based on those test drives. After spending a little time behind the wheel of each one, Stan knew which one was right. Not until he saw the car in action did he know whether it was the right one. (For a more formal introduction to Stan, see this book's Introduction.)

The process that Stan went through to buy a car is similar to the process of developing successful applications. Our clients never know what they want until they get it, just as Stan didn't know what car he wanted until he test-drove them all. Rather than complaining, "Why didn't you tell us you wanted this before we started?," we use wireframes to deliver the application to clients before writing a single line of code.

In this chapter, we will imagine we are working with Stan to build the wireframe for Janice's site (`www.thirdwheelbikes.com`). We will cover the basics of wireframing, including what wireframing is, the differences of wireframing and flowcharting, and some wireframing tools. We will also cover syntax while we build our wireframe.

What Is a Wireframe?

A *wireframe* is a page-by-page, plain-text representation of what a finished application will do. Devoid of techno-babble such as UML, flowcharts, or data models, the wireframe is extremely fast to develop, is readable by everyone, and answers the oft-overlooked question of what the application needs to do. As soon as a client begins identifying her requirements, it is quite tempting to open up a new Access file and begin the preliminary database schema. Let's face it—we are all geeks, so writing code and thinking in application systems is what we do best.

However, if we are lulled into thinking about architectural subsystems before we fully understand what the finished system is supposed to do, then it is likely that we will subconsciously rearrange the requirements into something that is easily coded. This is dangerous because by giving the client what we think she wants, we almost never give her what she actually wants. We do not know anything about Janice's requirements other than that she needs to sell bikes online. Is the shipping coming directly from the manufacturer? Is this for consumers and resellers? We just do not know yet.

Step away from your favorite code editor and close your flowcharting program. Wireframing is wonderfully simple, and it can be done on brown grocery bags, dry-erase boards, or a nifty wireframe tool, discussed later. Figure 12.1 shows a sample wireframe page.

By avoiding discussion of colors, page layouts, and menu systems, we get to the heart of the system—who the users are, what those users can do, what pages they see, and what clicks take them where. At this point in the development process, we cannot be concerned with getting the page content correct. That is a distraction from the process. We also cannot be concerned with capturing all the input fields of user-based forms. It is easy to add form fields or rearrange the layout of a page in the next phase, which is presented in Chapter 13, "Prototyping and DevNotes." Trying to tackle anything other than page flows and general functionality reduces the chance of creating the finished product that we mean to create.

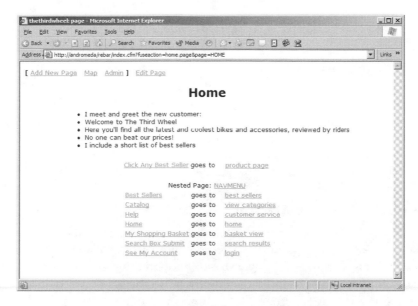

Figure 12.1   A sample wireframe page.

Because we are just trying to tackle page flows and major features, why not use flowcharts?

Wireframe Versus Flowchart

Flowcharts have been used for many years to aid in planning computer pro-grams. They are wonderful for visualizing complex algorithms and processes. In fact, the symbols used (oval, diamond, and rectangle) are well suited to those purposes. However, flowcharts are not good at determining total application functionality. Those same symbols are difficult to understand for some clients. Flowcharting a web site usually requires specific user scenarios to be determined.

If you are familiar with flowcharting, you might find that wireframing is similar to it. Of course, the tools used are different, and wireframing might seem a little less precise in its accomplishments, but wireframing has been especially designed for the task of determining page flows for web pages. Flowcharting is still powerful, and we sometimes find ourselves using it to work through a complex section of logic in an action fuse. However, its usage has focused, and wireframing is more productive for the initial phases of your web projects.

What Is Involved in Wireframing?

Wireframing can be tough work for programmers. Luckily, most programmers like a good challenge. Our minds are usually thinking about tailoring technical solutions to the client's specific needs. In reality, however, we can accomplish just about anything that a client can dream up. Sure, some things are easier than others, but if Janice just "has to have" a complex report page that we think will require a SQL query joining every table in the database, we had better deliver that report to her. Uninhibited by what is possible, our client is free to discuss what she and the project need to become successful.

The First Wireframe Meeting

The wireframing meeting is similar to a brainstorming session. Janice will do the talking, and we will build the wireframe in real-time as she tells us want she wants. This is a process that we share; although the primary responsibility for describing what needs to be included is up to the client, we would be shirking our duties as experienced developers if we did not jump in at opportune moments. If Janice wants a way for people to log in but has not yet identified an administrative component to manage user accounts, we can bring it up now, while changes are cheap. It's okay to expand the scope of the project during the wireframing process. Keep in mind that you probably should not have already quoted the client a fixed price for the project; that way, the more detailed you make the project now, the happier you both will be.

After spending an hour or so on the wireframe, you might think that you are nearly complete. Although this might be the case, carefully consider that the amount of time you spend on the wireframe is proportional to the amount of time and headaches you save in the later phases. It is important to have as much "face time" as possible with the client during the wireframe process. You cannot guess what the client wants, even if it is something as "simple" as an e-commerce site. Maybe she did not tell you about the unique partnering her business has that complicates the shipping process, or she might have forgotten the bit about needing to process checks by mail as well as credit cards.

Wireframing Alone

Getting hours of one-on-one contact with Janice is not practical. She is busy; so are we. In most cases, after the first couple of hour-long meetings to start out the wireframing process, you can retire back to the office to work on it alone. Be careful not to put too many words into the client's mouth. You might spend a lot of time developing a wireframe for a system that the client does not want. Worse yet, the client might think that she does really want it, but only after final delivery of the finished product does she realize that you (maybe inadvertently) hijacked the wireframing process. If you have to work on the wireframe alone, it is safest to flesh out a few pages that you previously created but left as "stubs." Maybe there is a certain three-page routine for looking up forgotten passwords that you left empty. That sort of functionality is pretty generic, so based on the few notes you took while with the client, you can finish it off by yourself.

Also, be especially wary of clients who "just don't have the time" to spend with you. If they do not have the time to spend figuring out what they want, how can the final result possibly be what they want? Most clients are overjoyed to see such a structured process occurring to increase their chance of success, but some clients might need a bit of an explanation of the benefits of wireframing before committing to the process. You might also suggest that your busy client turn the project over to an assistant who does have time to work with your process.

Now that you understand what a wireframe is, how do we build one? Janice is waiting, so let's quickly review our options for wireframing tools.

Wireframing Tools

Before we start building our wireframe, let's figure out what tool to use. Because the task of creating a wireframe is not complex but the importance of getting it right is high, a certain methodology for creating it needs to be employed.

Paper-Based Wireframes

One way (albeit not the best way) to create wireframes is on paper. Avoiding computers while wireframing can be very nice; that way, you are not seduced into downloading new wallpaper when the client is not looking, or taking too many breaks to play *Quake 3 Arena*. You can make web page representations very rapidly—often faster than you and the client can think them up.

Paper-based wireframes have problems, though. It is hard to update them without a big eraser, sharing them means making more paper copies, and you cannot easily transfer them to the computer for later phases. The biggest problem with paper-based wireframes is that no matter what kind of wizardry the wireframer employs, it is impossible to accurately represent a web application with links in a browser, on paper. For these reasons, we cannot recommend making paper-based wireframes unless you are stuck with the client during a rolling blackout.

Design Tools

You might already have a wireframe editor incorporated into another development tool. Visio has a variety of templates that might be suitable for wireframing. If you are a whiz with Dreamweaver or another visual IDE for the web, you might be able to create a wireframe quickly, including the basic content for the page as well as all the necessary links between pages. Using a visual development tool entices us to add a splash of color or rearrange the menu to be on the left side rather than the top. As we have discussed earlier, making these kinds of decisions at this point in the game serves only to mask the requirements of the system. The time to decide the shade of background blue comes later, after the wireframe is completed.

Wireframe Editors

Design tools like Dreamweaver and Visio are decent, but wireframing is such a specific job that the process greatly benefits from a dedicated wireframe editor. The original dedicated wireframe editor was created by Hal Helms and is available from his site:

```
http://www.halhelms.com/
```

Lee Borkman borrowed the concept that Hal introduced, removed the need for a database, and released a nice tool, Wireframe Editor/Viewer, which has now gone open-source and is available at this URL:

```
http://www.sourceforge.com/projects/wireframe
```

Rebar

Building on this tradition of wireframe editors to meet the needs of the job, Erik Voldengen and Nat Papovich recently released Rebar, available at the following:

```
http://www.fusium.com/go/rebar
```

Although we will be using Rebar in our examples during the rest of the chapter, any of the preceding wireframe editors will work and be relevant to the wireframing process. All three of these editors are similar in design and use, so if you are not using Rebar, this chapter is still relevant to you. The process of creating wireframe pages to simulate the finished application is the same even if you are using crayons on paper.

The finished wireframe data files are available to download at the following URL:

```
http://www.thirdwheelbikes.com/book
```

The wireframe data files that Rebar creates are in an open and generic format, so the wireframe can run on the other wireframe editors. Rebar has some nice features, including easier page creation, better interface, and cross-wireframe linking. In addition, although the completed wireframe files are not in a format compatible with tools like Visio or Dreamweaver, Rebar generates the beginning HTML prototype, which provides a jumpstart to the next phase in the Fusebox Lifecycle Process: prototyping. Both Wireframe Editor/Viewer and Rebar are written in Fusebox and ColdFusion, so you'll need to have ColdFusion running to use either editor.

Wireframing in Action

Before we begin the wireframing process, we need to set up and familiarize ourselves with Rebar. You should follow along with a copy of Rebar. Because we have the zip file for Rebar on our local computer, we will unzip the contents into a folder below the web root named `rebar`. When you do this, it should look something like our directory structure, as shown in Figure 12.2.

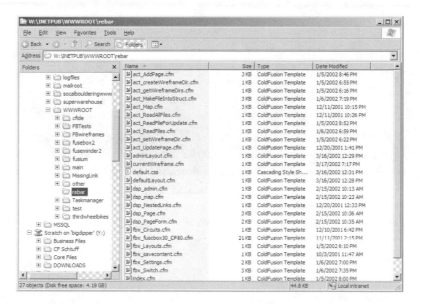

Figure 12.2   Rebar directory structure.

Now we are ready to start creating the wireframe; no more installation is needed. If you have installation or configuration problems, see the `readme` file that is included in the Rebar zip file.

We will run Rebar by opening a browser window to the root of the `rebar` folder into which we created and unzipped Rebar. Figure 12.3 shows the Rebar Administration page, where we can switch between available wireframes as well as create new wireframes.

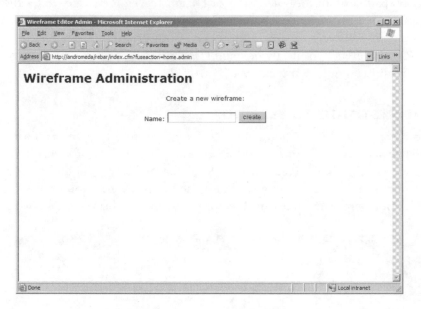

Figure 12.3   Rebar Administrator.

Because no wireframes are available to work with, we are going to create the wireframe `thethirdwheel` and click `Create`. Now we are looking at the Site Map page for our application. It is empty because we have not made wireframe pages yet. Notice the three links on the top of the editor. `Map` takes us to this same map. If we click it, nothing changes; we are still looking at an empty map. If we click `Admin`, we can go back to the Rebar Admin page, which looks familiar. Finally, `Add New Page` lets us make new wireframe pages. Janice is waiting for us to get ready, so we will click that link and begin creating pages.

Wireframe Syntax

The wireframe syntax is easy to learn. Figure 12.4 shows the page creation screen.

This large text area is where we create the wireframe pages. If you have ever worked with Windows .ini files, the text displayed should not be too foreign. If you have never worked with .ini files, fear not; the syntax is extremely simple. In fact, there are only three commands. Because wireframes are designed to be simple and fast, three commands are all that we need.

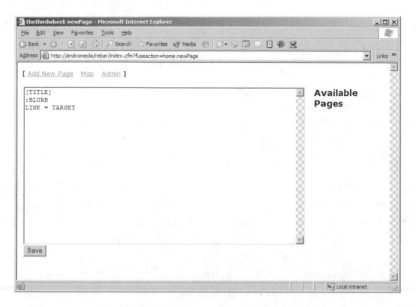

Figure 12.4   Rebar wireframe page creation.

The Title

Janice wants to work on the first page that a user sees, so let's create that page. Starting at the top of the text area, we see this:

    [TITLE]

As you could guess, this is the title of the page. It serves two purposes—what name to display at the top of the page and how to reference this page when linking. Remember: The goal of wireframing is to create a text-based representation of the web site consisting of page responsibilities and links—nothing more. Because we are making the first page of the web site, we are going to name this page HOME and replace [TITLE] for [HOME]. When rendered by Rebar's viewer, the text inside the square brackets becomes the page title. Only one title can be used per page; subsequent titles are ignored.

The Body

The next line showcases the semi-colon command:

    ;BLURB

This command allows us to write text on the page. You can add as many lines of semi-colons as you want. Janice has some ideas about what this page should do, so we are going to remove the `;BLURB` line and add our own text about this page:

```
;I meet and greet the new customer:
;Welcome to The Third Wheel
;Here you'll find all the latest and coolest bikes and accessories,
➥reviewed by riders
;No one can beat our prices!
;I include a short list of best sellers
```

Notice how we write these lines in first-person. It might be tempting to begin writing content in the wireframe, but that is not the point here. We are striving to determine *what* the application does and *what* each page does, not *how* it goes about accomplishing its task. At this point in the process, Janice has good ideas about how to word the content of each page, and that is fine. Hold onto those ideas, and do not waste time getting them right in the wireframe. The wireframing process is fast and furious, so keep the content of each page to a minimum.

Links and Nested Pages

The final line is an example link:

```
LINK = TARGET
```

On the left side of the equal sign is the link that will be displayed on the page. The text on the right side of the equal sign is the page where the link goes. Because you know HTML, we will tell you now that this line translates into something like this:

```
<a href="target">link</a>
```

Janice wants a few links on this page, so we are going to replace that example link with two new links:

```
Click Any Best Seller=Product Page

NavMenu
```

These two lines look quite different. One is a name=value pair, whereas the other is just a name. The name=value pair makes a link something like this:

```
<a href="product page">Click Any Best Seller</a>
```

What does `NavMenu` do? Janice has told us that her site is going to need a global navigation menu, available on any page. Because a wireframe page is supposed to show every link that the finished application page does, we need to represent those global links. Of course, we could type every global link on every page, but then if we needed to add one new link to the global navigation, we would be forced to duplicate that link on every page, which is not in the best interest of the lazy programmer. By typing just the value of a page without a corresponding name, we can nest a page in another page, similar to `<cfinclude>`.

(Although we refer to the ColdFusion tag `<cfinclude>`, it is important to remember that we are not writing code here, nor are we determining how the final ColdFusion logic will be written.)

The Completed Wireframe Page

We will talk a bit more about nesting pages in a minute, but we want to see the wireframe page just created by clicking `Save`. Figure 12.5 shows the completed wireframe page output.

Figure 12.5 Viewing a created wireframe page.

Notice that the title at the top was translated from [HOME] and how each semicolon line became a bullet item. Also, check out the links section and how our `name=value` pair became a link. The section that says `Nested Page: NAVMENU` does not look quite right because we have not yet created the `NAVMENU` wireframe page. Rebar knows which pages you have created and which ones you have not, so you can safely place links to wireframe pages that do not exist and come back to create them later. For now, though, Janice is satisfied with the page. Let's go to the site map by clicking Map at the top.

Site Map

Figure 12.6 shows a site map of the wireframe that we are creating with Rebar.

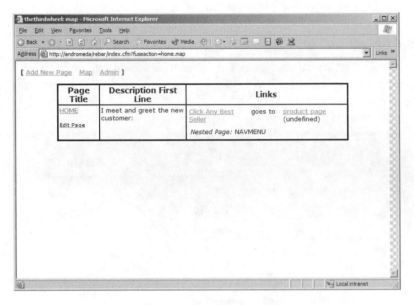

Figure 12.6   The Rebar site map page.

Although it might seem a bit complex at first, this page is crucial to the development of a wireframe. Every page in our wireframe is captured in one row in the site map. The far-left column displays the name of the page as entered in the [TITLE] for that page along with a link to edit that page. The middle column shows the first of the semi-colon lines for that page. The other semi-colon lines are still saved, but for brevity, only one is shown on the site map. Finally, the far-right column shows all the links for the page. If a link goes to a page that is not yet created, a reminder is displayed next to the link that says (undefined). Also in the right column is the name of any nested pages. Unlike the actual page view, the links for nested pages are not shown on the site map, but you can easily scroll down the page to see the links of the nested page, if you so choose.

More Wireframe Pages

By taking a look at the current site map, we know that we have one page
that is undefined (product page), and we can also tell that we have not made
NAVMENU yet. When we click on the link for product page, Rebar shows us a
basic and empty page. Now by clicking on the link Create this page, we can
easily create the missing page, based on the concept that Janice has for this
page.

```
[product page]
;I give summary information about this product
;I also show the latest review of this product
complete technical specs for this product=product detail
read reviews=product review
write a review for this product=write review
buy this product=basket view
navmenu
```

After completing this page, we can go back to the map and see that our new
page is added to the site map. Now the link from HOME to product page no
longer has the (undefined) reminder next to it. However, now we have four
more pages to create as links from PRODUCT PAGE. Before creating those pages,
we want to create the NAVMENU page. We already have two pages that nest this
undefined page, and we know that almost every page will nest it also, so it is
wise for us to complete this nested page now. It is important to keep nested
pages updated because so many other pages reference a nested page. By clicking Add New Page, we can create the NAVMENU page.

```
[NAVMENU]
See my account=login
Home=home
Browse the store=view categories
Best sellers=best sellers
Customer Service=customer service
search box submit=search results
my shopping basket=basket view
```

We did not add semi-colon lines to this page because Janice doesn't want text
displayed along with these links on every page. Unlike name=value pair links,
Rebar will not display semi-colon denoted text in nested pages. The purpose
of nested pages is only to provide common links to a large set of wireframe
pages.

   After saving this NAVMENU page, we can use the map to go to the HOME page
view. We see the nested links at the bottom of the page.

   Figure 12.7 shows us how Rebar interprets the nested page command into
output. NAVMENU shows up below the normal links for the HOME page.

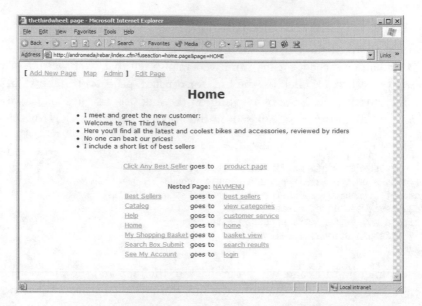

Figure 12.7   Viewing a nested wireframe page.

It's That Easy

After just a few minutes, we have created three pages of our budding application. The syntax was not hard to learn, and because Rebar provides us with an example of the syntax during page creation, we do not have to memorize anything. In fact, the process of wireframing is so simple that programmers are not the ideal people to be doing it.

Who Should Wireframe?

Business analysts are a better choice for wireframing, but if you are a one-man shop or your development team does not include someone with formal business-analysis experience, then you should consciously switch hats when making a wireframe with a client to avoid thinking in technical terms.

The wireframe syntax is so simple that occasionally we feel comfortable enough letting a client make it. It might be tough to imagine such tech-savvy clients, but they do exist. When you find a computer-savvy client who knows what he wants, the best thing you can do is start the wireframe together, and then let the client have at it. You absolutely need to check up on the client frequently, and you will want to carefully review the entire wireframe together to make sure everything the client is creating is feasible, but when a client is empowered to tell you what he wants, the chance of project success is high. We are going to continue to build the wireframe for Janice; she is not ready to work on it herself.

If you work in a corporate environment, wireframes are an excellent tool for managers and your intra-business customers. You can set up a brown bag lunchtime seminar to go over how to create wireframes and the syntax that is required. After your customers and managers become proficient at wireframes, all your requests for improvements and work orders can come in the form of wireframes. Although the current version of Rebar does not come with role-based access built in, you can easily add this functionality because Rebar is a Fusebox 3-compliant application. You can even embed Rebar in an existing Fusebox 3 intranet by drag-and-drop and updating the `fbx_circuits.cfm` file.

Limiting Wireframe Complexity

While you're adding pages, you might be wondering why Rebar does not allow you to change the color schemes or fonts to be used. Although it might be tempting to change the color for different projects, the client will think that you are beginning development of the layout and look and feel of the application. It might be tempting to use a visual development tool to create wireframes so that you can quickly add form elements to wireframe pages. After all, form-only pages are different from content-only pages. But in our experience, including anything other than plain text might lead to a conversation like this:

> "Focus on the application and the pages, not the colors," you say.
>
> "Okay, this page is great, but can you scoot up the password box so it's even with the username box? They really need to be on the same line," says Janice, completely unaware of the real task at hand.
>
> "No, hold on, you're not getting it. Those form elements are there just as an example of what would be on this page. Later in the process, we will decide where they should go. Hold onto those ideas," you reply, hoping she understands.
>
> "Okay, well I don't want to forget the fact that we need a drop-down box for company logins on this page too. Can you just add that? It's an important part of this page."
>
> Grumbling, you give up. "Fine. I'll stick that in."

Then your speedy wireframe brainstorming session becomes a nitpicking session. That select box you added to appease Janice most likely will not make it into the final application. Maybe it will be abandoned in favor of IP subclass lookups, or maybe each login will be associated with one company, removing the need for company identification. However it ends up, that interchange was not a good use of valuable face time. This is why Rebar and the open data file syntax do not allow complex page creation. Save that stuff for the prototype.

More Wireframe Pages

We are going to make a few more wireframe pages for Third Wheel Bikes. Which pages do we need to make? By reviewing the site map, we see that we are missing 10 pages. We are going to pick the basket view page, which links from PRODUCT PAGE and NAVMENU. By clicking on that link and then clicking Create this page, we can create the wireframe page with these lines:

```
[basket view]
;I show all the items in the basket
;I also show upsell/cross-sell best seller items like "wanna buy a
↳helmet with your new bike?"
;customer can change quantity of the items in basket here
update quantity=basket view
continue shopping (goes back to the previous page)=product page
continue checkout=checkout page one
navmenu
```

By this time, you can probably look at those lines and tell exactly what is going to be displayed on the basket view page, but Figure 12.8 shows us the output.

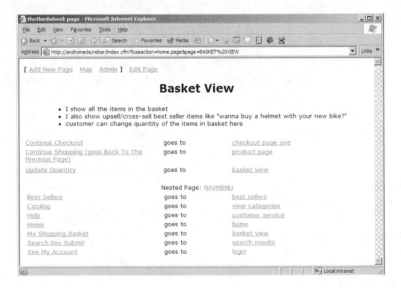

Figure 12.8   Basket view page.

We are going to continue the checkout process by clicking the link for `checkout page one` and creating it with this data:

```
[checkout page one]
;I gather billing name, address, etc
;I gather shipping information (include javascript to copy billing
➥fields to shipping fields)
;I also let customer enter credit card information
review order=checkout one decision
navmenu
```

On this page, we made a note about a JavaScript function that should be in use on this page. You might be tempted to bang out that function right now, but just making a note of it is best. While you are creating wireframe pages, if you ever encounter notes about the page, you should stick them on a semi-colon line. If you need to remember that a page references an external system, such as `http://www.weather.com` for the current forecast, then that note should become a bullet item by adding it as a semi-colon line.

One of the links on this page goes to an action page. What is an action page?

Action Pages

We also made a link to a page called `checkout one decision`. Any time we make a link to a page with the word *decision* in the title, we know that it is a page that won't show up in the final application, but for now, it reflects an important behind-the-scenes piece of logic that determines which page the user sees next. We are going to create the `checkout one decision` page like this:

```
[checkout one decision]
;ACTION PAGE
;validate the information in the form on the previous page
bad information=checkout page one
all good=checkout page two
```

The preceding code example shows us how to create the action page. Figure 12.9 shows how the action page looks when displayed.

The first bullet item on this page says ACTION PAGE. This is our alert that the user will not be able to see this page in the end. This page has only two links, and the rest of the text describes what this page does. On the previous page (`checkout page one`), the customer will enter a credit card along with other information such as billing and shipping details. In the finished application, what should happen if some of the information entered is wrong? What if the credit card entered is not a valid credit card? What should the system do if the customer forgets to enter a shipping address? This ACTION PAGE is used to emulate two different states: one of the customer entering something wrong or

missing something, and the second of the customer entering everything correctly. Notice where the two links go. If something is wrong, the customer
goes to checkout page one. If everything is good, the customer goes to
checkout page two, which looks like this:

```
[checkout page two]
;I give a summary of the order including costs, estimated shipping
➥times, and a review of the customer data.
buy something else=basket view
place order=checkout thank you
navmenu
```

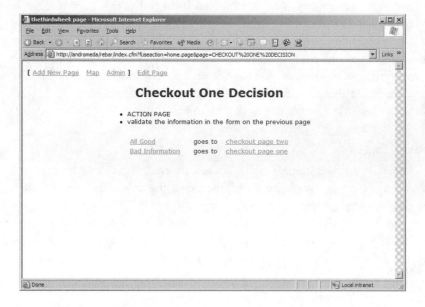

Figure 12.9   An action wireframe page.

Notice in Figure 12.10 how the NAVMENU page is being nested in every page so
far. Because we have created the NAVMENU once, all we have to do is include it
in the pages and it will show up. Also, you might have noticed that we tend to
mix up our cases in the wireframe data files. Rebar is not case sensitive, so the
only thing that matters is spelling. Now the customer is just one click away
from completing the order, so let's finish it up with the page where the place
order link goes: checkout thank you:

```
[checkout thank you]
;I advise the customer to print out this page since it contains the
➥order number, etc
;I thank the customer for placing the order
back home=home
navmenu
```

The wireframe code displays the final wireframe page in the checkout process. Figure 12.11 shows how Rebar outputs the page.

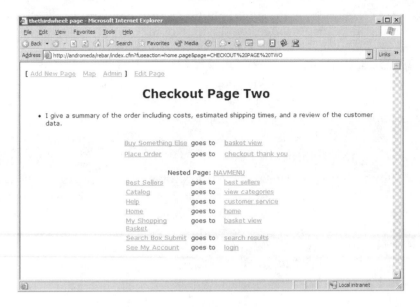

Figure 12.10   Checkout page two.

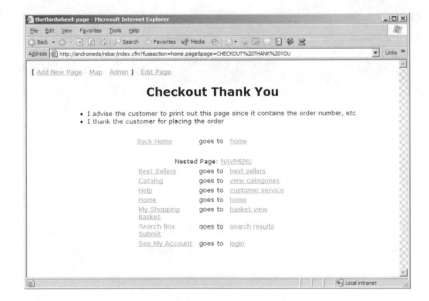

Figure 12.11   The final wireframe page in the checkout process.

Closing Thoughts

We have finished one part of the wireframe in a short amount of time. This process is fast, but most applications you develop are going to be larger than Third Wheel Bikes. How long should wireframing take? It is difficult to quantify exactly, but we have found that for a two-month project, the wireframe can take a week to develop. You might get nervous spending so much valuable development time without doing coding, but remember that the amount of time you spend wireframing is proportional to the amount of time you save from making changes in the following phases, including development.

Generating the Prototype

Rebar allows you to generate an HTML prototype so that it can run without ColdFusion. In fact, you do not have to wait until the wireframe is complete to create a prototype. You can do periodic "builds" to show others who are involved in the project how the wireframing is progressing. Using Rebar to generate HTML prototypes is also an excellent way to get a jump-start on the next phase: prototyping. Use the Rebar Admin to generate the prototype, as shown in Figure 12.12.

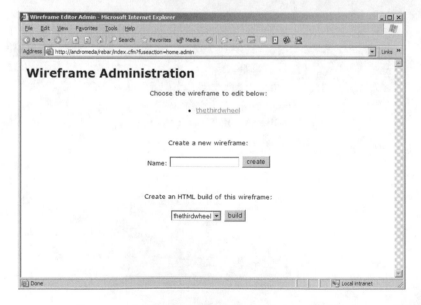

Figure 12.12   Rebar HTML prototype generation.

Although we did not complete the entire wireframe for our site, you can download the sample wireframe data files to complete the collection. After the wireframe is complete, it is helpful to run through it a few times. You might have missed a few things, or the client might want more added to the wireframe. What you do at this point is up to you.

Some people find it helpful to get the wireframe written in stone before moving on to the next phase. Others only use the wireframe for a few hours even on large projects, preferring to jettison the tool in favor of a prototype after the baseline functionality is explored. We prefer something of the middle ground. Use the wireframe until you or the client becomes tired of the process. Wireframing is difficult and mentally exhausting if you spend too long on it.

Leaving wiggle room in a completed wireframe is fine. You can use the HTML prototype generated by Rebar to start the next phase, prototyping, in which no wiggle room exists. By the time you finish the wireframe, you probably will have some ideas brewing about color schemes and layouts. Wireframing might be too limiting after the application starts forming in your mind.

In the next phase, prototyping, we fully explore the site's layout and navigation. Most importantly, our decisions are driven by the functional needs that we have identified while wireframing.

"Oft expectation fails, and most oft there Where most it promises"

—William Shakespeare, *All's Well That Ends Well*, Act II, Scene 1

Prototyping and DevNotes

13

STAN'S ANXIETY LEVEL ABOUT STARTING A NEW project had always been rather high. After all, it was impossible to know whether the application he built would meet with the client's approval. It seemed like most of the time, he would finish the job only to have the client say, "Well, that's not really what I wanted." But this time things would be different. After the positive reaction he got from Janice in the wireframing meeting, Stan was excited about working on the prototype of the application. (For a proper introduction to Stan, Brody, and Janice, see this book's Introduction.)

Instead of jumping right into the coding process with the information gathered using a wireframe, Stan would have Brody work with Janice to build a prototype based on the business processes that were discovered in the wireframe. By working through the issues of layout, appearance, and presentation on the prototype, Stan and Brody could avoid changes after the code development had begun and changes became expensive.

This chapter is about one of the most important aspects of creating a web application—the human interface. The prototyping process is all about taking the concept that is constructed in the wireframing process and fleshing it out with a front end. We'll look at the concept and purpose of prototyping, some techniques and tools for prototyping, a practical example from Third Wheel Bikes, and how to use the prototype as the starting point for coding the application.

Introducing Prototypes

Many engineering and development disciplines use prototypes, but not all mean the same thing when they use the term. Before we get too deeply involved in the nuts and bolts of application prototyping, we need to get a handle on the Fusebox definition of the term.

A Fusebox *prototype* is a working front end for the application that has no ColdFusion code working behind it. Whereas some disciplines use the term prototype to mean the first working version of an item in development, we use the term to mean a version that is non-working but identical in every other way. That is, the version looks and feels like a running application, but it doesn't interact with a database, communicate with other systems, process credit cards, and so on. In many ways, it's like a full-scale model of a concept car; it looks like it's all there, but it doesn't have an engine under the hood.

Fusebox prototypes should be indistinguishable from the final application as far as the user experience is concerned. This might sound like an impossible idea without a database working, but certain techniques allow us to model the behavior of the database without having one. We'll discuss that in more detail later.

Prototyping provides us with two vital capabilities in the development process. The first is clear communication with the client, and the second is a way to manage the age-old enemy of projects everywhere: scope creep. The next two sections look at communication and scope creep and how prototypes allow us to master them both.

Communicating Through the Prototype

The prototype is a means of communicating with the client. As with the old adage, "A picture is worth a thousand words," prototypes are intended to communicate volumes of information about Brody's understanding of Janice's wishes. Instead of sitting down and creating a laundry list of requirements to be formalized in a design document and hashed over before Janice ever sees anything, Brody starts by working off the wireframe and creating an HTML presentation that satisfies the business model it represents. He also spends some time talking with Janice about sites she likes, the intended audience, and so on.

After the initial prototype has been created, it becomes the centerpiece of an ongoing conversation between Janice and Brody, being continually modified until it ultimately becomes what Janice wants to see in an application. By presenting Brody's interpretation of Janice's requests, the prototype becomes an evolving question that asks Janice, "Is this what you want?" The goal of the prototype is to continually change until Janice's answer to the question is, "Yes."

This communicative process is the Fusebox Lifecycle Process (FLiP) method for dealing with scope creep. Instead of trying to avoid scope creep, we invite scope creep into the project on our own terms.

Productive Scope Creep

Scope creep refers to the tendency of clients to think of requirements for a system after the initial requirements, or scope, of the project have been determined. It is a familiar situation for most developers. Requirements gathering is a difficult task, particularly if it's done without the benefit of some kind of modeling to help the client think about the proposed system. To combat scope creep, many software shops resort to strict forms of control and fees that discourage clients from "changing their minds" after development has begun.

The problem with this approach is that it ignores the fact that it's practically impossible to successfully discover all the requirements of a system up front. For lack of a better solution, however, treating scope creep as the enemy is the most prevalent means of dealing with it.

FLiP, on the other hand, encourages us to invite scope creep in at a point in the development process where dealing with it is comparatively inexpensive. That point is during the prototyping phase.

We create a prototype that we think will satisfy the client's requirements. When presented with the prototype, the client will do one of two things: either point out what's been left out or what isn't quite right; or accept the prototype as satisfactory. It's then our job to either incorporate the new requirements into the prototype or explore whether the client is approving the prototype too quickly.

Yes, that's right—even if the client agrees to the first prototype straight off, we want to help the client consider every aspect of it. Walk through it, follow each action the user can do, talk about what goes on behind the scenes. As experienced web developers, we should provide our expertise as a benefit to the client. Keep in mind that it is less expensive to make the changes to the prototype than it is to make changes to the application after development has begun.

Now that we know something about where we're trying to go with prototypes, we can look at the process that is involved in creating them.

Creating a Prototype

To create a prototype, we start with the wireframe. It becomes a sort of check-list for the features that need to be included in the prototype. Armed with this information and other design preferences from the client, our HTML designer sets out to model a site that will meet the wireframe's requirements and the client's preferences. The end result of the process is a clickable prototype.

Clickable Prototype

A clickable prototype is a "looks great, does nothing for real" model of the application. When we say "does nothing," though, we mean that it does nothing relative to the underlying application, data model, database, and so on. In fact, the prototype, as the phrase "clickable prototype" implies, does respond to mouse and keyboard events in just the same way you would expect to see the live application behave.

Few restrictions are imposed on the choice of tools for creating a prototype. There are as many design tools out there as there are designers—probably more. The most frequently used tool will be HTML because that's the means we generally use to present data on the screen.

Of course when creating an application with a Flash-based front end, you can certainly create your prototype using Flash if that works for you.

Also, although we're in the design phase, we are still able to use CFML within prototype screens to a certain extent. For example, we might use a CFLOOP to generate the appearance of a long list of data. We need to be somewhat careful, though, about how much ColdFusion we allow at this point. It is important to stay focused on the design aspects of the prototype and not get led into coding considerations. Beware, though, that CFML used in the prototype should be commented as prototype code; that way, it is not accidentally preserved in the final application. Listing 13.1 shows a piece of CFML in a prototype template that is commented in this fashion.

Listing 13.1   **CFML in Prototype Template**

```
<!--- Start prototype code block; remove in live app --->
<cfif url.role = 'Admin'>
  Welcome Admin User<br>
</cfif>
<!--- End prototype code block --->
```

Stan is fortunate in this sense; he can leave the design concerns to Brody, who doesn't know ColdFusion. This tends to lead to an application that is designed the way Janice wants, rather than in a manner that is pleasing to a programmer. Of course Stan remains available in his capacity as the application architect to help Brody deal with technical issues like when to use radio buttons instead of check boxes. The bottom line of prototyping is to listen carefully to the client and to interfere with the design only when something that seriously threatens the feasibility of the project is suggested.

Client Coordination

As Brody works his way through the creation of the prototype, he'll want to be in close communication with Janice and Stan. This is the only way he can hope to successfully create a prototype that will meet Janice's expectations while adhering to the technical parameters of the project. As the project's architect, Stan is kept in the loop as a matter of course.

Unfortunately, staying in close communication is somehow never as easy as it seems it should be. Even in the age of the Internet, scheduling time to talk with a client is one of those tasks that just doesn't seem to get easier. Compound that by the iterative changes that are necessary to design a successful prototype and you have a recipe for frustration. A strategy to assist the flow of information will ease the task greatly.

DevNotes

DevNotes is a ColdFusion-based system that is built on a Hal Helms idea and augmented by several members of the ColdFusion community. It is designed to leverage the Internet as a means to communicate with the client about prototypes and store comments in a meaningful way.

You can also use DevNotes to establish client interaction for just about any web-based topic you would like. For now, though, we'll limit the discussion to their use relative to prototypes. In this arena, DevNotes are used to create a sort of bulletin-board functionality on the prototype site, allowing everyone who is involved in the project to comment on the prototype as it develops.

DevNotes Explained

Wouldn't it be cool to have a place at the bottom of every page in the site (in our case, the prototype) that allows the client to enter comments? That's what DevNotes does. What's more, it keeps track of which comments belong to each URL in the site, who made the comment and when, and even allows replies to comments. It's a lot like having a little bulletin board system right at the bottom of every page.

Every web designer has had the experience of trying to pry out of a client his reactions to, or requirements for, a site under development. We've all received that email that lists a bunch of bullet points for items that "need to be fixed" on the site. The points may range from "Change the color of that button to cornflower blue" to "This whole navigation scheme stinks; put it in frames with a floating remote control window." Generally, each bullet contains a reference to a page. If we're lucky, it'll be the page URL. Most of the time, though, it's something less helpful like "on the second page after you log in."

Implementing DevNotes

Through its history, DevNotes has undergone several implementations. Originally, it was a simple custom tag that provided a list of notes and a new note entry box. Later versions from various authors saw the DevNotes concept expanded into complete development-tracking systems.

For our demonstrations, we'll use DevNotes from `GrokFusebox.com`, a marriage of the original custom tag concept and some of the more professional display characteristics of other versions. This version of DevNotes uses a pair of custom tags and the `<cfx_make_tree>` custom tag by Michael Dinowitz.

Setting up DevNotes on a site is a fairly simple process. Just unpack the files, set up an ODBC source, and register the `cfx_make_tree.cfm` custom tag. Then insert the `<cf_DevNotes>` tag in your prototype pages with an `OnRequestEnd.cfm` template. Using `OnRequestEnd.cfm` prevents the need to insert a custom tag call in every file in the prototype. As long as the prototype files are named with the `.cfm` extension, the custom tag call in `OnRequestEnd.cfm` will do the job for every page.

The following How To steps through setting up DevNotes.

How To: Install and Configure DevNotes

1. Unzip the tag files from the DevNotes archive file to the ColdFusion custom tags directory (see Figure 13.1).

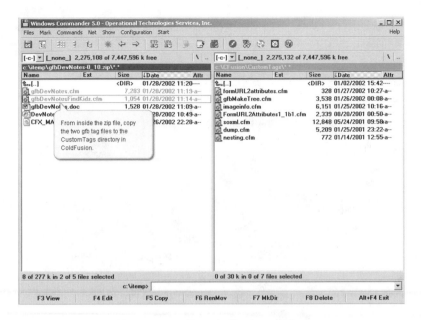

Figure 13.1   Step 1: Unzip tag files.

2. Unzip the database file to a directory of your choice (see Figure 13.2).

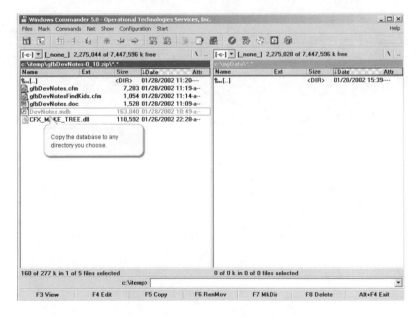

Figure 13.2   Step 2: Unzip the database file.

3. Unzip the `CFX_MAKE_TREE.CFM` from the MakeTree archive file to the ColdFusion custom tags directory (see Figure 13.3).

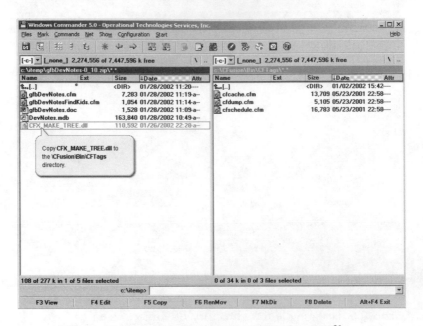

Figure 13.3 Step 3: Unzip `CFX_MAKE_TREE.CFM` file.

4. Register the `CFX_MAKE_TREE` tag. Note that the name you give the CFX tag is arbitrary; it must be `CFX_Make_Tree` for DevNotes to work properly (see Figure 13.4).

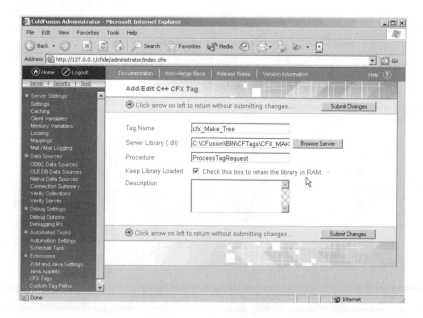

Figure 13.4 Step 4: Register CFX_MAKE_TREE.

5. Set up an ODBC datasource for the database that was unzipped in step 2 (see Figure 13.5).

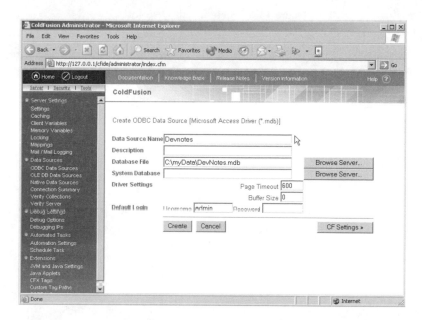

Figure 13.5 Step 5: Set up ODBC DSN.

6. Create `OnRequestEnd.cfm` and put a call to `<cf_DevNotes>` in it. If
    `Application.cfm` doesn't exist in the prototype directory, make an
    `Application.cfm` file that contains only a comment. `Application.cfm`
    causes ColdFusion to use `OnRequestEnd.cfm` (see Figure 13.6).

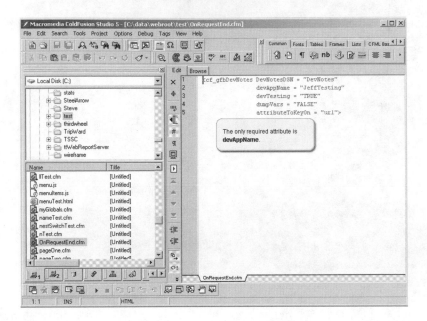

Figure 13.6   Step 6: Call DevNotes.

7. We're now ready to comment on the prototype. The DevNotes interface
    appears at the bottom of every prototype page (see Figure 13.7).

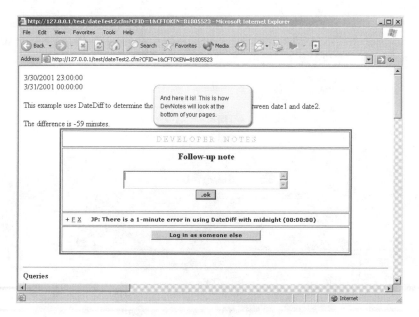

Figure 13.7   DevNotes in action.

DevNotes provides a way to communicate easily with a client about the appearance of the prototype. The ability to enter a follow-up note permits threaded comments, which are displayed in hierarchical format. The notes are stored in a database that can be used to generate reports about the notes that were collected during the prototyping phase.

Using DevNotes

After you've installed DevNotes, you can jump right into reviewing the prototype and leaving comments on its pages. To get some practice using DevNotes, we suggest placing an `OnRequestEnd.cfm` file with a DevNotes tag in a directory that you use for test files. This will present the DevNotes interface at the bottom of every ColdFusion page that you run from that directory. Besides providing practice with using DevNotes, this technique also builds a nice database of test notes for you while you experiment with ColdFusion. Remember this important safety tip: If the directory where you're using `OnRequestEnd.cfm` doesn't have an `Application.cfm` file, create one that only contains a comment. If `Application.cfm` doesn't exist, ColdFusion won't run `OnRequestEnd.cfm`.

The first time that DevNotes is run in a session, the form in Figure 13.8 appears. It allows the user to enter his initials or some other string to identify his notes, and a note.

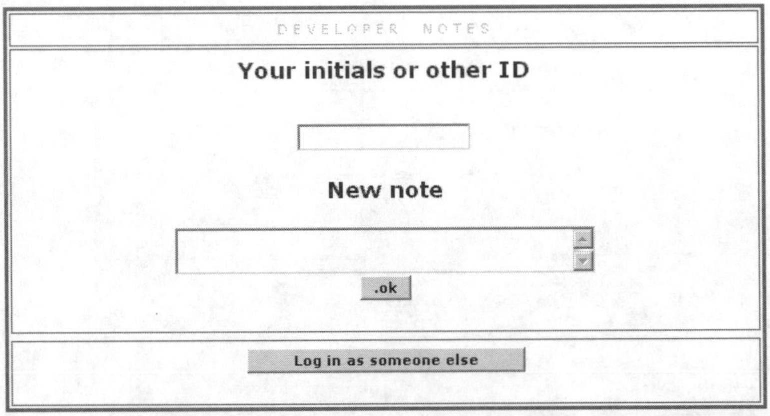

Figure 13.8   First DevNotes form.

After a note has been entered, the form in Figure 13.9 appears. The text box for initials or another ID has disappeared now that the user has been identified.

Figure 13.9   In-session DevNotes form.

The note appears, preceded by two letters (F and X) and the user's ID. The two letters are command links. Clicking on the F (follow-up) link takes the user to the form in Figure 13.10. Clicking on the X (delete) link deletes the note and all its descendants.

Figure 13.10   DevNotes follow-up form.

When a follow-up note is entered, it appears in a hierarchical manner beneath its parent, as shown in Figure 13.11. Follow-ups can be added as far as desired in the manner of a threaded conversation.

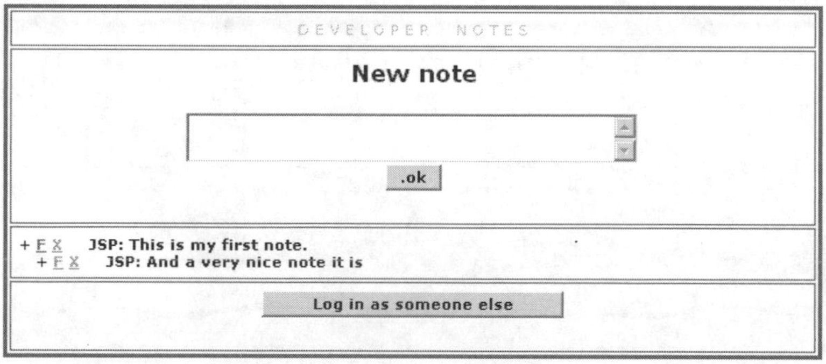

Figure 13.11   DevNotes with follow-up.

The follow-up in Figure 13.11 might not make much sense because it was posted by the same person who posted the original note. You can easily change the identity of the user by clicking the Log In As Someone Else button, which calls up the original form shown in Figure 13.8. If the user wants to change the current ID and then enter a follow-up, the procedure is simple:

1. Click Log In As Someone Else.
2. Enter a new set of initials; leave the Note field blank.
3. Click OK.
4. Click on the follow-up link (F) for the desired note.
5. Enter a comment.
6. Click OK.

We're now thoroughly familiar with DevNotes and keeping track of our prototyping efforts. Let's get back to the development project at Third Wheel Bikes and see how things are going.

DevNotes for Third Wheel Bikes

Stan and Brody have decided to make use of DevNotes for the Third Wheel Bikes job. After Brody has created an initial design for the site prototype (remembering to use .cfm file extensions for DevNotes' benefit), Stan posts the site on a web server where Janice can view the design. Janice agrees to review the design over the course of the next couple of days, as her schedule permits. Her first comments on the home page of the project are shown in Figure 13.12.

Figure 13.12   DevNotes on Third Wheel Bikes prototype.

Being the responsive team that they are, Stan and Brody are quick to provide answers to Janice's comments and alterations to the prototype. Figure 13.13 shows the threads that have been created over the home page.

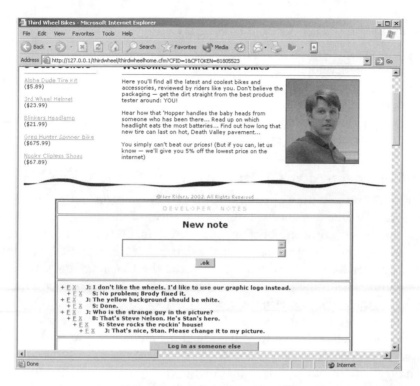

Figure 13.13   DevNotes threads.

Notice that when Stan and Brody make a change to the prototype in response to Janice's comments, they don't delete her comments. Adding a follow-up acknowledging the change means that Stan and Brody have a record in their DevNotes database of the request from Janice and their response to it. Depending on the client, you might get to the point on a page in which there are so many notes that it gets tough to view through them all. When this happens, you might want to delete some of the less important threads. Prior to doing so, we suggest you back up the DevNotes database. This will give you a record of the threads and allow you to clean up the page as well.

Taking advantage of tools like DevNotes allows us to create methods for avoiding problems that the Comment-Alter Cycle causes.

Prototype and Get It Right

The prototype portion of the application design phase is one of the most critical parts of the development life cycle. This is the opportunity to fine-tune the information that is collected during the wireframing and sharply hone the client's understanding of his proposed application. In reality, we're inviting scope creep in the front door and making it happen when we want it to happen, instead of later in the project when it would be much more expensive.

The Comment-Alter Cycle: Befriending Scope Creep

For most clients and most applications, the prototype turns out to be a revealing operation. Often, clients will discover nuances of the proposed system that they hadn't really considered before. The more information that Stan and Brody can help uncover at this phase, the better. For this reason, the prototype phase is an iterative process, using what we call the *Comment-Alter cycle*; the client comments on the current state of the work, and the designer responds by altering the work to satisfy the comments. Just as we often use the term front end to refer to a prototype, we use the term Comment-Alter cycle because it is less threatening to a client than the anxiety-producing term scope creep.

The real hazard of the Comment-Alter cycle comes if it is allowed to occur during coding instead of during design. This is classic scope creep. If it happens, the project can get stuck in the cycle on a permanent basis. In fact, this is where many projects that don't use a solid design methodology remain throughout their life spans. If coding starts before the design is locked down, the effort can easily wind up in a perpetual scope creep, never able to satisfy the requirements. Some developers see this as job security (assuming the client is willing to pay the never-ending bills), but more often it's a fast track to insanity.

Fortunately, because we're dealing with a prototype during the Comment-Alter cycle, responding to comments is a trivial matter and we can make real design progress instead of constantly worrying about the operational impact of proposed alterations and getting mired in classic scope creep. This does not mean, though, that the cycle is without hazards.

Prototype Freeze and Signoff

One major pitfall is inherent to the Comment-Alter cycle. That pitfall is the simple fact that it is a cycle. Unless you can stop the cycle that is built into the process, you'll keep going in circles. We call the brake on the Comment-Alter cycle *prototype freeze*. At every iteration of the cycle, you check with the client to see if the resulting alterations satisfy all his requirements. If so, you've arrived at prototype freeze, and the Comment-Alter cycle is ended.

All this sounds great so far, but beware. Sometimes a client will be willing to sign off on the first prototype that is put in front of them. This is a dangerous proposition because it's a pretty fair indicator that they haven't really considered the prototype in depth. This is particularly true of clients who are not familiar with network-based technologies and who are depending on the architect for expertise. At this point, it's up to the architect to help explore the prototype in detail and make sure the client doesn't want to make changes. Prototype freeze should be a mutual agreement; both the developer and the client must feel that the prototype represents an application that will satisfy the client's needs and can be successfully built.

There are two vital aspects of coordinating prototype freeze. First, there must be some way to indicate in no uncertain terms that comments on the prototype will no longer be accepted. Removing DevNotes from the prototype is an excellent way to do this; if the client is unable to enter comments, it's fairly clear that something momentous has occurred.

Second, there must be a way to record the client's agreement that prototype freeze has been reached and that you will be developing the application based on the state of the prototype at that time. We call this *signoff*. Probably the best way to record signoff is to print a hard copy of the prototype, including each page in the application. Include these hard copies in a signoff package and present it to the client for signature. The client should sign or initial every page of the hard copy prototype. In case of future disputes over what was to be developed, you can refer back to the prototype signoff document as the authoritative source.

The prototype signoff document should also include a checklist of backend functions that the system is to perform. These are not immediately apparent on the prototype because they don't involve user interaction. For example, a background process might exist that looks up a user in the company's LDAP directory or verifies a credit card through an external verification service. One of the most overlooked of these types of processes is the administration aspect of the application. Most applications need a way to manage users, modify settings, and so on; these functions are often overlooked. It is important to note and get agreement on these "invisible" processes at the same time we get agreement on the visible prototype.

Prototype Considerations

Whereas the wireframing phase was concerned with the business processes that are involved in the application, the prototype phase is concerned with design and delivery. These areas are more closely linked to the application that will actually be delivered because the decisions made around them will directly impact the design of the code model.

In an ideal world, every development team would have someone like Brody available to handle the design aspects of prototyping. It is practically impossible to overestimate the value of a trained graphic designer.

Unfortunately, only a small percentage of development shops are large enough to keep a designer on staff full-time. For the rest of us, design can be a difficult matter. Although we're by no means design professionals, the next few sections suggest some areas to discuss with your client while you're working out the design aspects of the application.

Design Elements

Before we mention too much on the subject of design, understand that this is not a book about designing web sites, nor are we professional designers. However, it is important that everyone who intends to manage the development of a web site or application have some basic understanding of the areas to consider when designing a site.

The next few subsections touch on three of the aesthetic areas to consider when designing a site—form, color, and impact. We intend them to be jumping-off points for further investigation into design issues.

Form

Mention the word "form" to a web developer, and the immediate concept that comes to mind is an HTML form for collecting user input.

When it comes to design, though, *form* refers to where things are going to be on the screen. This is one of the most important aspects of design, and one that is often overlooked. It's a good idea to pay careful attention to sites you like as a learning tool. Take notes about where navigational controls are located, the relative importance of items placed in various locations around the screen, and so on. The more you expose yourself to a wide variety of designs, the more you'll begin to recognize the good, the bad, and the absolutely nonfunctional.

When discussing form with the client, ask about what sorts of controls are desired, where to place them, and so on. The client might have a well-formed idea of what he wants or no idea at all. In either case, our job is to listen and help build a model of something the client likes.

Sometimes, the desired result will be a site that is "just like the one XYZ Corporation built." Starting points like this are helpful for understanding the client's wishes, but care must be taken to avoid copyright issues. Besides, who wants to be known for a site that's an obvious rip-off of someone else's work?

Color

Color is another important area to discuss with the client. A defined color style guide for corporate publications might already be established. If so, this guide can be extremely useful in making color decisions early in the prototyping process.

If the client is ambivalent about color, you'll probably have to resort to creating sample pages in a variety of color palettes and allowing the client to respond to each of them. This is where the talents of a good designer can be extremely helpful. Put together the various pages and include them in your prototyping efforts, including DevNotes on them (assuming you're using DevNotes). The use of style sheets can make altering color palettes a much easier task.

In the absence of a good designer, take to the Net or visit your local library. Hundreds of sites and books on graphic design are available.

Form and color contribute to the overall characteristic of a site that we think of as impact. Every site has its own impact; some are stronger than others. If we mention eBay, nearly everyone will have in immediate reaction based on the impact of that site on him.

Impact

Impact is the purely emotional reaction that a user has when visiting a site, especially for the first time. Just as the old bit of advice says that first impressions are most important, so it goes with web sites.

Impact depends on a wide variety of factors, ranging from form and color to download time. All these factors contribute to the "gut reaction" that a user experiences.

One of the most effective ways to get in touch with the concept of impact is to keep notes while surfing the Net. First, just make notes about the first reaction you have to new sites as you visit them. Later, go back and examine the site more carefully. Try to analyze what it is about the site that caused you to react the way you did.

Impact can also be a good starting point when exploring design with a client. Full color printouts of a variety of sites (or screen shots if you have a projector handy) make good jumping-off points for discussing form, color, and other design issues.

Although graphic design issues comprise the most-stressed aspect of prototyping, we should not overlook delivery during this phase.

Delivery Considerations

Delivery is everything that contributes to the mechanism by which the application will be delivered to the user. In most cases, this refers to HTML-based pages that are delivered to a standard browser. In some cases, delivery is through a Flash-based interface, also delivered through a standard browser. In addition, delivery includes factors such as browser software and version, audience limitations, and targeted platforms.

It is easy to overlook these factors while prototyping. We'll explore each of them at a surface level just to offer some things to think about when discussing the front end with our clients.

Multiple Platforms

An increasing number of sites are being developed for delivery to non-standard platforms. Cell phones and PDAs offer an entirely new (and quite large) market for web development, and Fusebox is certainly a great way to address either of them. Of course the most common variation in platform is the need to deliver an application that is compatible with Microsoft Internet Explorer and Netscape Navigator. We should ask the client what browser(s) she wants targeted and discuss the cost impact of developing for multiple browser compliance.

When designing in the prototype phase, if there is an expressed desire to deliver to multiple platforms, a prototype should be developed for each platform. If Pocket PCs are being targeted, then screen designs should take its tall-and-narrow form factor into consideration. If the application is to be accessed through cell phones, a prototype of the Wireless Markup Language (WML) version should be created. See www.wapforum.org for more information on the Wireless Access Protocol (WAP) and WML.

Wherever possible, the basis for these alternate representations should be the same as that of the browser-based model. Technologies such as XML and XSL can go a long way toward making these sorts of multiplatform solutions possible. Visit www.xml.org for more information on these subjects.

Asking a handful of well-placed questions regarding delivery of the application will prevent major headaches at the end of the project when the client says, "This is great! Now all we need is to send it to our cell phones."

All of these areas of consideration go into making the prototype phase work for us. We'll say it again: Scope creep in this phase is cheap, and we want and encourage it to happen here. The goal is to put together a complete prototype that addresses all the client's needs and points the way to a successful application.

ADA and Section 508

The Americans with Disabilities Act (ADA) has focused a great deal of attention on giving due consideration in the workplace to people who have disabilities. It has resulted in workplace alterations in a wide variety of areas, from physical access to ergonomics. Section 508 is a piece of federal legislation that has focused similar attention on electronic systems in general, and web sites in particular. It sets requirements for federal systems, but it also offers some insight into areas of consideration for all web developers.

Section 508 is formally known as Section 508 of the Workforce Investment Act of 1998. It requires that federal employees and public users of federal information systems "have access to and use of information and data that is comparable to the access to and use of the information and data by [others] who are not individuals with disabilities." [Section 508, sections (a)(1)(A)(i) and (ii)]

This broad definition is currently being interpreted to mean that developers of information systems on behalf of the U.S. government must exercise due diligence in making their systems accessible to users who have disabilities. Some of the points of consideration include these:

- Using `alt` attributes on `img` tags to support screen readers
- Avoiding use of color as a carrier of information (for example, color-coding priorities without providing a textual version of the same information)
- Providing a text-only version of information for access by screen readers

Section 508 only applies for government clients, but its intent should be taken into consideration when developing any application. As with every other aspect of design, the audience should be the primary consideration in designing an effective interface.

As of the writing of this book, no legal cases have been decided over Section 508; therefore, compliance is still a fairly nebulous question. More information can be found at www.section508.gov.

Platform is another important aspect of audience characteristics. *Platform* is the actual hardware and software combination that the application's audience will use to view it.

Put It All Together

It is impossible to overstress the importance of the prototyping step of the FLiP methodology. This is where it gets down to brass tacks as far as design is concerned. The more time you spend on this step, getting inside the client's head, the better chance that you will produce a successful application.

Even though the prototype development phase might seem like endless circles at the beginning, it is far better to work through numerous iterations of the system design while prototyping than to get stuck in classic scope creep during code development.

For the die-hard code jockeys, the next step in FLiP will be the most fun. We finally get to start coding. Every programmer has his own collection of best-loved tools and methods, but we'll make some suggestions in the next chapter that might change the way you think about "banging out code." FLiP gives us great control over every other aspect of the development lifecycle, and coding is no different.

"He who loves practice without theory is like the sailor who boards ship without a rudder and compass and never knows where he may cast."

—Leonardo da Vinci

14

Construction and Coding

PROTOTYPE FREEZE IS OUR FAVORITE PART of any project. Only then do we actually know what we are building. Only then do we become technical and start thinking about arrays and schemas and architecture and variables. Hey! We get to start talking about arrays and schemas and architecture and variables! Yippee!

If you feel like we do, coding can be fun. Indeed, we think of it as the time when we are most productive. You sit in your comfy chair, turn the tunes up really loud, and code for hours on end. Getting hungry? Take a break—you have something to show for it. Another form now works or a circuit is completed.

But wait! It gets even better! After prototype freeze, your communication with that pesky client slows down. Of course, your business sense might insist that you maintain an open dialogue about the current project status, but we have been in situations where our clients had enough faith in us to say, "See you in a couple weeks." And we had enough faith in the process to believe that we could sequester ourselves in the coffee shop, far away from phones, email, and instant messengers, and come out with something to show for it.

Because our prototype for Third Wheel Bikes is absolutely complete, Janice knows what she is getting (a working version of the car-with-no-engine prototype). (For a proper introduction to Janice and her counterparts, see this book's Introduction.) We know what we are delivering. Changes that the client needs can be included now, but at a much higher cost, usually involving a *change order*. This means the change request is clearly defined with a written estimate to cover the additional development costs. Usually, change orders are done after the initial program has been developed.

Now that we have a fake version of the application completed, where do we start? We have a lot of HTML pages. Should we open up an HTML page in ColdFusion Studio and start recoding it with CFML? No, the Fusebox Lifecycle Process (FLiP) has an easier way to segue from prototyping to coding.

This chapter will cover the steps to creating a Fusebox application. You should already be familiar with the way the framework operates from Part 2, "Fusebox Coding." In this chapter, we get to put all that code to work, creating a finished application.

There are six steps to follow, in this order:

1. Identify each prototype page's exit points and take notes about the interaction between the pages.

2. Assemble the pages into logical collections of functionality.

3. Mind Map the application, identifying circuits, fuseactions, and fuses.

4. Run Fuseminder2 to create the skeleton.

5. Create the fusestubs.

6. Code the fuses.

We will discuss each step and work on Third Wheel Bikes together, but for brevity, we will not code the entire application in this chapter. We call this the "cooking show" style. Together, we will start each step of the process, and you can pull the completed masterpiece "out of the oven," so to speak, by downloading the files from http://www.thirdwheelbikes.com. This will provide a good blend of hands-on work without being unnecessarily exhaustive.

Identifying Exit Points

Exit points are the places where a user can "escape" from a page. Take the page in Figure 14.1, for example.

The roughly circled sections in Figure 14.1 were done on top of the prototype page. The top menu has six exits to other parts of the site, the search box has a Submit button, the logo on the left is clickable to send the user home, the left side has links to popular helmets, and the body of the page has links to buy this item, read reviews, and write a new review. One link that should be an exit is the email link `john@doe.com`. This link does not go back to our application—it goes to an external system, which in most cases, is the user's default email client. That means that we can circle it now to be complete, but we will not end up doing any more work on it.

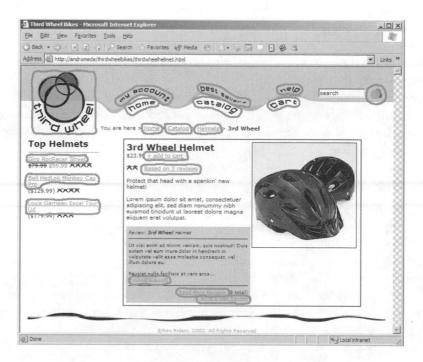

Figure 14.1   Exit points.

We print the prototype pages (in color if we can afford it) and go through each one by hand, circling all the exit points with a fat red magic marker. This helps us begin to visualize all the different tasks that our application needs to accomplish. It might seem strange to print them, but you will find it helpful to have paper copies of your prototype. Some of us are lucky enough to have dual monitors, but nothing beats paper for instantaneous marking and note taking. Because the prototype is frozen, no changes will be made to the layout and page content, so we will not be continually printing updated copies of the pages at this point.

Follow along with us, if you like. The complete prototype is available from http://www.thirdwheelbikes.com. Use crayons or a pencil—anything to identify each exit on each page. Don't have access to a printer? Do too many pages in your prototype make managing all the paper difficult? One great trick is to use dry erase markers on your screen. Don't worry—it will not hurt the monitor. (Despite the fact that it always comes off for us, we are not responsible for any damage resulting from this advice; please don't try this if you have a flat panel display.) Go to each page in your application and, using a dry-erase marker, circle the exit points on your monitor. Then, write down each exit point, grouped by page.

The result is the same: written documentation of more than half of all fuseactions in your application. Imagine that—no coding (heck, hardly even any thinking), and you have already identified most of the actions that your application can perform.

Variables on Exit

In addition to circling every exit point, we also jot down notes about some of them. Flip back to that screen shot and notice the left-hand Top Helmets section.

You see three links, but each one does basically the same thing. In fact, our prototype does not differentiate at all. Each link in our prototype goes to the static HTML page thirdwheelhelmet.html. But in the finished application, what will make these links go to different places? Some kind of variable, right? Beside each link, we scribble this:

```
?productID=xxx
```

This alerts us that a variable is passed here (the product ID of each of the top three products). It also furthers the complete (maybe subconscious) picture of the application we are cultivating.

Not all exits warrant a note scribbled beside them. Look at the navigation menu on the top. It goes to the major sections of the site. There is nothing unique about those links—they are the same on every page, for every user.

Here is another prototype page (see Figure 14.2). Find all the exit points and circle them.

You should have found 15 exit points. Eight are on the top section, similar to the previous example. One is in the breadcrumb trail by clicking Home. The final six are in the body of the page—the date link goes to the review and the product link goes to the product for each of the three rows. Now what about some notes scribbled for some of the links? Each review link might need a variable like this:

```
?reviewID=xxx
```

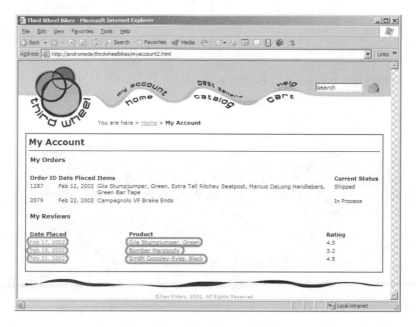

Figure 14.2   Find the exit points.

Each product link might need a variable like this:

```
?productID=xxx
```

It is important to understand that we are not holding ourselves to decisions about variable naming or data schemas now. We are just brainstorming. The initial stages of architecting are the first times that we look at the application with our coder hats on, so we are bound to make a few mistakes along the way. Because we are not committed to any code now, we can brainstorm all we want.

Other Variables

So far, we have focused on variables accompanying XFAs. However, a page often references many more variables. Circling XFAs in one color and making notes of incoming variables in another color helps identify even more functionality. We know that `productID` is attached to XFAs, but where does it come from? Make a note that this page needs to get a list of products somewhere. That will help you identify hidden fuses that don't appear in the prototype, such as query and action fuse types. Other variables could include `reviewDate` and `productName`.

Although circling the XFAs is an excellent way to define the exit points, circling the variables is an excellent way to begin to define the Fusedocs.

Grouping Fuseactions

Take a look at Figures 14.3 and 14.4. See if you notice a similar theme in the functionality of these pages.

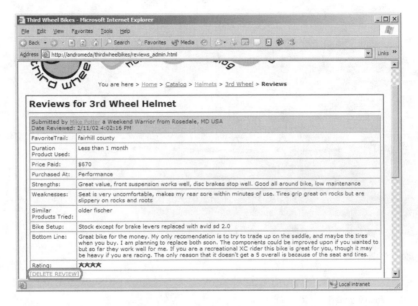

Figure 14.3   Product review listing.

We might call the fuseaction in the page shown in Figure 14.3 showReviews, but it has a link at the bottom: [DELETE REVIEW]. This link goes to another fuseaction. That one might be called deleteReview. That makes two fuseactions that we have found on one page. deleteReview is a secured fuseaction—only admins can use it. Make a note of that on the page.

The second page (shown in Figure 14.4) also gives clues about two fuseactions. The fuseaction to display this page might be called reviewForm. But the Submit button (just off the screen) at the bottom goes somewhere, too—it doesn't just drop the user off of a cliff. That button should take the contents of the form and store it for future use. Maybe it is in a database; maybe it is in a WDDX-encoded flat file. Maybe it is a web services post to a remote server. We are not thinking about how it does the job right now. We are just thinking about the name of that fuseaction. Let's think of it as addReview for now.

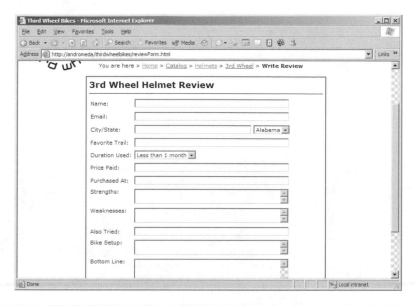

Figure 14.4 Product review entry form.

We have taken care of two screens (out of about 30 screens in the prototype), and we have identified four fuseactions that seem similar. They all deal with product reviews, and one is secured only to admins. No more pages deal with reviews. An undiscovered fuseaction might be needed to do some behind-the-scenes work, but for now, remember those four fuseactions. They are closely tied to each other.

Another Kind of Group: Wizards

For the most part, Third Wheel Bikes is free of multistep wizards. The one exception is the checkout process. Let's take a look at the three pages that a customer sees during a checkout. The first page appears after a user begins the checkout from his Cart page, shown in Figure 14.5.

After clicking the Review Your Order button, a confirmation page appears, as shown in Figure 14.6.

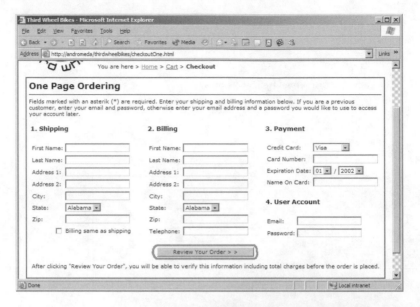

Figure 14.5   Order details.

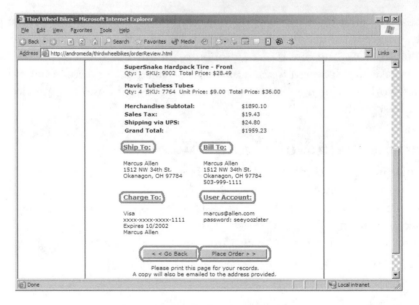

Figure 14.6   Order confirmation.

Figure 14.6 shows a page where the customer is ready to place the order and clicks the Place Order button. The order is placed and the Thank You page appears, as shown in Figure 14.7

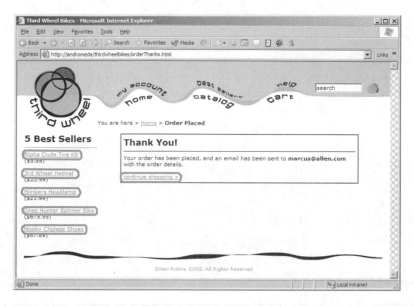

Figure 14.7   Thank you page.

These pages shown in Figures 14.5, 14.6, and 14.7 might be considered a "wizard." There are forward and backward buttons, each page assumes that the previous page has been already executed in sequence, and the final result creates the order with data collected from the other pages. Let's think about the fuseactions for these pages.

The fuseaction that displays the first page (`checkoutOne.html`) might be called `checkoutOne`. This page links to `orderReview.html`. Should some behind-the-scenes processing be taking place? Probably so. We need some way to capture the values entered in the previous form. Make a note of that on the printed page for this form by circling the Submit button and jotting down something along the lines of "store user input values."

Now the second page is displayed. We need a fuseaction for that, too. We could just tack it on the end of the previous fuseaction that we made a note about—the one that stored the form fields. We will tell you from experience, though, that that would not be a good idea. Therefore, a new fuseaction will probably be used. Let's call it `checkoutTwo`.

The bottom of this page has two buttons: Go Back and Place Order. The Go Back button goes to a previous fuseaction that we already discovered and documented: `checkoutOne`. The Place Order button goes to a new fuseaction, and the next page thanks the user for ordering. It would be wise to separate the display of the thank you page from the code that actually places the order. One fuseaction runs code to validate the prices of the items, store the order in the database, and send emails to the customer and the store administrator. The other fuseaction just displays a page. Because the purpose of those two fuseactions is so fundamentally different, they deserve to be split.

We will call the fuseaction that places the order `placeOrder` and the fuseaction that displays the thank you page `checkoutFinal`.

Keep an eye out for this kind of multistep process while circling and noting exit points in the prototype. It is a good sign that those fuseactions should be collected into one circuit.

Identifying Circuits

So far, we have covered seven pages and found a lot of fuseactions. Some fuseactions seem to be naturally similar, such as the checkout process and the reviews pages. Those collections of fuseactions are ideal candidates for becoming circuits.

By grouping fuseactions into circuits, we can concentrate code in one location. For example, the checkout process should not occur unless the shopper's basket has five items. In addition, certain sections of the site are only accessible to administrators.

Let's take a look at four more pages (Figures 14.8–14.11) to identify the fuseactions and group them into circuits. Note that we did not circle the menu links at the top (including My Account, Home, Best Sellers, and so on). It is easy to see that these are part of the global layout, which is not part of each page.

Figure 14.8 shows a Browse page, where the user can see all the different product categories.

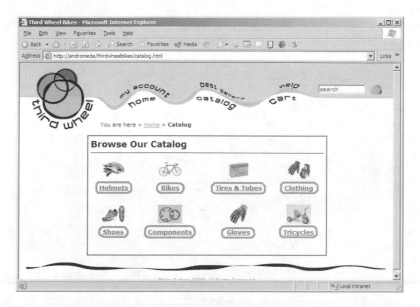

Figure 14.8   All categories list.

After drilling down, Figure 14.9 shows the products for one category.

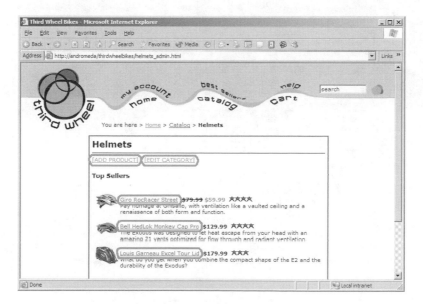

Figure 14.9   One category list.

Figure 14.10 is a screen that is available only to admins. It allows the admin to edit details about a category.

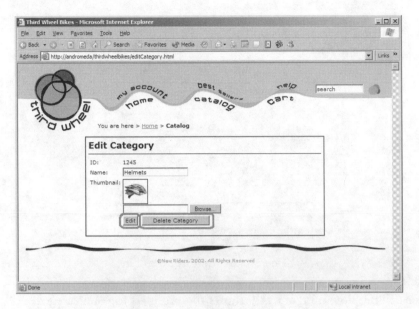

Figure 14.10   Edit a category.

Figure 14.11 shows a page where admins can create new categories.

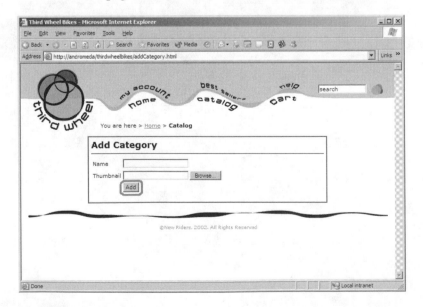

Figure 14.11   Add a category.

Having circled the exit points for each of those pages, we see a trend: They all deal with the catalog. Some of them are admin-only access (add and edit category), whereas the others are available to all users. When grouping fuseactions together, we group by functionality, not by user role. That means that we do not create a separate circuit for the admin fuseactions for product reviews, apart from the general review fuseactions. This is because there might be overlap with users.

The first page is reached by clicking the catalog link on the top navigation. The grouping is more than just in the display. Categories need to be created via the Add page (Figure 14.11) before they can be edited (Figure 14.10). All categories show up in the category list (Figure 14.8), and each category can be viewed individually (along with the products in that category (Figure 14.8). All these pages (`listCategories`, `oneCategory`, `addCategory` (admin), `editCategory` (admin)) and all the hidden fuseactions on these pages (`updateCategory` (admin), `deleteCategory` (admin), `insertCategory` (admin)) combine to make up the `catalog` circuit.

Feel free to work your way through each prototype page, circling the exit points and making notes about fuseactions and circuit grouping. For right now, we are done. The rest of the prototype is available from `http://www.thirdwheelbikes.com`. Let's move on from the paperwork and into our first real coding exercise.

Mind Mapping/Fuseminder

Okay, so we lied a little. Mind Mapping is not coding. In fact, the creator of Mind Mapping would probably say it is far from coding. You are not confined to a rigid, awkward syntax in Mind Mapping. Developed in the late 1960s by Tony Buzan, millions of people around the world use Mind Mapping for a multitude of purposes. Fusebox developers use it to create the skeleton of the entire application. Similar to a road map, a Mind Map provides an overview of the entire application, enables us to visualize connections between different points, contains a massive amount of data in a portable format, and is extremely fast to develop by using one of the Mind Mapping software tools on the market today.

> **Note**
> Mind Map and Mind Mapping are registered trademarks of Tony Buzan and the Buzan Organization. More information on Mind Mapping can be found at `http://www.mind-map.com`.

For the purposes of this book, we are going to use MindMapper 3.0 Professional by SimTech Systems. A demo copy of this product is available from `http://www.thirdwheelbikes.com` and can also be downloaded directly from `http://www.MindMapper.com`.

Other Mind Map tools are available. A Google search for "mind map" returns millions of hits (like most searches), but the top results should be other tools, including Visual Mind (`http://www.visual-mind.com`) and MindJet (`http://www.mindjet.com`). The benefit that MindMapper 3.0 has over the other tools is that it outputs the Mind Map in a plain text format that Fuseminder can read.

Introduction to Fuseminder

Fuseminder is a custom tag-based tool, written in ColdFusion and originally created by Jeff Peters. We have combined our efforts to release Fuseminder2, compatible with Fusebox version 3. This custom tag reads a Mind Map text outline and converts all the data into a basic Fusebox structure. Much Fusebox code consists of the `<cfswitch>`/`<cfcase>` tags in the `fbx_switch.cfm` files, along with a many `<cfinclude>` tags for each fuse. Instead of writing all that code by hand, we use MindMapper to create the outline and then let Fuseminder create the start of our application for us. We will cover Fuseminder after we make the Mind Map of our site, coming up next.

Starting a Mind Map

Open MindMapper and begin a new Mind Map. By highlighting and pressing Enter on any node, you can change the title. Change the title in the center to `ThirdWheelBikes`. Your Mind Map should now look like the one in Figure 14.12, with a simple title in the center.

`ThirdWheelBikes` becomes the container for all the circuits in our application. Now we need to identify every circuit by adding it as a branch on the Mind Map. With the center node highlighted, type **cReviews**. MindMapper senses the keystrokes and automatically creates a new branch. The "c" denotes that this node is a circuit, and any branches underneath it will be either other circuits or fuseactions.

Continue adding all the other circuits we have identified until your Mind Map looks like the one pictured in Figure 14.13.

Figure 14.12   Start of the Mind Map.

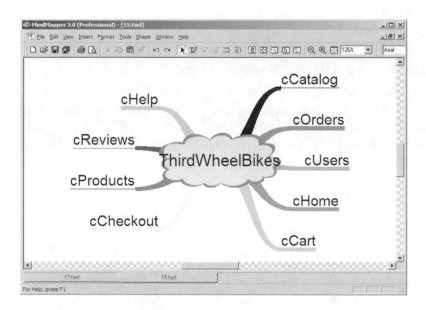

Figure 14.13   All the circuits completed.

Your Mind Map might have the circuits rearranged on the screen or have different color branches. What's important is that all the circuits are on the same level, one beneath the root node, and that each circuit node is prefixed with a "c." How did we decide to use those specific circuits?

Although FLiP provides solid guidelines to increase the likelihood of project success, and although Fusebox also provides a framework to ease the complexity of applications, one thing Fusebox does not do is make your applications for you.

Knowing when to split one circuit into two circuits or when to nest one circuit inside another are skills that you will acquire as you gain experience. Have you been lucky enough (or cursed enough) to be able to review the first application you ever created? "What the heck was I thinking?" you probably said. We all have those reactions to projects we have completed. Often, while we're halfway through a project, we strike upon a better way to organize it all. Most of the time, it is too late to incorporate those changes. No matter how much preplanning you do, it is bound to happen that way eventually.

Don't let those situations cause you grief. Learn from those revelations and use them to improve your future architectures.

For now, just trust us. We know that this architecture is a good one. It will serve our purposes well.

Analyzing Fuseaction Steps

We already identified the fuseactions in the reviews circuit by circling exit points and jotting down fuseaction names on paper. Let's add those to the Mind Map. Highlight the cReviews node and start typing the name of the first fuseaction fAddReview. A new branch and node are quickly added beneath the circuit. Add the rest of the fuseactions in the reviews circuit until your Mind Map looks like Figure 14.14.

We added a small lock from the legends toolbar (View, Toolbar, Legend) to denote that we have one admin-only fuseaction. This is nothing more than a visual clue.

How did we know which fuseactions we needed in the reviews circuit? How are we confident that a fuseaction does a well-defined job?

One tactic we like to employ is to name the fuseactions well. Each reviews fuseaction accomplishes a single task and is named for that task. We do not have a fuseaction called reviewsAction. That would be awfully ambiguous. What exactly is it that the reviewsAction fuseaction does? Does it process a form somehow? By reading the names of each fuseaction, we can begin to construct in our heads what fuses are needed to create a fuseaction. We will talk more about fuses in a second.

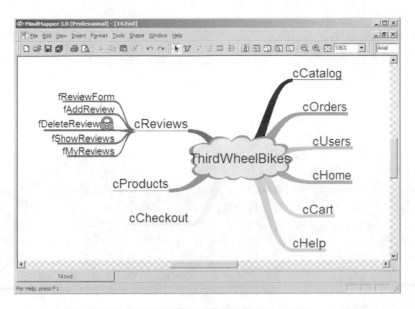

Figure 14.14   Adding fuseactions to a circuit.

In our application, we have one wizard: the checkout process. The three steps contain a total of five fuseactions: three display fuseactions and two behind-the-scenes fuseactions. The fuseactions have to occur in order, though. How do we ensure the correct sequence?

One good tactic when organizing wizards is to set them in their own circuit. You should not group other fuseactions with wizard fuseactions. By doing this, we can write code that requires any access to a fuseaction in this circuit to go through the first step: `checkoutOne`. Placing this code in the `fbx_settings.cfm` for this circuit will manage directional access to fuseactions in a wizard:

```
1 <cfset variables.checkoutWizard="start,checkoutOne,checkoutTwo,
  ➥checkoutThree,checkoutFour,checkoutFinal">
2 <cfparam name="client.checkoutWizard"
  ➥default="#ListGetAt(variables.checkoutWizard,2)#">
3 <cfset currentPosition=ListFind(variables.checkoutWizard,
  ➥client.checkoutWizard)>
4 <cfif ListGetAt(variables.checkoutWizard,currentPosition+1)
  ➥neq fusebox.fuseaction AND
5   ListGetAt(variables.checkoutWizard,currentPosition-1)
    ➥neq fusebox.fuseaction AND
6   ListGetAt(variables.checkoutWizard,currentPosition)
    ➥neq fusebox.fuseaction>
7 <cfset client.checkoutWizard=ListGetAt(variables.checkoutWizard,2)>
```

continues

```
8   <cflocation url="#request.self#?fuseaction=checkout.checkoutOne"
    ➥addtoken="Yes">
9 <cfelse>
10   <cfset client.checkoutWizard=fusebox.fuseaction>
11 </cfif>
```

The first line establishes the fuseaction order of the wizard. Any fuseaction can reference this list to determine its own position relative to the other steps. We can also easily create the Forward/Backward buttons based on this list. If a new step needs to be added, a minimum of code has to change to accommodate it.

Line 2 defaults the initial starting position of the wizard. Notice that we do not start at the first position. That step is not a real fuseaction. It exists only to "prime" the wizard process for the real first step: checkoutOne.

Line 3 determines the last fuseaction to run in the wizard, which should be the previous fuseaction in the list from the current request. If the user requests checkoutThree, she has already completed checkoutTwo. The value of client.checkoutWizard is checkoutTwo when checkoutThree has been requested. Consequently, the first time into the checkout process, client.checkoutWizard is start, so currentPosition is 1.

Lines 4, 5 and 6 determine whether the requested fuseaction is one forward, one backward, or is the last requested fuseaction. Users can go forward or backward one fuseaction at a time in the variables.checkoutWizard list. Users can also rerequest the same fuseaction if they reload the page.

If the user is requesting a fuseaction out of the order of the wizard, her client.checkoutWizard value is set to the first fuseaction in the wizard (which is actually the second element in the list), and she is redirected to that fuseaction.

If the user is requesting a valid fuseaction in the sequence, then client.checkoutWizard is updated to the current position and processing of the fuseaction continues.

Now we are done with wizards. Later in the chapter, we will show how one of the fuseactions in this sequence is actually just a "shell" fuseaction, calling a fuseaction in a different circuit. Using fuseactions in this style can be compared to Model-View-Controller (MVC), a popular design pattern used in software engineering. MVC allows us to maintain the wizard sequencing while reusing fuseactions in other circuits.

Finish off the rest of the Mind Map with all the fuseactions for each circuit. While you are deeply engrossed in Mind Mapping, be mindful of accelerating the rate at which you input data on the map. We find that constantly switching from mouse to keyboard and back again is frustrating. As you map, more of the application comes into your mind's eye. You notice the relationships between circuits and fuseactions. You can easily catch "hidden" fuseactions.

As you are doing this, explore some of the keyboard shortcuts and additional functionality of MindMapper 3.0. For example, use the arrow keys to navigate the map. F5 centers the map on the current node. Ctrl+up arrow and Ctrl+down arrow collapse and expand branches, one level at a time, which is handy for managing a large map. Ctrl+Enter hides all sibling and parent nodes, allowing you to focus on one circuit free of distractions.

When completed, your Mind Map should look like the one shown in Figure 14.15.

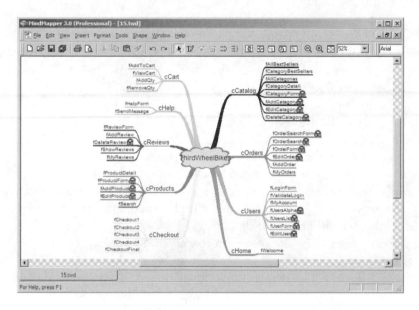

Figure 14.15   All fuseactions and circuits are completed.
Admin-only fuseactions are noted with a lock.

Remember: The completed Mind Map files are available from `http://www.thirdwheelbikes.com`. Looking at this Mind Map, you might be wondering where the nested circuits are. Fusebox 3 is all about the power of nesting circuits. This is a good opportunity to use the handy drag-and-drop features of MindMapper. Click the `cCheckout` node and drag it just to the outside of the `cCart` node. A small arrow pointing away appears to let you know that if you drop the branch in this spot, it will go out from this node, becoming a child branch. Now we have a nested circuit. The `fbx_settings.cfm` in the `cart` circuit will be run for any fuseactions that are called in the `checkout` circuit. In addition, any layouts that the `cart` circuit applies can be applied to the `checkout` circuit as well. We will take advantage of this hierarchy later.

Labeling Fuses

Now that all the fuseactions are added to the Mind Map, the only thing left to do is identify the fuses. Remember that Fuseminder2 will create the circuits, all the circuit files, and all the fuses, as well as put all the fuses in the correct order in the fuseactions. It is faster for us to use MindMapper than to make files by hand.

Determining the fuses needed for a fuseaction is simple. Just remember the rules about fuses from Chapter 5, "The Fuses." Each fuse should be small and accomplish a discrete task. Go through each fuseaction and add one branch for every fuse that makes up that fuseaction. Let's start off with the reviews circuit.

The first fuseaction we will work on is `showReviews`. This fuseaction should display the page of all reviews for any given product. That means two steps are involved: Get all the reviews from the database, and output them to the browser.

Using MindMapper the same way that you create fuseactions, create two fuses as sub-branches of the `showReviews` fuseaction and title them `qry_getReviewsByProductID.cfm` and `dsp_reviews.cfm`. Remember that you can just start typing when a fuseaction is highlighted and the fuse becomes added to the branch. That is all there is to it!

Let's make fuses for a few more fuseactions in the reviews circuit. `reviewForm` just displays a form to the user, so we need one fuse called `dsp_reviewForm.cfm`. That was a simple fuseaction. Any fuseaction that displays a form can be only one fuse long. This might seem like overkill, but as we get further along, we find this to be the exception rather than the rule. Most form-based fuseactions use two fuses or more: one to retrieve a recordset and one to display a form.

Another fuseaction is `myReviews`. This fuseaction displays all the reviews that one user has created. Where in the prototype is this fuseaction used? No pages display only a user's reviews.

Embedded Fuseactions

This is our first example of an embedded fuseaction, and it is not called alone. Instead, an otherwise empty display fuse in a user's My Account page calls it. See Figure 14.16.

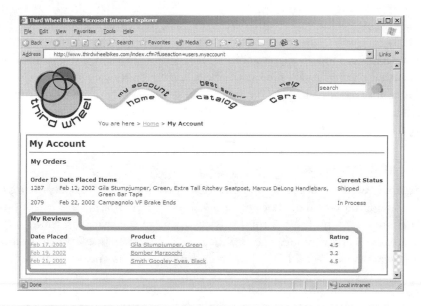

Figure 14.16 Two embedded fuseactions.

We circled the embedded myReviews fuseaction, but you might also notice that the top of this page shows a user's orders. That is also an embedded fuseaction, this time to the orders circuit's myOrders. These embedded fuseaction calls are performed using code like this:

```
<!--- in fbx_switch.cfm --->
<cfcase value="myAccount">
  <cfmodule template="#request.self#"
    fuseaction="reviews.myReviews"
    userID="#client.userID#"
    return="leftcell">
  <cfmodule template="#request.self#"
    fuseaction="orders.myOrders"
    userID="#client.userID#"
    return="rightcell">
</cfcase>

<!--- in dsp_myAccount.cfm --->
<table>
  <tr><td>
  #leftcell#
</td></tr>
  <tr><td>
  #rightcell#
</td></tr>
</table>
```

The <cfcase> for the fuseaction myAccount calls two different fuseactions. Those fuseactions return their contents in the value that is specified in the return attribute. Those variables contain the output of each fuseaction, which is outputted in the display file for the fuseaction: dsp_myAccount.cfm.

Those fuseactions produce the individual components to make up one page. Those of you who are familiar with MVC might find this scenario similar to that design pattern.

MVC and Fusebox

Sometimes, while building web applications, we find ourselves organizing the system in such a way that it poorly models the real-world system it is supposed to be simulating. The most natural way to organize the real world into our applications (real customers, real products, real customers buying real products) is not always how we do it. We have a customer's orders and we have reviews of a product. Those are separate objects, right? They should show up on separate pages with separate controls.

However, a customer on our web site wants to see the real world identically modeled on the site. She wants one screen to see different objects—objects that we would normally contain in separate pages.

It is times like these when MVC shines. The "model" represents the real-world objects like orders and reviews. The "view" displays results to and gathers data from the user. The "controller" interprets the user-inputted data to determine which models and views to command. In short, our actions are completely removed from our displays.

Fusebox lends itself well to this paradigm. Instead of gathering all the code to step through the checkout process, some of it resides in a different circuit—the orders circuit. The fbx_switch.cfm file for the checkout circuit can act as a controller, commanding the addOrder fuseaction in the orders circuit to assist in the user's request to place an order. As a result, the addOrder fuseaction needs to be coded in such a way as to allow this interaction. Download the code from www.newriders.com to see the code for the checkout circuit for an example of the benefits of MVC applied to Fusebox.

At this point, our Mind Map is complete and should look like Figure 14.7.

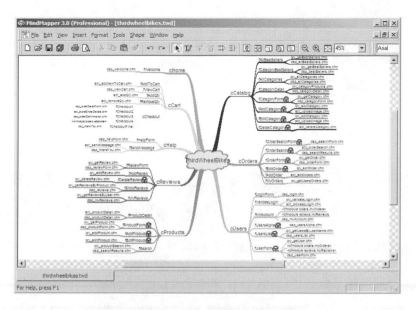

Figure 14.17   Our finished Mind Map.

Fuseminder2: Just Like Magic

We have already mentioned Fuseminder2 and how it is going to create our skeleton for us. Well, now is the time to do just that. MindMapper has taken us as far as it can go. Now we have to start using ColdFusion.

After saving the Mind Map in its normal format, save the map as a text file (.txt). This saves the entire map as an outline file, similar to the outline style you might have used to take notes in high school. Because of the format that MindMapper uses, Fuseminder2 can convert all the tab spaces and node names into a skeleton. After running Fuseminder2 on the text file, a complete directory structure is created. Every circuit's framework files are created. The `fbx_switch.cfm` file is built for each circuit, complete with a `<cfcase></cfcase>` set for each fuseaction. A template is made for each fuse, and they are all `<cfincluded>` in order in the fuseaction. The `fbx_settings.cfm` and default layout files are created. The `circuits` structure is even written out in the root `fbx_circuits.cfm` file. In fact, Fuseminder2 creates blank Fusedocs for you to fill in and writes any notes you made in the Mind Map into the right fuse. It is truly a sight to behold. Talk about saving some time! You have only barely opened ColdFusion Studio, and you already have every fuse started as a fusestub. Just to prove it, Figure 14.18 shows our new application's directory after running Fuseminder2.

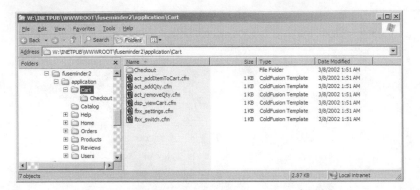

Figure 14.18   Fuseminder2-built application skeleton.

You can find Fuseminder2 at http://www.fusium.com/go/fuseminder2.

Create Fusestubs with Fusedocs

Although Fuseminder2 creates the fuses you identified in the Mind Map, it
does not write Fusedocs for you. Creating Fusedocs for all your fuses is the
next step. Fusedocs were covered at length in Chapter 7, "Fusedocs," so we
will not discuss how to write them here.

We have all the fuses (58, to be exact) that we need to write Fusedocs for.
That could take a long time. What is the best way to organize your efforts?

We tend to take Fusedoc writing one circuit at a time. We also start with
the smallest, most unconnected circuit first. That way, our first circuit can be
completed quickly. Even though it is a small part of the entire application,
starting off on the right foot is important. Let's write the Fusedocs for the
help circuit.

The help circuit has two fuseactions: helpForm (consisting of
dsp_helpForm.cfm) and sendMessage (consisting of act_sendMessage.cfm and
dsp_thankYou.cfm). Open up the fbx_switch.cfm file for the help circuit. You
can see that the <cfswitch>/<cfcase> statements are already written, and that
the first fuse is dsp_helpForm.cfm. When you open that file, you can see
that the Fusedoc is already started. We just have to fill in the <io>,
<responsibilities> and <history> sections.

Also, because this fuse is a display fuse, we can copy the HTML from the
prototype page into this page. Be careful to copy only the part of the prototype that is unique to this fuseaction. Do not copy the opening HTML tags
or any of the supporting layouts. We only want the form. The HTML written
in the prototype just gets reused in the fusestubs, so no previous efforts are
wasted.

What does this fuse do? It displays a form to the user. Write this in the
`<responsibilities>` section:

```
<responsibilities>I present a form to the user to take their name,
➥email, and message. Some friendly text tells the user how to use
➥this page.</responsibilities>
```

This fuse only needs one variable to do its job: an XFA. That means that the
`<io>` section looks like this:

```
<in>
  <string name="xfa.submit" comments="form action" />
</in>
<out>
<string name="name" scope="formOrUrl" />
  <string name="email" scope="formOrUrl" />
  <string name="message" scope="formOrUrl" />
<out>
```

This fuse is complete, but where do these variables go? What fuseaction
processes them?

Change the `fbx_switch.cfm` to add an XFA for this fuseaction:

```
<cfcase value="helpform">
  <cfset xfa.submit="#fusebox.thisCircuit#.sendmessage">
  <cfinclude template="dsp_helpForm.cfm">
</cfcase>
```

We are sending the submission of this form to the `sendMessage` fuseaction in
the `help` circuit. The fuses that we have identified for that fuseaction are
`act_sendMessage.cfm` and `dsp_thankYou.cfm`.

We tend to think of form and form-processing pages as the most closely
related fuses in all of Fusebox. The variables that `dsp_helpForm.cfm` created
(`name`, `email`, and `message`) become `<in>` variables for its companion fuse. Copy
the `<out>` variables from `dsp_helpForm.cfm` and paste them into the `<in>` section of `act_sendMessage.cfm`. That is pretty simple; the variables come out of
one fuse and go into another.

Update the `<responsibilities>` tag of `act_sendMessage.cfm` to read as
follows:

```
<responsibilities>Upon receiving a message, I send it to
➥cusomtersupport@thirdwheelbikes.com.</responsibilities>
```

This fuse is complete. The responsibilities plainly state what it is supposed to
do, and all variables are accounted for. This fuse has no exit, so an XFA isn't
defined in the fusedoc.

The last fuse in this circuit is the second fuse to process in the `sendMessage` fuseaction. Open `dsp_thankYou.cfm` and update the responsibilities section to this:

```
<responsibilities>I thank the customer for the comment and assure
➥them to wait patiently.</responsibilities>
```

This fuse has no `<io>` section. The page has no XFAs, and no variables are outgoing. It is the simplest kind of fusedoc to write. Before it becomes a real fusestub, though, it needs something. Remember that all display and layout fuses already have their HTML code written in the prototype. Open the complementary page and copy-paste the body of it into this fuse. Now it is complete; it contains a fusedoc and the HTML.

That is all the Fusedocing we will do; the completed fusestub collection is available from `http://www.thirdwheelbikes.com`. When writing fusestubs, remember the 10 rules of fuses (Chapter 5) and all the guidelines for proper Fusedocs (Chapter 7). Good luck!

Distributing Code to Developers

After all the fusestubs are completed, the only thing left to do is write the code. You are probably thinking, "The *only* thing? That's the biggest part!" Maybe you are right, but it all depends on your point of view.

Because we have created such tight Fusedocs, we have ensured the successful integration of all the pieces. That means that someone with no knowledge of the complete system can create the fuses. Just because you architected the application does not mean that you have to write it. By transferring that documentation to the Fusedocs, you give each fuse the power to assemble itself outside of the system.

Steve Nelson's `SecretAgents.com` aims to accomplish that very task— subcontracting fusecoders who know nothing of the complete application but who work in "black boxes" where they get a Fusedoc and turn around a completed fuse. You can also have several coders working on an application at once. The other phases of FLiP might take a long time compared to coding. For more information, check out `http://www.secretagents.com`.

Inevitable Changes

You finished all your Fusedocs and are getting a hand at writing the code from some other developers when one of them raises a good question. "I'm supposed to output a search results list, but it could be really long. There isn't anything mentioned about a 'next-n' system, but I think it's going to be needed."

It is a good thing that the developer spoke up now. The prototype did not accurately reflect a situation in which dozens or hundreds of results are returned from a search. What should you do?

You have two choices: Ignore the idea and mark it down for phase two, or recalibrate the search results fuse and any other fuses that might be affected. The option you choose is up to you; neither is right or wrong. In fact, you might choose to ignore some issues that show up and fix others. When you decide to fix issues, you have to update the Fusedocs and maybe even the Mind Map. You really should try to keep the Mind Map up to date because it can serve as a wonderful reference to the entire application, similar to a site map for the completed site.

Update the Fusedoc and Mind Map, taking care not to introduce additional unknown variables into the situation, and let the fusecoder have another go at the fuse.

Coding Like a Cooking Show

Because writing fuses is primarily ColdFusion (not Fusebox), we are not going to write fuses together. Instead, you can get the completed application for Third Wheel Bikes from `http://www.thirdwheelbikes.com`.

A Job Well Done

Congratulations! You went from a pile of HTML pages created in Dreamweaver to airtight fuses, each one neatly fitting together to create one application. The circuits are well defined, and the fuseactions are complete. Most of the job was accomplished without even using ColdFusion Studio.

The prototypes serve as a fantastic bridge into the coding phase; however, Mind Mapping saves us countless hours and makes the architecting process kind of fun. In addition, because we used a visual method of circuit, fuseaction, and fuse organization, the likelihood is good that what we came up with is the right solution, or at least *one of* the right solutions.

If you decide to write the fuses, that is great. We are coders, too, and find a certain level of enjoyment in being able to produce code rapidly, confident that it all is good code and will not need to be taped together in the application. We feel like the digital cowboy—mouse and keyboard in hand and Mind Map in our back pocket.

"It won't work; it never does."

—Eeyore

15

Unit Testing

L OOKING UP FROM THE ERROR MESSAGE GLARING stark black-on-white across the screen, Stan briefly flashed back to a past project when he almost lost a client.

Everything went as it was supposed to during the development of the application, or so Stan thought. We can only empathize with the jolt of sheer cold terror that ran through poor Stan when, upon demonstrating the new live application for his client, he was presented with a raw ColdFusion error screen three clicks into the application.

Snapping back to the present, Stan thanked all the faceless names on the Fusebox list who had cajoled him into a worthwhile testing habit.

Thinking About Testing

One thing that's obvious about the software development world is that programmers aren't testers. Programmers are artistic inventors who like to create new ways to "do stuff." They know the thrill of a really cool logic technique that is well applied. They willingly sit up through the dark nights, fueled by any food that can be delivered lest concentration be broken, poking and prodding an idea until it springs into the shape of a wonderful piece of code.

But they aren't testers.

Testers are adventurers—warriors on a quest to break things. They are focused, diligent, effective breakers of all things created by programmers. They seek the weak points of a program with the assurance of a martial artist who knows the specific location of every pressure point on the human body.

But good testers aren't easy to find, and they are often expensive.

So we have a bit of a problem. If programmers prefer invention to testing, then it's difficult to make them test their work thoroughly. We need to find a way to help programmers who aren't testers test at some level before their code becomes part of the system as a whole.

We call this unit testing, and there are some great techniques for unit testing Fusebox applications. To get to these techniques, we'll take a look at testing in general, just to get into a testing frame of mind and see how Fusebox unit testing compares with other types of testing we've used.

Web application development is different from traditional application development; the end product is part document and part interface, and it's often difficult to differentiate between the two at first glance. Consequently, the idea of testing web applications in much the same way that we test traditional programs might not be readily apparent. The rest of this chapter explores general testing concepts, unit testing in Fusebox, constructing test harnesses, and performing unit test procedures. By the time we're done, there won't be a fuse imaginable that can escape our testing prowess.

If you typically go about the testing/debugging process by running your program and rewriting code until the whole thing seems to work the way you want it to, this is the chapter where you should focus. Find a nice comfortable thought-conducive place to read, lock the doors, turn off the phone/email/ICQ/IRC/AIM/YIM/telegraph, and ride along as we take a quick look at a few types of testing.

Types of Testing

Any time you start a discussion of testing, it is vital to define just what you mean by the term. *Testing* is the practice of critical evaluation, or examining something to see whether it meets expectations. Wide varieties of testing disciplines are used throughout the development life cycle. Our purpose in this book is not to address every kind of testing you might imagine. In fact, the only type of testing we're going to discuss in detail is unit testing. Where does unit testing fit into the whole idea of testing in general? Let's look at some types of testing and see how unit testing fits.

Use Testing

Use testing is a means of finding out how people perform a particular type of activity. Use testing is designed to find out how users work with respect to an application, either existing or proposed. It's a good way to look at existing applications with an eye toward creating an upgrade or replacement application, or to examine the activities that must be modeled in a proposed application. Typically, in a use-testing scenario, the tester is responsible for observing or questioning users of a system, whether that system is electronic or physical. For example, you might collect a series of screen shots to follow a user's progress through an application, or design a set of questionnaires to determine what aspects of a paper-based system are most important to each worker or category of workers.

Stress Testing

Stress testing or *load testing* tests an application in as close to a production loaded environment as possible. The idea is to find out how well the system as a whole will perform when the heat is on, so to speak. In many cases, stress testing will involve the use of much higher usage levels than are expected from the production application. This allows some degree of assurance that the system will work as expected when it is implemented in the normal production environment. Stress testers usually take advantage of a variety of software packages to test the system under load and generate statistics about performance. When stress testing, it is generally assumed that non–stress-related bugs have been removed from the system.

Application Testing

Application testing checks to see whether the application does the jobs it is designed to do. It makes sure that each action does what's expected and that users can be expected to learn the application given the available support (training, help files, and so on). When we talk about "alpha test" and "beta test," we're generally talking about application testing. This is what most developers think of when the topic of testing comes up. Application testers are typically responsible for designing test plans that will exercise each part of the system, running the tests specified by the plans, recording the results, and reporting back to the development staff.

Whether formal or casual, application testing is part of every development project. Sometimes application tests show the system to be complete and healthy, and sometimes they show weaknesses and shortcomings. Unless otherwise prevented, avoidable errors can show up in application testing, too. The goal of unit testing is to prevent errors at the earliest possible point.

Unit Testing

Unit testing ensures that an individual piece, or unit, of code performs the work for which it was designed. Effective unit testing by the development staff greatly reduces the number of bugs that turn up during application testing. Because the amount of back–and–forth traffic between programming and testing is reduced, the overall development schedule is accelerated.

To be most effective, unit testing should be performed at a program's atomic level. The *atomic level* is the level at which an application cannot be broken down into smaller pieces. This is usually defined as the function level for function-based languages, such as C++, Java, and Visual Basic. As we'll see in a moment, atomic level becomes a critical issue for us in the Fusebox world.

Why Unit Test?

It is sometimes difficult to help someone understand why coders should spend time on unit testing. After all, you're going to perform applicaton tests before you release the program, so what's the point?

The reasons for unit testing are many. First, smaller chunks of code are easier to test. It is much easier to isolate a problem if you know it's in 30 lines of code than if it's somewhere in the midst of 30,000 lines.

Second, if you've performed a good unit testing cycle, then when you integrate the application, you'll be testing application functionality and not unit logic. This is an important distinction. If you spend your application testing schedule fixing unit logic bugs, you won't have spent a sufficient amount of time in making sure your application meets the client's requirements.

Finally, unit testing is highly distributable. Individual coders can unit test their code, so the project's unit tests are run in parallel. This represents yet another way you can take advantage of the calendar when working toward those tight deadlines.

Unit testing is good. However, to unit test fuses, we have to consider the essence of a Fusebox application and its atomic level.

Atomic Level and Fusebox

We mentioned a little earlier that unit tests deal with a program's atomic level. Let's consider this for a moment. What is a Fusebox application's atomic level?

As we've already seen, atomic level is defined as that level at which a program can be broken into no smaller pieces. For ColdFusion in general, this would logically seem to be the template, or file, level. It makes sense that we should be able to test each code file as a unit.

This is a good assumption; in fact, it is exactly the approach we want to take. However, the Fusebox environment seems to have an atomic level somewhere above the individual code file (fuse). That is, it appears that we cannot take a single fuse file in isolation and run it. After all, the Fusebox file is basically a collection of `include` statements and a collection of files working together to generate the code that is rendered for any given fuseaction. A high degree of interdependence exists between the parts of a fuseaction. How can we possibly unit test this thing at a code file level? It certainly seems as though the fuse is below the atomic level where Fusebox is concerned.

How, if the fuse is below the atomic level, can we possibly expect a coder to be able to test it? The use of test harnesses solves this problem by letting us run an individual fuse file separately from the Fusebox application.

Units and Test Harnesses

A *unit* is an individual, group, or other entity regarded as an elementary part of a whole. Where Fusebox is concerned, this definition could fit anything from the entire application down to the individual fuse, including circuits or fuseactions along the way. Unit testing in FLiP, though, is concerned with the smallest available unit: the fuse.

To test a fuse independently of other code in the application (that might or might not even be developed yet), a means must exist for running the fuse separately from the application. This is the sole purpose of a test harness.

What Is a Test Harness

The idea behind a test harness is simple. A *test harness* provides the environment with a unit of code that is needed to run. The term originates from the electronics industry, where a "wiring harness" is a collection of wires prefabricated to fit a particular application. To test portions of a complete system, smaller collections of wires connected to test equipment were created. These were naturally called test harnesses. Because the world of software development was originally populated with folks primarily from electronics disciplines, the term test harness was adopted to refer to a piece of software designed to test part of a software system.

After you understand what a test harness is, the first question that you might have is, "How do you know what the environment should look like?" This question sends us immediately back to our old friend, the Fusedoc.

When you create a Fusedoc, you write all the information that a coder needs to write that piece of code. Therefore, this should also be all the information that a test harness needs to test that piece of code. With a couple of rules, this is true.

Rule 1: Fuse files are called from the Fusebox file.

Rule 2: Common variables are established in the fbx_Settings file.

These two factors work together to give us the basis for creating test harnesses. Rule 1 tells us that we can create a file to simulate the Fusebox file (the immediate application environment) for unit-testing purposes. This is the test harness. Rule 2 tells us that we need to include the fbx_Settings file so that common variables are available.

With these two things done, we can then write CFSET statements to create the input variables that are specified in the Fusedoc. When we run the test harness, we'll be able to observe the results of its processing, thereby verifying that the unit works as expected.

Creating a Test Harness

Let's go through the process of creating a test harness. We'll use a simple Fusedoc to try to keep things as clear as possible.

To create a test harness for this fuse, we follow a fairly straightforward procedure:

1. Create a test harness file. A good naming convention is tst_*fuse-to-test.cfm*. We're going to test dsp_Login.cfm, so the test harness is tst_dsp_Login.cfm.

2. Set the "self" variable to redirect output calls. This is one of the most important parts of unit testing. Instead of directing page exits back to the Fusebox, a test harness directs exits to a template that will dump the output to the screen for review. We'll use ShowAttributes.cfm for this purpose:

   ```
   <cfset self="ShowAttributes.cfm">
   ```

3. Set variable values for each input variable that is specified in the Fusedoc:

   ```
   <cfset XFA.onSubmitForm = "XFA.onSubmitForm">
   ```

4. Add an include line for the template to be tested:

   ```
   <cfinclude template="dsp_Login.cfm">
   ```

That's it. The finished test harness looks like Figure 15.1.

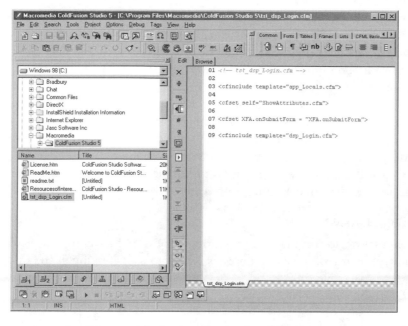

Figure 15.1   Test harness for dsp_Login.cfm.

As you can see, a great deal of labor is involved in creating test harnesses. Our little example here is an extremely simple one. Most test harnesses will have several lines of CFSETs to simulate all expected inputs. Each harness is a combination of unchanging template and specific variable assignments for the individual fuse. Fortunately, thanks to Fusedoc, the creation of test harnesses could be farmed out to the coders who are responsible for creating the code.

Of course, some of us aren't willing to leave well enough alone. The first time Jeff (your humble author) had to create test harnesses for the fuses he was writing, he was just about fit to be tied. There was so much repetitious coding, and his creative side was becoming extremely frustrated. We find this is often the state of mind that inspires ideas for new tools, and that was indeed the case here. Frustration became the mother of Harness2.

Harness2: More Anti-Drudgery

Some have accused Jeff of being a major contender for the title of World's Laziest Programmer, often going to great lengths to avoid the need to type something he's already typed once. Other people think that means he's highly motivated to create cool automation tools. Call it what you will; the end result is that things like Harness2 get created.

Written by Jeff Peters, Harness2 is the obvious successor to the Harness utility. It's available from www.grokfusebox.com.

The Harness idea grew out of the need to rapidly create test harnesses for an entire Fusebox application. Harness was designed to read classic Fusedocs and generate test harnesses based on their requirements. Harness2 does the same thing for Fusebox applications that use the Fusedoc 2 syntax.

Simply put, Harness2 is a recursive utility that writes test harnesses for each of the templates in a directory tree. It's a simple utility to run, and it provides a nice detailed report of all the work it's done. Let's look at how to use Harness2 and what it does, and then we'll dig into how it works. Before we're done, we should have a good understanding of some of the power offered by Fusedocs.

Running Harness2

The easiest way to run Harness2 is through the use of a calling template. At its simplest, all Harness2 needs to know is where to start looking at the directory tree. Here's a sample call:

```
<cf_harness verbose="yes"
  rootDir="#GetDirectoryFromPath(GetCurrentTemplatePath())#">
```

The utility starts in the specified directory, locating all Fusebox template files. It then reads each file's Fusedoc and creates a test harness file based on the information found in the Fusedoc. It repeats this process for any subdirectories of the starting directory, and so on down the directory tree. The output from the process (assuming the verbose attribute is set to "yes") is shown in Figure 15.2.

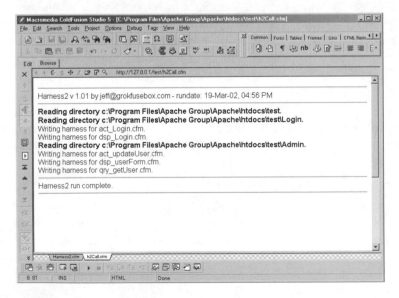

Figure 15.2   Harness2 output.

Although Harness2 is primarily a timesaving device, it also has some interesting things to teach us about the power of Fusedocs in our applications. For this information, we need to look at its inner workings.

The Inner Workings of Harness2

Although we could spend a great deal of time talking about *how* Harness2 works, we think it's much more important to take a look at *why* it works. In other words, what makes it possible for tools like this to exist in the first place?

Understanding the guts of Harness2 will give us some insight into the power that is inherent in Fusedocs. The information in Fusedocs provides the basis for innumerable tools that, like Harness2, provide development leverage based on that information. After looking through Harness2's methods, we'll be able to take advantage of Fusedocs to build similar tools.

Because we know what to expect in terms of how variables are documented in any given Fusedoc, we can write tools to process the information in just about any way we can imagine. For the sake of clarity, let's look at a sample Fusedoc and see how Harness2 takes it apart and uses it to build a test harness file. Listing 15.1 shows a sample Fusedoc.

Listing 15.1 **Sample Fusedoc**

```
02 <fusedoc fuse="dsp_Login.cfm">
03   <responsibilities>
04     I provide a login form for users.
05   </responsibilities>
06   <properties>
07     <history author="Jeff Peters"
08               date="2001.07.13"
09               email="jeff.peters@bigfoot.com"
10               type="create"/>
11   </properties>
12   <io>
13     <in>
14       <string name="self" />
15       <string name="appName" scope="attributes" />
16       <string name="XFA.onSubmitForm"/>
17     </in>
18     <out>
19       <string name="userName" />
20       <password name="password" />
21       <string name="XFA.fuseaction" />
22     </out>
23   </io>
24 </fusedoc>
```

Listing 15.2 shows a sample `harness2.ini` file.

Listing 15.2   **Sample *harness2.ini* File**

```
[Globals]
LineCount=3
Line1=<cfset self="ShowAttributes.cfm">
Line2=<cfset request.imgroot="images/">
Line3=<cfset request.queries="queries/">
```

The first thing Harness2 does in creating a test harness for this Fusedoc is to get the generic lines specified in the `harness2.ini` file. These lines are simply copied from the ini file and written to the test harness file. They make sure the expected local environment is in place.

Perhaps the most important aspect of the local environment is the use of the "self" variable. In a working Fusebox application, this variable contains a reference to the Fusebox file (index.cfm). In a test harness, we reset the variable to contain a reference to some code that will reveal the contents of the program's environment after the template in question has run. This is how we enable the test harness to provide monitoring of the fuse's output. A number of custom tag templates can be used for this purpose, including Dump.cfm, DumpAll.cfm, and ShowAttributes.cfm. If you have a preferred way of displaying the program environment, you're free to use it as well. Simply edit the `harness2.ini` file to reflect the template of choice.

The true work done by Harness2 is accomplished by reading the input variable specifications in the Fusedoc. In our sample, the inputs are in lines 14–16. Each of these lines is read in turn, and the following lines are created in the test harness:

```
<cfset attributes.appName="attributes.appName" />
<cfset XFA.onSubmitForm="XFA.onSubmitForm">
```

You might be wondering why the first line doesn't cause an input variable to be created. This is because Harness2 keeps track of the variables that were set by the lines included from the ini file. Because a variable named "self" is already present in the harness file, no new line is created. The second line, defined as a string variable in the Fusedoc, causes a CFSET line for the named variable to be created in the test harness. Because no default value for the variable was specified, Harness2 uses the variable's name as its value. In similar fashion, if an integer variable is required, its value is set to 1; if a number (floating point) variable is required, its value is set to 1.0.

Thanks to the XML specification for Fusedoc 2.0, Harness2 is also capable of something that the original Harness tool was not: auto-generating fully specified complex datatypes such as structures and arrays.

With the power of Harness2 at our disposal, we can worry less about the work of writing test harnesses and more about working with them. Let's look at a test harness for Third Wheel Bikes.

A Test Harness From Third Wheel Bikes

We'll have a quick look at a fuse and its test harness from our ThirdWheelBikes.com site. Listing 15.3 shows the fuse, act_Login.cfm; Listing 15.4 shows its test harness.

Listing 15.3   **Third Wheel Fuse**—*act_Login.cfm*

```
<!-- act_Login.cfm by jeff@grokfusebox.com -->
<!---
<fusedoc fuse="act_Login.cfm" language="ColdFusion"
➥specification="2.0">
  <responsibilities>
  I check the user's ID and password with qryValidateUser.  If the user
  ➥is valid,
  I set some client variables.  If the user is not valid, I clear the
  ➥client variables.
  </responsibilities>
  <properties>
    <history author="jeff@grokfusebox.com" role="Architect" date="02
    ➥Jan 2002" />
  </properties>
  <io>
    <in>
      <string name="XFA.onSuccess" scope="attributes" comments="Use if
      ➥validation succeeds." />
      <string name="XFA.onFailure" scope="attributes" comments="Use if
      ➥validation fails." />
      <recordset name="qryValidateUser" comments="contains no records
      ➥if validation failed">
        <string name="userID" />
        <string name="lastName" />
        <string name="firstName" />
        <string name="email" />
        <string name="region" />
        <string name="roles" />
      </recordset>
    </in>
    <out>
      <string name="userID" scope="client" oncondition="validation
      ➥succeeds" comments="delete if validation fails"  />
```

continues

Listing 15.3   **Continued**

```
            <string name="userName" scope="client" oncondition="validation
        ⇒succeeds" comments="firstName lastName; delete if validation fails" />
            <string name="email" scope="client" oncondition="validation
        ⇒succeeds" comments="delete if validation fails" />
            <string name="region" scope="client" oncondition="validation
        ⇒succeeds" comments="delete if validation fails" />
            <string name="roles" scope="client" oncondition="validation
        ⇒succeeds" comments="delete if validation fails" />
        </out>
    </io>
</fusedoc>
--->

<cfif isdefined("qryValidateUser.userID")>
  <cfset client.userID = #qryValidateUser.userID#>
  <cfset client.userName = "#qryValidateUser.lastName#,
  ⇒#qryValidateUser.firstName#">
  <cfset client.region = #qryValidateUser.region#>
  <cfset client.roles = #qryValidateUser.roles#>

  <script>
  window.location="<cfoutput>#request.self#?fuseaction=
  ⇒#attributes.XFA.onSuccess#</cfoutput>"
  </script>
<CFELSE>
  <cfset IsDeleteSuccessful=DeleteClientVariable("client.userID")>
  <cfset IsDeleteSuccessful=DeleteClientVariable("client.userName")>
  <cfset IsDeleteSuccessful=DeleteClientVariable("client.region")>
  <cfset IsDeleteSuccessful=DeleteClientVariable("client.roles")>
  <script>
  window.location="<cfoutput>#request.self#?fuseaction=
  ⇒#attributes.XFA.onFailure#</cfoutput>"
  </script>
</cfif>
```

A one-to-one correspondence exists between the `<in>` section of the fuse's Fusedoc and the `<cfset>` lines in the test harness. Compare the `<in>` section from Listing 15.3 with the `<cfset>` lines in Listing 15.4.

Listing 15.4   **Test Harness for** *act_Login.cfm*

```
<!-- tst_act_login.cfm -->
<!--- --->
<fusedoc fuse="tst_act_login.cfm" language="ColdFusion"
⇒specification="2.0">
  <responsibilities>
    I am a test harness for the act_Login.cfm fuse.
```

```
    </responsibilities>
    <properties>
      <history author="Jeff Peters" email="jeff@grokfusebox.com"
      ↪role="Architect" type="Create"/>
    </properties>
  </fusedoc>
--->

<!--- ********************************************************** --->
<!--- Set the Fusebox API variables.  This creates a valid    --->
<!--- Fusebox environment.                                    --->
<!--- ********************************************************** --->
<cfinclude template="fbx_Settings">
<cfset fusebox = StructNew()>
<cfset fusebox.IsCustomTag = No>
<cfset fusebox.IsHomeCircuit = Yes>
<cfset fusebox.IsTargetCircuit = Yes>
<cfset fusebox.Circuit = Foo>
<cfset fusebox.Fuseaction = Login.doLogin>
<cfset fusebox.HomeCircuit = Foo>
<cfset fusebox.TargetCircuit = Login>
<cfset fusebox.ThisCircuit = Login>
<cfset fusebox.ThisLayoutPath = "">
<cfset fusebox.currentPath = "">
<cfset fusebox.rootPath = "/test">
<cfset self="ShowAttributes.cfm">

<!--- ********************************************************** --->
<!--- Here's the stuff from the in section of the Fusedoc      --->
<!--- ********************************************************** --->
<cfset attributes.XFA.onFailure = "WoeIsMe">
<cfset attributes.XFA.onSuccess = "TaRaRaBoomDeeAy">
<cfset attributes.userID="JPeters">
<cfset attributes.password="x">
<!--- ********************************************************** --->
<!--- Now include the fuse we're testing                       --->
<!--- ********************************************************** --->
<cfinclude template="actLogin.cfm">
```

After generating the test harness for a fuse, actual unit testing can be conducted. A basic unit test is simply running the test harness and observing the results. If the result has problems, the code is adjusted and the unit test is run again.

However, there is much more to unit testing in a shop that intends to produce quality systems. We need to conduct the test, but we also need to keep track of test results and which fuses have been tested. As with any kind of testing, unit testing involves a disciplined process.

The Process of Unit Testing

Whether Harness2 is used to create test harnesses or they are coded by hand, the process of actually performing the test is the same. Variables required by the fuse are set in the test harness, and the test harness is called in a browser.

It might seem that if the fuse runs successfully, the test is complete and the coder can move on to another fuse. However, it's important to examine the fuse's Fusedoc for indications of how the fuse's inputs might vary, and run additional tests accordingly. For example, the Fusedoc might specify that if a certain input variable is above a given value, one output variable should be created; if the input variable is below the value, a different output variable should be created. Both of these scenarios should be run through the unit test.

Following are some common tests we can consider when unit testing. These should be used as inspiration for your own tests, not as an exhaustive list:

- Set numeric variables to negative values.
- Set numeric variables to positive values outside the expected bounds (four-digit person's age, for example).
- Set numeric variables to zero.
- Set numeric variables to string values.
- Set string variables to numeric values.
- Set all variables to empty strings ("").
- Set date variables to non-date values ("March First 2000").
- Set recordsets to empty (no records returned).

This is the aspect of unit testing that most resembles the work that application testers do. Creating test harnesses based on Fusedocs provides the programmer with a great set of instructions for unit testing and reinforces the discipline necessary for effective testing.

Unit Testing Discipline

Test harnesses and unit testing should be a required part of your development life cycle, and they are certainly important steps in FLiP. Not only will the end product be more complete, stable, and bulletproof by incorporating these steps, but fusecoders will also have a great tool available to ensure their code does what's expected, even though they might have no idea what the application as a whole will do.

If you're a fusecoder, life is good at this point. You get an assignment that includes a fuse stub with complete Fusedoc and a test harness. When you've finished writing the code, just drop the test harness and the code file into a test directory on your development server (in this case, it's usually your coding box running the single-IP version of ColdFusion) and run the test harness. You'll see a result page something like Figure 15.3, which shows output using the ShowAttributes custom tag.

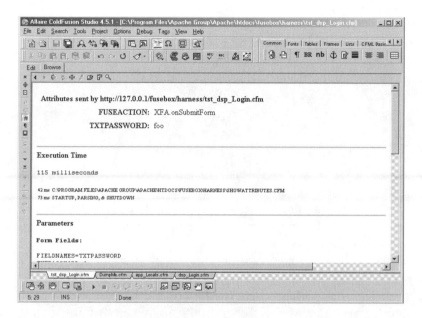

Figure 15.3   ShowAttributes output.

By examining the output, we can see that we got the expected fuseaction, but we have some problems with the other output variables. The Fusedoc tells us we're supposed to get three outputs: username, password, and fuseaction. The unit test results show the outputs fuseaction and txtPassword. It looks like it's time to fix this fuse and test it again—before it gets integrated and somebody else is forced to chase down and swat these bugs. After we have successfully run the unit test battery and verified the outputs of the fuse, we can send it back to the application architect with confidence that the fuse behaves as expected.

Unit Tests Aren't Guarantees

Unit testing suffers from one great hazard: the assumption that if every fuse is properly unit tested, the application will work the first time the fuses are put together in a circuit.

Test harnesses, though, depend on Fusedocs. If the Fusedocs aren't right or if they have inconsistent specifications across the application, even completely exhaustive unit testing won't make the circuit work correctly.

For example, imagine an application with two circuits. In one circuit, the architect writes a Fusedoc that specifies an output variable called `client.userID`. In the other circuit, the architect writes a Fusedoc that specifies an input variable called `client.user_ID`. The two fuses are given to two different coders, who both produce excellent code. Both fuses unit-test perfectly. However, when the application is integrated, a failure occurs when the fuse that tries to read `client.user_ID` finds that it doesn't exist.

This bug is not due to an error on the part of either of the programmers, but to the architect's inconsistency.

All Tests Completed, Houston

In some respects, the use of test harnesses is analogous to returning to your first days as a ColdFusion developer. Think back to the time before you knew every tag by heart, the time before you instinctively knew when to use the `item` attribute instead of the `index` attribute in a CFLOOP. (If you're still in those days, that's all the better.)

Remember banging together a template and then running it to see what happened? The code-test-code-test-code-until-it-does-what-I-want method is an experience we've all had. Using test harnesses is like that, although it's a bit more refined. It's reducing the process to the atomic level and working with it until it does exactly what you want it to do. By examining and testing each part of the application at an atomic level, confidence in the overall application is built from the ground up.

Throughout this chapter, we've looked at unit testing, a responsibility of fusecoders. Now the FLiP process brings to a point where we must step back into the shoes of the application architect. The fuses are starting to roll in from the developers, they've been unit tested, and we start putting them together into circuits. The application's code is filling in behind the prototype, and things are starting to get interesting.

The next step in the FLiP process is deployment and integration. If we've done everything else well, this phase should be practically anti-climactic. With the amount of planning, careful work, and testing we've done, the final deployment doesn't represent the kind of fear-inspiring experience that Stan was remembering at the beginning of this chapter. We must consider certain issues any time we turn to deployment, though, so on we go.

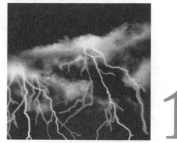

"Now the general who wins a battle makes many calculations in his temple ere the battle is fought."

—Sun Tzu

16

Application Integration and Deployment

FOR MANY OF US PROGRAMMERS, IT MIGHT seem that all the work has been done by the time we get through the FLiP unit testing phase. The application is well conceived and well designed, the code has all been written and unit tested, and we can go relax and congratulate ourselves on a job well done.

This is a problem.

As far as Janice is concerned, we haven't done anything yet. After all, she's waiting to have an application installed or available at her location. The job is not done until the program runs properly as a whole, and has been shown to do so for the client. In other words, the application is not done until it has been successfully integrated and deployed. Stan knows this all too well, as his memory spins back to a near-career-ending disaster…

Coaxing the last half-swallow from his fourth Mountain Dew of the night, Stan checks his watch and shakes his head in dismay. With only four hours left until the site is due to go live, everything was going wrong.

It all started the previous evening when Stan installed the finished site on his client's production server. The last of the code had been completed just that day. Satisfied with a completed job, he sat down at a browser to cruise through the site in preparation for the next day's unveiling. That's when it started. The first indication of a problem was a `datasource not found` error. "Oh. I forgot to set up the DSN," thought Stan, turning to the server to correct his oversight. A few mouse clicks later, and the difficulties began in earnest.

"Access 97? Access *97*?!! They said, 'Use the latest version of Access!' I developed for 2002! What am I supposed to do with 97?' Where's the phone?!"

And downhill it went from there. As the night wore on, Stan became increasingly certain that he would never again be hired for anything related to web development. After fixing the database problem, more errors popped up. Squashing one bug seemed to create two more.

By the time the 9:00 a.m. rollout arrived, Stan was worn to a nub. He had managed to fix (he thought) all the major errors, and he informed the client of a few minor ones that would be fixed later in the day. All the while, he kept thinking to himself, "If only I'd taken more time to make sure it all worked."

Stan had made the mistake of thinking that the application was finished when the coding was done. He was not yet familiar with the finishing steps that every good application needs.

The first of these finishing steps is integration. *Integration* is a 5-cent word for putting the entire application together and making sure it runs. This sounds simplistic, and in a way it is. Many times, developers get caught up in the excitement of finishing the code and fail to perform a solid test of the whole system prior to deployment.

The second step is *deployment*, or making sure the application runs in the production environment. Like Stan's problem with database versions, variances between the development environment and the production environment are among the most common deployment barriers. Fortunately, we can take measures to minimize the variances.

This chapter will give you some insights into approaching integration and deployment in a way that will ensure success. We'll look at integration testing and debugging, followed by some considerations and techniques for deployment, including the use of development and staging environments. These techniques will help us minimize the problems we might encounter when rolling out a new application.

Integration

Integration is the point in the development process when Stan, as the application architect, takes all the wonderful code created by his "army" of developers and assembles it into the final application.

Putting the code together might seem to be a trivial matter. After all, the fuses have all been unit tested and certified to operate correctly. Therefore, it's tempting to think that when the fuses and circuits are dropped together on the server, the application will run correctly as well. In an ideal case, following appropriate integration testing, that would be true. Stan would drop all the fuses into their appropriate directories, fire up his browser, point it at the application's starting page, and watch his beautiful new application run without errors or hiccups.

For small applications, this might even happen on occasion. When it does, it's truly a marvelous thing to see, and it's a testimony to all the hard work the team put into wireframing, prototyping, Fusedocs, coding, and unit testing, as well as the Fusebox concept in general.

In most cases, though, some problems will arise when it's all put together. The likely problems will vary, but a few common ones can be expected.

Sometimes a query refers to an incorrect field name in the database. This might be caused by programmer error in creating the query simulation that was used in the unit test (see Chapter 17, "Best Practices," for more on query sims), or by architect error in documenting the field name for the simulation.

Disconnects sometimes occur between outputs from one fuse that become inputs for the next fuse. This usually occurs because the architect failed to be consistent when creating the Fusedocs for the two fuses.

Regardless of the cause of the error, the responsibility for resolving integration errors falls to the architect. Depending on the size of the project and the organization of the development team, the architect might have integration coders who will handle these bug fixes. Many times, the architect is the integration coder. Of course, if you're a one-man shop, you're doing it all yourself anyway. Whichever your circumstance, the architect needs to be the one making decisions about fixing integration bugs.

Finding the Bugs

The central issue in integration is finding and eradicating the bugs that pop up when you start putting the components together. It makes sense, then, to put things together in a way that allows you to isolate problems at the lowest possible level.

Because Fusebox is such a well-organized hierarchical model, you have a great opportunity to create thorough integration-testing scenarios. You already have experience with unit testing, so you can now start integrating and testing at each level from the bottom up.

The next level from the bottom is the fuseaction, which is contained in a circuit. Thanks to the Fusebox concept, each circuit can run as an independent unit. You can create a list of tests to run based on the fuseactions that are in the circuit's Fusebox file. The goals of this step are to make sure that each fuseaction runs properly, and that the circuit successfully handles all of its fuseactions.

After the circuits have been individually tested, you can then run a series of full application-integration tests. These tests are what you might think of as "alpha tests" in the traditional application-development world. The goal at this point is to make sure the application does what it is supposed to do, without unexpected errors, for all types of users who will be using the system.

Test Reports

At each step of integration testing, predesigned test cases should be used to make sure testing is thorough. Test cases are just written descriptions of what you're going to test. As the case is tested, notes of any problems that occur are made and documented on a test report. This report is given to the coder who will be fixing the problem.

Writing up all these notes and reports might sound like unnecessary legwork, but it's definitely necessary. Test reports provide documentation for us to present if a question comes up as to the procedures we've used to create the system. Test reports not only help us build better products, but they also protect us from potential disputes with clients.

Test reports don't have to be incredibly detailed, although some firms do create rather intricate ones. The reports should contain enough information to clearly explain what we were testing, and to describe either the problem that was encountered or successful completion of the test. We should also record the date and time of the test on every report. For example, if we were testing a circuit, we would want to record the circuit name, fuseaction, and any variables used to test the fuseaction. If we were doing an application test, we would want to record what case we were testing, the user we were logged in as (assuming our system requires login), and what we were doing at the time of the error.

Some shops handle test reports on paper, and some create in-house systems for recording tests in a central database. You can handle it in whatever way best suits you and your client. The point isn't the form the integration tests take; it's the assurance to be had from doing them.

Following are a couple of sample test reports, just to give an idea of what it's all about.

The Circuit Test Report Form in Figure 16.1 shows a possible format for recording findings of a circuit test. Include all details about the actions taken and the results observed. In particular, we don't want to overlook successful completion of a test. Stating "Meets all requirements" is much more informative than stating "OK."

Circuit Test Report
Circuit Name: Catalog
Fuseaction: showListing
Variables: UserID=23
                    Section=Shoes

Results

No errors

Figure 16.1   Circuit Test Report Form.

In Figure 16.2, the Application Test Report Form shows a similar reporting concept, but for a higher level of testing. At the application testing level, we're looking for problems with the overall behavior of the application, as opposed to the more specific features that are tested during circuit testing. The report reflects this focus.

Application Test Report
Use Case: View Catalog List
User: JPublic
Actions: Click "Shoes" button on main catalog screen

Results

The listing is successfully presented, but it shows the Hats section instead of Shoes.

Figure 16.2   Application Test Report Form.

After the bugs have been identified and reported, they obviously must be fixed. You might be wondering exactly how this is going to work because we've made a lot of noise about Fusebox enabling remote coders.

Fixing the Bugs

If the architect has taken advantage of the ease of distributing the coding work to remote coders, it can be quite cumbersome to use the original developers to fix integration bugs. For this reason, integration bug killing most often involves either the application architect or an in-house debugging programmer or team.

In most cases, this isn't really a big deal because the purpose of integration testing is really just ironing out minor bugs to get all the fuses working together properly. In a way, there is poetic justice to having the application architect involved at this point in the development cycle. The more complete and well designed the Fusedocs were before coding, the fewer bugs will occur during the integration test. If the architect did a great job on Fusedocs, he won't have much to fix during integration testing. Again, the responsibility for fixing integration bugs lies with the architect, even if he is fortunate enough to have a coder or two to actually write the required changes.

Deployment, on the other hand, can be much more of an adventure than many developers ever expected it to be. One of the objectives of the Fusebox Lifecycle Process (FLiP) is to make deployment as uneventful as possible. If that's going to be the case, we need to be careful about how we approach it.

Deployment

For every development project, a best-case scenario exists for development environments. That scenario is to have separate and identical server environments for development, testing, staging, and production.

In practice, it is the rare client who is willing to provide four separate and equivalent duplications of the server environment. Consequently, it is quite common to set up individual environments for development, testing, and sometimes staging on one server, and production on another. Production servers should never be used for development, testing, or staging.

If development, testing, and staging areas are to be configured on the same box, then separate directory structures should exist for each, as well as separate databases. A different datasource name for each database will be needed; the DSN name for the staging area should be the same as the DSN name on the production server. The other two areas can use arbitrary DSNs, thanks to our well-loved practice of using the `request.DSN` variable to store the DSN name (see Chapter 17).

Just What Is Staging?

Most developers are familiar with having separate development and testing environments. Many, however, are not as familiar with the concept of staging.

A staging environment is simply an exact duplicate of the production environment. When a new version of software is ready for release to production, it is first installed in the staging environment. This offers several advantages over going from testing to production.

First, it provides you with an opportunity to make sure all the "move to production" adjustments, such as setting the appropriate DSN, have been done properly without impacting the production application.

Second, it provides a place to maintain a ready backup of the production code. If the production code suffers a disaster, the staging environment is ready for immediate implementation. In a worst-case scenario, the staging server can be loaded with recent backup data to replace the failed production server until the production server can be replaced.

Finally, it allows testers to implement any of the variety of testing tools in the testing environment without concern for causing difficulty when going to production. For example, a test tool might drop a directory into each circuit to store test result datasets. Naturally, these directories would have to be removed prior to moving into production. Rather than trying to develop a procedure that makes sure this happens during the move to production, this can be done during the move to staging where there is no impact on production if the moving process encounters problems.

Even for the first release of a new application, the staging environment is important. It is the place where deployment and acceptance testing can occur without exposing the application to the public.

Preparing for Deployment and Acceptance Testing

Deployment and acceptance (D&A) testing are the final steps in the FLiP development cycle. *Deployment testing* is the opportunity you have to make sure the migration from the development environment to the production environment goes smoothly. *Acceptance testing* is the client's opportunity to verify that the application performs as he expects it to.

To prepare for successful deployment and acceptance testing, install the application to the staging environment. This includes installing all the software that will be present on the production server in support of the application, in exactly the same configuration. Be as thorough as time allows during installation; you'll be glad you did.

Install the web server software that will be on the production server. If production uses Internet Information Services, don't put Apache on the staging server. Make sure all the server configuration settings are the same between staging and production, such as default index page name, directory listing authorization, and so on.

Install the database software, again paying attention to configuration. Access on the staging server and SQL Server for production is a forbidden combination. It might help to think of mirroring here. If the production server is already in place, use it as a reference for setting up the staging environment. If the staging and production servers are being configured simultaneously, keep careful notes so that both configurations are the same.

Install ColdFusion in the same configuration. It's hard to believe, but some shops have one version of ColdFusion on the staging server and a different version on the production server. Even more astonishing are the places that have ColdFusion Entreprise Single-IP (from ColdFusion Studio) on the testing server and ColdFusion Express in production—with no staging environment. Check to make sure the available custom tags are identical.

Finally, install your application code. Make sure it goes into the same directory structure it will be in on the production server. Double-check DSN names in your code.

After all the software is installed and configuration is thoroughly checked, the staging environment is ready for testing.

Deployment Testing

Deployment testing is really nothing more than one final application test with all the pieces in place in the staging environment. If you like, you can use the same test cases you used during application testing for deployment testing.

There's no magic formula to decide how many or what kind of tests you need to perform during deployment testing. You can test as little or as much as you choose. Bear in mind, though, that it will be the client's acceptance tests that are critical to successful completion of the project.

If the application is going to be on a high-volume public access site, it's a good idea to consider load testing as part of the deployment test. A variety of web load testing software packages and services are available; if you're beginning your research, use your favorite search engine to search for "web load testing." If you know from the start of the project that performance is a critical issue, it's a good idea to explore the client's expectations so that you can test for compliance during deployment testing.

Sometimes a client's expectations are based on assumptions that don't bear out under scrutiny. We once had a client who wanted to "load test" the application prior to deployment. As it turned out, what he really wanted to know was whether everyone on his corporate intranet could see the application server; load had nothing to do with the requirement. Of course, answering that requirement was much less expensive than load testing would have been. As always, explore the client's requirements and make as few assumptions as possible.

Upon completion of deployment tests, you're ready to offer the system for acceptance testing.

Acceptance Testing

Acceptance testing can be exceptionally tense or warmly reassuring, depending on many factors. Foremost among these are the client's expectations and how they've been communicated to you during the project's development.

Sometimes, the client has hidden expectations for performance or program behavior. If this is the case, acceptance testing can be a rough ride. Complaints might arise over issues that you had no idea even existed.

Fortunately, the FLiP methodology is designed specifically to minimize this sort of hidden expectation. Having gone through the prototyping process, you have the assurance of the prototype specification to resolve any disputes over look and feel. The explorative process of wireframing has provided a chance to talk about expectations, audience, and performance. In fact, the amount of time spent on the planning process as a whole normally tends to build a strong cooperative relationship with the client. This helps make any difficulties discovered during acceptance testing relatively easy to handle.

Sometimes, a client might have a plan for acceptance testing based on his internal requirements, but typically a client will have no such plan. Clients depend on you as the architect to make sure your system works. In these situations, your deployment test cases can contribute to the basis for acceptance testing, responding to requirements that are established at prototype freeze (see Chapter 13, "Prototyping and DevNotes").

Signoff

Signoff on a project is simply the client's acknowledgment that the application development is finished. Depending on your arrangement with the client, this might occur immediately following acceptance testing, or it might be delayed until the application has been placed on a production server.

It is best to agree that signoff on the completed application development will occur as a result of completed acceptance testing. Because most clients will have their own staff who is responsible for maintaining in-house servers or will have technical contacts for outsourced sites, monitoring the production activity is not normally the developer's responsibility. After all, you were hired to build an application, not monitor its production run. Of course, you might have contracted for follow-on production monitoring or maintenance of the application. If so, that's another phase of the project; the development phase needs to be completed and signed off before you continue into production monitoring.

We have a colleague we'll call Carol. Carol had contracted to build a personnel intranet application for a private company. She successfully built the application, installed it on the client's server, and saw it through acceptance testing. Thinking her job completed, Carol went back to her office and waited for the check to arrive.

Unfortunately, as the client continued to use the system, some unexpected behaviors on the part of users began to occur. Undesired data formats were being used in text fields, and the users were making requests for added features. The client called Carol and demanded that she come back and update the system, saying that payment would be withheld until "the system is right."

Because Carol didn't have an agreement in place as to what would constitute completion of the development, she had to either work with the client until he was happy, or forego payment for the work she'd already done. Fortunately, she managed to work out a reasonably fair deal for the additional work. Had Carol had a solid agreement for acceptance testing and signoff prior to beginning the development, she would have been in a much better position to contract for follow-on maintenance after the initial development was complete.

We Have Lift-Off

Having learned his lesson from past nightmares, Stan has naturally incorporated a thorough integration testing and deployment phase into Janice's project. Following integration tests and the correction of a few minor bugs, Stan ran the acceptance tests and shared the results with Janice. Impressed with Stan's thorough coverage of the requirements, Janice asked to see the application working live and then proceeded to announce its availability to her customers.

Integration and deployment are the final stages of the FLiP development cycle. If we have done a good job from wireframing through unit testing, integration and deployment should be singularly unexciting experiences.

Integration, as a process of combining parts and testing at successively higher levels of integration, is the portion of the cycle during which all our work comes to fruition. Test reports at the circuit and application level provide an opportunity to eradicate integration bugs and evidence of quality work.

Deployment is not just the task of copying the application to a production server. Using a staging environment and proper care, along with deployment and acceptance testing, we can offer the client not only a finished application, but a high degree of confidence that it is robust, stable, and reliable.

We've finished our tour of FLiP, following our intrepid development team, Stan and Brody, through the steps of designing, developing, and deploying an e-commerce site for Janice, the owner of Third Wheel Bikes. We are now well equipped to use the FLiP model on other development projects.

The next chapter takes us away from the FLiP process to have a look at some best practices that are related to Fusebox development. These are not formal parts of Fusebox, but rather some of the techniques that we use to make our lives as developers easier or more productive, or our code more consistent and stable.

"They didn't want it good, they wanted it Wednesday."

—Robert Heinlein

17

Best Practices

Our Fusebox application is coded, tested, and launched. We saved countless headaches by following an established process for determining the basic goals of the application while wireframing. We saved even more time by prototyping the application in HTML. We were able to reuse that HTML to create our fusestubs after Mind Mapping the architecture of the application. Fuseminder2 wrote a lot of code for us. The whole process was pretty painless.

Fusebox does not end there, though. The basic goal of Fusebox is to increase the chance of quickly completing successful projects. The community of Fusebox users has formalized many ideas and practices into the framework and FLiP. However, many more ideas have yet to be formalized or would not fit in with the rest of formalized Fusebox. Most of these topics are not Fusebox-specific in nature, either. All members of the community do not use them, so incorporating them would be overkill and would dilute the power of Fusebox. We will cover some of those topics in this chapter, including security and Fusebox, encrypted URLs, search engine safe (SES) URLs, and some popular custom tags.

Security and Fusebox

Some struggling developers discover Fusebox and expect it to do more than it does. Fusebox is hard to define; it is a set of core files, it is a specification, and it is a methodology. Arguably, Fusebox is many things to many people. One thing that Fusebox does not address, however, is application security.

Many solutions that are incorrectly compared to Fusebox contain a built-in security system. Spectra utilizes an elaborate roles-based system to manage access to content objects. But Spectra's usefulness proved very slim. Few companies found that their business model fit into what Spectra offered.

Spectra is an example of the limitations of most universal security systems. ColdFusion developers tend to create custom security solutions for their applications again and again. Each developer has a different way of creating the system, whether it means bitwise operations, complex database matrix tables, or flat XML storage. Why is the security solution so complex?

Even when the same developer creates a security system for the same kind of client twice, the results are often different because each system is integrated with its application environment. A security system tightly coupled with the application makes for better security.

Can Fusebox provide a universal security model that will fit every kind of application that can be built?

Basic and Common Security Systems

A universal security model for Fusebox is probably impossible, but that does not mean that attempts to standardize security would be fruitless. After all, security boils down to controlling access to pieces of code. We can attempt to define a universal methodology explaining what can be secured in a Fusebox application, and the community can offer potential solutions.

Although the following code is not a Fusebox standard, it is a good starting place. ·

If a customer is not supposed to be able to change the status of his order, then the database query that does that job needs to be wrapped in some logic like this:

```
<cfif IsDefined("client.isAdmin")>
  <cfquery name="updateStatus" datasource="#request.DSN#">
    update order set status=#attributes.status#
where orderID=#attributes.orderID#
  </cfquery>
</cfif>
```

This code is not complex, but it is a good representation of the most common kinds of security used. If a certain user belongs to a certain group or has a certain role, then some code can be run. How does Fusebox come into play?

In a Fusebox application, security can be applied in three places and with two methods.

What to Secure	How to Secure It
Circuit-wide, including all fuseactions, fuses, and nested circuits	Place code in fbx_settings.cfm
One fuseaction	Place code in the `<cfcase>` tag for the secure fuseaction
Section of a fuse	Place code in the fuse

Security Need	Employment Method
No access to the requested operation	Relocate user if failed validation
Hide a piece of code	Wrap the secured code in a validation routine

The way that you store your security is up to you. Maybe you have a database schema like the one shown in Figure 17.1.

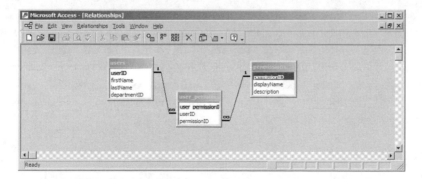

Figure 17.1   Simple security schema.

This common solution allows users to have multiple permissions. Sometimes the users table is replaced by a groups table, which contains users. That extra level of abstraction boils down to the same thing: Certain users are able to do certain things.

What would the ColdFusion code look like if a fuseaction needed to be secured to users with a `permissionID` of 18? The following code demonstrates:

```
<cfcase value="thisFuseaction">
  <cfquery name="securityCheck" datasource="northwind">
    SELECT user_permissionID FROM user_permission
    WHERE permissionID=18 AND userID=#client.userID#
  </cfquery>
  <cfif not securityCheck.recordCount>
    <cflocation url="#request.self#?fuseaction=users.login&message=
    ⇥#URLEncodedFormat("This is a secured action, available only to
    ⇥system administrators")#">
  <cfelse>
    ...fuseaction code here...
  </cfif>
</cfcase>
```

What if only a portion of a fuse needed to be secured? The same code could be used, with a few modifications:

```
<cfif securityCheck.recordCount>
  ...code to be secured...
</cfif>
```

The code to check a user's security permissions might be called quite frequently. Shouldn't it be wrapped into a custom tag?

Securing Code with *<cf_secure>*

The functionality of custom tags provides an excellent way to encapsulate this functionality. Although many developers have created similar tags, Hal Helms' `<cf_secure>` tag (available from `http://halhelms.com`) is a popular version.

Helms' tag can be used with a closing tag to secure a section of code, or it can be called standalone, with a fuseaction to go to if the validation fails. Helms also has a whitepaper discussing the tag's use, available from his site.

Although the likelihood of creating a universal security model is slim, an understanding of security and Fusebox, combined with `<cf_secure>`, can solve most security problems.

SES URLs

What makes a URL "search engine safe"? Better yet, what makes a URL not "search engine safe"?

All major search engines (MSN, Yahoo!, Lycos, and so on) have traditionally had trouble indexing highly dynamic, template-driven sites. Because the site is dynamic, it is feasible that a search engine spider might get lost in a never-ending loop of links, unable to leave or to properly index the site.

Because of this, search engine spiders have avoided links with ? or & in the URLs. This has been a way to differentiate dynamic sites from static sites. As a result, most content in a ColdFusion site would not be indexed. There has to be a way around this. If search engines do not like the ? and & symbols, can we recode our links to pass variables a different way?

That is exactly what we do for SES. Here is how a "normal" link looks:

```
<a href="index.cfm?fuseaction=reviews.read&productID=1409&start=15">
```

Here is the same link, recoded for SES compatibility:

```
<a href="index.cfm/fuseaction/reviews.read/productID/1409/start/15">
```

Writing the code for all our links that way is simple, but how is that "improper" query string converted into the appropriate name=value pairs so that we can use them on the calling template?

That is where SESConverter.cfm comes into play. Steve Nelson created the first version of this file and wrapped it into <cf_formURL2attributes>. The SES converter code has undergone significant changes since its original release. Notably, support for Apache was added as well as optimization of the parsing and updating for use with Fusebox 3.

Now called as a <cfinclude> in index.cfm, SESConverter.cfm parses the value of cgi.request_uri (which contains the query string) and converts the slashes into & and =. That way, the string fuseaction would be pulled out of the earlier query string and assigned the value reviews.read. The same thing would happen for productID (getting the value 1409) and start (value of 15). For an example of this method of variable passing being used, go to Amazon.com and look at the URL when viewing a product. All the slashes are being converted to usable variable name=value pairs, while keeping the URLs easily indexed.

As we mentioned previously, early search engines didn't catalog URLs with ? and &. That is not the case anymore. Starting with Google, it appears that all the other engines have caught up and are now indexing fully dynamic URLs. That doesn't mean that this technique is useless, though. In fact, many people use SES URLs to enable web-logging tools to collect accurate data on page views.

MediaHouse's LiveStats and WebTrends's Log Analyzer are two of the most commonly used site usage analysis and reporting tools, especially in shared hosting environments. These tools do not correctly display usage and page hit statistics for "normal" URLs much for the same reason that search engines do not index them. These tools consider the actual page requested (index.cfm) to be the "hit" for the request, regardless of the variables passed.

Although it is unfortunate, these tools are not designed to report on query strings. (WebTrends has a number of products that do allow reporting based on query strings. Log Analyzer continues to be their most popular product though.) We can, however, fool those reporting tools into thinking that users are requesting individual pages rather than one page with variables appended to the URL by using SES. Appending a fake suffix or a fake filename to the URL string aids the reporting. Look at this URL:

```
<a href="index.cfm/fuseaction/reviews.read/productID/1409/faker.htm">
```

WebTrends thinks this request is for the file `faker.htm` in the folder `1409`, which is nested in a number of other folders, starting with the folder `index.cfm`. (It is okay to have dots in folder names.) The dummy filename at the end is a mismatched pair. If you count the number of elements in the query string, you see there is an odd number. `SESConverter.cfm` recognizes this too and knows that `faker.htm` is just a placeholder and should not be converted to a name=value pair.

Now when reviewing page hits, both Log Analyzer and LiveStats think that page requests are unique. They all request a file called `faker.htm`, but that file is in many different directories. You can accurately see the hits your site is getting.

`SESConverter.cfm` has many other features, including the ability to recognize dummy filenames or just dummy extensions. It also allows passing name=null pairs by passing the string value `null`, which will be converted to an empty string. Erik Voldengen and Bert Dawson currently maintain `SESConverter.cfm`. The latest version—including an example application and an extensive whitepaper on SES—can be found at `http://www.fusium.com/go/ses`.

Encrypted URLs

One misconception that we periodically hear is Fusebox's dependence on URL variables. "Fusebox can't be secured," some misinformed developers say. The truth of the matter is that Fusebox might be considered more secure than traditional ColdFusion applications. Sure, we rely on one more variable in the URL string (`?fuseaction=circuit.fuseaction`), but because of the security code that goes in `Application.cfm` mentioned in Chapter 3, "The Fusebox Framework," our applications are less open to malicious users.

Nonetheless, some people are concerned about URL hacking, and Fusebox is just as susceptible to it as any dynamic application that relies on variables, whether variables are passed in a form or on the URL string. Take, for example, this URL:

```
<a href="index.cfm?fuseaction=users.myAccount&userID=109">
```

That would be a remarkably bad URL to make. The `users.myAccount` fuseaction displays the account information that matches the `userID` passed on the URL. Users are only supposed to see their own accounts, but by modifying the `userID` variable to, say, `110`, a user can see someone else's account.

This kind of poor programming has nothing to do with Fusebox, so the solutions are not Fusebox based. First and foremost, developers need to be aware of this kind of programming error. But it sounds harder than it must be because hackers have a history of compromising Authorize.net by manipulating merchant accounts and passwords this way.

Even after you secure all your URLs and form variables to hackers, the possibility still exists for a user to "session jump" by stealing someone else's `CFID` and `CFToken`. If you do not use cookies to store these variables and instead pass them on the URL string, then any user who is using any browser can act as another user if he sets `CFID` and `CFToken` to another user's values. But just how hard is it to jump into another session?

ColdFusion uses sequential numbering to generate a `CFID` for each user. The first user to a site gets the number 1, the second user gets 2, and so on. This variable is not meant to be secure; instead, it is meant only to identify the user. The second variable, `CFToken`, is a highly random number that ColdFusion generates and assigns to each user. When `CFID` and `CFToken` are combined, you can be relatively assured that session jumpers have their work cut out for them. After all, they have to guess the `CFToken` of a user who is currently active—and `CFToken` is eight numbers long. A hacker has a 1 in 100 million chance of guessing it. Tough odds, right?

Those certainly are tough odds, but they might not be tough enough. What happens if someone session jumps in a stock trading application? Major financial ramifications could result if that 1 in 100 million chance occurs.

However, finances are not the major reason that developers are concerned about URL security. Mostly, we do not want users to see parts of the application that they should not see. Our applications might throw ColdFusion bombs if a user messes with the URL enough. The error message displayed might contain debugging information that enables the hacker to make more focused URL hacking attempts, eventually compromising our application.

Fusebox and Frames

Regardless of whether frames strike your personal fancy, they can be a great way to create highly responsive web applications. Users can maintain a single page in their browser while only selected portions retrieve data and reload.

Implementing a frames-based application using Fusebox is simple as long as you remember the principle rule of Fusebox: All requests go through `index.cfm`.

Figure 17.2 is a screen shot of a frames-based Fusebox example.

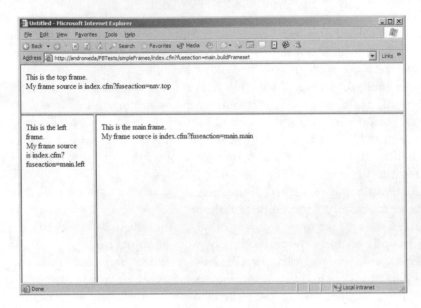

Figure 17.2   Simple frames example.

The fuseaction that generates the whole page is `main.buildFrameset`. Let's take a look at that fuseaction:

```
<cfcase value="buildFrameset">
  <cfinclude template="fra_main.cfm">
</cfcase>
```

Pretty simple, right? This fuseaction just `<cfinclude>`s a file that contains the `<frameset>` tag. Notice the `fra_` prefix. This does not follow the standard Fusebox fuse-naming conventions. Remember though that one of the guiding principles of fuse prefix naming is that if you need a custom prefix, you should use it. In the case of frames, you will notice that many developers call frameset fuses with the `fra_` prefix. `fra_main.cfm` looks like this:

```
<cfoutput>
<frameset rows="100,*">
  <frame src="#request.self#?fuseaction=nav.top">
  <frame src="#request.self#?fuseaction=main.buildSubFrameset">
</frameset>
</cfoutput>
```

See how the frame sources point to the Fusebox framework? Form actions do it, hrefs do it, and `<cflocation>`s do it. Why should frame sources do it differently? The two fuseactions called look like this:

```
<!--- in nav circuit --->
<cfcase value="top">
  <cfinclude template="dsp_top.cfm">
</cfcase>

<!--- in main circuit --->
<cfcase value="buildSubFrameset">
  <cfinclude template="fra_sub.cfm">
</cfcase>
```

The first fuseaction calls a fuse to fill the top frame. The second fuseaction is slightly more complicated. It introduces a nested frameset. It `<cfinclude>`s another `fra_` file. Here is what `fra_sub.cfm` looks like:

```
<cfoutput>
<frameset cols="150,*">
  <frame src="#request.self#?fuseaction=main.left">
  <frame src="#request.self#?fuseaction=main.main">
</frameset>
</cfoutput>
```

This frameset fills its frames with two more fuseactions. Those fuseactions are simple, though; they only `<cfinclude>` single fuses.

To generate a frameset and fill all the frames, a request to the Fusebox must be made once for each frame and once for each frameset. After you build a Fusebox and frames application, it is easy to understand how all the pieces fit together. A sample application using Fusebox and frames can be found at `http://fusium.com`.

Popular Custom Tags

Although with the release of version 3 Fusebox needs no custom tags to operate, Fuseboxers have still found a few tags to be on our "must-have" list. These are tags that we make sure are on every ColdFusion server we use. Most of these tags are used in our example application, Third Wheel Bikes. All of these custom tags are available from `fusebox.org`.

<cf_reuseForm> to Reuse Forms

Frequently, we have fuseactions in our applications that display a form page that we reuse for creating a new record and editing an existing record. After all, why should we create two copies of essentially the same file? Here is a very small example form used for creating a new record:

```
<form method="post" action="index.cfm?fuseaction=#xfa.submit#">
  First Name: <input type="Text" name="firstName"><br>
  Last Name: <input type="Text" name="lastName"><br>
  <input type="Submit">
</form>
```

Here is a form used for editing the same record:

```
<form method="post" action="index.cfm?fuseaction=#xfa.submit#">
  First Name: <input type="Text" name="firstName"
  value="#query.firstName#"><br>
  Last Name: <input type="Text" name="lastName"
  value="#query.lastName#"><br>
  <input type="Submit">
</form>
```

Because we have removed the hard-coded form post–fuseaction (by using XFAs), the only thing different about these two forms is the value of two fields. It seems silly to create and maintain two files that are so similar. This is where <cf_reuseForm>, created by Steve Nelson, helps out. Here is an example of this tag in use:

```
<!--- the <cfcase> tags for fuseactions using <cf_reuseForm> --->
<cfcase value="edituser">
  <cfinclude template="qry_getuser.cfm">
  <cf_reuseform action="query" fieldlist="firstName,lastName"
    queryname="getuser">
  <cfinclude template="dsp_user.cfm">
</cfcase>
<cfcase value="newuser">
  <cf_reuseform action="new" fieldlist="firstName,lastName">
  <cfinclude template="dsp_user.cfm">
</cfcase>

<!--- qry_getuser.cfm --->
<cfparam name="attributes.userid" default="0">
<cfquery name="getuser" datasource="#request.DSN#">
  SELECT firstname, lastname FROM users
  WHERE userid=#attributes.userid#
</cfquery>
<!--- end query fuse --->

<!--- dsp_user.cfm - Note the value of each field is coming from the
<cf_reuseform> tag. The action will determine where the data comes
from, i.e. blank, query data, form data or url data (the last two
are for data validation). --->
<form method="post" action="index.cfm?fuseaction=#xfa.submit#">
  First Name: <input type="Text" name="firstName"
  value="#firstname#"><br>
  Last Name: <input type="Text" name="lastName" value="#lastname#"><br>
  <input type="Submit">
</form>
```

As we can see from the preceding example, `<cf_reuseForm>` does more than provide a method to reuse a form for creating new and editing existing records. It also makes it easy to populate a form with values that are available from the form or URL scope. When is this beneficial?

Imagine that a user is filling out a long order form that has dozens of fields. This situation can prove to be a troublesome user interface on two occasions. The first occasion is when she tries to navigate the whole form. Too many fields make a form difficult to fill out properly. The second occasion occurs after she thinks she filled it all in properly. Clicking Submit, she is greeted by an error message stating that she did not fill in all the fields correctly. What's even worse, though, is that all the data she previously entered is gone. The form is blank now, and she will have to fill in that long form again.

By calling `<cf_reuseForm action="form">`, you can populate all the values previously entered. Sure, you could do this by hand, but `<cf_reuseForm>` also lets you use the same form for creating new records and editing existing records. You actually can serve three purposes with one form.

This tag is a powerful boon to reuse efforts and will certainly become a well-used tool in your development toolbox.

<cf_returnFuseaction> to Control Flow

Have you ever been looking at a web page, clicked a link to continue, were prompted to log in, and after your successful log in, were sent to the home page of the site? This can be frustrating for users. Just because your application requires users to be logged in to access certain fuseactions does not mean that they should be penalized for not already being logged in. We need some way to hold onto the current position before redirecting users to the login form. Then, after the login completes, send the users back to where they were, no matter where that was on the site. `<cf_returnFuseaction>` is another custom tag to rescue.

`<cf_returnFuseaction>`, developed by Steve Nelson, operates in two modes: set and return. You use the set action before relocating the user to the login form to store the current location; you use the return action after the login processes, to return the user to where they previously were. Here is the syntax of the tag:

```
<cf_returnfuseaction action="set|return" gotoURL="http://"
⮑returnURL="http://">
```

Here is a more thorough example. A user starts on a product detail page, looking at a new car. She clicks a link that says, Create a Testimonial.

She goes to the testimonial circuit, which requires all users to be logged in first. `<cf_returnFuseaction>` is used like this:

```
<cf_returnfuseaction action="set" gotoURL=
"http://www.myCarSite.com/index.cfm?fuseaction=users.login">
```

The custom tag redirects her to the login process. After she finishes the login process, she goes back to the testimonials fuseaction where she came from, like this:

```
<cf_returnfuseaction action="return">
```

`<cf_returnFuseaction>` is not limited to logging in users. It can also be used to interrupt a wizard to perform a subwizard. A fuseaction that requires another fuseaction to occur first can make good use of `<cf_returnFuseaction>`.

<cf_location> Replaces *<cflocation>*

We can only guess how many hours ColdFusion developers have scratched their heads, wondering why their cookies were not being set after running code like this:

```
<cfcookie name="userID" value="#userID#" expires="NEVER">
<cflocation url="index.cfm?fuseaction=#xfa.continue#">
```

Macromedia has always maintained that the fact that you cannot set a cookie and use `<cflocation>` on the same page is not a bug. Regardless of Macromedia's position on the subject, we think this is one of the most unnecessary causes of gray hair in the world of ColdFusion. The most common solution involves using code like this:

```
<cfcookie name="userID" value="#userID#" expires="NEVER">
<cfheader name="Refresh" value="0;URL=index.cfm?fuseaction=#xfa.
↪continue #">
```

Using `<cfheader>` does not come naturally to most developers. In fact, we did not write that code; we got it from someone who got it from someone else. Knowing header commands is not something that most ColdFusion developers can claim. Why is it that `<cflocation>` cannot behave like we expect it should?

It is a little known fact that if you put an underscore in the tag name, it will work. Well, that, and you need Jordan Clark's magnificent `<cf_location>` replacement tag in your custom tags folder. We are convinced that it is only because of backward compatibility that Macromedia does not fix `<cflocation>`.

What is the syntax for this custom tag? Well, that is the great part about it—
`<cf_location>` and `<cflocation>` are the same. It is a true replacement. A new
version (3.0) of `<cf_location>` is due to be released sometime soon with powerful new features, including closer interaction with Fusebox. `<cf_location>`
can be found on the Macromedia Developer's Exchange.

Learn from Experience

Although the Fusebox framework provides a standard way of writing your
applications, and FLiP identifies a process that is likely to increase the success
of the project as a whole, Fusebox developers have created or discovered a
multitude of things to make coding easier. The discussion of a universal security model has proven valuable because some basic principles have been agreed
upon, yielding well-used custom tags. Fuseboxers developed the URL encryp-
tion utilities, even though they are not specifically Fusebox-related. You can
also take advantage of the exiting SES tools to increase traffic to your site.
Some best practices for using Fusebox and frames have been established, and a
few custom tags have proven immensely valuable to general ColdFusion and
Fusebox-specific development. These are only a small fraction of the wonderful tools available.

Have a good tool that would benefit Fuseboxers? Join the community
and share it. Custom tags and links to external resources are available from
`fusebox.org`.

"Ignorance is like a delicate exotic fruit; touch it and the bloom is gone."

—Oscar Wilde,
The Importance of Being Earnest, Act I

18

Fusebox Exotica

THIS ENTIRE BOOK HAS BEEN ABOUT FUSEBOX and ColdFusion—and rightly so because this book is titled *Fusebox: Developing ColdFusion Applications*. However, just because you are writing in ColdFusion now does not mean you will *always* be writing in ColdFusion. In fact, we promise you that, as it exists now, ColdFusion will not be widely used in 15 years (Yes, we are predicting the future. You just wait and see.) Do you still hope to be a web or computer programmer in 15 years? Change is inevitable. All languages die eventually, even the mighty Fortran.

Fusebox is language independent. That means that the skills we acquire now in architecting applications with Fusebox can be easily transferred to another language. Some developers wonder if the latest release of ColdFusion will "kill Fusebox," as though there were something magic about the current environment that makes Fusebox possible. Fusebox is far more than a collection of ColdFusion code, though. At its heart, Fusebox is a collection of ideas about how to approach application development. From that perspective, it's easy to see that, in essence, Fusebox will never die. After a developer has absorbed and internalized the ideas that make up Fusebox and the Fusebox Lifecycle Process (FLiP), the application of those ideas to other environments becomes practically second nature.

In fact, Fusebox is already used in two popular languages other than ColdFusion: PHP and JSP. Devoted Fuseboxers took on the effort required to port the core file functionality to these two languages. Fusebox will also be ported to Microsoft's .NET framework if investigative efforts currently under way are continued. Finally, Fusebox plays nicely with ColdFusion MX's new component model, CFCs.

These are exciting developments for the Fusebox community. The ability to implement a set of ideas in any of a variety of languages represents an increased value to a broader clientele. Let's take a look at how Fusebox is used in these environments; perhaps your next project is waiting in these pages. Our first stop on this "multicultural" tour is PHP.

PHP Fusebox

PHP has become the second most popular web environment in existence, according to an informal page-count survey using the Google search engine in March 2002. Its low entry cost makes it particularly appealing to shoestring operations and non-profit organizations. Like ColdFusion, PHP provides a tag-based language for creating server-side processing of HTTP requests. It was only natural that Fuseboxers who had a taste of PHP would want to use their favorite framework there as well as in ColdFusion.

The beauty of Fusebox is that the concepts are simple. Early versions of Fusebox were powerful guidelines backed by good tools. In comparison, though, the fully mature Fusebox 3.0 framework makes its ancestors seem awkward and clumsy.

Fusebox 3.0 eliminated dependence on ColdFusion custom tags. As a result, the Fusebox framework is far easier to translate to other languages. In fact, Fusebox for PHP is not a different "version" of Fusebox at all, but simply a translation. All the basic concepts are identical: fuses, the switch in the Fusebox file, the API, and so on. Nothing has changed except that you have to write your code in a different language. That seems like an exaggeration, but there is more truth to it than you might think.

What Is the Same?

The following PHP files perform the same functions as their ColdFusion counterparts. One important thing to remember with PHP is that filenames and variables are case sensitive.

fbx_Fusebox3.0_PHP4.0.6.php

This is the core file for PHP Fusebox. Just like different versions of the core exist for different versions of ColdFusion, this is the version of the core for PHP. The core sets up the API variables and performs the main processing of the Fusebox application. The core is required for every request to the Fusebox application.

fbx_Circuits.php

This file is where the mappings for the application's circuits are set up. Mappings point circuit aliases to directory paths and place them in the $Fusebox["circuits"] associative array. This file is required in the application's home circuit.

```php
<?php
$Fusebox["circuits"]["home"]      = "home";
$Fusebox["circuits"]["downloads"] = "home/downloads";
$Fusebox["circuits"]["search"]    = "home/search";
$Fusebox["circuits"]["news"]      = "home/news";
?>
```

fbx_settings.php

This is where application-wide configuration is done. A circuit application that is not the home application can have its own fbx_settings.php file. This file serves the same purpose as fbx_settings.cfm.

fbx_switch.php

This is the "Fusebox." The switch file delegates processing to the appropriate fuses for the requested fuseaction. The fbx_Switch.php file is required for every circuit in the application.

```php
<?php
switch($Fusebox["fuseaction"]) {
    case "main":
    case "Fusebox.defaultFuseaction":
        $pageTitle = "Welcome";
        include("dsp_main.php");
        break;

    case "about":
        $pageTitle = "About";
        $XFA["links"] = "links.";
        $XFA["downloads"] = "downloads.";
        include("dsp_about.php");
        break;
    default:
```

continues

```
                    print "I received a fuseaction called <b>"
                    .$Fusebox["fuseaction"]
                    ."</b> that the circuit <b>"
                    .$Fusebox["circuit"]
                    ."</b> does not have a handler for.";
                    break;
        }
    ?>
```

fbx_layouts.php

This is where a circuit can set up its own layout file. This file is not required, but it performs the same job as the ColdFusion version.

What Is Different?

Apart from the obvious language distinction, PHP Fusebox has some requirements that ColdFusion Fusebox does not.

fbx_listFunctions.php

This file is a function library. The PHP list functions are re-creations of the list functions from ColdFusion. This file is used in PHP Fusebox for three reasons:

- The list functions are extremely useful tools in general.
- PHP has no built-in list functions.
- In translating the Fusebox core code, it was clear that the code would be far simpler and more elegant using the list functions.

Because the core code requires the list functions, you can use the functions in your PHP Fusebox programming as if you were using the same functions in ColdFusion.

fbx_saveContent.php

This is the code for saving page content to a variable. This file is similar to the file by the same name used by ColdFusion Fusebox for versions before ColdFusion 5.0. However, the implementation of the concept is different in PHP because of the way the language works. This file is required in the root circuit of the application.

ColdFusion is tag based, which means that most of its functions are written as tags that look like HTML. PHP is more strictly a script-based language, much like CFScript or JavaScript. Code sections must be separated from non-PHP code using delimiters: `<?php` to begin and `?>` to end. Therefore, ColdFusion's concept of custom tags does not apply to PHP.

```php
<?php
//code goes in here...
?>
```

Instead, some of the features of custom tags can be mimicked in PHP by creating custom objects. One important part of a custom tag is that it runs in a protected namespace, meaning that it can write and read its own variables without worrying about overwriting variables elsewhere in the application. Objects have the same property: Variables that are set within a class and its derived objects are in a local scope that will not infringe on the global scope.

Hence the `SaveContent` class defined in `fbx_SaveContent.php`. Instantiating the object starts an output buffer; anything that would normally go directly to the browser is stored in memory until further instructions are given. After the class is "opened," you have to close it to get the contents back out:

```php
<?php
require_once("fbx_SaveContent.php");
$SaveContent = new SaveContent;
// generate some output
print "Hello, Stan!";
$content = $SaveContent->close();
// now output saved content
print $content;
?>
```

The `SaveContent` class, just like the `<cfsavecontent>` tag in ColdFusion 5, makes it possible to do such things as nested layouts and modularized content.

A further extension in the `fbx_SaveContent.php` file is the custom `Location()` function, which re-creates ColdFusion's built-in `<cflocation>` tag as well as the popular `<cf_location>` custom tag. (`<cf_location>` is discussed in Chapter 17, "Best Practices.") If no content (and therefore no header) has been sent to the browser yet, the `Location()` function takes the URL you pass in and redirects the browser to that page by sending an HTTP redirect header. This is just like the native `<cflocation>` function. However, if some content (such as a cookie) has been sent to the browser already, the function will instead send a META redirect because HTTP headers can only be sent once.

Finally, the `fbx_SaveContent.php` file contains a custom PHP function, `Module()`, which is a mimic of the functionality of `<cfmodule>`. Remember though, that PHP is not tag based, so the PHP `Module()` function does not have a way to include an "end tag." However, in Fusebox for ColdFusion, `<cfmodule>` is frequently used to include content from a fuseaction other than the one that the user specifically requests. The PHP `Module()` function is perfect for this:

```
//includes the login form within the layout of the main app
Module("index.php", array("fuseaction"=>"users.loginForm"));
```

Why PHP?

If Fusebox works the same in ColdFusion, JSP, and PHP, how do you choose which language to use when building a Fusebox application? PHP does not (yet) have a reputation of being a solid, robust enterprise web development platform. Its humble beginnings might have started PHP out on the wrong foot; PHP originally stood for "personal homepage," although it now recursively stands for "hypertext preprocessor." And PHP faces many of the same prejudices as other open source projects: "If it is free, how can it be any good?" But now, as the computing world is recognizing the stability and robustness available in open source software—and especially with PHP's latest upgrade to version 4—PHP is giving developers reason to reconsider its power.

There are several specific reasons to use PHP. It is free; and because it is an extremely active open source project, any bugs that are found are fixed quickly. PHP is also widely available on hosted servers, and when it is running on an Apache web server, it is customizable using `.htaccess` files and setting simple configuration flags. Some would argue that PHP is not a fully realized object-oriented (OO) language, but others would rebut that intense OO application development has little place in a stateless environment like the web. Either way, to the extent that you can define classes and create custom objects in your applications, PHP's simulated object-oriented nature gives the developer broader options in his code.

PHP is not right for every project, but neither is ColdFusion or JSP. Deciding which environment and platform to build your application on depends on a number of different factors. In most cases, it comes down to selecting the right tool for the job.

Why PHP Fusebox?

If you are a PHP developer, you might realize that many freely distributed applications are available to you. In addition, you can adopt several frameworks; PHP-Nuke is a popular portal framework, and some popular template engines are available as well, such as FastTemplate. Why use Fusebox?

Of the frameworks and applications that are available for PHP developers, most are trying to solve a specific problem. PHP-Nuke is specifically tuned toward building portal sites, and FastTemplate is strictly a way to simplify the integration of variables on the front end of an application for non-programmers (a.k.a. "HTML Jockeys"). Other free applications available are written by various individuals, usually not following a standardized coding style or architecture. Integrating such applications into your web site is usually a complicated mess of stripping the code down to its essential functionality and then rewrapping it with your own site's look and feel, hopefully not breaking the application in the process.

Fusebox is specifically designed to be versatile, allowing for code reuse and adaptability. Integrating a Fusebox circuit application into your site can be as simple as copying the files to your server and adding a link to the new circuit. With nested layouts, the new application will look as if you built it yourself because your site look and feel will automatically wrap around the new application. Plus, the types of circuit applications that can be built or added to your web application is limitless. You could just as easily build a portal site using Fusebox as you could an e-commerce application.

Additionally, when you are integrating someone else's Fusebox code, you can expect that the code and the files will be organized in a familiar way. Fusebox is known for being easy to debug, and this is never more necessary than when working with someone else's code.

Fusebox has been proven as a powerful, scalable web application framework. The number of sites built and thriving on Fusebox continues to grow, as does the number of developers in the community and number of available applications. Now, that power and community are available to PHP developers.

Resources

Many Fusebox and PHP resources are available online, as spelled out in this section.

bombusbee.com

Run by David Huyck, bombusbee.com (`http://bombusbee.com`) is devoted to the development and support of Fusebox for PHP. In addition to the core PHP Fusebox files, busbee.com has sample applications, tutorials and articles, and other useful PHP and Fusebox code.

SourceForge.net

SourceForge.net has great tools for open source software projects, and it currently hosts the Fusebox for PHP project at

```
http://sourceforge.net/projects/php-fusebox/
```

In addition to the latest core code, sample code and a conversion template for search engine safe (SES) URLs are available.

PHP.net

PHP.net (`http://www.php.net/`) is where to get all you need to begin developing PHP applications. Download the latest binaries or source code, and access the vast documentation for the PHP language.

As you can see, the jump from ColdFusion to PHP isn't particularly long for an experienced Fuseboxer. In fact, we think the similarities between the ColdFusion implementation of Fusebox and the PHP implementation provide an excellent opportunity for ColdFusion-conversant Fuseboxers to learn PHP. As both languages continue to mature, strengths are available in each that can benefit the other as long as developers who are familiar with both are around.

Just as PHP is one of the hottest web technologies out there today, Java is perhaps the hottest (and most misunderstood) overall language to come down the pipe since Niklaus Wirth introduced Forth. Fortunately for us, there are some keen minds at work in the laboratories of a few "mad Fuseboxers"—developers who see Fusebox as a great way to develop within the J2EE platform.

Fusebox and Java (J2EE Fusebox)

Although Fusebox was originally developed for the ColdFusion platform, the Fusebox architecture and FLiP methodology also make a great combination in the Java enterprise world. J2EE Fusebox (formerly known as JSP-Fusebox) brings together the benefits of Fusebox and the industrial strength of the Java 2 Enterprise Edition (J2EE) platform.

Two primary goals of the J2EE Fusebox project are to create a Java implementation of Fusebox that aligns closely with the ColdFusion Fusebox standard, and to combine the benefits of Fusebox with the Java platform.

JavaServer Pages (JSP) technology is similar to ColdFusion. JSP allows developers to build dynamic web applications using a combination of a powerful programming language (Java) and other standard Internet technologies, such as HTML and XML.

J2EE Fusebox developers who are familiar with ColdFusion yet new to the J2EE platform will realize that little has changed in Fusebox besides syntax. One difference in implementations is worth noting, though; with J2EE Fusebox, all of the resources of the J2EE environment can be brought to bear. A simple yet powerful example of these benefits is the scenario in which a standard query fuse implemented in JSP calls an Enterprise Java Bean (EJB) method rather than directly querying a database.

J2EE Fusebox provides benefits to Java and ColdFusion developers alike. With Neo coming out soon and the future of ColdFusion and Java growing closer together, J2EE Fusebox gives ColdFusion developers a great on-ramp to the world of enterprise Java. And for experienced Java developers, J2EE Fusebox provides a powerful, flexible, proven architecture and methodology to tame the complexity of J2EE.

The Components of J2EE Fusebox

The J2EE Fusebox framework consists of JSP files, a small tag library, and compiled classes. The JSP files are similar to their ColdFusion relatives. Similar to PHP Fusebox, all that has changed is the syntax.

fbx_fusebox.jsp

The fbx_Fusebox.jsp file acts as the main controller of a Fusebox system. It provides the core processing of a Fusebox request, and it is required in the home circuit of an application. Typically, this file will be suffixed with a version number. For instance, fbx_fusebox301.jsp denotes Fusebox version 3.01.

fbx_circuits.jsp

The fbx_cirucuits.jsp file maps circuit aliases to directory paths and sets them in the Fusebox.circuits structure. This file is required in the home circuit of a Fusebox application. Here is example code from an fbx_circuits.jsp file:

```
<%
    fusebox.circuits.put( "home", "home" );
    fusebox.circuits.put( "Login", "home/Login" );
%>
```

fbx_switch.jsp

Just like the ColdFusion Fusebox file of the same name, `fbx_switch.jsp` acts as a circuit's controller, mapping each fuseaction that a circuit handles to specific fuses to be executed. This file is required in every circuit directory. Here is an example from an `fbx_switch.jsp` file (the `fbx:` prefix on a tag indicates that it is a Fusebox Tag class):

```
<fbx:saveContent variable="fusebox.layout">
<fbx:switch value="<%= fusebox.fuseaction %>">
   <fbx:case value="editProfile">
      <%@ include file="qry_getProfile.jsp" %>
      <%@ include file="act_restoreProfile.jsp" %>
      <%@ include file="dsp_ProfileEdit.jsp" %>
   </fbx:case>
</fbx:switch>
</fbx:saveContent>
```

fbx_settings.jsp

Used to set application configuration information, each circuit might optionally have its own `fbx_settings.jsp` file. This is what an `fbx_settings.jsp` file looks like:

```
<%
   String defaultFuseaction = "home.main";
   fusebox.suppressErrors = false;
   if( fusebox.isHomeCircuit )
   {
     application.setAttribute( "name", "FuseboxApp" );
   }
%>
```

fbx_layouts.jsp

The `fbx_layouts.jsp` is used to set a circuit's layout file and directory information. This file is optional. Here is an example `fbx_layouts.jsp` file:

```
<%
   fusebox.layoutDir = "";
   fusebox.layoutFile = "TypicalLayout.jsp";
%>
```

fbx_include.jsp

When included in a fuse (using the include directive), this file makes sure that the request's Fusebox object is available in local scope and that the Fusebox Tag Library can be accessed. This file does not have a ColdFusion cousin. It is a utility file for the Fusebox/JSP environment. Typically, this file will reside in an application's WEB–INF directory, where it can be referenced easily with a relative URI. This is what `fbx_include.jsp` looks like:

```
<%@ taglib uri="/WEB-INF/fusebox.tld" prefix="fbx" %>
<%@ page import="org.fusebox.Fusebox, java.util.*" %>
<%
    Fusebox fusebox = (Fusebox) request.getAttribute( Fusebox.FUSEBOX );
%>
```

fusebox.tld

`fusebox.tld` describes the Fusebox Tag Library (TLD stands for tag library descriptor). Refer to the J2EE specification for more information on TLD files.

web.xml

This standard JSP web application configuration file is necessary to define the Fusebox Tag Library. Refer to the J2EE specification for more information on `web.xml` files.

fusebox-j2ee.jar

This file conveniently packages the compiled Fusebox classes and makes them available to the JSP environment.

Custom JSP Tags

The J2EE Fusebox framework requires the use of some custom JSP tags for operation. These tags also are available for general development use. A brief overview of the standard tags is provided next.

fbx:fusedoc

The `fbx:fusedoc` tag is used to enclose a fuse's XML Fusedoc. Here is an example of this file in conjunction with a Fusedoc:

```
<fbx:fusedoc>
<fusedoc fuse="act_queryServer.jsp">
   ...
</fusedoc>
</fbx:fusedoc>
```

fbx:saveContent

The `fbx:saveContent` tag stores its translated body content in a request scope variable. Its most common use is for caching display fuse output for use in a nested layout. Here is an example usage of the `saveContent` tag:

```
<fbx:saveContent variable="fusebox.layout">
    JSP Output…
</fbx:saveContent>
```

fbx:switch

The `fbx:switch` tag works in conjunction with the `fbx:case` tag to provide standard switch/case execution logic. This tag is most commonly used in Fusebox `fbx_switch.jsp` files, but it also is used in `fbx_layous.jsp`.

fbx:case

The `fbx:case` tag requires being a child of an `fbx:switch` tag. The body of only one `fbx:case` will be executed within an `fbx:switch` tag, just like ColdFusion's `<cfswitch>` and `<cfcase>`. Each fuseaction appears as an instance of this tag in a circuit's `fbx_switch.jsp` file.

Java Class Files

J2EE Fusebox does require the use of a few compiled classes. The use of compiled classes might be somewhat foreign to ColdFusion developers, but most classes are used behind the scenes, and a Fusebox developer will not have to directly access them.

The last class file we'll mention here is `org.fusebox.Fusebox`; it provides access to the Fusebox API. An instance of this class is created for every Fusebox request and used by the core `fbx_fusebox.jsp` page.

Fusebox in the J2EE Framework Landscape

Along with the J2EE specification, Sun Microsystems released two different J2EE programming models known as Model 1 and Model 2. Both models were released as generic development patterns, not as specific standards. Model 1 designs are page centric, usually consisting of a collection of JSP pages that more or less work independently of each other. Model 2 architectures follow the Model-View-Controller (MVC) design pattern and are typically more complex than page-based systems. Both Model 1 and Model 2 designs have their advantages.

Model 1 systems are conceptually less complex and usually easier to build. However, purely page-based designs generally suffer from some inherent problems. One problem is that pages become difficult to maintain. The entangling of different scripting routines requires that developers who are working on a page be skilled in multiple programming languages and concepts. Another problem is that Model 1 code assets are difficult to reuse. Without a high-level architecture to structure the pieces, individual files are often handcrafted for their specific role within one system.

Model 2 architectures seek to eliminate the problems of purely page-based designs. By nature, MVC provides a clean separation of business logic and display logic, similar to Fusebox. This separation allows individual components to be reused and integrated easily with other components. The biggest disadvantages of such a system are complexity and reliance on compiled classes. Frequently, these issues translate to limited customization and difficulty in modifying existing code.

J2EE Fusebox combines the simplicity of Model 1 with the modularity and power of Model 2. J2EE Fusebox is JSP centric, but fuses are separable and meant to be kept simple, with well-defined roles. Fusebox is also a structured hub-and-spoke system, keeping presentation, control, and business logic separated. This maintains modularity and means that independent circuits can be reused easily. As a result, J2EE Fusebox allows developers to enjoy the major benefits of a Model 2 architecture, but with the simplicity offered by Model 1 designs.

Some additional features of J2EE Fusebox are not found in other J2EE frameworks. XML-based Fusedocs are a unique facet of Fusebox that works to keep the components of a Fusebox implementation clear and maintainable. In J2EE Fusebox, configuration files are coded in JSP, can contain logic, and are applied with every request. For a developer, this means that a J2EE Fusebox system needing modifications does not need to be rebuilt. A new circuit module can be added to an application by updating only one Fusebox system file. This ability to drag and drop components to existing applications equals an unparalleled level of code reuse. Additionally, the scalable circuit structure and use of layout templates in Fusebox means it is the first standards-based J2EE framework that legitimately solves the pervasive problem of nested layouts.

J2EE Fusebox Resources

A growing number of tools and resources are available for J2EE Fusebox developers, as this section details.

SourceForge

SourceForge.net is the world's largest open source development web site and current home of the J2EE Fusebox development project, found at

```
http://www.sourceforge.net/projects/j2ee-fusebox
```

The J2EE Fusebox project web site provides several useful resources for developers, such as documentation, sample applications, and the latest code releases. It is also the best place to learn how to get involved in the J2EE Fusebox development effort.

Synthis

Synthis Corporation's (`http://www.synthis.com`) Adalon is an analysis, modeling, and design tool that helps unify development phases. It is the first tool built from the ground up to support business process design for web applications, and it is the only commercial tool capable of generating code skeletons in J2EE Fusebox and ColdFusion Fusebox. Synthis writes code for you, and it also allows modifications to the code generators through XSLT style sheets.

The J2EE implementation of Fusebox has come a long way in a short period of time, clearly indicating the depth of work that preceded it in the ColdFusion community. Even in this most "techie" of development worlds, Fusebox's simplicity brings clarity, focus, and power.

What a Ride!

As we've seen through our tour of the more exotic lands of this chapter, Fusebox is not a ColdFusion-dependent framework. Fusebox is a mindset—a way of working that offers an opportunity to better analyze, design, and build web-based projects in a variety of environments.

The Fusebox community has really only scratched the surface of these alternative environments, and the benefits are being realized already. We as Fuseboxers have the opportunity to respond to requests for system development in three of the most popular development languages available today, all without abandoning the techniques that have come to serve us so well. We can only imagine where the ride could lead in years to come.

Our next (and final) chapter is a bit of a change from the rest of the book. Instead of taking the usual tech-manual summary approach to closing the book, we decided to check in on Stan and Brody in the aftermath of the Third Wheel Bikes project, just to see how things are going. Stay tuned as the adventure continues.

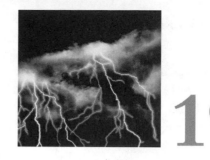

19

The Adventure Continues

Shootin' Hoops

The hoop thrummed its complaint as Stan's shot rebounded away, missing the target. Brody grabbed the ball and headed back to half-court, thinking about Janice's project as he and Stan faced each other in their daily lunchtime ritual. Brody dribbled the ball, contemplating game strategy and the job they had just finished.

"So why do you think Janice's project went so well?" Brody asked Stan.

"Mainly because we handled it completely differently from anything we've done before. It's Fusebox, dude," remarked Stan.
Brody took the opportunity to lunge past Stan, heading straight in for a clean lay-up. He tossed the ball and a question to Stan.

"You really think Fusebox made that much difference? I mean, sure it was great to get all the design stuff worked out up front, but it seemed like Janice was just a lot easier to deal with than other clients we've had."

"Brody, before we started using Fusebox, how did we handle a project?" Stan kept an eye on Brody, trying to decide how he might find a path through the key.

"Whaddya mean? We just did it. We know what we're doing."
Brody knew Stan was trying to distract him from the game, but it
wasn't working. He hadn't lost to Stan yet, and he didn't intend to
start now.

"That's just it, though. We just did it. We started out talking to
the client, played it by ear as we went along, and just hoped everything would work out." Stan feinted for the hoop, and then pulled
up and launched a long, high-arcing airball. Brody snickered under
his breath and chased the ball.

"Yeah," said Stan, "I guess it was sort of like your shooting—aim
for the hole and pray."

"Thanks," Brody muttered sarcastically.

"Any time," said Stan with satisfaction.

"Seriously, Brody, when we decided to use Fusebox on Janice's
project, it was like opening up a playbook for the project. We knew
everything we were going to do before we even started."

"And you think that made a difference in the way Janice acted
toward us?" questioned Brody.

"Of course it did. We were able to talk about the whole process
like we knew exactly what to expect. We came off looking like
pros, instead of like we were just feeling our way along. That had to
make her feel more comfortable trusting us with the work. Hey!"
Stan jumped to cut off Brody, who had slid past the lecturing Stan
and headed down the half court. As usual, Stan was a half-step
slower and could do nothing but watch as Brody sunk another
well-practiced two-pointer.

"No fair! You got me thinking about the project," Stan com-
plained.

"Too bad, man. Besides, I've put that move past you a thousand
times. You should have seen it coming." Brody's well-placed bounce
pass slipped through Stan's fingers and caught him in the stomach.

"Kind of like FLiP, huh? You always know what comes next."
Stan was having a hard time concentrating on the game. His mind
kept returning to the way the Third Wheel Bikes site seemed to just
grow by itself.

"Yeah, I guess you're right. It was really nice to know what was
going to happen after I finished doing the prototype," Brody
replied, once again setting up his defense.

"But it's more than just the prototyping. Sure, that's the part you like, but you're the designer. But FLiP made the whole project easier for everybody." Stan stood at half court with his hands on his knees, catching his breath.

"Even Janice?" asked Brody.

"Especially Janice." Stan started a slow walking dribble down court.

"Why 'especially' her? We did all the work."

"Sure, but think about it. Our clients in the days before Fusebox had to take our word for what was going on after the initial requirements gathering. Unless we made special efforts to tell the clients what was going on, they didn't really have a clue. They just hoped that when the deadline rolled around, we would have their site ready." Stan reversed course and started back toward half court, considering his next move.

"But Janice knew what we were going to do next because we told her up front how FLiP works." Brody followed, keeping a careful eye on Stan.

"Right. Starting from the first wireframing session, she could see the project take shape and make progress." Stan paused, changed course again, and headed for the basket.

"She really liked seeing my prototype, too." Brody neatly matched strides with Stan, waiting for him to make his move.

"Of course she did. That's the part that makes it really come alive. And even though she took a while to make up her mind about some of the appearance issues, none of it impacted me while you two were working it out. I finished the coding on two other projects while you were finalizing the prototype." Stan put up another high arcing shot, this time narrowly missing his target. The rebound favored him, though, and he stepped back with the ball, trying to find a line past Brody.

"I was really worried that after we had the prototype frozen, she would think everything was done. I really liked your idea to render the whole thing in shades of gray and turn their colors on as the coding was completed for each feature. That was an excellent way to let her see the coding progress." Brody liked working with Stan because of considerate notions like this.

"I read about doing that on a mail list. I thought it would work for us, and because you base everything on style sheets anyway, I figured it would be pretty easy to do." Stan decided on the direct route, and charged the basket. His lay-up didn't exactly have style, but it went in. Brody took the ball out and checked it to Stan. With the ball back in his hands, Brody planned his partner's demise.

"Definitely cool. Janice really liked checking in every day to see what else was 'colorized.' I did, too, because I was working on that other project and it let me see how you were doing on my site." Brody took three long strides and launched himself into the air, ending his flight with a resounding jam.

"Slam-dunk! Just like coding with Fusedocs," cheered Stan. Defeat at Brody's hands was a daily occurrence, and Stan didn't mind as long as Brody showed him a trick or two.

"Fusedocs?! What's that got to do with slammin'?" Brody tossed Stan the ball and stood on the court, waiting for Stan to explain his point.

"Everything. Because of Fusedocs, I could architect the site based on your prototype and then work on slammin' out the code. After all the fuses were documented, the big e-picture thinking was done, and I could just tune out the world and concentrate on writing awesome code." Stan's analogy had temporarily distracted Brody, allowing Stan a quick jog to the net. He didn't have enough vertical jump to slam like Brody, but the points counted just the same. Brody was a little confused. "I thought Fusedocs were supposed to help if you had a bunch of coders working on the project. You mean they helped you even though you did all the coding?"

"Sure. With everything I needed to know for each fuse already packaged in its Fusedoc, I didn't need to go anywhere else for information while I was coding. I could focus on each fuse and not worry about anything else. It's really cool—kind of like being 'in the zone' when you're playing—nothing to worry about except the game."

"I hear ya. I love it when I can do my thing without getting distracted."

As if on cue, Brody loped under the backboard, leapt, and turned in mid-air, executing a reverse lay-up that made Stan wish he could jump.

"Yep. Nothing like leaving the distractions behind," Stan grinned, realizing his focus had once again wandered from the game, this time to memories of coding `ThirdWheelBikes.com`.

"How did you know what fuses to write Fusedocs for in the first place?" Brody wondered aloud as he tossed the ball to Stan.

"It's not like my prototype told you any of that."

"Well, not in so many words," Stan admitted, "but it was all there just the same. All I had to do was go over each page of the frozen prototype looking for exit points. That gave me a good idea of all the things the application had to do. Then I just started organizing exit points and page contents into logical groups. That gave me ideas for fuseactions and circuits. After I had the circuits and fuse-actions figured out, I could decide what fuses I would need for each fuseaction."

"So every Fusebox architect would have come up with that design, huh?" asked Brody.

"No way. No two architects would come up with the same design," explained Stan.

"Even using the same prototype?" Brody wondered.

"Even using the same prototype. We all think a little bit differently and organize circuits a little differently. That's one of the great things about Fusebox, though. It lets the architect decide how to structure the application and doesn't restrict you solely on an organizational basis. I'm sure that if Hal Helms or Steve Nelson designed Third Wheel from your prototype, they'd each come up with a different design." Stan was warming to his subject now, as was always the case when someone showed interest in his work.

"But all three would still look and work the way Janice decided she wanted it to work in the prototype?" asked Brody.

"Yep," Stan said. "That's the test they would all need to pass."
Brody was impressed. "That is so cool. I guess it's kind of like when some of my web design friends get together and talk about style sheets and things. We each have our favorite methods for achieving a certain appearance. They're all different, but they all work. Come on, you gonna play or talk?"

"Keep your shirt on." Stan generally spent more time thinking about playing than actually playing. "Sure, everybody has his own way of working. We're always more concerned with *what* we're supposed to do, not *how* we're going to do it."

"Yeah," remarked Brody. "I've noticed you saying that repeatedly over the past few weeks. I thought maybe you'd joined a cult or something…"

"Well, it's true," Stan went on. When you're not so worried about the *how*, the *what* becomes really easy to figure out.

Just then, a sporty Honda two-door appeared at the corner. Janice pulled into the parking lot adjacent to the court and stepped out of her car. She walked toward Stan and Brody, thinking how nice it must be to have your own outdoor gym right next door to the office.

"Hi, guys!" Janice waved as she approached.

"Janice! Hi!" Stan and Brody met her halfway.

"What brings you by?" asked Stan.

"I just thought I'd drop off the last payment for `ThirdWheelBikes.com`. Thanks again, guys."

"Oh, no problem. We had a ball working with you." Stan quipped, tossing the basketball to Brody.

"Stan, you're sick, you know it?" Brody said, shaking his head at his partner's pun. "It's true, though, Janice. We really did have a great time working with you. It's been one of our best projects ever."

"Well, thanks. I was worried about how it was going to go, but you guys made it seem easy. Every step of the way, you knew exactly what was going on."

Stan exchanged an "I told you so" glance with Brody, glad to see his theory proven.

"Brody and I were just talking about the project and how well it went. We're really glad you feel the same way."

"Oh, definitely. I wish all the business dealings I have would go as well."

"What was the best part about the project, in your opinion?" Stan inquired.

Janice responded, "I really liked the way you built the front end along with me, helping me make decisions about everything. I'm still not sure I entirely understand what happened after the front end was done, when you were doing the daily work that made it change from grays back to full color, but I really enjoyed watching that happen. I felt like I could always go look and see what was happening, without making you guys feel like I was always checking up on you."

Stan agreed. "Yeah, it was nice to be able to work like that. I really enjoyed the final delivery date. Seeing the site go live as `ThirdWheelBikes.com` was really cool."

"I suppose so," replied Janice, "but it didn't seem like such a big deal to me. After all, it was just the same stuff you'd been showing me all along. No big deal."

"Yeah, no big deal," Brody said. He and Stan couldn't help thinking about some of their past projects where final delivery had been a huge, painful, costly deal.

"Anyway, thanks again, guys. I'll give you a call when I need more help. Oh, and I have a friend who owns a department store downtown. He's interested in looking into a web site with online sales. I told him to give you a call." Janice returned to her car and drove off, leaving Stan and Brody grinning like idiots.

"All right! Referral business!" Stan put his hand up for the well-deserved high-five.

"This Fusebox thing was definitely the ticket, Stan."

"Don't I know it, Bro," Stan agreed.

"So what do we do now? Is there more to do, or learn, or what?" Brody was anxious to get going on more projects if they were going to follow the pattern set by Third Wheel.

"Well, I go onto the Fusebox mailing lists. They're a big help, and..." Stan started.

"How hard is that?" interrupted Brody, "Getting on the mailing lists, I mean."

"Oh, it's a piece of cake," Stan explained. "You just send an email to the address for the list you want. It's `subscribe-fusebox@topica.com` for the Fusebox list, `subscribe-fbcommunity@topica.com` for the Fusebox Community list, and `subscribe-SteerFB@topica.com` for the Steering list. Easy."

"Excellent. And what do you get there?" Brody hadn't had much experience with email lists, but he was curious.

"Whatever discussion happens each day," said Stan. "You can start your own discussions, too. Everybody's there, too—all the members of the Fusebox Council, and Fuseboxers from all over the world."

"Cool. You mean you can actually ask Hal Helms a question and he'll answer you?" Brody imagined this to be somewhat akin to asking for fashion tips from Tommy Hilfiger.

"Sure." Stan was nonchalant. "He and Steve and the rest of 'em are always answering questions."

"So when do you get to be one of the bigwigs?" Brody enjoyed teasing Stan.

"Maybe in time…" Stan had thought about this before. I'm not ready to run for the Steering Committee or anything, but one of these days I might think about it."

"They let you do that?" Brody asked with awe. I mean, you can decide what's going to be in Fusebox in future versions?"

"Sort of, yeah." Stan went on, "Everybody's encouraged to explore and try new ideas. That's a big part of what Fusebox is all about."

"Sounds good to me!" exclaimed Brody.

"Yeah," agreed Stan, "and I just heard about a new book that's coming out. It's supposed to be all about Fusebox and FLiP, and it features a fictitious development team with an architect-coder and a designer. The book follows them through building a web app."

"Cool. Sounds kind of like us," thought Brody.

"Yeah, but I'll bet they're a lot cooler than us," said Stan.

"Probably. Hey, what's the score?" Brody tossed Stan the ball and headed back for the court.

"13-0, my lead." Stan tossed out his usual "We now return to the game already in progress" score.

"In your dreams, programmer geek!" teased Brody.

"Yeah, okay, designer dude. Watch this!" Stan pulled back and launched a one-armed three-point attempt from half-court. He and Brody both watched slack-jawed as it hurtled through the cool afternoon air and swished through the hoop, "Nothin' but net."

Some Final Words

We hope that you have enjoyed reading this book as much as we have enjoyed bringing it to you. It has been more than a year in the making, but the result is truly fun to see.

As you can tell from this final chapter, for us, Fusebox is more than just a way to work. Fusebox is a way to think, a way to plan, a way to build, and a way to honestly enjoy the creative work of web application development.

All of this creativity happens mainly because Fusebox allows us to focus on the task at hand, wherever we might be in the project. If we're doing "architect stuff," we can focus on thinking like architects. If we're designing, we can focus on designing and making sure the client likes what he sees. If we're writing code, we can focus on writing code. Regardless of your role in the project, Fusebox clarifies it.

The coding aspects of Fusebox, like exit fuseactions and fuse purpose and naming conventions, help reinforce coding habits that will benefit all our work, from a standalone custom tag on up. Fusedocs give us a basis not only for documenting, but also for monitoring and reporting on our development projects.

The development process aspects of the Fusebox Lifecycle Process (FLiP) help reinforce the way we analyze new problems and projects and the way we go about building solutions to those problems.

Regardless of whether you're a die-hard ColdFusion fan, or you're experimenting with Fusebox in some of its more exotic incarnations, FLiP makes the whole process more manageable.

And, of course, there's the Fusebox community, that worldwide gang of coders who somehow seem to be up at all hours, day or night, waiting for someone to post something interesting on one of the email lists. A large part of the reason we enjoy working in Fusebox is the people we get to meet and work with. It is truly a dynamic and inspiring group. We strongly encourage you to actively participate in whatever way you like. Start at `fusebox.org` and go from there.

Finally, we'd like to thank you for buying this book and sticking with us through it. We hope you've enjoyed the trip as much as we've enjoyed going through it with you. Don't forget to drop by `ThirdWheelBikes.com` to see Janice's application live (although you can't buy anything real there). You can also visit the book's site from there.

Good luck in your Fuseboxing. Drop us a note and let us know how your adventure is coming along.

—Jeff Peters and Nat Papovich

*"The last thing that we find in making a
book is to know what we must put first."*

—Blaise Pascal

4

Appendixes

Fusebox 3.0 Specification Reference

P ART 2 OF THIS BOOK, "FUSEBOX CODING," serves as a complete reference to the Fusebox Framework. However, that Part is eight chapters and many pages long. This appendix will serve as a quick reference to the Fusebox framework and should be helpful for experienced Fusebox developers just learning the new files. It will also serve well as condensed reference for developers creating their first Fusebox application who need to "jog their memory."

We will cover five topics in this appendix, including the framework files (fbx_ prefixed files), fuse uses and their rules, exit fuseactions (XFAs), and Fusedocs. We will also briefly cover the basics of nested circuits and nested layouts, including the execution order of a Fusebox request.

The Framework Files

There are seven Fusebox framework files. Using the Fusebox framework allows you to leverage the experience and hard work of the entire Fusebox community. Less time spent developing a framework to contain your code means less time spent working. Table A.1 shows each file, the order in which it is processed, and a brief description about it.

Table A.1   **The Framework Files**

Processing Order	Filename	Description
1	fbx_fusebox30_CFxx.cfm	Commonly referred to as "the core file," this file sets up the entire Fusebox framework that calls the other core files and fuses. The xx denotes ColdFusion version-specific files.
2	fbx_circuits.cfm	This file establishes the relationship of circuits to each other by "registering" circuits with the application.
3	fbx_settings.cfm	One per circuit, this file allows circuit-wide (and child circuit) settings and inheritance.
4	fbx_switch.cfm	Little more than a `<cfswitch>`/`<cfcase>` statement, this file controls the application flow, based on the fuseaction.
5	fbx_layouts.cfm	One per circuit, this file controls which layout file to use for the request.
N/A	fbx_savecontent.cfm	Fusebox relies on `<cfsavecontent>`, introduced in CF5. This file emulates the native tag's functionality.

More information about the Framework files can be found in Chapters 3, "The Fusebox Framework," and 4, "Handling a Fuseaction."

Fuse Rules

Fuses follow specific rules of use and employ standard naming prefixes (shown in Table A.3). Following the rules shown in Table A.2, your code is more easily reused, debugged, extended with new features, and provides a level of self documentation.

Table A.2 **Fuse Rules**

Rule Number	Description
Rule 1	A fuse is length challenged. Code should be short and concise. Try to fit each fuse's code on one screen.
Rule 2	A fuse is reusable. Fuses should only contain one atomic action, which is carefully defined.
Rule 3	A fuse by any other prefix isn't a fuse. All fuses must contain a prefix (see Table A.3 for a list) that denotes its role.
Rule 4	A fuse can be a naming rebel. Try to follow the standard naming practices and fuse types. However, if your environment needs another prefix, use it.
Rule 5	A fuse has a sense of self. Some types of code should not be in certain types of fuses. For example, display code should only be used for display fuses.
Rule 6	Fuse types congregate together. Fuses can be stored in their own subdirectories below the circuit.
Rule 7	A fuse contains Fusedocs. Fusedocs guide the fuse, determining its role and available variables. Fuses cannot live without Fusedocs.
Rule 8	A fuse is clueless. Fuses should not be tightly integrated into other fuses, nor should they rely heavily on external resources.
Rule 9	A fuse should watch its back. Fuses might get bad data or expect different datatypes than that which is provided. Code accordingly and expect the unexpected.
Rule 10	A fuse has a good name. In addition to prefixes, fuses should be named explicitly. `dsp_loginForm.cfm` is better than `dsp_clSm_frm.cfm`.

Fuse Types

There are three standard fuse types. Each type has a usage, with certain code allowed in that type. In addition, each fuse type is identified by a prefix, such as `dsp_loginForm.cfm`. Table A.3 shows the fuse types.

Table A.3 **Fuse Types**

Fuse Type	Prefix	Usage
Action	act_filename.cfm	No display; can only contain CFML logic and service calls.
Query	qry_filename.cfm	No display; only database interaction with this fuse.
Display	dsp_filename.cfm	Only fuse type that can present output to the client; should contain a minimal amount of ColdFusion logic.
Fusebox Framework	fbx_filename.cfm	Fusebox framework file. These are established files, most of which you modify very little.
Layout	lay_filename.cfm	Layout files contain the final output of the fuseaction and include any "wrapper" layout.

Because Fusebox limits certain kinds of code to specific fuse types, the result is a complete separation of display from logic. Due to this separation, debugging is easier and development is faster. Complete coverage of fuses, including rules for use and different fuse types, can be found in Chapter 5, "The Fuses."

Exit Fuseactions

Fuses should be designed so that they contain as few dependencies on the rest of the application as possible. This is why we use XFAs rather than hard-coded fuseactions. Following is a sample hard-coded fuseaction:

```
<form action="index.cfm?fuseaction=users.login" method="post">
```

Here is a sample XFA:

```
<form action="index.cfm?fuseaction=#xfa.submit#" method="post">
```

XFAs are nothing more than fuseaction values as variables. They are set in the fbx_switch.cfm just before <cfinclude>ing the fuse:

```
<cfcase value="privacy">
  <cfset xfa.continue="policy.payments">
  <cfset xfa.back="policy.security">
  <cfinclude template="dsp_privacy.cfm">
</cfcase>
```

This allows the `fbx_switch.cfm` file to control where each fuse it calls is allowed to go next. By using XFAs, we can write the fuse once but use it in different locations, and the links can go to different places. XFAs are covered fully in Chapter 6, "Exit Fuseactions."

Fusedocs

Because an individual fuse is supposed to be designed and coded as if it were unaware of the larger application using it, a formalized method should exist to describe everything that the fuse can assume and everything that it cannot. By carefully documenting every variable that a fuse is allowed to reference and every variable that a fuse is supposed to create, we can be assured minimum coupling by our most discrete units.

A Fusedoc appears at the top of every fuse. Here is an example Fusedoc:

```
<!---
<?xml version="1.0" encoding="UTF-8"?>
<!DOCTYPE fusedoc SYSTEM "http://fusebox.org/fd4.dtd">
<fusedoc fuse="act_deleteTask.cfm" language="ColdFusion"
➥specification="2.0">
  <responsibilities>I delete a task and any user_tasks associated with
  ➥that task.</responsibilities>
  <properties>
    <history author="Nat Papovich" date="08/10/2001"
    ➥email="nat@fusium.com" role="Architect" type="Create"/>
  </properties>
  <io>
    <in>
      <list name="taskID" scope="attributes" optional="False"/>
    </in>
    <out>
      <boolean name="success" scope="variables"/>
    </out>
  </io>
</fusedoc>
--->
```

Starting at the top, the `<fusedoc>` tag wraps the whole Fusedoc. Next, the `<responsibilities>` tag describes what this fuse accomplishes, in plain English. The `<history>` tag is like a stamp of who did what when to this fuse. This example shows the creator of the fuse. The final section describes the input and output (I/O) of the fuse—what variables are coming in and what variables need to go out. Fusedocs are exhaustively covered in Chapter 7, "Fusedocs."

Nested Circuits

The fuseaction variable always contains two values in what we refer to as a *compound fuseaction*. The first part determines the circuit that contains that fuseaction, and the second part is the actual fuseaction.

If a fuseaction is called in a circuit below the root, the `fbx_settings.cfm` file is run in the root as well as in every other circuit that is a parent of the target circuit. If a circuit is a sub-circuit, nested three deep from the root, then a total of four `fbx_settings.cfm` files are run, enabling a system of inheritance of variables. Nested circuits concepts are discussed in Chapter 8, "Nesting Circuits."

Nested Layouts

Similar to the way that nested circuits allow `fbx_settings.cfm` files to be executed in order, from the root circuit to the target circuit, nested layouts allow the output of the fuseaction to be nested in layouts that are applied by the parent circuits. `fbx_layouts.cfm` determines which layout file to use (one that uses the `lay_` prefix).

This allows one site-wide layout to be applied to all fuseactions (from the root `fbx_layouts.cfm` and layout file). Circuits can add their own layouts nested inside the root circuit. Additionally, the layout file can act as an "assembler," collecting multiple fuseactions from different circuits into one layout file, enabling portal-style page creation. The power and application of nested layouts are discussed in Chapter 9, "Nested Layouts."

B

Fusebox Glossary

action fuse A template that does not present data to the user or interact with the database. Usually has act_ as its prefix. For more information, see Chapter 3, "The Fusebox Framework."

architect The person responsible for the development of a Fusebox application. Oversees the entire project, and is responsible for circuit design and Fusedocs.

child circuit A circuit that is nested beneath another circuit. Sometimes called a sub-circuit. For more information, see Chapter 8, "Nesting Circuits."

circuit A collection of fuseactions. Circuits are groups of program behavior arranged according to common behavior. For example, all fuseactions having to do with management of user accounts might be placed in a circuit called Users. Deciding which fuseactions belong in which circuits is part of the architect's job. For more information, see Chapter 3, "The Fusebox Framework."

circuits file The file where circuit aliases are assigned (fbx_circuits.cfm). For more information, see Chapter 3, "The Fusebox Framework."

container circuit Within the context of a fuseaction, a circuit that falls within the hierarchy between the main circuit and the target circuit. For more information, see Chapter 9, "Nested Layouts."

container folder The directory or folder where a container circuit's files are stored.

core file   The file that handles the "heavy lifting" that is central to Fusebox processing. For ColdFusion in Windows, it's named `fbx_fuseboxNN_CFXX.cfm`, where NN is the Fusebox version and XX is the ColdFusion version. For ColdFusion in UNIX/Linux, it's named `fbx_fusebox30_CF50_nix.cfm`, with the same numerics. For more information, see Chapter 3, "The Fusebox Framework."

daily build   The result of each day's writing of code. Daily builds can be plugged into the prototype to demonstrate progress to the client. For more information, see Chapter 14, "Construction and Coding."

designer   The person who is responsible for the visual design of a Fusebox application.

DevNotes   A small utility used to provide discussion and feedback capability at the bottom of prototype pages. For more information, see Chapter 13, "Prototyping and DevNotes."

display fuse   A template that provides information to the user or allows user interaction. Display fuses do not interact with the database. Usually has `dsp_` as its prefix. For more information, see Chapter 3, "The Fusebox Framework."

exit fuseaction (XFA)   A variable that contains a fuseaction that can be used to exit a given fuse. For example, if a fuse uses a button named Save, the architect might create an XFA named `XFA.btnSave`, with the value "users.saveUser" stored in it. This allows fuses to be coded with variable destinations, such as fuseaction=#XFA.btnSave#, instead of being hard coded. For more information, see Chapter 6, "Exit Fuseactions."

exit point   A place where processing leaves a fuse, such as a form action or redirection. For more information, see Chapter 6, "Exit Fuseactions."

front end   Sometimes used to refer to a prototype. Because a Fusebox prototype becomes the front end for the finished application, this term is often used when talking to clients. For more information, see Chapter 13, "Prototyping and DevNotes."

fuse   An individual code file that contributes to processing a fuseaction. One or more fuses can contribute to a fuseaction. Typically divided into display, action, query, and sometimes URL categories. For more information, see Chapter 3, "The Fusebox Framework."

fuse file   The file that holds a fuse. In ColdFusion, a fuse file is a single CFML template. For more information, see Chapter 3, "The Fusebox Framework."

fuseaction   A collection of fuses that perform an action within a Fusebox application. For example, a fuseaction might consist of a query fuse to fetch data from a database and a display fuse to present the data to the user. For more information, see Chapter 3, "The Fusebox Framework."

fusebox file   The file that manages control of the application through use of the fuseaction variable. In Fusebox 3.0, this function is performed by `fbx_circuits.cfm`. For more information, see Chapter 3, "The Fusebox Framework."

Fusebox Lifecycle Process (FLiP)   A web development methodology that includes wireframes, prototypes, DevNotes, distributed coding, and unit testing. For more information, see Part 3, "Fusebox Lifecycle Process (FLiP)."

Fuseboxer   A person who uses Fusebox.

fusecoder   A person who writes the code for a fuse, as specified in its Fusedoc.

Fusedoc   A specification for documenting the inputs and outputs to be used by a fuse. Also refers to the documentation block at the top of a fuse file. The architect is responsible for creating the Fusedoc, and the fusecoder is responsible for writing the fuse's code according to its Fusedoc. For more information, see Chapter 7, "Fusedocs."

home circuit   The top-level circuit in a Fusebox application. Also called the main circuit. For more information, see Chapter 9, "Nested Layouts."

layout   The presentation HTML that surrounds the HTML produced by a circuit's fuseactions. For more information, see Chapter 9, "Nested Layouts."

layout file   A file that generates a circuit's layout. Usuaully has `lay_` as its prefix. A circuit's layout files are specified in its `fbx_layout.cfm` file. For more information, see Chapter 9, "Nested Layouts."

main circuit   Another name for the home circuit. For more information, see Chapter 8, "Nesting Circuits."

parent circuit   A circuit that is above another circuit in a nested hierarchy. For more information, see Chapter 8, "Nesting Circuits."

prototype   A static representation of the final application. A prototype looks and acts in every way, except the presence of production data, as the final application will. Uses query sims to mimic the presence of a database. For more information, see Chapter 13, "Prototyping and DevNotes."

prototype freeze   The point in time at which the client accepts the prototype as the plan for development. For more information, see Chapter 13, "Prototyping and DevNotes."

query fuse   A template that interacts with the database. Usually has `qry_` as its prefix. For more information, see Chapter 3, "The Fusebox Framework."

query sim   A query simulation. Query sims use Hal Helms' `QuerySim` tag to generate ColdFusion recordsets. They are used in place of live queries until the database has been constructed. For more information, see Chapter 14, "Construction and Coding."

settings file   Another name for `fbx_settings.cfm`. For more information, see Chapter 3, "The Fusebox Framework."

sub-circuit   Another name for a child circuit. For more information, see Chapter 8, "Nesting Circuits."

target circuit   In the context of a fuseaction, the circuit where the requested fuseaction is located. For more information, see Chapter 8, "Nesting Circuits" and Chapter 9, "Nested Layouts."

test harness   A template that establishes a valid Fusebox environment for the purpose of testing a fuse file. Test harnesses are not part of the production application. For more information, see Chapter 15, "Unit Testing."

unit test   A test of an individual fuse file. Unit tests are performed using test harnesses. For more information, see Chapter 15, "Unit Testing."

wireframe   A text-based representation of the application's business logic. Wireframes are used to develop the application concept prior to prototyping. For more information, see Chapter 12, "Wireframing."

XFA   *See* exit fuseaction.

C

Fusedoc Data Type Definition

UNLIKE THE ORIGINAL SPECIFICATION FOR Fusedoc, Fusedoc 2.0 is an XML vocabulary. As such, it is governed by a data type definition (DTD) file. A DTD is a formal definition for a given XML vocabulary. In other words, the DTD for Fusedoc defines what we can say in a Fusedoc. This file specifies how a Fusedoc-compliant dataset might be formed.

For those who are unfamiliar with XML, keep the following points in mind when reading any DTD:

- XML datasets consist of hierarchical collections of elements. Each element is encoded in a tag.

- An XML dataset must start with a single root element. All other elements descend from the root.

- In the DTD, each element is specified by an `<!ELEMENT>` tag. Its definition lists the elements that can be enclosed within it.

- The vertical pipe symbol (|) represents an OR condition.

- The question mark indicates an optional element.

- The plus sign (+) indicates the presence of one or more of the corresponding element(s).

- The asterisk (*) indicates the presence of zero or more of the corresponding element(s).
- Parentheses are used to logically group options.
- The descriptor "#PCDATA" indicates the ability to enter free text.
- The <!ATTLIST> tag lists the attributes that can be used with an element.

Armed with this information, we can rely on the DTD for Fusedoc to define the boundaries for us. Based on this specification, we know what to expect when we're dealing with Fusedoc datasets. Listing C.1 contains the complete Fusedoc 2.0 DTD. For more information on Fusedocs, refer to Chapter 7, "Fusedocs."

Listing C.1   **Fusedoc 2.0 DTD**

```
<?xml version="1.0" encoding="US-ASCII"?>
<!-- edited with XML Spy v3.5 NT (http://www.xmlspy.com) by Hal Helms
(HHI) -->
<!ELEMENT fusedoc (responsibilities | (properties? | io? |
assertions?)+)>
<!ATTLIST fusedoc
  specification CDATA #FIXED "2.0"
  fuse CDATA #REQUIRED
  language CDATA #FIXED "ColdFusion"
>
<!ELEMENT responsibilities (#PCDATA)>
<!ELEMENT properties ((history* | property* | note*)+)>
<!ELEMENT history (#PCDATA)>
<!ATTLIST history
  type (create | update) "create"
  date CDATA #IMPLIED
  author CDATA #IMPLIED
  role CDATA #IMPLIED
  email CDATA #IMPLIED
  comments CDATA #IMPLIED
>
<!ELEMENT property EMPTY>
<!ATTLIST property
  name CDATA #REQUIRED
  value CDATA #REQUIRED
  comments CDATA #IMPLIED
>
<!ELEMENT note (#PCDATA)>
<!ATTLIST note
  author CDATA #IMPLIED
  date CDATA #IMPLIED
>
```

```
<!ELEMENT io ((in* | out* | passthrough*)+)>
<!ELEMENT in ((string* | number* | boolean* | datetime* | array* |
↪structure* | recordset* | list* | cookie* | file*)+)>
<!ELEMENT out ((string* | number* | boolean* | datetime* | array* |
↪structure* | recordset* | list* | cookie* | file*)+)>
<!ELEMENT passthrough ((string* | number* | boolean* | datetime* |
↪array* | structure* | recordset* | list* | cookie* | file*)+)>
<!ELEMENT string EMPTY>
<!ATTLIST string
  name CDATA #REQUIRED
  scope (application | attributes | caller | cgi | client | form |
  ↪formOrUrl | request | server | session | url | variables)
  ↪"variables"
  comments CDATA #IMPLIED
  mask CDATA #IMPLIED
  onCondition CDATA #IMPLIED
  format (CFML | WDDX) "CFML"
  optional (true | false) "false"
  default CDATA #IMPLIED
>
<!ELEMENT number EMPTY>
<!ATTLIST number
  name CDATA #REQUIRED
  scope (application | attributes | caller | cgi | client | form |
  ↪formOrUrl | request | server | session | url | variables)
  ↪"variables"
  comments CDATA #IMPLIED
  precision (decimal | integer) #IMPLIED
  onCondition CDATA #IMPLIED
  format (CFML | WDDX) "CFML"
  optional (true | false) "false"
  default CDATA #IMPLIED
>
<!ELEMENT boolean EMPTY>
<!ATTLIST boolean
  name CDATA #REQUIRED
  scope (application | attributes | caller | cgi | client | form |
  ↪formOrUrl | request | server | session | url | variables)
  ↪"variables"
  comments CDATA #IMPLIED
  onCondition CDATA #IMPLIED
  format (CFML | WDDX) "CFML"
  optional (true | false) "false"
  default CDATA #IMPLIED
>
<!ELEMENT datetime EMPTY>
<!ATTLIST datetime
  name CDATA #REQUIRED
  scope (application | attributes | caller | cgi | client | form |
  ↪formOrUrl | request | server | session | url | variables)
  ↪"variables"
```

continues

Listing C.1   **Continued**

```
  mask CDATA "m/d/yy"
  comments CDATA #IMPLIED
  onCondition CDATA #IMPLIED
  format (CFML | WDDX) "CFML"
  optional (true | false) "false"
  default CDATA #IMPLIED
>
<!ELEMENT recordset ((string* | number* | boolean* | datetime* |
➥list*)+)>
<!ATTLIST recordset
  name CDATA #REQUIRED
  scope (application | attributes | caller | cgi | client | form |
➥formOrUrl | request | server | session | url | variables)
➥"variables"
  primarykeys CDATA #IMPLIED
  comments CDATA #IMPLIED
  onCondition CDATA #IMPLIED
  format (CFML | WDDX) "CFML"
  optional (true | false) "false"
>
<!ELEMENT list EMPTY>
<!ATTLIST list
  name CDATA #REQUIRED
  delims CDATA "comma"
  scope (application | attributes | caller | cgi | client | form |
➥formOrUrl | request | server | session | url | variables)
➥"variables"
  comments CDATA #IMPLIED
  onCondition CDATA #IMPLIED
  format (CFML | WDDX) "CFML"
  optional (true | false) "false"
  default CDATA #IMPLIED
>
<!ELEMENT array ((string* | number* | boolean* | datetime* | array* |
➥structure* | recordset* | list*)+)>
<!ATTLIST array
  name CDATA #REQUIRED
  scope (application | attributes | caller | cgi | client | form |
➥formOrUrl | request | server | session | url | variables)
➥"variables"
  comments CDATA #IMPLIED
  onCondition CDATA #IMPLIED
  format (CFML | WDDX) "CFML"
  optional (true | false) "false"
>
<!ELEMENT structure ((string* | number* | boolean* | datetime* | array*
➥| structure* | recordset* | list*)+)>
<!ATTLIST structure
  name CDATA #REQUIRED
```

```
   scope (application | attributes | caller | cgi | client | form |
   ↪formOrUrl | request | server | session | url | variables)
   ↪"variables"
   comments CDATA #IMPLIED
   onCondition CDATA #IMPLIED
   format (CFML | WDDX) "CFML"
   optional (true | false) "false"
>
<!ELEMENT file EMPTY>
<!ATTLIST file
   path CDATA #REQUIRED
   action (read | write | append | overwrite | delete | available)
   ↪"available"
   comments CDATA #IMPLIED
   onCondition CDATA #IMPLIED
   optional (true | false) "false"
   default CDATA #IMPLIED
>
<!ELEMENT cookie EMPTY>
<!ATTLIST cookie
   name CDATA #REQUIRED
   expires (now | never | CDATA) #IMPLIED
   secure (true | false) "false"
   comments CDATA #IMPLIED
   onCondition CDATA #IMPLIED
   format (CFML | WDDX) "CFML"
   optional (true | false) "false"
   default CDATA #IMPLIED
>
<!ELEMENT assertions (assert+)>
<!ELEMENT assert EMPTY>
<!ATTLIST assert
   that CDATA #REQUIRED
   on (client | server) "server"
   else CDATA #IMPLIED
   comments CDATA #IMPLIED
   onCondition CDATA #IMPLIED
>
```

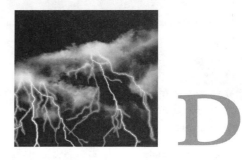

Fusebox Version 2 to Version 3 Comparison

L EARNING VERSION 3 OF FUSEBOX IF YOU already know version 2 might seem like an intimidating process because of all the apparent differences, but it is actually quite simple. A couple of new features are available in version 3, as well as a few new framework files to use. The way you use some of the previous files has changed, too. Let's take these one at a time.

Two New Features of Fusebox 3

Fusebox 3 contains all of the same elements as Fusebox 2, but they are implemented differently, for greater efficiency (faster and easier to reuse) and functionality (more powerful features). Fusebox 3 introduces two brand-new elements: Exit Fuseactions (XFAs) and XML-based Fusedocs.

XFAs

An *exit* is simply an exit point of a template, such as `<a href>` links, form actions, and JavaScript redirects. Exits in a typical template look like this:

```
<b>Envision your question to the Magic Eight Ball...</b><br>

<a href="#request.self#?fuseaction=eightball.answer">VIEW YOUR
⇒ANSWER</a>
<br>

<a href="#request.self#?fuseaction=home.cover">back to main menu</a>
```

XFAs are simply the dynamically declared fuseactions of the fuse's exits. For example, the fuseactions of the preceding example code are `eightball.answer` and `home.cover`.

The main concept of XFAs is simple—reference all exit fuseactions with variables. XFAs are defined in each `<cfcase>` statement of the Fusebox code (that is, the fuseaction):

```
<cfcase value="question">
  <cfset XFA.menu = "home.cover">
  <cfset XFA.submit = "eightball.answer">
  <cfinclude template="dsp_question.cfm">
</cfcase>
```

XFAs are then referred to in the fuse code:

```
<b>Envision your question to the Magic Eight Ball...</b><br>

<a href="#request.self#?fuseaction=#XFA.submit#">VIEW YOUR ANSWER</a>
<br>


<a href="#request.self#?fuseaction=#XFA.menu#">back to main menu</a>
```

Because only one file (the file containing the `<cfswitch>` statement) needs to be modified to change any of its fuse's exits, exit fuseactions make code maintenance and reuse more efficient. This is one of the many reasons that XFAs are part of the Fusebox 3 specification. See more about XFAs in Chapter 6, "Exit Fuseactions." The second element introduced to Fusebox in version 3 is XML Fusedocs.

XML Fusedocs

Fusedocs are basically the blueprint of a fuse, residing as comments at the beginning of your code. You should be able to know everything about the functionality of a fuse simply by reading its Fusedoc. The syntax of Fusedocs is outside the scope of this appendix but is covered in depth in Chapter 7, "Fusedocs." Fusebox 2 recommended the use of Fusedocs in the Extended Backus-Naur Form (EBNF) format. Machines found that this syntax was cryptic and difficult to read. A great deal of guesswork also was involved in reading Fusedocs because the language was not complete. An example EBNF Fusedoc looks like this:

```
<!---
|| BEGIN FUSEDOC ||
|| Properties ||
Name: dsp_question.cfm
Author: nat@fusium.com
|| Responsibilities ||
I display a link that says "ask a question" and links to xfa.answer
|| Attributes ||
--> xfa.mainMenu
-->xfa.answer
++> request.self
|| END FUSEDOC ||
--->
```

In Fusebox 3, XML-based Fusedocs are a required element. Using XML, we cannot run out of symbols to accurately describe the data, and it is easy to use XML validators to check the formatting of Fusedocs. Following is an XML Fusedoc:

```
<!---
<fusedoc language="ColdFusion" specification="2.0"
➥fuse="dsp_question.cfm">
  <responsibilities>
    I display a link that says "ask a question" and links to xfa.answer
  </responsibilities>
  <properties>
    <history author="Nat Papovich" email="nat@fusium.com"
    ➥role="Architect" type="Create" />
  </properties>
  <io>
    <in>
      <string name="self" scope="request" />
      <structure name="xfa" scope="variables">
        <string name="mainMenu" />
        <string name="answer" />
      </structure>
    </in>
  </io>
</fusedoc>
--->
```

Like XFAs, Fusedocs make Fusebox more efficient by enabling programmers to review the functionality of a fuse without reading a single line of code. Now that we have covered the two new elements introduced into Fusebox with version 3, let's get into some nuts and bolts.

Version 2 and Version 3 Framework Files

Fusebox 3 uses a reserved file prefix for key configuration files. All of these files use the same prefix to make development simpler. Any file having an `fbx_` prefix is described in the Fusebox 3 specification. `fbx_` files are similar to the application files commonly used in Fusebox 2, and they have taken over most of their functionality. Let's review the Fusebox 2 and Fusebox 3 framework files.

Fusebox 2 Framework Files

Table D.1 shows the framework files that were commonly used in Fusebox 2 along with their Fusebox 3 counterparts.

Table D.1 **Fusebox 2 Framework Files**

Filename	Description	Similar to Fusebox 3 File
index.cfm	Contains the `<cfswitch>` statement, and `<cfinclude>`s a few files.	fbx_switch.cfm
app_globals.cfm	Contains application-wide (global) settings.	Root fbx_settings.cfm
app_locals.cfm	Contains circuit-specific (local) settings.	Child fbx_settings.cfm
`<cf_formURL2 Attributes>`	Copies all URL and form variables to the attributes scope.	Embedded in fbx_ fusebox30_CFxx.cfm
`<cf_bodyContent>` and app_layout.cfm	Used for layouts in Fusebox 2.	fbx_layouts.cfm and layout file, as well as embedded in fbx_fusebox30_CFxx.cfm

The functionality of each of these files is duplicated in Fusebox 3, but the new framework files add some important features. Let's look at the new framework files for Fusebox 3.

Fusebox 3 Framework Files

Each file is explained in detail in Chapters 3, "The Fusebox Framework," and 4, "Handling a Fuseaction," but Table D.2 shows each file and how it relates to Fusebox 2. The Fusebox spec currently has seven fbx_ files.

Table D.2　**Fusebox 3.0 Framework Files**

Filename	Description	Similar to Fusebox 2 file
fbx_fusebox31_CFxx.cfm	Handles processing of the other framework files; the core file.	None
fbx_circuits.cfm	Registers circuits in the root circuit.	None
fbx_settings.cfm	Handles circuit-wide settings.	app_globals.cfm and app_locals.cfm
fbx_switch.cfm	Performs the switch on the fuseaction, including needed fuses.	index.cfm
fbx_layouts.cfm	Determines which layout file to use.	Partially in app_layouts.cfm
fbx_saveContent.cfm	Custom tag replacement for ColdFusion 5's native <cfsavecontent>.	bodycontent.cfm

You can see that not all the Fusebox 3 files have comparable files in the Fusebox 2 framework. This is because Fusebox 3 introduces the concept of nested circuits and nested layouts, something that Fusebox 2 did not do. Also Fusebox 2 relied on a number of custom tags that have been integrated into the Fusebox 3 core file, fbx_fusebox31_CFxx.cfm.

A Code Comparison of FB2 and FB3

Now we are going to deconstruct a version 2 index.cfm file and show you the translation to version 3.

Following is a sample Fusebox 2 index.cfm:

```
1 <cfinclude template="app_locals.cfm">
2 <cf_bodycontent>
3 <cfswitch expression = "#attributes.fuseaction#">
3  <cfcase value="cover">
     <cfinclude template="dsp_cover.cfm">
```

continues

```
3  </cfcase>
3  </cfswitch>
2  </cf_bodycontent>
2  <cfinclude template="#request.fuse_root#/app_layout.cfm">
```

Let's go through each section, starting with section 1:

```
1  <cfinclude template="app_locals.cfm">
```

The functionality of a circuit's `app_locals.cfm` is now performed by
`fbx_settings.cfm`. Each circuit has its own `fbx_settings.cfm` file, just
as each circuit contained an `app_locals.cfm` in Fusebox 2.

Thanks to the nested circuit functionality of Fusebox 3, this file also
takes the place of `app_globals.cfm`. The root `fbx_settings.cfm` file (the
`fbx_settings.cfm` in the root directory of your Fusebox application) contains
application-wide settings. This is all explained in great detail in Chapters 3
and 4.

The Differences in Layouts

Section 2 prepares for and implements a layout:

```
2  <cf_bodyContent>…</cf_bodyContent> and 2 <cfinclude
⇒template="#request.fuse_root#/app_layout.cfm">
```

The layout management of `<cf_bodycontent>` and `app_layout.cfm` is
now contained in `fbx_layouts.cfm` and your chosen layout file, and the
`fbx_fusebox31_CFxx.cfm` file facilitates it. The headers and footers commonly
used in Fusebox 2 have been replaced with a single layout file. The
`fbx_layouts.cfm` file contains the layout settings for each circuit, such as the
location of the layout file and the name of that file.

The following line is a very simple example of the `fbx_layouts.cfm` file:

```
<cfset fusebox.layoutfile="blackLayout.cfm">
```

The layout file called by the `fbx_layouts.cfm` above looks like this:

```
<HTML>
<HEAD>
  <TITLE>Hello World</TITLE>
</HEAD>
<BODY BGCOLOR="black" TEXT="white">
#fusebox.layout#
</BODY>
</HTML>
```

Fusebox 3 introduces nested layouts. If a circuit has a parent, then it will inherit its layout. Check out Chapter 9, "Nested Layouts," for more information on nested layouts.

Section 3 manages the conditional logic based on the fuseaction:

```
3 <cfswitch expression = "#attributes.fuseaction#">
3 <cfcase value="cover">
    <cfinclude template="dsp_cover.cfm">
3 </cfcase>
3 <cfdefaultcase>
    Sorry, unknown fuseaction.
3 </cfdefaultcase>
3 </cfswitch>
```

The `<cfswitch>` statement used to switch on the fuseaction still exists, but it's completely removed from the `index.cfm`, where it was in Fusebox 2. In Fusebox 3, the `fbx_switch.cfm` file contains the `<cfswitch>` tag. Just as each Fusebox 2 circuit has its own `index.cfm`, each circuit in a Fusebox 3 application contains an `fbx_switch.cfm`. The `<cfswitch>` code in this file is pretty much the same as in Fusebox 2; only the file holding the code has changed.

What Happened to *index.cfm*?

All the elements from the example Fusebox 2 `index.cfm` have been moved to other files. However, `index.cfm` is not a blank, unused file. Just as in previous versions of Fusebox, all requests are channeled through `index.cfm`. What is different in Fusebox 3 is that `index.cfm` now `<cfinclude>`s the Fusebox 3 core file, and there is only one `index.cfm` file per application, in the root. Each circuit does not get an `index.cfm` because no circuit but the root should receive requests.

The core Fusebox file handles the functionality of nested circuits and layouts. It also takes the place of the custom tags `<cf_formurl2attributes>` and `<cf_bodycontent>` that were used in Fusebox 2. If you are familiar with XFB, the core file also handles the functionality of `<cf_nesting>`. This code has been highly optimized and should be considered read-only. As long as everyone uses the same core file (or a core file with identical functionality), we all gain increased industry acceptance, plug-and-play Fusebox applications, and much more. These files are currently maintained and available free of charge from `http://www.fusebox.org`.

Updating Your Skills and Applications

In the real world, not every organization will be ready to switch to Fusebox 3 instantly. If you are in this situation, you can transition in phases:

1. **XFAs**—Implement XFAs in your future Fusebox 2 projects.
2. **Fusedocs**—Add Fusedocs, becoming familiar with the process of getting the architectural thinking done before any code is written.
3. **Dive in 100%**—Get the core files and make a Fusebox 3 application from scratch.

Migrating to Fusebox 3 is not as intimidating as it might seem. Fusebox 3 includes the same elements and functionality of Fusebox 2. They are simply implemented differently, with increased efficiency and functionality. In fact, most Fusebox developers who were previously familiar with version 2 have had a smooth transition to the new version and consider it easier than Fusebox 2. Good luck!

E

Fusebox Resources

AS MENTIONED IN CHAPTER 2, "Is Fusebox Right for You?," several categories of great resources are available to Fusebox developers. The first and perhaps foremost of these is the community. Fuseboxers are a great bunch of folks, with all kinds of experience to offer. The best place to meet up with them is on the Fusebox email lists. Two primary lists are available:

- **Fusebox List (fusebox@topica.com)**—The list for all Fusebox-specific threads. You can subscribe by visiting http://www.topica.com or sending a blank email to fusebox-subscribe@topica.com.

- **Fusebox Community List (fbcommunity@topica.com)**—The list for all threads initiated by Fuseboxers. This is the place to go for all those off-topic posts that don't really belong on the Fusebox List. You'll see plenty of regulars here, just like your favorite hangout. You can subscribe by visiting http://www.topica.com or sending a blank email to fbcommunity-subscribe@topica.com.

> **Note**
>
> Although the Fusebox lists are hosted at topica.com as of the writing of this book, plans are under way to move them onto a server that is more specific to the community. By the time you read this, the lists might have moved; check fusebox.org for updates.

You can also find plenty of information at various Fusebox-related web sites. Check out the Official Fusebox Site, as well as some sites hosted by Fusebox Council members:

- **www.fusebox.org**—The Official Fusebox Site is the home of the latest Fusebox specification. You can also find supporting information such as whitepapers, presentations, sample code, and links to other resources. This is the site to visit if you're interested in formally participating in the future of Fusebox.

Council Sites

The Fusebox Council is the primary organizational element of the Fusebox community. These are people who pushed, molded, and maintained Fusebox prior to the formal community organization in early 2002. Council members' sites are not necessarily Fusebox exclusive, but they do have a wide variety of resources available:

- **www.secretagents.com (Steve Nelson)**—Steve's site is aimed at the application architect and the idea of using an "army of fusecoders." Some nice downloads and online training are available here.

- **www.halhelms.com (Hal Helms)**—Hal's site has several areas, including some of his writing and a collection of the code he has discussed in various venues.

- **www.grokfusebox.com (Jeff Peters)**—GrokFusebox.com is about "getting it." You will find links to resources about Fusebox and ColdFusion in general. Be sure to visit Grok's Goodies, where you can download Fusebox-related utilities; and participate in the "I Had This Great Snippet" project.

- **www.fusium.com (Nat Papovich/Erik Voldengen)**—Nat and Erik have combined forces to offer Fusebox development and consulting along with developer resources and tools. Find improved Fusebox core files, fuseminder2, and Rebar at fusium.com.

Community Sites

You will also find sites hosted by various members of the Fusebox community, many of which come and go on a regular basis. The best place to keep up with these sites is the Fusebox Community List. A German Fusebox site (www.fusebox.de) is available, as well as a broad spectrum of international attendees at the annual Fusebox Conference. CFConf (www.cfconf.org) has information about Fusebox and ColdFusion conferences and training worldwide.

Finally, one of the more interesting Fusebox resources on the web is Fusewiki (`meta-magic.com/cgi-bin/fusewiki`), headed by Patrick McElhaney. If you haven't visited a wiki before, drop by soon.

Commercial Sites

Some companies have been instrumental in Fusebox's rise to the forefront of ColdFusion development. Among the most active are these:

- **TeraTech (`www.teratech.com`)**—TeraTech is a Washington, D.C.-based company that provides development services and training in ColdFusion and Fusebox. TeraTech's president is Michael Smith, whose work you might have read in ColdFusion Developer's Journal. TeraTech helped organize the first two Fusebox conferences and remains one of Fusebox's strongest supporters.

- **Synthis (`www.synthis.com`)**—Synthis was the first company to bring out a commercial development environment targeted for the Fusebox community: Adalon. It continues to improve Adalon's Fusebox compatibility with each release.

You Be the Resource

Of course, you can be a great resource, too. Set up a site, offer some cool stuff, and let us know about it.

Index

D

F

creating, 256
  clickable prototypes, 256-257
  client coordination, 257, 268-269
  freeze, 268-269
  signoff, 269
delivery, 272
  Americans with Disabilities Act (ADA), 273-274
  platforms, 272-273
  Section 508, 273-274
design, 270
  color, 271
  forms, 270-271
  impact, 271-272
design architecture, 363
scope creep, 255
wireframes, generating, 250-251

publications, ColdFusion Developer's Journal, 397

Q

qry files, 96, 103-104
  developers, 104
  QuerySims, 105-106

qry fuses, 15-16

qry_filename.cfm file, 374

qry_validateUser.cfm fuse, 95-96

query fuses, 103-104, 374
  developers, 104
  QuerySims, 105-106

QuerySetCell() function, 104

QuerySims, 105-106

R

Rebar, 236-237
  Action pages, 247-249
  Add New Page page, 238, 243
  Administration, 238

  Administration page, 238
  Basket View page, 246
  body page, 239-240
  Checkout Page One page, 247
  directory structure, 237
  Home page, 243
  links, 240-241
  nested pages, 240-241
  page creation, 238
  prototypes, 250-251
  Site Map page, 238, 242
  title page, 239
  viewing completed pages, 241-242

recordset element (Fusedoc), 155-156

recycling fuses, 95-96

report, test, 322-323

repurposing circuits, 130

requests, starting, 51
  Application.cfm, 51-52
  index.cfm, 52-55

reserved fbx files, 111-112

resources, 395-397
  commercial web sites, 397
  community web sites, 396
  email lists, 395
  Fusebox Council sites, 396
  Fusebox web site, 396
  J2EE, 357-358
  PHP, 351
    PHP.net, 352
    SourceForge.net, 352

Responsibilities element (Fusedoc), 138-139

reverse circuit structure, 69-71

Roffman, Gabe, 4

role attribute (History element), 140

X-Z

VOICES THAT MATTER

VISIT OUR WEB SITE

WWW.NEWRIDERS.COM

On our web site, you'll find information about our other books, authors, tables of contents, and book errata. You will also find information about book registration and how to purchase our books, both domestically and internationally.

EMAIL US

Contact us at: **nrfeedback@newriders.com**

- If you have comments or questions about this book
- To report errors that you have found in this book
- If you have a book proposal to submit or are interested in writing for New Riders
- If you are an expert in a computer topic or technology and are interested in being a technical editor who reviews manuscripts for technical accuracy

Contact us at: **nreducation@newriders.com**

- If you are an instructor from an educational institution who wants to preview New Riders books for classroom use. Email should include your name, title, school, department, address, phone number, office days/hours, text in use, and enrollment, along with your request for desk/examination copies and/or additional information.

Contact us at: **nrmedia@newriders.com**

- If you are a member of the media who is interested in reviewing copies of New Riders books. Send your name, mailing address, and email address, along with the name of the publication or web site you work for.

BULK PURCHASES/CORPORATE SALES

The publisher offers discounts on this book when ordered in quantity for bulk purchases and special sales. For sales within the U.S., please contact: Corporate and Government Sales (800) 382-3419 or **corpsales@pearsontechgroup.com**. Outside of the U.S., please contact: International Sales (317) 581-3793 or **international@pearsontechgroup.com**.

WRITE TO US

New Riders Publishing
201 W. 103rd St.
Indianapolis, IN 46290-1097

CALL/FAX US

Toll-free (800) 571-5840
If outside U.S. (317) 581-3500
Ask for New Riders
FAX: (317) 581-4663

WWW.NEWRIDERS.COM

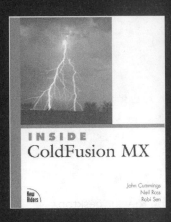

Solutions from experts you know and trust.

www.informit.com

New Riders has partnered with **InformIT.com** to bring technical information to your desktop. Drawing on New Riders authors and reviewers to provide additional information on topics you're interested in, **InformIT.com** has free, in-depth information you won't find anywhere else.

- **Master the skills you need, when you need them**

- **Call on resources from some of the best minds in the industry**

- **Get answers when you need them, using InformIT's comprehensive library or live experts online**

- **Go above and beyond what you find in New Riders books, extending your knowledge**

As an **InformIT** partner, **New Riders** has shared the wisdom and knowledge of our authors with you online. Visit **InformIT.com** to see what you're missing.

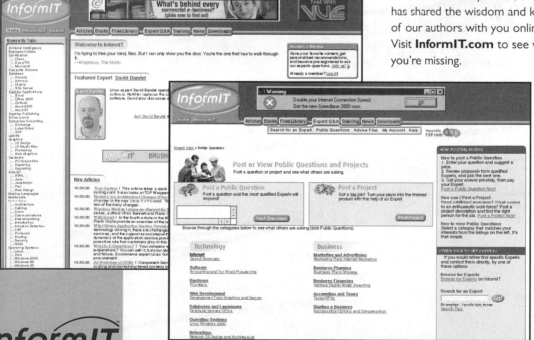

New Riders

Colophon

The photo of a lightning storm on the cover was captured by Don Farrell (PhotoDisc). Just like the storm's magnificent power, Fusebox has a set of powerful features that can make your development process more efficient. With the Fusebox framework, you can unleash dynamic features such as variable inheritance, nested layout control, and the nested circuit model of unit testing. These capabilities make your ColdFusion projects better organized and more efficient, and the elimination of typical frustrations allows you to write more complex and specialized code.

This book was written and edited in Microsoft Word, and laid out in QuarkXPress. The fonts used for the body text are Bembo and MCPdigital. It was printed on 50# Husky Offset Smooth paper at VonHoffmann Graphics, Inc. in Owensville, MO. Prepress consisted of PostScript computer-to-plate technology (filmless process). The cover was printed at Moore Langen Printing in Terre Haute, Indiana, on 12pt, coated on one side.